# PRAISE FOR
## *OBJECT-ORIENTED PYTHON*

"This book is both entertaining and educational, and a great stocking stuffer, especially for anyone involved with data analysis."

—THE *VANCOUVER SUN*

"If only I could have learned programming with this book! Any sufficiently advanced Python code will work with classes and Irv Kalb has provided a useful, fun introduction to Object-Oriented Programming (OOP). The projects start simple and build upon each other, always with a specific outcome in mind. For example, the first example is a basic card game written in procedural Python. A dozen chapters later, you'll be including card graphics and keeping track of the state of the deck with OOP concepts like encapsulation, polymorphism, and inheritance—all without reading a dry textbook. *Object-Oriented Python* is a fun way for new coders to level up their skills."

—ADAM DUVANDER, EVERYDEVELOPER

"The projects for the most part are real-world appropriate and easily understandable for multiple levels of expertise of the readers . . . Anyone who is interested in learning Python Object-Oriented Programming would benefit by having this book in their library. Kudos to both Mr. Kalb and No Starch Press for this book!"

—FULL CIRCLE MAGAZINE

"A guide to mastering object-oriented programming from the ground up. Irv Kalb covers the basics of building classes and creating objects, and puts theory into practice using the pygame package with clear examples that help visualize the object-oriented style."

—I PROGRAMMER

# OBJECT-ORIENTED PYTHON

## PYTHON

### Master OOP by Building Games and GUIs

by Irv Kalb

**no starch press**

San Francisco

**OBJECT-ORIENTED PYTHON.** Copyright © 2022 by Irv Kalb.

Printed in the United States of America

Third printing

27 26 25 24 23     3 4 5 6 7

ISBN-13: 978-1-7185-0206-2 (print)
ISBN-13: 978-1-7185-0207-9 (ebook)

Publisher: William Pollock
Managing Editor: Jill Franklin
Production Manager: Rachel Monaghan
Production Editor: Kate Kaminski
Developmental Editor: Liz Chadwick
Cover Illustrator: James L. Barry
Interior Design: Octopod Studios
Technical Reviewer: Monte Davidoff
Copyeditor: Rachel Head
Compositor: Maureen Forys, Happenstance Type-O-Rama
Proofreader: Paula L. Fleming
Indexer: Valerie Haynes Perry

The following images are reproduced with permission:

Figure 2-1, photo by David Benbennick, printed under the Creative Commons Attribution-Share Alike 3.0 Unported license, *https://creativecommons.org/licenses/by-sa/3.0/deed.en*.

For information on distribution, bulk sales, corporate sales, or translations, please contact No Starch Press, Inc. directly at info@nostarch.com or:

No Starch Press, Inc.
245 8th Street, San Francisco, CA 94103
phone: 1.415.863.9900
www.nostarch.com

*Library of Congress Cataloging-in-Publication Data*

Names: Kalb, Irv, author.
Title: Object-oriented Python: master OOP by building games and GUIs / Irv Kalb.
Description: San Francisco : No Starch Press, [2021] | Includes index. |
Identifiers: LCCN 2021044174 (print) | LCCN 2021044175 (ebook) | ISBN
    9781718502062 (print) | ISBN 9781718502079 (ebook)
Subjects: LCSH: Object-oriented programming (Computer science) | Python
    (Computer program language)
Classification: LCC QA76.64 .K3563 2021 (print) | LCC QA76.64 (ebook) |
    DDC 005.1/17--dc23
LC record available at https://lccn.loc.gov/2021044174
LC ebook record available at https://lccn.loc.gov/2021044175

To my wonderful wife, Doreen.
You are the glue that keeps
our family together.

Many years ago, I said, "I do,"
but what I meant was, "I will."

## About the Author

Irv Kalb is an adjunct professor at UCSC Silicon Valley Extension and the University of Silicon Valley (formerly Cogswell Polytechnical College), where he teaches introductory and object-oriented programming courses in Python. Irv has a bachelor's and a master's degree in computer science, has been using object-oriented programming for over 30 years in a number of different computer languages, and has been teaching for over 10 years. He has decades of experience developing software, with a focus on educational software. As Furry Pants Productions, he and his wife created and shipped two edutainment CD-ROMs based on the character Darby the Dalmatian. Irv is also the author of *Learn to Program with Python 3: A Step-by-Step Guide to Programming* (Apress).

Irv was heavily involved in the early development of the sport of Ultimate Frisbee®. He led the effort of writing many versions of the official rule book and co-authored and self-published the first book on the sport, *Ultimate: Fundamentals of the Sport.*

## About the Technical Reviewer

Monte Davidoff is an independent software development consultant. His areas of expertise include DevOps and Linux. Monte has been programming in Python for over 20 years. He has used Python to develop a variety of software, including business-critical applications and embedded software.

# BRIEF CONTENTS

# CONTENTS IN DETAIL

# PART I: INTRODUCING OBJECT-ORIENTED PROGRAMMING

## 1
## PROCEDURAL PYTHON EXAMPLES                                            3

## 2
## MODELING PHYSICAL OBJECTS WITH OBJECT-ORIENTED PROGRAMMING                                                          21

# PART II: GRAPHICAL USER INTERFACES WITH PYGAME

**7**
# PYGAME GUI WIDGETS 143

# PART III: ENCAPSULATION, POLYMORPHISM, AND INHERITANCE

**8**
# ENCAPSULATION 163

**9**
# POLYMORPHISM 183

# PART IV: USING OOP IN GAME DEVELOPMENT

# ACKNOWLEDGMENTS

I would like to thank the following people, who helped make this book possible:

Al Sweigart, for getting me started in the use of pygame (especially with his "Pygbutton" code) and for allowing me to use the concept of his "Dodger" game.

Monte Davidoff, who was instrumental in helping me get the source code and documentation of that code to build correctly through the use of GitHub, Sphinx, and ReadTheDocs. He worked miracles using a myriad of tools to wrestle the appropriate files into submission.

Monte Davidoff (yes, the same guy), for being an outstanding technical reviewer. Monte made excellent technical and writing suggestions throughout the book, and many of the code examples are more Pythonic and more OOP-ish because of his comments.

Tep Sathya Khieu, who did a stellar job of drawing all the original diagrams for this book. I am not an artist (I don't even play one on TV). Tep was able to take my primitive pencil sketches and turn them into clear, consistent pieces of art.

Harrison Yung, Kevin Ly, and Emily Allis, for their contributions of artwork in some of the game art.

The early reviewers, Illya Katsyuk, Jamie Kalb, Gergana Angelova, and Joe Langmuir, who found and corrected many typos and made excellent suggestions for modifications and clarifications.

All the editors who worked on this book: Liz Chadwick (developmental editor), Rachel Head (copyeditor), and Kate Kaminski (production editor). They all made huge contributions by questioning and often rewording and reorganizing some of my explanations of concepts. They were also extremely helpful in adding and removing commas [do I need one here?] and lengthening my sentences as I am doing here to make sure that the point comes across cleanly (OK, I'll stop!). I'm afraid that I'll never understand when to use "which" versus "that," or when to use a comma and when to use a dash, but I'm glad that they know! Thanks also to Maureen Forys (compositor) for her valuable contributions to the finished product.

All the students who have been in my classes over the years at the UCSC Silicon Valley Extension and at the University of Silicon Valley (formerly Cogswell Polytechnical College). Their feedback, suggestions, smiles, frowns, light-bulb moments, frustrations, knowing head nods, and even thumbs-up (in Zoom classes during the COVID era) were extremely helpful in shaping the content of this book and my overall teaching style.

Finally, my family, who supported me through the long process of writing, testing, editing, rewriting, editing, debugging, editing, rewriting, editing (and so on) this book and the associated code. I couldn't have done it without them. I wasn't sure if we had enough books in our library, so I wrote another one!

# INTRODUCTION

This book is about a software development technique called *object-oriented programming (OOP)* and how it can be used with Python. Before OOP, programmers used an approach known as *procedural programming*, also called *structured programming*, which involves building a set of functions (procedures) and passing data around through calls to those functions. The OOP paradigm gives programmers an efficient way to combine code and data into cohesive units that are often highly reusable.

In preparation for writing this book, I extensively researched existing literature and videos, looking specifically at the approaches taken to explain this important and wide-ranging topic. I found that instructors and writers typically start by defining certain key terms: *class, instance variable, method, encapsulation, inheritance, polymorphism,* and so on.

While these are all important concepts, and I'll cover all of them in depth in this book, I'll begin in a different way: by considering the question, "What problem are we solving?" That is, if OOP is the solution, then what is the problem? To answer this question, I'll start by presenting a few examples of programs built using procedural programming and identifying complications inherent in this style. Then I'll show you how an object-oriented approach can make the construction of such programs much easier and the programs themselves more maintainable.

## Who Is This Book For?

This book is intended for people who already have some familiarity with Python and with using basic functions from the Python Standard Library. I will assume that you understand the fundamental syntax of the language and can write small- to medium-sized programs using variables, assignment statements, if/elif/else statements, while and for loops, functions and function calls, lists, dictionaries, and so on. If you aren't comfortable with all of these concepts, then I suggest that you get a copy of my earlier book, *Learn to Program with Python 3* (Apress), and read that first.

This is an intermediate-level text, so there are a number of more advanced topics that I will not address. For example, to keep the book practical, I will not often go into detail on the internal implementation of Python. For simplicity and clarity, and to keep the focus on mastering OOP techniques, the examples are written using a limited subset of the language. There are more advanced and concise ways to code in Python that are beyond the scope of this book.

I will cover the underlying details of OOP in a mostly language-independent way, but will point out areas where there are differences between Python and other OOP languages. Having learned the basics of OOP-style coding through this book, if you wish, you should be able to easily apply these techniques to other OOP languages.

## Python Version(s) and Installation

All the example code in this book was written and tested using Python version 3.9. All the examples should work fine with version 3.9 or newer.

Python is available for free at *https://www.python.org*. If you don't have Python installed, or you want to upgrade to the latest version, go to that site, find the Downloads tab, and click the **Download** button. This will download an installable file onto your computer. Double-click the file that was downloaded to install Python.

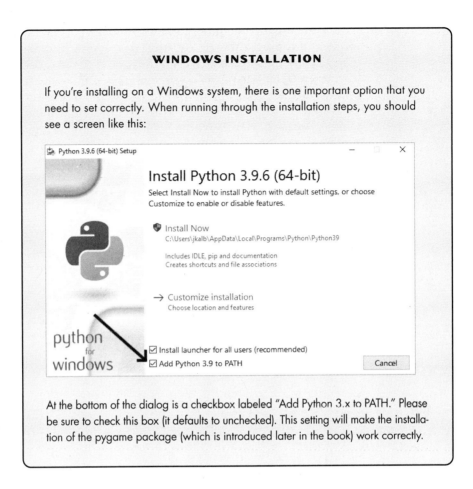

**WINDOWS INSTALLATION**

If you're installing on a Windows system, there is one important option that you need to set correctly. When running through the installation steps, you should see a screen like this:

At the bottom of the dialog is a checkbox labeled "Add Python 3.x to PATH." Please be sure to check this box (it defaults to unchecked). This setting will make the installation of the pygame package (which is introduced later in the book) work correctly.

**NOTE** *I am aware of the "PEP 8 – Style Guide for Python Code" and its specific recommendation to use the snake case convention (snake_case) for variable and function names. However, the document starts by saying that the convention is "for the Python code comprising the standard library." I fully applaud this consistency. I have been using the camel case naming convention (camelCase) for many years before the PEP 8 document was written and have become comfortable with it during my career. Therefore, all variable and function names in this book are consistently written using camel case.*

## How Will I Explain OOP?

The examples in the first few chapters use text-based Python; these sample programs get input from the user and output information to the user purely in the form of text. I'll introduce OOP by showing you how to develop text-based simulations of physical objects in code. We'll start by creating representations of light switches, dimmer switches, and TV remote controls as objects. I'll then show you how we can use OOP to simulate bank accounts and a bank that controls many accounts.

Once we've covered the basics of OOP, I'll introduce the *pygame* module, which allows programmers to write games and applications that use a *graphical user interface (GUI)*. With GUI-based programs, the user intuitively interacts with buttons, checkboxes, text input and output fields, and other user-friendly widgets.

I chose to use pygame with Python because this combination allows me to demonstrate OOP concepts in a highly visual way using elements on the screen. Pygame is extremely portable and runs on nearly every platform and operating system. All the sample programs that use the pygame package have been tested with the recently released pygame version 2.0.

I've created a package called pygwidgets that works with pygame and implements a number of basic widgets, all of which are built using an OOP approach. I'll introduce this package later in the book, providing sample code you can run and experiment with. This approach will allow you to see real, practical examples of key object-oriented concepts, while incorporating these techniques to produce fun, playable games. I'll also introduce my pyghelpers package, which provides code to help write more complicated games and applications.

All the example code shown in the book is available as a single download from the No Starch website: *https://www.nostarch.com/object-oriented-python/*.

The code is also available on a chapter-by-chapter basis from my GitHub repository: *https://github.com/IrvKalb/Object-Oriented-Python-Code/*.

## What's in the Book

This book is divided into four parts. Part I introduces object-oriented programming:

- Chapter 1 provides a review of coding using procedural programming. I'll show you how to implement a text-based card game and simulate a bank performing operations on one or more accounts. Along the way, I discuss common problems with the procedural approach.

- Chapter 2 introduces classes and objects and shows how you can represent real-world objects like light switches or a TV remote in Python using classes. You'll see how an object-oriented approach solves the problems highlighted in the first chapter.

- Chapter 3 presents two mental models that you can use to think about what's going on behind the scenes when you create objects in Python. We'll use Python Tutor to step through code and see how objects are created.

- Chapter 4 demonstrates a standard way to handle multiple objects of the same type by introducing the concept of an object manager object. We'll expand the bank account simulation using classes, and I'll show you how to handle errors using exceptions.

Part II focuses on building GUIs with pygame:

- Chapter 5 introduces the pygame package and the event-driven model of programming. We'll build a few simple programs to get you started with placing graphics in a window and handling keyboard and mouse input, then develop a more complicated ball-bouncing program.

- Chapter 6 goes into much more detail on using OOP with pygame programs. We'll rewrite the ball-bouncing program in an OOP style and develop some simple GUI elements.

- Chapter 7 introduces the pygwidgets module, which contains full implementations of many standard GUI elements (buttons, checkboxes, and so on), each developed as a class.

Part III delves into the main tenets of OOP:

- Chapter 8 discusses encapsulation, which involves hiding implementation details from external code and placing all related methods in one place: a class.

- Chapter 9 introduces polymorphism—the idea that multiple classes can have methods with the same names—and shows how it enables you to make calls to methods in multiple objects, without having to know the type of each object. We'll build a Shapes program to demonstrate this concept.

- Chapter 10 covers inheritance, which allows you to create a set of subclasses that all use common code built into a base class, rather than having to reinvent the wheel with similar classes. We'll look at a few real-world examples where inheritance comes in handy, such as implementing an input field that only accepts numbers, then rewrite our Shapes example program to use this feature.

- Chapter 11 wraps up this part of the book by discussing some additional important OOP topics, mostly related to memory management. We'll look at the lifetime of an object, and as an example we'll build a small balloon-popping game.

Part IV explores several topics related to using OOP in game development:

- Chapter 12 demonstrates how we can rebuild the card game developed in Chapter 1 as a pygame-based GUI program. I also show you how to build reusable Deck and Card classes that you can use in other card games you create.

- Chapter 13 covers timing. We'll develop different timer classes that allow a program to keep running while concurrently checking for a given time limit.

- Chapter 14 explains animation classes you can use to show sequences of images. We'll look at two animation techniques: building animations from a collection of separate image files and extracting and using multiple images from a single sprite sheet file.

- Chapter 15 explains the concept of a state machine, which represents and controls the flow of your programs, and a scene manager, which you can use to build a program with multiple scenes. To demonstrate the use of each of these, we'll build two versions of a Rock, Paper, Scissors game.

- Chapter 16 discusses different types of modal dialogs, another important user interaction feature. We then walk through building a full-featured OOP-based video game called Dodger that demonstrates many of the techniques described in the book.

- Chapter 17 introduces the concept of design patterns, focusing on the Model View Controller pattern, then presents a dice-rolling program that uses this pattern to allow the user to visualize data in numerous different ways. It concludes with a short wrap-up for the book.

## Development Environments

In this book, you'll need to use the command line only minimally for installing software. All installation instructions will be clearly written out, so you won't need to learn any additional command line syntax.

Rather than using the command line for development, I believe strongly in using an interactive development environment (IDE). An IDE handles many of the details of the underlying operating system for you, and it allows you to write, edit, and run your code using a single program. IDEs are typically cross-platform, allowing programmers to easily move from a Mac to a Windows computer or vice versa.

The short example programs in the book can be run in the IDLE development environment that is installed when you install Python. IDLE is very simple to use and works well for programs that can be written in a single file. When we get into more complicated programs that use multiple Python files, I encourage you to use a more sophisticated environment instead; I use the JetBrains PyCharm development environment, which handles multiple-file projects more easily. The Community Edition is available for free from *https://www.jetbrains.com/*, and I highly recommend it. PyCharm also has a fully integrated debugger that can be extremely useful when writing larger programs. For more information on how to use the debugger, please see my YouTube video "Debugging Python 3 with PyCharm" at *https://www.youtube.com/watch?v=cxAOSQQwDJ4&t=43s/*.

## Widgets and Example Games

The book introduces and makes available two Python packages: pygwidgets and pyghelpers. Using these packages, you should be able to build full GUI programs—but more importantly, you should gain an understanding of how each of the widgets is coded as a class and used as an object.

Incorporating various widgets, the example games in the book start out relatively simple and get progressively more complicated. Chapter 16 walks you through the development and implementation of a full-featured video game, complete with a high-scores table that is saved to a file.

By the end of this book, you should be able to code your own games—card games, or video games in the style of Pong, Hangman, Breakout, Space Invaders, and so on. Object-oriented programming gives you the ability to write programs that can easily display and control multiple items of the same type, which is often required when building user interfaces and is frequently necessary in game play.

Object-oriented programming is a general style that can be used in all aspects of programming, well beyond the game examples I use to demonstrate OOP techniques here. I hope you find this approach to learning OOP enjoyable.

Let's get started!

# PART I

## INTRODUCING OBJECT-ORIENTED PROGRAMMING

This part of the book introduces you to object-oriented programming. We'll discuss problems inherent in procedural code, then see how object-oriented programming addresses those concerns. Thinking in objects (with state and behavior) will give you a new perspective about how to write code.

Chapter 1 provides a review of procedural Python. I start by presenting a text-based card game named Higher or Lower, then work through a few progressively more complex implementations of a bank account in Python to help you better understand common problems with coding in a procedural style.

Chapter 2 shows how we might represent real-world objects in Python using classes. We'll write a program to simulate a light switch, modify it to include dimming capabilities, then move on to a more complicated TV remote simulation.

Chapter 3 gives you two different ways to think about what is going on behind the scenes when you create objects in Python.

Chapter 4 then demonstrates a standard way to handle multiple objects of the same type (for example, consider a simple game like checkers where you have to keep track of many similar game pieces). We'll expand the bank account programs from Chapter 1, and explore how to handle errors.

# 1

## PROCEDURAL PYTHON EXAMPLES

Introductory courses and books typically teach software development using the procedural programming style, which involves splitting a program into a number of functions (also known as procedures or subroutines). You pass data into functions, each of which performs one or more computations and, typically, passes back results. This book is about a different paradigm of programming known as *object-oriented programming (OOP)* that allows programmers to think differently about how to build software. Object-oriented programming gives programmers a way to combine code and data together into cohesive units, thereby avoiding some complications inherent in procedural programming.

In this chapter, I'll review a number of concepts in basic Python by building two small programs that incorporate various Python constructs. The first will be a small card game called Higher or Lower; the second will be a simulation of a bank, performing operations on one, two, and multiple accounts. Both will be built using procedural programming—that is, using the standard techniques of data and functions. Later, I'll rewrite these programs using OOP techniques. The purpose of this chapter is to demonstrate some key problems inherent in procedural programming. With that understanding, the chapters that follow will explain how OOP solves those problems.

## Higher or Lower Card Game

My first example is a simple card game called Higher or Lower. In this game, eight cards are randomly chosen from a deck. The first card is shown face up. The game asks the player to predict whether the next card in the selection will have a higher or lower value than the currently showing card. For example, say the card that's shown is a 3. The player chooses "higher," and the next card is shown. If that card has a higher value, the player is correct. In this example, if the player had chosen "lower," they would have been incorrect.

If the player guesses correctly, they get 20 points. If they choose incorrectly, they lose 15 points. If the next card to be turned over has the same value as the previous card, the player is incorrect.

### Representing the Data

The program needs to represent a deck of 52 cards, which I'll build as a list. Each of the 52 elements in the list will be a dictionary (a set of key/value pairs). To represent any card, each dictionary will contain three key/value pairs: 'rank', 'suit', and 'value'. The rank is the name of the card (Ace, 2, 3, ... 10, Jack, Queen, King), but the value is an integer used for comparing cards (1, 2, 3, ... 10, 11, 12, 13). For example, the Jack of Clubs would be represented as the following dictionary:

```
{'rank': 'Jack', 'suit': 'Clubs', 'value': 11}
```

Before the player plays a round, the list representing the deck is created and shuffled to randomize the order of the cards. I have no graphical representation of the cards, so each time the user chooses "higher" or "lower," the program gets a card dictionary from the deck and prints the rank and the suit for the user. The program then compares the value of the new card to that of the previous card and gives feedback based on the correctness of the user's answer.

### Implementation

Listing 1-1 shows the code of the Higher or Lower game.

**NOTE**    *As a reminder, the code associated with all the major listings in this book is available for download at* https://www.nostarch.com/object-oriented-python/ *and* https://github.com/IrvKalb/Object-Oriented-Python-Code/. *You can either download and run the code or type it in yourself.*

## File: HigherOrLowerProcedural.py

```python
# HigherOrLower

import random

# Card constants
SUIT_TUPLE = ('Spades', 'Hearts', 'Clubs', 'Diamonds')
RANK_TUPLE = ('Ace', '2', '3', '4', '5', '6', '7', '8', '9', '10', 'Jack',
'Queen', 'King')

NCARDS = 8

# Pass in a deck and this function returns a random card from the deck
def getCard(deckListIn):
    thisCard = deckListIn.pop() # pop one off the top of the deck and return
    return thisCard

# Pass in a deck and this function returns a shuffled copy of the deck
def shuffle(deckListIn):
    deckListOut = deckListIn.copy()   # make a copy of the starting deck
    random.shuffle(deckListOut)
    return deckListOut

#  Main code
print('Welcome to Higher or Lower.')
print('You have to choose whether the next card to be shown will be higher or
lower than the current card.')
print('Getting it right adds 20 points; get it wrong and you lose 15 points.')
print('You have 50 points to start.')
print()

startingDeckList = []
❶ for suit in SUIT_TUPLE:
    for thisValue, rank in enumerate(RANK_TUPLE):
        cardDict = {'rank':rank, 'suit':suit, 'value':thisValue + 1}
        startingDeckList.append(cardDict)

score = 50

while True:   # play multiple games
    print()
    gameDeckList = shuffle(startingDeckList)
  ❷ currentCardDict = getCard(gameDeckList)
    currentCardRank = currentCardDict['rank']
    currentCardValue = currentCardDict['value']
    currentCardSuit = currentCardDict['suit']
    print('Starting card is:', currentCardRank + ' of ' + currentCardSuit)
    print()

    ❸ for cardNumber in range(0, NCARDS):   # play one game of this many cards
        answer = input('Will the next card be higher or lower than the ' +
                       currentCardRank + ' of ' +
                       currentCardSuit + '?  (enter h or l): ')
```

```
        answer = answer.casefold()  # force lowercase
❹ nextCardDict = getCard(gameDeckList)
  nextCardRank = nextCardDict['rank']
  nextCardSuit = nextCardDict['suit']
  nextCardValue = nextCardDict['value']
  print('Next card is:', nextCardRank + ' of ' + nextCardSuit)

❺ if answer == 'h':
      if nextCardValue > currentCardValue:
          print('You got it right, it was higher')
          score = score + 20
      else:
          print('Sorry, it was not higher')
          score = score - 15

  elif answer == 'l':
      if nextCardValue < currentCardValue:
          score = score + 20
          print('You got it right, it was lower')

      else:
          score = score - 15
          print('Sorry, it was not lower')

  print('Your score is:', score)
  print()
  currentCardValue = nextCardValue
  currentCardSuit = nextCardSuit

❻ goAgain = input('To play again, press ENTER, or "q" to quit: ')
  if goAgain == 'q':
      break

print('OK bye')
```

*Listing 1-1: A Higher or Lower game using procedural Python*

The program starts by creating a deck as a list ❶. Each card is a dictionary made up of a rank, a suit, and a value. For each round of the game, I retrieve the first card from the deck and save the components in variables ❷. For the next seven cards, the user is asked to predict whether the next card will be higher or lower than the most recently showing card ❸. The next card is retrieved from the deck, and its components are saved in a second set of variables ❹. The game compares the user's answer to the card drawn and gives the user feedback and points based on the outcome ❺. When the user has made predictions for all seven cards in the selection, we ask if they want to play again ❻.

This program demonstrates many elements of programming in general and Python in particular: variables, assignment statements, functions and function calls, if/else statements, print statements, while loops, lists, strings, and dictionaries. This book will assume you're already familiar with everything shown in this example. If there is anything in this program that is unfamiliar or not clear to you, it would probably be worth your time to review the appropriate material before moving on.

### Reusable Code

Since this is a playing card–based game, the code obviously creates and manipulates a simulated deck of cards. If we wanted to write another card-based game, it would be great to be able to reuse the code for the deck and cards.

In a procedural program, it can often be difficult to identify all the pieces of code associated with one portion of the program, such as the deck and cards in this example. In Listing 1-1, the code for the deck consists of two tuple constants, two functions, some main code to build a global list that represents the starting deck of 52 cards, and another global list that represents the deck that is used while the game is being played. Further, notice that even in a small program like this, the data and the code that manipulates the data might not be closely grouped together.

Therefore, reusing the deck and card code in another program is not that easy or straightforward. In Chapter 12, we will revisit this program and show how an OOP solution makes reusing code like this much easier.

## Bank Account Simulations

In this second example of procedural coding, I'll present a number of variations of a program that simulates running a bank. In each new version of the program, I'll add more functionality. Note that these programs are not production-ready; invalid user entries or misuse will lead to errors. The intent is to have you focus on how the code interacts with the data associated with one or more bank accounts.

To start, consider what operations a client would want to do with a bank account and what data would be needed to represent an account.

### Analysis of Required Operations and Data

A list of operations a person would want to do with a bank account would include:

- Create (an account)
- Deposit
- Withdraw
- Check balance

Next, here is a minimal list of the data we would need to represent a bank account:

- Customer name
- Password
- Balance

Notice that all the operations are action words (verbs) and all the data items are things (nouns). A real bank account would certainly be capable of many more operations and would contain additional pieces of data (such as the account holder's address, phone number, and Social Security number), but to keep the discussion clear, I'll start with just these four actions and three pieces of data. Further, to keep things simple and focused, I'll make all amounts an integer number of dollars. I should also point out that in a real bank application, passwords would not be kept in cleartext (unencrypted) as it is in these examples.

## Implementation 1—Single Account Without Functions

In the starting version in Listing 1-2, there is only a single account.

### File: Bank1_OneAccount.py

```
# Non-OOP
# Bank Version 1
# Single account

❶ accountName = 'Joe'
accountBalance = 100
accountPassword = 'soup'

while True:
  ❷ print()
    print('Press b to get the balance')
    print('Press d to make a deposit')
    print('Press w to make a withdrawal')
    print('Press s to show the account')
    print('Press q to quit')
    print()

    action = input('What do you want to do? ')
    action = action.lower()  # force lowercase
    action = action[0]  # just use first letter
    print()

    if action == 'b':
        print('Get Balance:')
        userPassword = input('Please enter the password: ')
        if userPassword != accountPassword:
            print('Incorrect password')
        else:
            print('Your balance is:', accountBalance)

    elif action == 'd':
        print('Deposit:')
        userDepositAmount = input('Please enter amount to deposit: ')
        userDepositAmount = int(userDepositAmount)
        userPassword = input('Please enter the password: ')

        if userDepositAmount < 0:
```

```
                print('You cannot deposit a negative amount!')

            elif userPassword != accountPassword:
                print('Incorrect password')

            else:  # OK
                accountBalance = accountBalance + userDepositAmount
                print('Your new balance is:', accountBalance)

        elif action == 's':  # show
            print('Show:')
            print('        Name', accountName)
            print('        Balance:', accountBalance)
            print('        Password:', accountPassword)
            print()

        elif action == 'q':
            break

        elif action == 'w':
            print('Withdraw:')

            userWithdrawAmount = input('Please enter the amount to withdraw: ')
            userWithdrawAmount = int(userWithdrawAmount)
            userPassword = input('Please enter the password: ')

            if userWithdrawAmount < 0:
                print('You cannot withdraw a negative amount')

            elif userPassword != accountPassword:
                print('Incorrect password for this account')

            elif userWithdrawAmount > accountBalance:
                print('You cannot withdraw more than you have in your account')

            else:  #OK
                accountBalance = accountBalance - userWithdrawAmount
                print('Your new balance is:', accountBalance)

print('Done')
```

*Listing 1-2: Bank simulation for a single account*

The program starts off by initializing three variables to represent the data of one account ❶. Then it displays a menu that allows a choice of operations ❷. The main code of the program acts directly on the global account variables.

In this example, all the actions are at the main level; there are no functions in the code. The program works fine, but it may seem a little long. A typical approach to make longer programs clearer is to move related code into functions and make calls to those functions. We'll explore that in the next implementation of the banking program.

## Implementation 2—Single Account with Functions

In the version of the program in Listing 1-3, the code is broken up into separate functions, one for each action. Again, this simulation is for a single account.

### File: Bank2_OneAccountWithFunctions.py

```python
# Non-OOP
# Bank 2
# Single account

accountName = ''
accountBalance = 0
accountPassword = ''

❶ def newAccount(name, balance, password):
    global accountName, accountBalance, accountPassword
    accountName = name
    accountBalance = balance
    accountPassword = password

def show():
    global accountName, accountBalance, accountPassword
    print('      Name', accountName)
    print('      Balance:', accountBalance)
    print('      Password:', accountPassword)
    print()

❷ def getBalance(password):
    global accountName, accountBalance, accountPassword
    if password != accountPassword:
        print('Incorrect password')
        return None
    return accountBalance

❸ def deposit(amountToDeposit, password):
    global accountName, accountBalance, accountPassword
    if amountToDeposit < 0:
        print('You cannot deposit a negative amount!')
        return None

    if password != accountPassword:
        print('Incorrect password')
        return None

    accountBalance = accountBalance + amountToDeposit
    return accountBalance

❹ def withdraw(amountToWithdraw, password):
    ❺ global accountName, accountBalance, accountPassword
    if amountToWithdraw < 0:
        print('You cannot withdraw a negative amount')
        return None
```

```
    if password != accountPassword:
        print('Incorrect password for this account')
        return None

    if amountToWithdraw > accountBalance:
        print('You cannot withdraw more than you have in your account')
        return None

❻ accountBalance = accountBalance - amountToWithdraw
    return accountBalance

newAccount("Joe", 100, 'soup')  # create an account

while True:
    print()
    print('Press b to get the balance')
    print('Press d to make a deposit')
    print('Press w to make a withdrawal')
    print('Press s to show the account')
    print('Press q to quit')
    print()

    action = input('What do you want to do? ')
    action = action.lower()  # force lowercase
    action = action[0]  # just use first letter
    print()

    if action == 'b':
        print('Get Balance:')
        userPassword = input('Please enter the password: ')
        theBalance = getBalance(userPassword)
        if theBalance is not None:
            print('Your balance is:', theBalance)

❼ elif action == 'd':
        print('Deposit:')
        userDepositAmount = input('Please enter amount to deposit: ')
        userDepositAmount = int(userDepositAmount)
        userPassword = input('Please enter the password: ')

❽     newBalance = deposit(userDepositAmount, userPassword)
        if newBalance is not None:
            print('Your new balance is:', newBalance)

--- snip calls to appropriate functions ---

print('Done')
```

*Listing 1-3: Bank simulation for one account with functions*

In this version, I've built a function for each of the operations that we identified for a bank account (create ❶, check balance ❷, deposit ❸, and withdraw ❹) and rearranged the code so that the main code contains calls to the different functions.

As a result, the main program is much more readable. For example, if the user types d to indicate that they want to make a deposit ❼, the code now calls a function named deposit() ❸, passing in the amount to be deposited and the account password the user entered.

However, if you look at the definition of any of these functions—for example, the withdraw() function—you'll see that the code uses global statements ❺ to access (get or set) the variables that represent the account. In Python, a global statement is only required if you want to change the value of a global variable in a function. However, I am using them here to make it clear that these functions are referring to global variables, even if they are just getting a value.

As a general programming tenet, functions should *never* modify global variables. A function should only use data that is passed into it, make calculations based on that data, and potentially return a result or results. The withdraw() function in this program does work, but it violates this rule by modifying the value of the global variable accountBalance ❻ (in addition to accessing the value of the global variable accountPassword).

## Implementation 3—Two Accounts

The version of the bank simulation program in Listing 1-4 uses the same approach as Listing 1-3 but adds the ability to have two accounts.

### File: Bank3_TwoAccounts.py

```
# Non-OOP
# Bank 3
# Two accounts

account0Name = ''
account0Balance = 0
account0Password = ''
account1Name = ''
account1Balance = 0
account1Password = ''
nAccounts = 0

def newAccount(accountNumber, name, balance, password):
❶   global account0Name, account0Balance, account0Password
    global account1Name, account1Balance, account1Password

    if accountNumber == 0:
        account0Name = name
        account0Balance = balance
        account0Password = password
    if accountNumber == 1:
        account1Name = name
        account1Balance = balance
        account1Password = password
```

```
def show():
❷ global account0Name, account0Balance, account0Password
    global account1Name, account1Balance, account1Password

    if account0Name != '':
        print('Account 0')
        print('      Name', account0Name)
        print('      Balance:', account0Balance)
        print('      Password:', account0Password)
        print()
    if account1Name != '':
        print('Account 1')
        print('      Name', account1Name)
        print('      Balance:', account1Balance)
        print('      Password:', account1Password)
        print()

def getBalance(accountNumber, password):
❸ global account0Name, account0Balance, account0Password
    global account1Name, account1Balance, account1Password

    if accountNumber == 0:
        if password != account0Password:
            print('Incorrect password')
            return None
        return account0Balance
    if accountNumber == 1:
        if password != account1Password:
            print('Incorrect password')
            return None
        return account1Balance

--- snipped additional deposit() and withdraw() functions ---

--- snipped main code that calls functions above ---

print('Done')
```

*Listing 1-4: Bank simulation for two accounts with functions*

Even with just two accounts, you can see that this approach gets out of
hand quickly. First, we set three global variables for each account at ❶, ❷,
and ❸. Also, every function now has an if statement to choose which set
of global variables to access or change. Any time we want to add another
account, we'll need to add another set of global variables and more if statements in every function. This is simply not a feasible approach. We need a
different way to handle an arbitrary number of accounts.

## Implementation 4—Multiple Accounts Using Lists

To more easily accommodate multiple accounts, in Listing 1-5 I'll represent
the data using lists. I'll use three parallel lists in this version of the program:
accountNamesList, accountPasswordsList, and accountBalancesList.

**File: Bank4_N_Accounts.py**

```python
# Non-OOP Bank
# Version 4
# Any number of accounts - with lists

❶ accountNamesList = []
accountBalancesList = []
accountPasswordsList = []

def newAccount(name, balance, password):
    global accountNamesList, accountBalancesList, accountPasswordsList
  ❷ accountNamesList.append(name)
    accountBalancesList.append(balance)
    accountPasswordsList.append(password)

def show(accountNumber):
    global accountNamesList, accountBalancesList, accountPasswordsList
    print('Account', accountNumber)
    print('      Name', accountNamesList[accountNumber])
    print('      Balance:', accountBalancesList[accountNumber])
    print('      Password:', accountPasswordsList[accountNumber])
    print()

def getBalance(accountNumber, password):
    global accountNamesList, accountBalancesList, accountPasswordsList
    if password != accountPasswordsList[accountNumber]:
        print('Incorrect password')
        return None
    return accountBalancesList[accountNumber]

--- snipped additional functions ---

# Create two sample accounts
❸ print("Joe's account is account number:", len(accountNamesList))
newAccount("Joe", 100, 'soup')

❹ print("Mary's account is account number:", len(accountNamesList))
newAccount("Mary", 12345, 'nuts')

while True:
    print()
    print('Press b to get the balance')
    print('Press d to make a deposit')
    print('Press n to create a new account')
    print('Press w to make a withdrawal')
    print('Press s to show all accounts')
    print('Press q to quit')
    print()

    action = input('What do you want to do? ')
    action = action.lower()  # force lowercase
    action = action[0]  # just use first letter
    print()
```

```
    if action == 'b':
        print('Get Balance:')
    ❺ userAccountNumber = input('Please enter your account number: ')
        userAccountNumber = int(userAccountNumber)
        userPassword = input('Please enter the password: ')
        theBalance = getBalance(userAccountNumber, userPassword)
        if theBalance is not None:
            print('Your balance is:', theBalance)

--- snipped additional user interface ---

print('Done')
```

*Listing 1-5: Bank simulation with a parallel lists*

At the beginning of the program, I set all three lists to the empty list ❶. To create a new account, I append the appropriate value to each of the three lists ❷.

Since I am now dealing with multiple accounts, I use the basic concept of a bank account number. Every time a user creates an account, the code uses the len() function on one of the lists and returns that number as the user's account number ❸, ❹. When I create an account for the first user, the length of the accountNamesList is zero. Therefore, the first account created will be given account number 0, the second account is given account number 1, and so on. Then, like at a real bank, to do any operation after creating an account (like deposit or withdraw funds), the user must supply their account number ❺.

However, this code is still working with global data; now there are three global lists of data.

Imagine viewing this data as a spreadsheet. It might look like Table 1-1.

**Table 1-1:** A Table of Our Data

| Account number | Name | Password | Balance |
|---|---|---|---|
| 0 | Joe | soup | 100 |
| 1 | Mary | nuts | 3550 |
| 2 | Bill | frisbee | 1000 |
| 3 | Sue | xxyyzz | 750 |
| 4 | Henry | PW | 10000 |

The data is maintained as three global Python lists, where each list represents a column in this table. For example, as you can see from the highlighted column, all the passwords are grouped together as one list. The users' names are grouped in another list, and the balances are grouped in a third list. With this approach, to get information about one account, you need to access these lists with a common index value.

While this works, it seems extremely awkward. The data is not grouped in a logical way. For example, it doesn't seem right to keep all users' passwords together. Further, every time you add a new attribute to an account, like an address or phone number, you need to create and access another global list.

Instead, what you really want is a grouping that represents a row in the same spreadsheet, as in Table 1-2.

**Table 1-2:** A Table of Our Data

| Account number | Name | Password | Balance |
|---|---|---|---|
| 0 | Joe | soup | 100 |
| 1 | Mary | nuts | 3550 |
| 2 | Bill | frisbee | 1000 |
| 3 | Sue | xxyyzz | 750 |
| 4 | Henry | PW | 10000 |

With this approach, each row represents the data associated with a single bank account. While this is the same data, this grouping is a much more natural way of representing an account.

## Implementation 5—List of Account Dictionaries

To implement this last approach, I'll use a slightly more complicated data structure. In this version, I'll create a list of accounts, where each account (each element of this list) is a dictionary that looks like this:

```
{'name':<someName>, 'password':<somePassword>, 'balance':<someBalance>}
```

**NOTE**  *In this book, whenever I present a value in angle brackets (<>), this means you should replace that item (including the brackets) with a value of your choosing. For example, in the preceding code line, <someName>, <somePassword>, and <someBalance> are placeholders and should be replaced with actual values.*

The code for the final implementation is presented in Listing 1-6.

**File: Bank5_Dictionary.py**

```
# Non-OOP Bank
# Version 5
# Any number of accounts - with a list of dictionaries

accountsList = [] ❶

def newAccount(aName, aBalance, aPassword):
    global accountsList
    newAccountDict = {'name':aName, 'balance':aBalance, 'password':aPassword}
    accountsList.append(newAccountDict) ❷
```

```python
def show(accountNumber):
    global accountsList
    print('Account', accountNumber)
    thisAccountDict = accountsList[accountNumber]
    print('        Name', thisAccountDict['name'])
    print('        Balance:', thisAccountDict['balance'])
    print('        Password:', thisAccountDict['password'])
    print()

def getBalance(accountNumber, password):
    global accountsList
    thisAccountDict = accountsList[accountNumber]  ❸
    if password != thisAccountDict['password']:
        print('Incorrect password')
        return None
    return thisAccountDict['balance']

--- snipped additional deposit() and withdraw() functions ---

# Create two sample accounts
print("Joe's account is account number:", len(accountsList))
newAccount("Joe", 100, 'soup')

print("Mary's account is account number:", len(accountsList))
newAccount("Mary", 12345, 'nuts')

while True:
    print()
    print('Press b to get the balance')
    print('Press d to make a deposit')
    print('Press n to create a new account')
    print('Press w to make a withdrawal')
    print('Press s to show all accounts')
    print('Press q to quit')
    print()

    action = input('What do you want to do? ')
    action = action.lower()  # force lowercase
    action = action[0]  # just use first letter
    print()

    if action == 'b':
        print('Get Balance:')
        userAccountNumber = input('Please enter your account number: ')
        userAccountNumber = int(userAccountNumber)
        userPassword = input('Please enter the password: ')
        theBalance = getBalance(userAccountNumber, userPassword)
        if theBalance is not None:
            print('Your balance is:', theBalance)

    elif action == 'd':
        print('Deposit:')
        userAccountNumber= input('Please enter the account number: ')
        userAccountNumber = int(userAccountNumber)
        userDepositAmount = input('Please enter amount to deposit: ')
```

```
        userDepositAmount = int(userDepositAmount)
        userPassword = input('Please enter the password: ')

        newBalance = deposit(userAccountNumber, userDepositAmount, userPassword)
        if newBalance is not None:
            print('Your new balance is:', newBalance)

    elif action == 'n':
        print('New Account:')
        userName = input('What is your name? ')
        userStartingAmount = input('What is the amount of your initial deposit? ')
        userStartingAmount = int(userStartingAmount)
        userPassword = input('What password would you like to use for this account? ')

        userAccountNumber = len(accountsList)
        newAccount(userName, userStartingAmount, userPassword)
        print('Your new account number is:', userAccountNumber)

--- snipped additional user interface ---

print('Done')
```

Listing 1-6: Bank simulation with a list of dictionaries

With this approach, all the data associated with one account can be found in a single dictionary ❶. To create a new account, we build a dictionary and append it to the list of accounts ❷. Each account is assigned a number (a simple integer), and that account number must be supplied when doing any action with the account. For example, the user supplies their account number when making a deposit, and the getBalance() function uses that account number as an index into the list of accounts ❸.

This cleans things up quite a bit, making the organization of the data more logical. But each of the functions in the program must still have access to the global list of accounts. As we'll see in the next section, granting functions access to all account data raises potential security risks. Ideally, each function should only be able to affect the data of a single account.

## Common Problems with Procedural Implementation

The examples shown in this chapter share a common problem: all the data the functions operate on is stored in one or more global variables. For the following reasons, using lots of global data with procedural programming is bad coding practice:

1.  Any function that uses and/or changes global data cannot easily be reused in a different program. A function that accesses global data is operating on data that lives at a different (higher) level than the code of the function itself. That function will need a global statement to access this data. You can't just take a function that relies on global data and reuse it in another program; it can only be reused in a program with similar global data.

2. Many procedural programs tend to have large collections of global variables. By definition, a global variable can be used or changed by any piece of code anywhere in the program. Assignments to global variables are often widely scattered throughout procedural programs, both in the main code and inside functions. Because variable values can change anywhere, it can be extremely difficult to debug and maintain programs written this way.

3. Functions written to use global data often have access to too much data. When a function uses a global list, dictionary, or any other global data structure, it has access to *all* the data in that data structure. However, typically the function should operate on only one piece (or just a small amount) of that data. Having the ability to read and modify any data in a large data structure can lead to errors, such as accidentally using or overwriting data that the function was not intended to touch.

## Object-Oriented Solution—First Look at a Class

Listing 1-7 is an object-oriented approach that combines all the code and associated data of a single account. There are many new concepts here, and I will get into all the details starting in the next chapter. While I am not expecting you to fully understand this example yet, notice that there is a combination of code and data in a single script (called a *class*). Here is your first look at object-oriented code.

### File: Account.py

```
# Account class

class Account():
    def __init__(self, name, balance, password):
        self.name = name
        self.balance = int(balance)
        self.password = password

    def deposit(self, amountToDeposit, password):
        if password != self.password:
            print('Sorry, incorrect password')
            return None

        if amountToDeposit < 0:
            print('You cannot deposit a negative amount')
            return None

        self.balance = self.balance + amountToDeposit
        return self.balance

    def withdraw(self, amountToWithdraw, password):
        if password != self.password:
            print('Incorrect password for this account')
            return None
```

```
        if amountToWithdraw < 0:
            print('You cannot withdraw a negative amount')
            return None

        if amountToWithdraw > self.balance:
            print('You cannot withdraw more than you have in your account')
            return None

        self.balance = self.balance - amountToWithdraw
        return self.balance

    def getBalance(self, password):
        if password != self.password:
            print('Sorry, incorrect password')
            return None
        return self.balance

    # Added for debugging
    def show(self):
        print('      Name:', self.name)
        print('      Balance:', self.balance)
        print('      Password:', self.password)
        print()
```

Listing 1-7: First example of a class in Python

For now, take a look at the functions and see how they're similar to our earlier procedural programming examples. The functions have the same names as in the earlier code—show(), getBalance(), deposit(), and withdraw()—but you'll also see the word self (or self.) peppered throughout this code. You'll learn what this means in the next chapters.

## Summary

This chapter started with a procedural implementation of the code for a card game called Higher or Lower. In Chapter 12, I will show you how to make an object-oriented version of the game with a graphical user interface.

I next introduced the problem of simulating a bank with one, then several bank accounts. I discussed several different ways to use procedural programming to implement the simulation and described some of the problems that this approach creates. Finally, I gave a first glimpse of what the code describing a bank account would look like if it were written using a class.

# 2

## MODELING PHYSICAL OBJECTS WITH OBJECT-ORIENTED PROGRAMMING

In this chapter, I'll introduce the general concepts behind object-oriented programming. I'll show a simple example program written using procedural programming, introduce classes as the basis of writing OOP code, and explain how the elements of a class work together. I'll then rewrite the first procedural example as a class in the object-oriented style and show how you create an object from a class.

In the remainder of the chapter, I'll go through some increasingly complex classes that represent physical objects to demonstrate how OOP fixes the problems of procedural programming we ran into in Chapter 1. This should give you a solid understanding of the underlying object-oriented concepts and how they can improve your programming skills.

# Building Software Models of Physical Objects

To describe a physical object in our everyday world, we often reference its attributes. When talking about a desk, you might describe its color, dimensions, weight, material, and so on. Some objects have attributes that apply only to them and not others. A car could be described by its number of doors, but a shirt could not. A box could be sealed or open, empty or full, but those characteristics would not apply to a block of wood. Additionally, some objects are capable of performing actions. A car can go forward, back up, and turn left or right.

To model a real-world object in code, we need to decide what data will represent that object's attributes and what operations it can perform. These two concepts are often referred to as an object's *state* and *behavior*, respectively: the state is the data that the object remembers, and the behaviors are the actions that the object can do.

## State and Behavior: Light Switch Example

Listing 2-1 is a software model of a standard two-position light switch written in procedural Python. This is a trivial example, but it will demonstrate state and behavior.

### File: LightSwitch_Procedural.py

```
# Procedural light switch

❶ def turnOn():
      global switchIsOn
      # turn the light on
      switchIsOn = True

❷ def turnOff():
      global switchIsOn
      # turn the light off
      switchIsOn = False

  # Main code
❸ switchIsOn = False   # a global Boolean variable

  # Test code
  print(switchIsOn)
  turnOn()
  print(switchIsOn)
  turnOff()
  print(switchIsOn)
  turnOn()
  print(switchIsOn)
```

Listing 2-1: Model of a light switch written with procedural code

The switch can only be in one of two positions: on or off. To model the state, we only need a single Boolean variable. We name this variable switchIsOn ❸ and we say that True means on and False indicates off. When the switch comes from the factory, it is in the off position, so we initially set switchIsOn to False.

Next, we look at the behavior. This switch can only perform two actions: "turn on" and "turn off." We therefore build two functions, turnOn() ❶ and turnOff() ❷, which set the value of the single Boolean variable to True and False, respectively.

I've added some test code at the end to turn the switch on and off a few times. The output is exactly what we would expect:

```
False
True
False
True
```

This is an extremely simple example, but starting with small functions like these makes the transition to an OOP approach easier. As I explained in Chapter 1, because we've used a global variable to represent the state (in this case, the variable switchIsOn), this code will only work for a single light switch, but one of the main goals of writing functions is to make reusable code. I'll therefore rebuild the light switch code using object-oriented programming, but I need to work through a bit of the underlying theory first.

## Introduction to Classes and Objects

The first step to understanding what an object is and how it works is to understand the relationship between a class and an object. I'll give formal definitions later, but for now, you can think of a class as a template or a blueprint that defines what an object will look like when one is created. We create objects from a class.

As an analogy, imagine if we started an on-demand cake-baking business. Being "on-demand," we only create a cake when an order for one comes in. We specialize in Bundt cakes, and we've spent a lot of time developing the cake pan in Figure 2-1 to make sure our cakes are not only tasty but also beautiful and consistent.

The pan defines what a Bundt cake will look like when we create one, but it certainly is not a cake. The pan represents our class. When an order comes in, we create a Bundt cake from our pan (Figure 2-2). The cake is an object made using the cake pan.

Using the pan, we can create any number of cakes. Our cakes could have different attributes, like different flavors, different types of frosting, and optional extras like chocolate chips, but all the cakes will come from the same cake pan.

Figure 2-1: A cake pan as a metaphor for a class

Figure 2-2: A cake as a metaphor for an object made from the cake pan class

Table 2-1 provides some other real-world examples to help clarify the relationship between a class and an object.

**Table 2-1:** Examples of Real-World Classes and Objects

| Class | Object made from the class |
| --- | --- |
| Blueprint for a house | House |
| Sandwich listed on a menu | Sandwich in your hand |
| Die used to manufacture a 25-cent coin | A single quarter |
| Manuscript of a book written by an author | Physical or electronic copy of the book |

# Classes, Objects, and Instantiation

Let's see how this works in code.

---

**class**    Code that defines what an object will remember (its data or *state*) and the things that it will be able to do (its functions or *behavior*).

---

To get a feel for what a class looks like, here is the code of a light switch written as a class:

```
# 00_LightSwitch

class LightSwitch():
    def __init__(self):
        self.switchIsOn = False

    def turnOn(self):
        # turn the switch on
        self.switchIsOn = True

    def turnOff(self):
        # turn the switch off
        self.switchIsOn = False
```

We'll go through the details in just a bit, but the things to notice are that this code defines a single variable, self.switchIsOn, which is initialized in one function, and contains two other functions for the behaviors: turnOn() and turnoff().

If you write the code of a class and try to run it, nothing happens, in the same way as when you run a Python program that consists of only functions and no function calls. You have to explicitly tell Python to make an object from the class.

To create a LightSwitch object from our LightSwitch class, we typically use a line like this:

```
oLightSwitch = LightSwitch()
```

This says: find the LightSwitch class, create a LightSwitch object from that class, and assign the resulting object to the variable oLightSwitch.

Another word that you'll come across in OOP is *instance*. The words *instance* and *object* are essentially interchangeable; however, to be precise, we would say that a LightSwitch object is an instance of the LightSwitch class.

---

**instantiation**    The process of creating an object from a class.

---

In the previous assignment statement, we went through the instantiation process to create a LightSwitch object from the LightSwitch class. We can also use this as a verb; we *instantiate* a LightSwitch object from the LightSwitch class.

## Writing a Class in Python

Let's discuss the different parts of a class and the details of instantiating and using an object. Listing 2-2 shows the general form of a class in Python.

```
class <ClassName>():

    def __init__(self, <optional param1>, ..., <optional paramN>):
        #  any initialization code here

    # Any number of functions that access the data
    # Each has the form:

    def <functionName1>(self, <optional param1>, ..., <optional paramN>):
        #  body of function

    #  ... more functions

    def <functionNameN>(self, <optional param1>, ..., <optional paramN>):
        #  body of function
```

*Listing 2-2: The typical form of a class in Python*

You begin a class definition with a class statement specifying the name you want to give the class. The convention for class names is to use camel case, with the first letter uppercase (for example, LightSwitch). Following the name you can optionally add a set of parentheses, but the statement must end with a colon to indicate that you're about to begin the body of the class. (I'll explain what can go inside the parentheses in Chapter 10, when we discuss inheritance.)

Within the body of the class, you can define any number of functions. All the functions are considered part of the class, and the code that defines them must be indented. Each function represents some behavior that an object created from the class can perform. All functions must have at least one parameter, which by convention is named self (I'll explain what this name means in Chapter 3). OOP functions are given a special name: *method*.

---

**method**    A function defined inside a class. A method always has at least one parameter, which is usually named self.

---

The first method in every class should have the special name __init__. Whenever you create an object from a class, this method will run automatically. Therefore, this method is the logical place to put any initialization code that you want to run whenever you instantiate an object from a class. The name __init__ is reserved by Python for this very task, and it must be written exactly this way, with two underscores before and after the word *init* (which must be lowercase). In reality, the __init__() method is not strictly required. However, it's generally considered good practice to include it and use it for initialization.

**NOTE**    *When you instantiate an object from a class, Python takes care of constructing the object (allocating memory) for you. The special __init__() method is called the "initializer" method, where you give variables initial values. (Most other OOP languages require a method named new(), which is often referred to as a* constructor.*)*

## Scope and Instance Variables

In procedural programming, there are two principal levels of scope: variables created in the main code have *global* scope and are available anywhere in a program, while variables created inside a function have *local* scope and only live as long as the function runs. When the function exits, all local variables (variables with local scope) literally go away.

Object-oriented programming and classes introduce a third level of scope, typically called *object scope*, though sometimes referred to as *class scope* or more rarely as *instance scope*. They all mean the same thing: the scope consists of all the code inside the class definition.

Methods can have both local variables and *instance variables*. In a method, any variable whose name does not start with self. is a local variable and will go away when that method exits, meaning other methods within the class can no longer use that variable. *Instance variables* have object scope, which means they are available to *all* methods defined in a class. Instance variables and object scope are the keys to understanding how objects remember data.

---

**instance variable**    In a method, any variable whose name begins, by convention, with the prefix self. (for example, self.x). Instance variables have object scope.

---

Just like local and global variables, instance variables are created when they are first given a value and do not need any special declaration. The __init__() method is the logical place to initialize instance variables. Here we have an example of a class where the __init__() method initializes an instance variable self.count (read as "self dot count") to zero and another method, increment(), that simply adds 1 to self.count:

```
class MyClass():
    def __init__(self):
        self.count = 0  # create self.count and set it to 0
    def increment(self):
        self.count = self.count + 1  # increment the variable
```

When you instantiate an object from the MyClass class, the __init__() method runs and sets the value of the instance variable self.count to zero. If you then call the increment() method, the value of self.count goes from zero to one. If you call increment() again, the value goes from one to two, and on and on.

Each object created from a class gets its own set of instance variables, independent of any other objects instantiated from that class. In the case of the LightSwitch class, there is only one instance variable, self.switchIsOn, so every LightSwitch object will have its own self.switchIsOn. Therefore, you can have multiple LightSwitch objects, each with its own independent value of True or False for its self.switchIsOn variable.

## Differences Between Functions and Methods

To recap, there are three key differences between a function and a method:

1. All methods of a class must be indented under the class statement.
2. All methods have a special first parameter that (by convention) is named self.
3. Methods in a class can use instance variables, written in the form self.<variableName>.

Now that you know what methods are, I'll show you how to create an object from a class and how to use the different methods that are available in a class.

## Creating an Object from a Class

As I said earlier, a class simply defines what an object will look like. To use a class, you have to tell Python to make an object from the class. The typical way to do this is to use an assignment statement like this:

```
<object> = <ClassName>(<optional arguments>)
```

This single line of code invokes a sequence of steps that ends with Python handing you back a new instance of the class, which you typically store into a variable. That variable then refers to the resulting object.

## THE INSTANTIATION PROCESS

Figure 2-3 shows the steps involved in instantiating a LightSwitch object from the LightSwitch class, going from the assignment statement into Python, then to the code of the class, then back out through Python again, and finally back to the assignment statement.

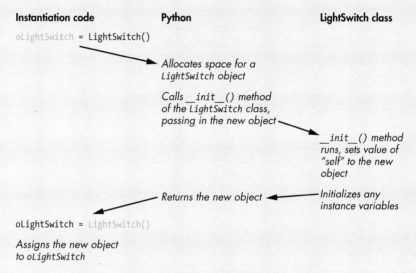

**Instantiation code**     **Python**     **LightSwitch class**

oLightSwitch = LightSwitch()

*Allocates space for a LightSwitch object*

*Calls __init__() method of the LightSwitch class, passing in the new object*

*__init__() method runs, sets value of "self" to the new object*

*Returns the new object*     *Initializes any instance variables*

oLightSwitch = LightSwitch()

*Assigns the new object to oLightSwitch*

Figure 2-3: The process of instantiating an object

The process consists of five steps:

1.  Our code asks Python to create an object from the LightSwitch class.
2.  Python allocates space in memory for a LightSwitch object, then calls the __init__() method of the LightSwitch class, passing in the newly created object.
3.  The __init__() method of the LightSwitch class runs. The new object is assigned to the parameter self. The code of __init__() initializes any instance variables in the object (in this case, the instance variable self.switchIsOn).
4.  Python returns the new object to the original caller.
5.  The result of the original call is assigned into the variable oLightSwitch, so it now represents the object.

You can make a class available in two ways: you can place the code of the class in the same file with the main program, or you can put the code of the class in an external file and use an import statement to bring in the contents of the file. I'll show the first approach in this chapter and the second approach in Chapter 4. The only rule is that the class definition must precede any code that instantiates an object from the class.

## Calling Methods of an Object

After creating an object from a class, to call a method of the object, you use the generic syntax:

---

`<object>.<methodName>(<any arguments>)`

---

Listing 2-3 contains the LightSwitch class, code to instantiate an object from the class, and code to turn that LightSwitch object on and off by calling its turnOn() and turnOff() methods.

### File: OO_LightSwitch_with_Test_Code.py

```python
# OO_LightSwitch

class LightSwitch():
    def __init__(self):
        self.switchIsOn = False

    def turnOn(self):
        # turn the switch on
        self.switchIsOn = True

    def turnOff(self):
        # turn the switch off
        self.switchIsOn = False

    def show(self):  # added for testing
        print(self.switchIsOn)

# Main code
oLightSwitch = LightSwitch()  # create a LightSwitch object

#  Calls to methods
oLightSwitch.show()
oLightSwitch.turnOn()
oLightSwitch.show()
oLightSwitch.turnOff()
oLightSwitch.show()
oLightSwitch.turnOn()
oLightSwitch.show()
```

*Listing 2-3: The LightSwitch class and test code to create an object and call its methods*

First we create a LightSwitch object and assign it to the oLightSwitch variable. We then use that variable to call other methods available in the LightSwitch class. We would read these lines as "oLightSwitch dot show," "oLightSwitch dot turnOn," and so on. If we run this code, it will output:

```
False
True
False
True
```

Recall that this class has a single instance variable named self.switchIsOn, but its value is remembered and easily accessed when different methods of the same object run.

## Creating Multiple Instances from the Same Class

One of the key features of OOP is that you can instantiate as many objects as you want from a single class, in the same way that you can make endless cakes from a Bundt cake pan.

So, if you want two light switch objects, or three, or more, you can just create additional objects from the LightSwitch class like so:

```python
oLightSwitch1 = LightSwitch()  # create a light switch object
oLightSwitch2 = LightSwitch()  # create another light switch object
```

The important point here is that each object that you create from a class maintains *its own version* of the data. In this case, oLightSwitch1 and oLightSwitch2 each have their own instance variable, self.switchIsOn. Any changes you make to the data of one object will not affect the data of another object. You can call any of the methods in the class with either object.

The example in Listing 2-4 creates two light switch objects and calls methods on the different objects.

### File: OO_LightSwitch_Two_Instances.py

```python
# OO_LightSwitch

class LightSwitch():
--- snipped code of LightSwitch class, as in Listing 2-3 ---

# Main code
oLightSwitch1 = LightSwitch()  # create a LightSwitch object
oLightSwitch2 = LightSwitch()  # create another LightSwitch object

# Test code
oLightSwitch1.show()
oLightSwitch2.show()
oLightSwitch1.turnOn() # Turn switch 1 on
# Switch 2 should be off at start, but this makes it clearer
oLightSwitch2.turnOff()
oLightSwitch1.show()
oLightSwitch2.show()
```

*Listing 2-4: Create two instances of a class and call methods of each*

Here's the output when this program is run:

```
False
False
True
False
```

The code tells oLightSwitch1 to turn itself on and tells oLightSwitch2 to turn itself off. Notice that the code in the class has no global variables. Each LightSwitch object gets its own set of any instance variables (just one in this case) defined in the class.

While this may not seem like a huge improvement over having two simple global variables that could be used to do the same thing, the implications of this technique are enormous. You'll get a better sense of this in Chapter 4, where I'll discuss how to create and maintain a large number of instances made from a class.

## Python Data Types Are Implemented as Classes

It might not surprise you that all built-in data types in Python are implemented as classes. Here is a simple example:

```
>>> myString = 'abcde'
>>> print(type(myString))
<class 'str'>
```

We assign a string value to a variable. When we call the type() function and print the results, we see that we have an instance of the str string class. The str class gives us a number of methods we can call with strings, including myString.upper(), myString.lower(), myString.strip(), and so on.

Lists work in a similar way:

```
>>> myList = [10, 20, 30, 40]
>>> print(type(myList))
<class 'list'>
```

All lists are instances of the list class, which has many methods including myList.append(), myList.count(), myList.index(), and so on.

When you write a class, you are defining a new data type. Your code provides the details by defining what data it maintains and what operations it can perform. After creating an instance of your class and assigning it to a variable, you can use the type() built-in function to determine the class used to create it, just like with a built-in data type. Here we instantiate a LightSwitch object and print out its data type:

```
>>> oLightSwitch = LightSwitch()
>>> print(type(oLightSwitch))
<class 'LightSwitch'>
```

Just like with Python's built-in data types, we can then use the variable `oLightSwitch` to call the methods available in the `oLightSwitch` class.

### Definition of an Object

To summarize this section, I'll give my formal definition of an *object*.

---

**object**  Data, plus code that acts on that data, over time.

---

A class defines what an object will look like when you instantiate one. An object is a set of instance variables and the code of the methods in the class from which the object was instantiated. Any number of objects can be instantiated from a class, and each has its own set of instance variables. When you call a method of an object, the method runs and uses the set of instance variables in that object.

## Building a Slightly More Complicated Class

Let's build on the concepts introduced so far and work through a second, slightly more complicated example in which we'll make a dimmer switch class. A dimmer switch has an on/off switch, but it also has a multiposition slider that affects the brightness of the light.

The slider can move through a range of brightness values. To make things straightforward, our dimmer digital slider has 11 positions, from 0 (completely off) through 10 (completely on). To raise or lower the brightness of the bulb to the maximum extent, you must move the slider through every possible setting.

This `DimmerSwitch` class has more functionality than our `LightSwitch` class and needs to remember more data:

- The switch state (on or off)
- Brightness level (0 to 10)

And here are the behaviors a `DimmerSwitch` object can perform:

- Turn on
- Turn off
- Raise level
- Lower level
- Show (for debugging)

The `DimmerSwitch` class uses the standard template shown earlier in Listing 2-2: it starts with a `class` statement and a first method named `__init__()`, then defines a number of additional methods, one for each of the behaviors listed. The full code for this class is presented in Listing 2-5.

**File: DimmerSwitch.py**

```python
# DimmerSwitch class

class DimmerSwitch():
    def __init__(self):
        self.switchIsOn = False
        self.brightness = 0

    def turnOn(self):
        self.switchIsOn = True

    def turnOff(self):
        self.switchIsOn = False

    def raiseLevel(self):
        if self.brightness < 10:
            self.brightness = self.brightness + 1

    def lowerLevel(self):
        if self.brightness > 0:
            self.brightness = self.brightness - 1

    # Extra method for debugging
    def show(self):
        print(Switch is on?', self.switchIsOn)
        print('Brightness is:', self.brightness)
```

*Listing 2-5: The slightly more complicated `DimmerSwitch` class*

In this __init__() method we have two instance variables: the familiar self.switchIsOn and a new one, self.brightness, which remembers the brightness level. We assign starting values to both instance variables. All other methods can access the current value of each of these. In addition to turnOn() and turnOff(), we include two new methods for this class: raiseLevel() and lowerLevel(), which do exactly what their names imply. The show() method is used during development and debugging and just prints the current values of the instance variables.

The main code in Listing 2-6 tests our class by creating a DimmerSwitch object (oDimmer), then calling the various methods.

**File: OO_DimmerSwitch_with_Test_Code.py**

```python
# DimmerSwitch class with test code

class DimmerSwitch():
--- snipped code of DimmerSwitch class, as in Listing 2-5 ---

# Main code
oDimmer = DimmerSwitch()

# Turn switch on, and raise the level 5 times
```

```
oDimmer.turnOn()
oDimmer.raiseLevel()
oDimmer.raiseLevel()
oDimmer.raiseLevel()
oDimmer.raiseLevel()
oDimmer.raiseLevel()
oDimmer.show()

# Lower the level 2 times, and turn switch off
oDimmer.lowerLevel()
oDimmer.lowerLevel()
oDimmer.turnOff()
oDimmer.show()

# Turn switch on, and raise the level 3 times
oDimmer.turnOn()
oDimmer.raiseLevel()
oDimmer.raiseLevel()
oDimmer.raiseLevel()
oDimmer.show()
```

Listing 2-6: DimmerSwitch class with test code

When we run this code, the resulting output is:

```
Switch is on? True
Brightness is: 5
Switch is on? False
Brightness is: 3
Switch is on? True
Brightness is: 6
```

The main code creates the oDimmer object, then makes calls to the various methods. Each time we call the show() method, the on/off state and the brightness level are printed. The key thing to remember here is that oDimmer represents an object. It allows access to all methods in the class from which it was instantiated (the DimmerSwitch class), *and* it has a set of all instance variables defined in the class (self.switchIsOn and self.brightness). Again, instance variables maintain their values between calls to methods of an object, so the self.brightness instance variable is incremented by 1 for each call to oDimmer.raiseLevel().

## Representing a More Complicated Physical Object as a Class

Let's consider a more complicated physical object: a television. With this more complicated example, we'll take a closer look at how arguments work in classes.

A television requires much more data than a light switch to represent its state, and it has more behaviors. To create a TV class, we must consider how a user would typically use a TV and what the TV would have to remember. Let's look at some of the important buttons on a typical TV remote (Figure 2-4).

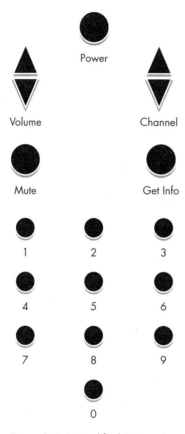

Figure 2-4: A simplified TV remote

From this, we can determine that to keep track of its state, a TV class would have to maintain the following data:

- Power state (on or off)
- Mute state (is it muted?)
- List of channels available
- Current channel setting
- Current volume setting
- Range of volume levels available

And the actions that the TV must provide include:

- Turn the power on and off
- Raise and lower the volume
- Change the channel up and down
- Mute and unmute the sound
- Get information about the current settings
- Go to a specified channel

The code for our TV class is shown in Listing 2-7. We include the __init__()
method for initialization, followed by a method for each of the behaviors.

## File: TV.py

```python
# TV class

class TV():
    def __init__(self): ❶
        self.isOn = False
        self.isMuted = False
        # Some default list of channels
        self.channelList = [2, 4, 5, 7, 9, 11, 20, 36, 44, 54, 65]
        self.nChannels = len(self.channelList)
        self.channelIndex = 0
        self.VOLUME_MINIMUM = 0     # constant
        self.VOLUME_MAXIMUM = 10    # constant
        self.volume = self.VOLUME_MAXIMUM // 2    # integer divide

    def power(self): ❷
        self.isOn = not self.isOn    # toggle

    def volumeUp(self):
        if not self.isOn:
            return
        if self.isMuted:
            self.isMuted = False  # changing the volume while muted unmutes the sound
        if self.volume < self.VOLUME_MAXIMUM:
            self.volume = self.volume + 1

    def volumeDown(self):
        if not self.isOn:
            return
        if self.isMuted:
            self.isMuted = False  # changing the volume while muted unmutes the sound
        if self.volume > self.VOLUME_MINIMUM:
            self.volume = self.volume - 1

    def channelUp(self): ❸
        if not self.isOn:
            return
        self.channelIndex = self.channelIndex + 1
        if self.channelIndex > self.nChannels:
            self.channelIndex = 0 # wrap around to the first channel

    def channelDown(self): ❹
        if not self.isOn:
            return
        self.channelIndex = self.channelIndex - 1
        if self.channelIndex < 0:
            self.channelIndex = self.nChannels - 1  # wrap around to the top channel

    def mute(self): ❺
        if not self.isOn:
```

```
        return
    self.isMuted = not self.isMuted

def setChannel(self, newChannel):
    if newChannel in self.channelList:
        self.channelIndex = self.channelList.index(newChannel)
    # if the newChannel is not in our list of channels, don't do anything

def showInfo(self): ❻
    print()
    print('TV Status:')
    if self.isOn:
        print('    TV is: On')
        print('    Channel is:', self.channelList[self.channelIndex])
        if self.isMuted:
            print('    Volume is:', self.volume, '(sound is muted)')
        else:
            print('    Volume is:', self.volume)
    else:
        print('    TV is: Off')
```

*Listing 2-7: The TV class with many instance variables and methods*

The __init__() method ❶ creates all the instance variables used in all the methods and assigns reasonable starting values to each. Technically, you can create an instance variable inside any method; however, it is a good programming practice to define all instance variables in the __init__() method. This avoids the risk of an error when attempting to use an instance variable in a method before it's been defined.

The power() method ❷ represents what happens when you push the power button on a remote. If the TV is off, pushing the power button turns it on; if the TV is on, pushing the power button turns it off. To code this behavior I've used a *toggle*, which is a Boolean that's used to represent one of two states and can easily be switched between them. With this toggle, the not operator switches the self.isOn variable from True to False, or from False to True. The mute() method code ❺ does a similar thing, with the self.muted variable toggling between muted and not-muted, but first has to check that the TV is on. If the TV is off, calling the mute() method has no effect.

One interesting thing to note is that we don't really keep track of the current channel. Instead, we keep track of the *index* of the current channel, which allows us to get the current channel at any time by using self.channelList[self.channelIndex].

The channelUp() ❸ and channelDown() ❹ methods basically increment and decrement the channel index, but there is also some clever code in them to allow for wrap-around. If you're currently at the last index in the channel list and the user asks to go to the next channel up, the TV goes to the first channel in the list. If you're at the first index in the channel list and the user asks to go the next channel down, the TV goes to the last channel in the list.

The showInfo() method ❻ prints out the current status of the TV based on the values of the instance variables (on/off, current channel, current volume setting, and mute setting).

In Listing 2-8, we'll create a TV object and call methods of that object.

## File: OO_TV_with_Test_Code.py

```
# TV class with test code

--- snipped code of TV class, as in Listing 2-7 ---

# Main code
oTV = TV()  # create the TV object

# Turn the TV on and show the status
oTV.power()
oTV.showInfo()

# Change the channel up twice, raise the volume twice, show status
oTV.channelUp()
oTV.channelUp()
oTV.volumeUp()
oTV.volumeUp()
oTV.showInfo()

# Turn the TV off, show status, turn the TV on, show status
oTV.power()
oTV.showInfo()
oTV.power()
oTV.showInfo()

# Lower the volume, mute the sound, show status
oTV.volumeDown()
oTV.mute()
oTV.showInfo()

# Change the channel to 11, mute the sound, show status
oTV.setChannel(11)
oTV.mute()
oTV.showInfo()
```

*Listing 2-8: TV class with test code*

When we run this code, here is what we get as output:

```
TV Status:
    TV is: On
    Channel is: 2
    Volume is: 5

TV Status:
    TV is: On
    Channel is: 5
    Volume is: 7

TV Status:
    TV is: Off
```

```
TV Status:
    TV is: On
    Channel is: 5
    Volume is: 7

TV Status:
    TV is: On
    Channel is: 5
    Volume is: 6 (sound is muted)

TV Status:
    TV is: On
    Channel is: 11
    Volume is: 6
```

All of the methods are working correctly, and we get the expected output.

## Passing Arguments to a Method

When calling any function, the number of arguments must match the number of parameters listed in the matching def statement:

```
def myFunction(param1, param2, param3):
    # body of function

# call to a function:
myFunction(argument1, argument2, argument3)
```

The same rule applies with methods and method calls. However, you may notice that whenever we make a call to a method, it appears that we are specifying one less argument than the number of parameters. For example, the definition of the power() method in our TV class looks like this:

```
def power(self):
```

This implies that the power() method is expecting one value to be passed in and whatever is passed in will be assigned to the variable self. Yet when we started by turning on the TV in Listing 2-8, we made this call:

```
oTV.power()
```

When we make the call, we don't explicitly pass anything inside the parentheses.

This may seem even stranger in the case of the setChannel() method. The method is written to accept two parameters:

```
def setchannel(self, newchannel):
    if newChannel in self.channelList:
        self.channelIndex = self.channelList.index(newChannel)
```

But we called setChannel() like this:

```
oTV.setChannel(11)
```

It appears that only one value is being passed in.

You might expect Python to generate an error here, due to a mismatch in the number of arguments (one) and the number of parameters (two). In practice, Python is doing a bit of behind-the-scenes work to make the syntax easier to follow.

Let's examine this. Earlier, I said that to make a call to a method of an object, you use the following generic syntax:

```
<object>.<method>(<any arguments>)
```

Python takes the `<object>` you specify in the call and rearranges it to become the first argument. Any values in the parentheses of the method call are considered the subsequent argument(s). Thus, Python makes it appear that you wrote this instead:

```
<method of object>(<object>, <any arguments>)
```

Figure 2-5 shows how this works in our example code, again using the setChannel() method of the TV class.

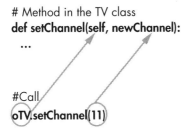

Figure 2-5: Calling a method

Although it looks like we're only providing one argument here (for newChannel), there are really two arguments passed in—oTV and 11—and the method provides two parameters to receive these values (self and newChannel, respectively). Python rearranges the arguments for us when the call is made. This may seem odd at first, but it will become second nature very quickly. Writing the call with the object first makes it much easier for a programmer to see which object is being acted on.

This is a subtle but important feature. Remember that the object (in this case, oTV) keeps the current settings of all of its instance variables. Passing the object as the first argument allows the method to run with the values of the instance variables of that object.

## Multiple Instances

Every method is written with self as the first parameter, so the self variable receives the object used in each call. This has a major implication: it allows any method within a class to work with *different* objects. I'll explain how this works using an example.

In Listing 2-9, we'll create two TV objects and save them in two variables, oTV1 and oTV2. Each TV object has a volume setting, a channel list, a channel setting, and so on. We'll make calls to a number of different methods of the different objects. At the end, we'll call the showInfo() method on each TV object to see the resulting settings.

### File: OO_TV_TwoInstances.py

```python
# Two TV objects with calls to their methods
class TV():
--- snipped code of TV class, as in Listing 2-7 ---
# Main code
oTV1 = TV()   # create one TV object
oTV2 = TV()   # create another TV object

# Turn both TVs on
oTV1.power()
oTV2.power()

# Raise the volume of TV1
oTV1.volumeUp()
oTV1.volumeUp()

# Raise the volume of TV2
oTV2.volumeUp()
oTV2.volumeUp()
oTV2.volumeUp()
oTV2.volumeUp()
oTV2.volumeUp()

# Change TV2's channel, then mute it
oTV2.setChannel(44)
oTV2.mute()

# Now display both TVs
oTV1.showInfo()
oTV2.showInfo()
```

*Listing 2-9: Creating two instances of the TV class and calling methods of each*

If we run this code, it will generate the following output:

```
Status of TV:
    TV is: On
    Channel is: 2
    Volume is: 7

Status of TV:
    TV is: On
    Channel is: 44
    Volume is: 10 (sound is muted)
```

Each TV object maintains its own set of the instance variables defined in the class. This way, each TV object's instance variables can be manipulated independently of those of any other TV object.

## Initialization Parameters

The ability to pass arguments to method calls also works when instantiating an object. So far, when we've created our objects, we've always set their instance variables to constant values. However, you'll often want to create different instances with different starting values. For example, imagine we want to instantiate different TVs and identify them using their brand name and location. This way, we can differentiate between a Samsung television in the family room and a Sony television in the bedroom. Constant values would not work for us in this situation.

To initialize an object with different values, we add parameters to the definition of the __init__() method, like this:

```
# TV class

class TV():
    def __init__(self, brand, location):  # pass in a brand and location for the TV
        self.brand = brand
        self.location = location
        --- snipped remaining initialization of TV ---
        ...
```

In all methods, parameters are local variables, so they literally go away when the method ends. For example, in the __init__() method of the TV class shown here, brand and location are local variables that will disappear when the method ends. However, we often want to save values that are passed in via parameters to use them in other methods.

In order to allow an object to remember initial values, the standard approach is to store any values passed in into instance variables. Since instance variables have object scope, they can be used in other methods in the class. The Python convention is that the name of the instance variable should be the same as the parameter name, but prefixed with self and a period:

```
def __init__(self, someVariableName):
    self.someVariableName = someVariableName
```

In the TV class, the line after the def statement tells Python to take the value of the brand parameter and assign it to an instance variable named self.brand. The next line does the same thing with the location parameter and the instance variable self.location. After these assignments, we can use self.brand and self.location in other methods.

Using this approach, we can create multiple objects from the same class but start each off with different data. So, we can create our two TV objects like this:

```
oTV1 = TV('Samsung', 'Family room')
oTV2 = TV('Sony', 'Bedroom')
```

When executing the first line, Python first allocates space for a TV object. Then it rearranges the arguments as discussed in the previous section and calls the __init__() method of the TV class with three arguments: the newly allocated oTV1 object, the brand, and the location.

When initializing the oTV1 object, self.brand is set to the string 'Samsung' and self.location is set to the string 'Family room'. When initializing oTV2, its self.brand is set to the string 'Sony', and its self.location gets set to the string 'Bedroom'.

We can modify the showInfo() method to report the name and location of the TV.

### File: OO_TV_TwoInstances_with_Init_Params.py

```
def showInfo(self):
    print()
    print('Status of TV:', self.brand)
    print('   Location:', self.location)
    if self.isOn:
        ...
```

And we'll see this as output:

```
Status of TV: Sony
   Location: Family room
   TV is: On
   Channel is: 2
   Volume is: 7

Status of TV: Samsung
   Location: Bedroom
   TV is: On
   Channel is: 44
   Volume is: 10 (sound is muted)
```

We made the same method calls as in the previous example in Listing 2-9. The difference is that each TV object is now initialized with a brand and a location, and you can now see that information printed in response to each call to the modified showInfo() method.

# Classes in Use

Using everything we've learned in this chapter, we can now create classes and build multiple independent instances from those classes. Here are a few examples of how we might use this:

- Say we wanted to model a student in a course. We could have a Student class that has instance variables for name, emailAddress, currentGrade, and so on. Each Student object we create from this class would have its own set of these instance variables, and the values given to the instance variables would be different for each student.

- Consider a game where we have multiple players. A player could be modeled by a Player class with instance variables for name, points, health, location, and so on. Each player would have the same capabilities, but the methods could work differently based on the different values in the instance variables.

- Imagine an address book. We could create a Person class with instance variables for name, address, phoneNumber, and birthday. We could create as many objects from the Person class as we want, one for each person we know. The instance variables in each Person object would contain different values. We could then write code to search through all the Person objects and retrieve information about the one or ones we are looking for.

In future chapters, I will explore this concept of instantiating multiple objects from a single class and give you tools to help manage a collection of objects.

# OOP as a Solution

Toward the end of Chapter 1, I mentioned three problems that are inherent in procedural coding. Hopefully, after working through the examples in this chapter, you can see how object-oriented programming solves all of those problems:

1. A well-written class can be easily reused in many different programs. Classes do not need to access global data. Instead, objects provide code and data at the same level.

2. Object-oriented programming can greatly reduce the number of global variables required, because a class provides a framework in which data and code that acts on the data exist in one grouping. This also tends to make code easier to debug.

3. Objects created from a class only have access to their own data—their set of the instance variables in the class. Even when you have multiple objects created from the same class, they do not have access to each other's data.

# Summary

In this chapter, I provided an introduction to object-oriented programming by demonstrating the relationship between a class and an object. The class defines the shape and capabilities of an object. An object is a single instance of a class that has its own set of all the data defined in the instance variables of the class. Each piece of data you want an object to contain is stored in an instance variable, which has object scope, meaning that it is available within all methods defined in the class. All objects created from the same class get their own set of all the instance variables, and because these may contain different values, calling the methods on different objects can result in different behavior.

I showed how you create an object from a class, typically through an assignment statement. After instantiating an object, you can use it to make calls to any method defined in the class of that object. I also showed how you can instantiate multiple objects from the same class.

In this chapter, the demonstration classes implemented physical objects (light switches, TVs). This is a good way to start understanding the concepts of a class and an object. However, in future chapters, I will introduce objects that do not represent physical objects.

# 3

## MENTAL MODELS OF OBJECTS AND THE MEANING OF "SELF"

Hopefully the new concepts and terminology I've introduced so far are starting to make sense. Some people new to OOP have trouble envisioning what an object is and how the methods of an object work with its instance variables. The specifics are fairly complex, so it can be helpful to develop a mental model of how objects and classes operate.

In this chapter, I'll present two mental models of OOP. Right up front, I want to be clear that neither of these models is an exact representation of how objects work in Python. Instead, these models are intended to give you a way to think about what an object looks like and what happens when you call a method. This chapter will also go into more detail about self and show how it is used to make methods work with multiple objects instantiated from the same class. Throughout the rest of the book, you'll gain a much deeper insight into objects and classes.

# Revisiting the DimmerSwitch Class

In the following examples, we'll continue with the DimmerSwitch class from Chapter 2 (Listing 2-5). The DimmerSwitch class already has two instance variables: self.isOn and self.brightness. The only modification we'll make is to add a self.label instance variable so each object we create can be identified easily in the output when we run our program. These variables are created and assigned initial values in the __init__() method. They are then accessed or modified in the five other methods of the class.

Listing 3-1 provides some test code to create three DimmerSwitch objects from the DimmerSwitch class, which we'll use in our mental models. I'll call various methods for each of the DimmerSwitch objects.

**File: OO_DimmerSwitch_Model1.py**

```python
# Create first DimmerSwitch, turn it on, and raise the level twice
oDimmer1 = DimmerSwitch('Dimmer1')
oDimmer1.turnOn()
oDimmer1.raiseLevel()
oDimmer1.raiseLevel()

# Create second DimmerSwitch, turn it on, and raise the level 3 times
oDimmer2 = DimmerSwitch('Dimmer2')
oDimmer2.turnOn()
oDimmer2.raiseLevel()
oDimmer2.raiseLevel()
oDimmer2.raiseLevel()

# Create third DimmerSwitch, using the default settings
oDimmer3 = DimmerSwitch('Dimmer3')

# Ask each switch to show itself
oDimmer1.show()
oDimmer2.show()
oDimmer3.show()
```

*Listing 3-1: Creating three DimmerSwitch objects and calling various methods on each*

When run with our DimmerSwitch class, this code gives the following output:

```
Label: Dimmer1
Light is on? True
Brightness is: 2

Label: Dimmer2
Light is on? True
Brightness is: 3

Label: Dimmer3
Light is on? False
Brightness is: 0
```

This is exactly what you would expect. Each `DimmerSwitch` object is independent of any other `DimmerSwitch` objects, and each object contains and modifies its own instance variables.

## High-Level Mental Model #1

In this first model, you can think of each object as a self-contained unit that contains a data type, a set of the instance variables defined in the class, and a copy of all the methods defined in the class (Figure 3-1).

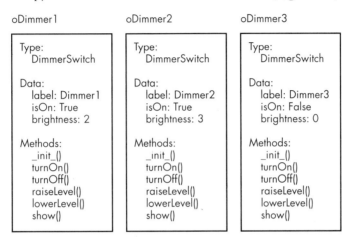

Figure 3-1: In mental model #1 each object is a unit that has a type, data, and methods.

The data and methods of each object are packaged together. The scope of an instance variable is defined as all the methods in the class, so all methods have access to the instance variables associated with that object.

If this mental model makes the concepts clear, then you're in good shape. While this is *not* the way objects are actually implemented, it's a perfectly reasonable way to *think about* how an object's instance variables and methods work together.

## A Deeper Mental Model #2

This second model explores objects at a lower level and will explain more about what an object is.

Every time you instantiate an object, you get back a value from Python. We typically store the returned value in a variable that refers to the object. In Listing 3-2, we create three `DimmerSwitch` objects. After creating each one, we'll add code to inspect the result by printing out the type and value of each variable.

**File: OO_DimmerSwitch_Model2_Instantiation.py**

```python
# Create three DimmerSwitch objects
oDimmer1 = DimmerSwitch('Dimmer1')
print(type(oDimmer1))
print(oDimmer1)
print()
oDimmer2 = DimmerSwitch('Dimmer2')
print(type(oDimmer2))
print(oDimmer2)
print()
oDimmer3 = DimmerSwitch('Dimmer3')
print(type(oDimmer3))
print(oDimmer3)
print()
```

*Listing 3-2: Creating three `DimmerSwitch` objects and printing the type and value of each*

Here is the output:

```
<class '__main__.DimmerSwitch'>
<__main__.DimmerSwitch object at 0x7ffe503b32e0>
<class '__main__.DimmerSwitch'>
<__main__.DimmerSwitch object at 0x7ffe503b3970>
<class '__main__.DimmerSwitch'>
<__main__.DimmerSwitch object at 0x7ffe503b39d0>
```

The first line in each grouping tells us the data type. Instead of a built-in type like integer or float, we see that all three objects are of the programmer-defined DimmerSwitch type. (The __main__ indicates that the DimmerSwitch code was found inside our single Python file, not imported from any other file.)

The second line of each grouping contains a string of characters. Each string represents a location in the memory of the computer. The memory location is where all the data associated with each object can be found. Notice each object is in a different location in memory. If you run this code on your computer, you will most likely get different values, but the actual values do not matter to understanding the concept.

All DimmerSwitch objects report the same type: class DimmerSwitch. The extremely important takeaway is that the objects all refer to the code of the same class, which really only exists in one place. When your program starts running, Python reads through all the class definitions and remembers the locations of all the classes and their methods.

The Python Tutor website (*http://PythonTutor.com*) provides some useful tools that can help you to visualize the execution of small programs by allowing you to step through each line of your code. Figure 3-2 is a screenshot from running the DimmerSwitch class and test code through the visualization tool, stopping execution before instantiating the first DimmerSwitch object.

In this screenshot, you can see that Python remembers the location of the DimmerSwitch class and all of its methods. While classes can contain hundreds or even thousands of lines of code, no object actually gets a copy of the class's code. Having only one copy of the code is very important, as it keeps the size of OOP programs small. When you instantiate an object,

Python allocates enough memory for each object to represent its own set of the instance variables defined in the class. In general, instantiating an object from a class is memory-efficient.

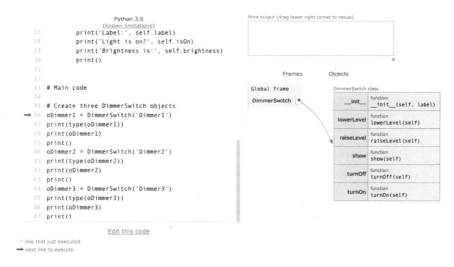

Figure 3-2: Python remembers all classes and all methods in each class.

The screenshot in Figure 3-3 shows the result of running all the test code in Listing 3-2.

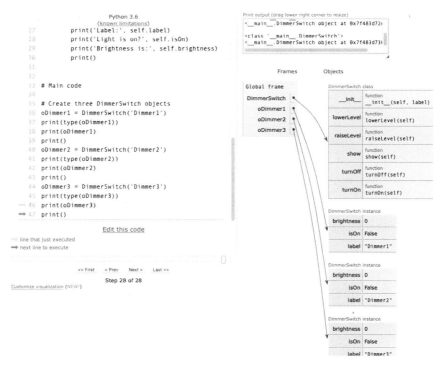

Figure 3-3: Running Listing 3-2 demonstrates that objects do not include code, in accordance with mental model #2.

This matches our second mental model. On the right side of this screenshot, the code for the DimmerSwitch class appears only once. Each object knows the class it was instantiated from and contains its own set of the instance variables defined in the class.

**NOTE**   *While the following is an implementation detail, it may help to further your understanding of objects. Internally, all instance variables of an object are kept as name/value pairs in a Python dictionary. You can inspect all the instance variables in an object by calling the built-in vars() function on any object. For example, in the test code from Listing 3-2, if you want to see the internal representation of the instance variables, you can add this line at the end:*

```
print('oDimmer1 variables:', vars(oDimmer1))
```

*When you run it, you'll see this output:*

```
oDimmer1 variables: {'label': 'Dimmer1', 'isOn': True, 'brightness': 2}
```

## What Is the Meaning of "self"?

Philosophers have struggled with this question for centuries, so it would be rather pretentious of me to try to explain it in just a few pages. In Python, however, the variable named self does have a highly specialized and clear meaning. In this section, I'll show how self is given a value and how the code of the methods in a class work with the instance variables of any object instantiated from the class.

**NOTE**   *The variable name self is not a keyword in Python but is used by convention—any other name could be used and the code would work fine. However, using self is a universally accepted practice in Python, and I will use it throughout this book. If you want your code to be understood by other Python programmers, use the name self as the first parameter in all methods of a class. (Other OOP languages have the same concept but use other names, such as this or me.)*

Suppose you write a class named SomeClass, then create an object from that class, like this:

```
oSomeObject = SomeClass(<optional arguments>)
```

The object oSomeObject contains a set of all the instance variables defined in the class. Every method of the SomeClass class has a definition that looks like this:

```
def someMethod(self, <any other parameters>):
```

And here is the general form of a call to such a method:

```
oSomeObject.someMethod(<any other arguments>)
```

As we know, Python rearranges the arguments in a call to a method, so that the object is passed in as the first argument. That value is received in the first parameter of the method and is put into the variable self (Figure 3-4).

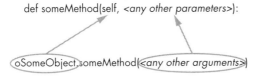

Figure 3-4: How Python rearranges arguments in a call to a method

Therefore, whenever a method is called, self will be set to the object in the call. This means that the code of a method can operate on the instance variables of *any* object instantiated from the class. It does so using the form:

```
self.<instanceVariableName>
```

This essentially says to use the object referred to by self and access the instance variable specified by *<instanceVariableName>*. Since every method uses self as the first parameter, every method in a class uses this same approach.

To illustrate this concept, let's use the DimmerSwitch class. In the following example, we'll instantiate two DimmerSwitch objects, then walk through what happens when we raise the brightness level of these objects by calling the raiseLevel() method with each.

The code of the method we're calling is:

```
def raiseLevel(self):
    if self.brightness < 10:
        self.brightness = self.brightness + 1
```

Listing 3-3 shows some example test code for two DimmerSwitch objects.

### File: OO_DimmerSwitch_Model2_Method_Calls.py

```
# Create two DimmerSwitch objects
oDimmer1 = DimmerSwitch('Dimmer1')
oDimmer2 = DimmerSwitch('Dimmer2')

# Tell oDimmer1 to raise its level
oDimmer1.raiseLevel()

# Tell oDimmer2 to raise its level
oDimmer2.raiseLevel()
```

Listing 3-3: Calling the same method on different DimmerSwitch objects

In this listing, we first instantiate two DimmerSwitch objects. Then we have two calls to the raiseLevel() method: first we call it with oDimmer1, then we call the same method using oDimmer2.

Figure 3-5 shows the result of running the test code in Listing 3-3 in Python Tutor, with execution stopped while making the first call to raiseLevel().

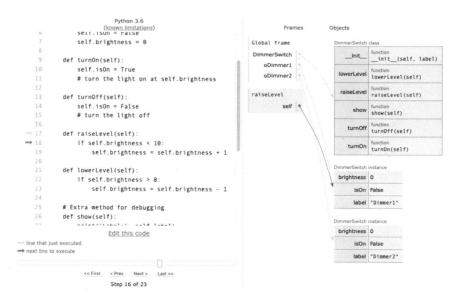

Figure 3-5: The program in Listing 3-3 stopped in call to oDimmer1.raiseLevel()

Notice that self and oDimmer1 refer to the same object. When the method executes and uses any self.*<instanceVariable>*, it will use oDimmer1's instance variables. Therefore, when this method runs, self.brightness refers to the brightness instance variable in oDimmer1.

If we continue to execute the test code in Listing 3-3, we get to the second call to raiseLevel() with oDimmer2. In Figure 3-6, I've stopped execution inside this method call.

Notice that this time, self refers to the same object as oDimmer2. Now, self.brightness refers to the brightness instance variable of oDimmer2.

No matter what object we use or which method we call, the value of the object is assigned to the variable self in the called method. You should think of self as meaning the current object—the object that the method was called with. Whenever a method executes, it uses the set of instance variables for the object specified in the call.

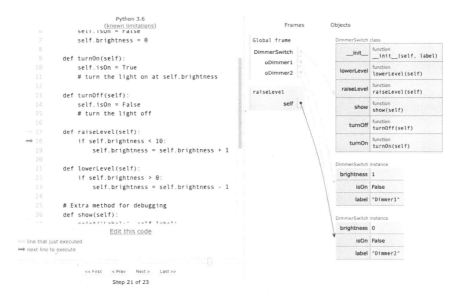

*Figure 3-6: The program in Listing 3-3 stopped in call to oDimmer2.raiseLevel()*

## Summary

In this chapter, I presented two different ways of thinking about objects. These mental models should help in developing a basic understanding of what happens when you instantiate multiple instances of an object from a class.

The first model showed how you can think of an object as having a set of all the instance variables and all the methods of a class wrapped up in a nice bundle.

The second model went into much greater detail about the implementation, explaining that the code of a class exists only in one place. An important takeaway is that creating new objects from a class is space-efficient. When you create a new instance of an object, Python allocates memory to represent the instance variables defined in the class. No duplicates of the class's code are made or required.

The key to how methods work with multiple objects is that the first parameter of all methods, self, is always set to the object used in a call to that method. With this approach, every method uses the instance variables for the current object.

# 4

## MANAGING MULTIPLE OBJECTS

This chapter will show you techniques for managing any number of objects instantiated from the same class. I'll first go through an OOP implementation of the bank account example from Chapter 1. The OOP approach allows the data and code of an account to be at the same level, eliminating the need to depend on global data. Then, I'll split the program into main code that provides a top-level menu and a separate Bank object that manages accounts, in addition to any number of Account objects. We'll also discuss a better way of handling errors using exceptions.

# Bank Account Class

Our bank account class will need, at a minimum, a name, password, and balance as its data. For behaviors, the user must be able to create an account, deposit and withdraw money, and check their balance.

We'll define and initialize the variables for the name, password, and balance, and build methods to implement each of the operations. We should then be able to instantiate any number of Account objects. Like the initial class from Chapter 1, this is a simplified Account class that only uses integers for the balance and keeps the password in cleartext. While you wouldn't use simplifications like these in a real banking application, they will allow us to concentrate on the OOP aspects involved.

The new code for the Account class is presented in Listing 4-1.

**File: Account.py**

```
# Account class

class Account():
❶ def __init__(self, name, balance, password):
        self.name = name
        self.balance = int(balance)
        self.password = password

❷ def deposit(self, amountToDeposit, password):
        if password != self.password:
            print('Sorry, incorrect password')
            return None

        if amountToDeposit < 0:
            print('You cannot deposit a negative amount')
            return None

        self.balance = self.balance + amountToDeposit
        return self.balance

❸ def withdraw(self, amountToWithdraw, password):
        if password != self.password:
            print('Incorrect password for this account')
            return None

        if amountToWithdraw < 0:
            print('You cannot withdraw a negative amount')
            return None

        if amountToWithdraw > self.balance:
            print('You cannot withdraw more than you have in your account')
            return None

        self.balance = self.balance - amountToWithdraw
        return self.balance
```

```
❹ def getBalance(self, password):
      if password != self.password:
          print('Sorry, incorrect password')
          return None
      return self.balance

   # Added for debugging
❺ def show(self):
      print('        Name:', self.name)
      print('        Balance:', self.balance)
      print('        Password:', self.password)
      print()
```

Listing 4-1: A minimal Account class

**NOTE**    *The error handling in Listing 4-1 is very simple. If we find an error condition, we print an error message and return a special value of None. Later in the chapter, I will show a better way of handling errors.*

Notice how these methods manipulate and remember data. Data is passed into each method through parameters, which are local variables that only exist while the method is running. Data is remembered in instance variables, which have object scope and therefore remember their values across calls to different methods.

First we have the \_\_init\_\_() method ❶, with three parameters. When an object is created from this class, three pieces of data are required: name, balance, and password. The instantiation might look like this:

```
oAccount = Account('Joe Schmoe', 1000, 'magic')
```

When we instantiate the object, the values of the three arguments are passed into the \_\_init\_\_() method, which in turn assigns these values to the similarly named instance variables: self.name, self.balance, and self.password. We'll access these instance variables in the other methods.

The deposit() method ❷ lets the user make a deposit into an account. After instantiating an Account object and saving it in oAccount, we could call the deposit() method like this:

```
newBalance = oAccount.deposit(500, 'magic')
```

This call says to deposit $500 and gives the password "magic". The method performs two validity checks on the deposit request. The first ensures that the password is correct by testing the password provided in the call against the password set when the Account object was created. This is a good example of how the original password saved in the instance variable self.password is used. The second validity check makes sure we aren't depositing a negative amount (which would actually be a withdrawal).

If either of those tests fails, for now we return the special value None to show that some error occurred. If both tests pass, we increment the instance variable self.balance by the amount of the deposit. Because the balance is stored in `self.balance`, it is remembered and is available for future calls. Finally, we return the new balance.

The `withdraw()` method ❸ works in a very similar way and would be called like this:

```
oAccount.withdraw(250, 'magic')
```

The `withdraw()` method checks that we've supplied the proper password by verifying it against the instance variable `self.password`. It also checks that we're not asking to withdraw a negative amount or more than we have in the account, using the instance variable `self.balance`. Once those tests pass, the method decrements `self.balance` by the amount to withdraw. It returns the resulting balance.

To check the balance ❹, we only need to supply the proper password for the account:

```
currentBalance = oAccount.getBalance('magic')
```

If the password supplied matches the one saved in the instance variable `self.password`, the method returns the value in `self.balance`.

Finally, for debugging, we added a `show()` method ❺ to display the current values of `self.name`, `self.balance`, and `self.password` saved for the account.

The `Account` class is our first example of representing something that is not a physical object. A bank account is not something that you can see, feel, or touch. However, it fits perfectly into the world of computer objects because it has data (name, balance, password) and actions that work on that data (create, deposit, withdraw, get balance, show).

## Importing Class Code

There are two ways to use a class you've built in your own code. As we've seen in previous chapters, the simplest way is to place all the code of the class directly in the main Python source file. But doing so makes it difficult to reuse a class.

A second approach is to place the code of the class in a file by itself and import it into a program that uses it. We've placed all the code for our `Account` class in *Account.py*, but if we try to run *Account.py* by itself, nothing happens, because it's just the definition of a class. To use our class code, we must instantiate one or more objects and make calls to the object's methods. As our classes become larger and more complicated, saving each of them as a separate file is the preferred way to work with them.

To use our `Account` class, we must build another *.py* file and import the code from *Account.py*, as we do with other built-in packages like `random` and `time`. Often, Python programmers name the main program that imports other class files *main.py* or *Main_<SomeName>.py*. We must then ensure that *Account.py* and the main program file are in the same folder. At the beginning of the main program, we bring in the Account code by starting with an import statement (notice that we leave off the *.py file extension):

```
from Account import *
```

Using the import statement with an asterisk (*) brings in the entire contents of the imported file. An imported file can contain multiple classes. In this case, where possible, you should specify the specific class or classes that you want to import, rather than importing the whole file. Here's the syntax for importing particular classes:

```
from <ExternalFile> import <ClassName1>, <ClassName2>, ...
```

There are two benefits to importing class code:

1. The module is reusable, so if we want to use *Account.py* in some other project, we just need to make a copy of the file and place it into that project's folder. Reusing code in this way is a staple of object-oriented programming.

2. If your class code is included in the main program, every time you run the program, Python compiles all the code in your class (translates it into a lower-level language that is more easily runnable on your computer), even if you have not made any changes to the class.

   However, when you run your main program with your class code imported, Python optimizes the compile step without you having to do anything. It creates a folder named *__pycache__* in the project folder, then compiles the code in your class file and saves the compiled code in the *__pycache__* folder with a variant of the original Python filename. For example, for the *Account.py* file, Python will create a file using the name *Account.cpython-39.pyc* (or similar, based on the version of Python you are using). The *.pyc* extension stands for *Python Compiled*. Python only recompiles your class file if the source of the class file changes. If the source of your *Account.py* has not changed, Python knows it doesn't need to recompile it and can more efficiently use the *.pyc* version of the file instead.

## Creating Some Test Code

We'll test our new class with four main programs. The first will create Account objects using separately named variables. The second stores the objects in a list, while the third stores the account numbers and objects in a dictionary. Finally, the fourth version will split the functionality so we have a main program that responds to the user and a Bank object that manages the different accounts.

In each example, the main program imports *Account.py*. Your project folder should contain the main program and the *Account.py* file. In the following discussion, the different versions of the main program will be named *Main_Bank_VersionX.py*, where *X* represents the version number.

## Creating Multiple Accounts

In this first version, we'll create two example accounts and populate them with viable data for testing. We'll save each account in an explicitly named variable representing the object.

### File: BankOOP1_IndividualVariables/Main_Bank_Version1.py

```
# Test program using accounts
# Version 1, using explicit variables for each Account object

# Bring in all the code from the Account class file
from Account import *

# Create two accounts
❶ oJoesAccount = Account('Joe', 100, 'JoesPassword')
  print("Created an account for Joe")

❷ oMarysAccount = Account('Mary', 12345, 'MarysPassword')
  print("Created an account for Mary")

❸ oJoesAccount.show()
  oMarysAccount.show()
  print()

# Call some methods on the different accounts
  print('Calling methods of the two accounts ...')
❹ oJoesAccount.deposit(50, 'JoesPassword')
  oMarysAccount.withdraw(345, 'MarysPassword')
  oMarysAccount.deposit(100, 'MarysPassword')

# Show the accounts
  oJoesAccount.show()
  oMarysAccount.show()
```

*Listing 4-2: A main program to test the Account class*

We create an account for Joe ❶ and an account for Mary ❷, and we store the results into two Account objects. We then call the show() method for the accounts to demonstrate that they were created correctly ❸. Joe deposits $50. Mary makes a withdrawal of $345 and then deposits $100 ❹. If we run the program now, this will be our output:

```
Created an account for Joe
Created an account for Mary
        Name: Joe
        Balance: 100
        Password: JoesPassword

        Name: Mary
```

```
        Balance: 12345
        Password: MarysPassword

Calling methods of the two accounts ...
        Name: Joe
        Balance: 150
        Password: JoesPassword

        Name: Mary
        Balance: 12100
        Password: MarysPassword
```

Now we'll extend the test program to create a third account interactively by asking for some input from the user. Listing 4-3 shows the code for this.

```
# Create another account with information from the user
print()
userName = input('What is the name for the new user account? ') ❶
userBalance = input('What is the starting balance for this account? ')
userBalance = int(userBalance)
userPassword = input('What is the password you want to use for this account? ')
oNewAccount = Account(userName, userBalance, userPassword) ❷

# Show the newly created user account
oNewAccount.show() ❸

# Let's deposit 100 into the new account
oNewAccount.deposit(100, userPassword) ❹
usersBalance = oNewAccount.getBalance(userPassword)
print()
print("After depositing 100, the user's balance is:", usersBalance)

# Show the new account
oNewAccount.show()
```

*Listing 4-3: An extension of the test program to create an account on the fly*

This test code asks the user for a name, a starting balance, and a password ❶. It uses these values to create a new account, and we store the newly created object in the variable oNewAccount ❷. We then call the show() method on the new object ❸. We deposit $100 into the account and retrieve the new balance by calling the getBalance() method ❹. When we run the full program, we get the output from Listing 4-2, as well as the following output:

```
What is the name for the new user account? Irv
What is the starting balance for this account? 777
What is the password you want to use for this account? IrvsPassword
        Name: Irv
        Balance: 777
        Password: IrvsPassword

After depositing 100, the user's balance is: 877
```

```
Name: Irv
Balance: 877
Password: IrvsPassword
```

The key thing to notice here is that each `Account` object maintains its own set of instance variables. Each object (`oJoesAccount`, `oMarysAccount`, and `oNewAccount`) is a global variable that contains a collection of three instance variables. If we were to expand our definition of the `Account` class to include information such as address, telephone number, and date of birth, each object would get a set of these additional instance variables.

## Multiple Account Objects in a List

Representing each account in a separate global variable works, but this is not a good approach when we need to handle a large number of objects. A bank would need a way to handle an arbitrary number of accounts. Whenever we need an arbitrary number of pieces of data, a list is the typical solution.

In this version of the test code, we'll start with an empty list of `Account` objects. Every time a user opens an account, we'll instantiate an `Account` object and append the resulting object onto our list. The account number for any given account will be the index of the account in the list, starting with 0. Again, we'll start by creating a test account for Joe and one for Mary, as shown in Listing 4-4.

### File: BankOOP2_ListOfAccountObjects/Main_Bank_Version2.py

```
# Test program using accounts
# Version 2, using a list of accounts

# Bring in all the code from the Account class file
from Account import *

# Start off with an empty list of accounts
accountsList = [ ] ❶

# Create two accounts
oAccount = Account('Joe', 100, 'JoesPassword') ❷
accountsList.append(oAccount)
print("Joe's account number is 0")

oAccount = Account('Mary', 12345, 'MarysPassword') ❸
accountsList.append(oAccount)
print("Mary's account number is 1")

accountsList[0].show() ❹
accountsList[1].show()
print()

# Call some methods on the different accounts
print('Calling methods of the two accounts ...')
accountsList[0].deposit(50, 'JoesPassword') ❺
accountsList[1].withdraw(345, 'MarysPassword') ❻
```

```
accountsList[1].deposit(100, 'MarysPassword') ❼

# Show the accounts
accountsList[0].show() ❽
accountsList[1].show()

# Create another account with information from the user
print()
userName = input('What is the name for the new user account? ')
userBalance = input('What is the starting balance for this account? ')
userBalance = int(userBalance)
userPassword = input('What is the password you want to use for this account? ')
oAccount = Account(userName, userBalance, userPassword)
accountsList.append(oAccount)   # append to list of accounts

# Show the newly created user account
print('Created new account, account number is 2')
accountsList[2].show()

# Let's deposit 100 into the new account
accountsList[2].deposit(100, userPassword)
usersBalance = accountsList[2].getBalance(userPassword)
print()
print("After depositing 100, the user's balance is:", usersBalance)

# Show the new account
accountsList[2].show()
```

_Listing 4-4: Modified test code to store objects in a list_

We start by creating an empty list of accounts ❶. We create an account for Joe, store the returned value into the variable oAccount, and immediately append that object onto our list of accounts ❷. Since this is the first account in the list, Joe's account number is 0. Like at a real bank, any time that Joe wants to do any transactions with his account, he supplies his account number. We use his account number to show the balance of his account ❹, make a deposit ❺, then show the balance again ❽. We also create an account for Mary with account number 1 ❸ and perform some test operations on her account at ❻ and ❼.

The results are identical to the test code from Listing 4-3. However, there is one highly significant difference between the two test programs: now there is only the single global variable accountsList. Each account has a unique account number, which we use to access a specific account. We have taken an important step in reducing the number of global variables.

Another important thing to note here is that we made some fairly major changes to the main program, but we did not touch anything in the Account class file. OOP often allows you to hide details at different levels. If we assume that the code of the Account class takes care of details related to an individual account, we can concentrate on ways to make the main code better.

Notice also that we're using the variable oAccount as a _temporary_ variable. That is, whenever we create a new Account object, we are assigning the result to the variable oAccount. Right after doing that, we append oAccount to our list of accounts. We never use the variable oAccount in calls to any method of a specific Account object. That way, we can reuse the variable oAccount to receive the value of the next account that is created.

## Multiple Objects with Unique Identifiers

The Account objects must be individually identifiable so each user can make deposits and withdrawals and get the balance of their specific account. Using a list for our bank accounts works, but there's a serious flaw. Imagine we have five accounts, numbered 0, 1, 2, 3, and 4. If the person who owns account 2 decides to close their account, we'd likely use a standard pop() operation on the list to delete account 2. This would cause a domino effect: the account that was in position 3 is now in position 2, and the account that was in position 4 is now in position 3. However, the users of these accounts still have their original account numbers, 3 and 4. As a result, the customer who owns account 3 will now get the information for the previous account 4, and account number 4 is now an invalid index.

To handle large numbers of objects with unique identifiers, we generally use a dictionary. Unlike a list, a dictionary will allow us to delete accounts without altering the account numbers associated with them. We build each key/value pair with an account number as the key and an Account object as the value. That way, if we need to eliminate a given account, no other account is affected. A dictionary of accounts would look like this:

```
{0 : <object for account 0>, 1 : <object for account 1>, ... }
```

We can then easily get the associated Account object and call a method like this:

```
oAccount = accountsDict[accountNumber]
oAccount.someMethodCall()
```

Alternatively, we could use the accountNumber directly to make a call to a method of an individual Account:

```
accountsDict[accountNumber].someMethodCall()
```

Listing 4-5 shows the test code using a dictionary of Account objects. Again, while we're making many changes to our test code, we're not changing a single line in the Account class. In our test code, rather than using hardcoded account numbers, we add a counter, nextAccountNumber, that we'll increment after creating a new Account.

### File: BankOOP3_DictionaryOfAccountObjects/Main_Bank_Version3.py

```
# Test program using accounts
# Version 3, using a dictionary of accounts

# Bring in all the code from the Account class file
from Account import *
```

```
accountsDict = {} ❶
nextAccountNumber = 0 ❷

# Create two accounts:
oAccount = Account('Joe', 100, 'JoesPassword')
joesAccountNumber = nextAccountNumber
accountsDict[joesAccountNumber] = oAccount ❸
print('Account number for Joe is:', joesAccountNumber)
nextAccountNumber = nextAccountNumber + 1 ❹

oAccount = Account('Mary', 12345, 'MarysPassword')
marysAccountNumber = nextAccountNumber
accountsDict[marysAccountNumber] = oAccount ❺
print('Account number for Mary is:', marysAccountNumber)
nextAccountNumber = nextAccountNumber + 1

accountsDict[joesAccountNumber].show()
accountsDict[marysAccountNumber].show()
print()

# Call some methods on the different accounts
print('Calling methods of the two accounts ...')
accountsDict[joesAccountNumber].deposit(50, 'JoesPassword')
accountsDict[marysAccountNumber].withdraw(345, 'MarysPassword')
accountsDict[marysAccountNumber].deposit(100, 'MarysPassword')

# Show the accounts
accountsDict[joesAccountNumber].show()
accountsDict[marysAccountNumber].show()

# Create another account with information from the user
print()
userName = input('What is the name for the new user account? ')
userBalance = input('What is the starting balance for this account? ')
userBalance = int(userBalance)
userPassword = input('What is the password you want to use for this account? ')
oAccount = Account(userName, userBalance, userPassword)
newAccountNumber = nextAccountNumber
accountsDict[newAccountNumber] = oAccount
print('Account number for new account is:', newAccountNumber)
nextAccountNumber = nextAccountNumber + 1

# Show the newly created user account
accountsDict[newAccountNumber].show()

# Let's deposit 100 into the new account
accountsDict[newAccountNumber].deposit(100, userPassword)
usersBalance = accountsDict[newAccountNumber].getBalance(userPassword)
print()
print("After depositing 100, the user's balance is:", usersBalance)

# Show the new account
accountsDict[newAccountNumber].show()
```

*Listing 4-5: Modified test code to store account numbers and objects in a dictionary*

Running this code yields results almost identical to those of the previous examples. We start with an empty dictionary of accounts ❶, and initialize our nextAccountNumber variable to 0 ❷. Every time we instantiate a new account, we add a new entry into the dictionary of accounts using the current value of nextAccountNumber as a key and the Account object as the value ❸. We do this for each customer, as you can see for Mary ❺. Every time we create a new account, we increment nextAccountNumber to prepare for the next account ❹. With account numbers as keys in a dictionary, if a customer closes their account, we can eliminate that key and value from the dictionary without affecting any other accounts.

## Building an Interactive Menu

With our Account class working correctly, we'll make the main code interactive by asking the user to tell us what operation they would like to do: get the balance, make a deposit, make a withdrawal, or open a new account. In response, our main code will gather the needed information from the user, starting with their account number, and call the appropriate method of the user's Account object.

As a shortcut, we will again prepopulate two accounts, one for Joe and one for Mary. Listing 4-6 shows our expanded main code, which uses a dictionary to keep track of all the accounts. I've omitted the code that creates the accounts for Joe and Mary and adds those to the dictionary of accounts for brevity, as it's the same as in Listing 4-5.

### File: BankOOP4_InteractiveMenu/Main_Bank_Version4.py

```
# Interactive test program creating a dictionary of accounts
# Version 4, with an interactive menu

from Account import *

accountsDict = {}
nextAccountNumber = 0

--- snip creating accounts, adding them to dictionary ---

while True:
    print()
    print('Press b to get the balance')
    print('Press d to make a deposit')
    print('Press o to open a new account')
    print('Press w to make a withdrawal')
    print('Press s to show all accounts')
    print('Press q to quit')
    print()

    action = input('What do you want to do? ') ❶
    action = action.lower()
    action = action[0]   # grab the first letter
```

```
print()

if action == 'b':
    print('*** Get Balance ***')
    userAccountNumber = input('Please enter your account number: ')
    userAccountNumber = int(userAccountNumber)
    userAccountPassword = input('Please enter the password: ')
    oAccount = accountsDict[userAccountNumber]
    theBalance = oAccount.getBalance(userAccountPassword)
    if theBalance is not None:
        print('Your balance is:', theBalance)

elif action == 'd':  ❷
    print('*** Deposit ***')
    userAccountNumber = input('Please enter the account number: ')  ❸
    userAccountNumber = int(userAccountNumber)
    userDepositAmount = input('Please enter amount to deposit: ')
    userDepositAmount = int(userDepositAmount)
    userPassword = input('Please enter the password: ')
    oAccount = accountsDict[userAccountNumber]  ❹
    theBalance = oAccount.deposit(userDepositAmount, userPassword)  ❺
    if theBalance is not None:
        print('Your new balance is:', theBalance)

elif action == 'o':
    print('*** Open Account ***')
    userName = input('What is the name for the new user account? ')
    userStartingAmount = input('What is the starting balance for this account? ')
    userStartingAmount = int(userStartingAmount)
    userPassword = input('What is the password you want to use for this account? ')
    oAccount = Account(userName, userStartingAmount, userPassword)
    accountsDict[nextAccountNumber] = oAccount
    print('Your new account number is:', nextAccountNumber)
    nextAccountNumber = nextAccountNumber + 1
    print()

elif action == 's':
    print('Show:')
    for userAccountNumber in accountsDict:
        oAccount = accountsDict[userAccountNumber]
        print('    Account number:', userAccountNumber)
        oAccount.show()

elif action == 'q':
    break

elif action == 'w':
    print('*** Withdraw ***')
    userAccountNumber = input('Please enter your account number: ')
    userAccountNumber = int(userAccountNumber)
    userWithdrawalAmount = input('Please enter the amount to withdraw: ')
    userWithdrawalAmount = int(userWithdrawalAmount)
    userPassword = input('Please enter the password: ')
    oAccount = accountsDict[userAccountNumber]
    theBalance = oAccount.withdraw(userWithdrawalAmount, userPassword)
```

```
    if theBalance is not None:
        print('Withdrew:', userWithdrawalAmount)
        print('Your new balance is:', theBalance)

else:
    print('Sorry, that was not a valid action. Please try again.')

print('Done')
```

*Listing 4-6: Adding an interactive menu*

In this version, we present the user with a menu of options. When the user selects an action ❶, the code asks questions about the intended transaction to gather all the information we need to make the call to the user's account. For example, if the user wants to make a deposit ❷, the program asks for the account number, the amount to deposit, and the password for the account ❸. We use the account number as a key into the dictionary of Account objects to get the appropriate Account object ❹. With that object, we then call the deposit() method, passing in the amount to deposit and the user's password ❺.

Once again, we have modified code at the main code level, and left our Account class untouched.

## Creating an Object Manager Object

The code in Listing 4-6 is actually doing two different things. The program first provides a simple menu interface. Then, when an action is chosen, it collects data and makes a call to a method of an Account object. Rather than having one large main program that does two different tasks, we can split this code into two smaller logical units, each with a clearly defined role. The menuing system becomes the main code that decides what action to take, and the rest of the code deals with the things a bank actually does. The bank can be modeled as an object that manages other (account) objects, known as an *object manager object.*

**object manager object**
An object that maintains a list or dictionary of managed objects (typically of a single class) and calls methods of those objects.

This split can be made easily and logically: we take all the code related to the bank and put it into a new Bank class. Then, at the beginning of the main program, we instantiate a single Bank object from the new Bank class.

The Bank class will manage a list or dictionary of Account objects. In this way, the Bank object will be the only code that communicates directly with Account objects (Figure 4-1).

To create this hierarchy, we need some main code that handles the highest-level menuing system. In response to a choice of action, the main code will call a method of the Bank object (for example, deposit() or withdraw()). The Bank object will gather the information it needs (account number, password, amount to deposit or withdraw), reach into its dictionary of accounts to find the matching user account, and call the appropriate method for that user's account.

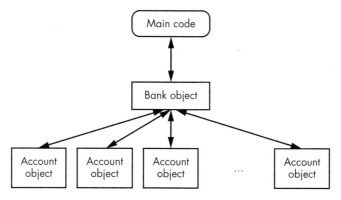

Figure 4-1: The main code manages a Bank object, which manages many Account objects.

There are three layers in this division of labor:

1. The main code that creates and talks to a single Bank object
2. The Bank object that manages a dictionary of Account objects and calls methods of those objects
3. The Account objects themselves

With this approach, we only have a single global variable, the Bank object. In fact, the main code has no idea that Account objects even exist. Conversely, each Account object has no clue (and does not care) what the top-level user interface of the program is. The Bank object receives messages from the main code and communicates with the appropriate Account object.

The key advantage of this approach is that we have broken down a much larger program into smaller subprograms: in this case, the main code and two classes. This makes it much easier to program each piece, since the scope of work is smaller and the responsibilities are clearer for each. Further, having only a single global variable ensures that lower-level code will not accidentally affect data at the global level.

In computer literature, the construct shown in Figure 4-1 is often known as *composition* or *object composition*.

---

**composition**    A logical structure in which one object manages one or more other objects

---

You can think of one object as being made up of other objects. An example is that a car object is made up of an engine object, a steering wheel object, some number of door objects, four wheel and tire objects, and so on. The discussion often centers around the relationships between objects. In this example, one would say that a car "has a" steering wheel, an engine, some number of doors, and so on. Therefore, the car object is a composite of other objects.

We'll have three separate files. The main code lives in its own file. It imports the code of our new *Bank.py* file that contains the Bank class (Listing 4-7). The Bank class imports the code of the *Account.py* file and uses it to instantiate Account objects as needed.

### Building the Object Manager Object

Listing 4-7 shows the code of the new Bank class, which is an object manager object.

**File: BankOOP5_SeparateBankClass/Bank.py**

```
# Bank that manages a dictionary of Account objects

from Account import *

class Bank():

    def __init__(self):
        self.accountsDict = {}  ❶
        self.nextAccountNumber = 0

    def createAccount(self, theName, theStartingAmount, thePassword):  ❷
        oAccount = Account(theName, theStartingAmount, thePassword)
        newAccountNumber = self.nextAccountNumber
        self.accountsDict[newAccountNumber] = oAccount
        # Increment to prepare for next account to be created
        self.nextAccountNumber = self.nextAccountNumber + 1
        return newAccountNumber

    def openAccount(self):  ❸
        print('*** Open Account ***')
        userName = input('What is the name for the new user account? ')
        userStartingAmount = input('What is the starting balance for this account? ')
        userStartingAmount = int(userStartingAmount)
        userPassword = input('What is the password you want to use for this account? ')

        userAccountNumber = self.createAccount(userName, userStartingAmount, userPassword)  ❹
        print('Your new account number is:', userAccountNumber)
        print()

    def closeAccount(self):  ❺
        print('*** Close Account ***')
        userAccountNumber = input('What is your account number? ')
        userAccountNumber = int(userAccountNumber)
        userPassword = input('What is your password? ')
        oAccount = self.accountsDict[userAccountNumber]
        theBalance = oAccount.getBalance(userPassword)
        if theBalance is not None:
            print('You had', theBalance, 'in your account, which is being returned to you.')
            # Remove user's account from the dictionary of accounts
            del self.accountsDict[userAccountNumber]
            print('Your account is now closed.')
```

```
def balance(self):
    print('*** Get Balance ***')
    userAccountNumber = input('Please enter your account number: ')
    userAccountNumber = int(userAccountNumber)
    userAccountPassword = input('Please enter the password: ')
    oAccount = self.accountsDict[userAccountNumber]
    theBalance = oAccount.getBalance(userAccountPassword)
    if theBalance is not None:
        print('Your balance is:', theBalance)


def deposit(self):
    print('*** Deposit ***')
    accountNum = input('Please enter the account number: ')
    accountNum = int(accountNum)
    depositAmount = input('Please enter amount to deposit: ')
    depositAmount = int(depositAmount)
    userAccountPassword = input('Please enter the password: ')
    oAccount = self.accountsDict[accountNum]
    theBalance = oAccount.deposit(depositAmount, userAccountPassword)
    if theBalance is not None:
        print('Your new balance is:', theBalance)


def show(self):
    print('*** Show ***')
    for userAccountNumber in self.accountsDict:
        oAccount = self.accountsDict[userAccountNumber]
        print('   Account:', userAccountNumber)
        oAccount.show()


def withdraw(self):
    print('*** Withdraw ***')
    userAccountNumber = input('Please enter your account number: ')
    userAccountNumber = int(userAccountNumber)
    userAmount = input('Please enter the amount to withdraw: ')
    userAmount = int(userAmount)
    userAccountPassword = input('Please enter the password: ')
    oAccount = self.accountsDict[userAccountNumber]
    theBalance = oAccount.withdraw(userAmount, userAccountPassword)
    if theBalance is not None:
        print('Withdrew:', userAmount)
        print('Your new balance is:', theBalance)
```

*Listing 4-7: The Bank class with separate methods for different bank operations*

I'll focus on the most important things to notice in the Bank class.
First, in its __init__() method, Bank initializes two variables: self.accountsDict
and self.nextAccountNumber ❶. The prefix self. designates these as instance variables, meaning the Bank class can refer to these variables in any of its methods.

Second, there are two methods for creating an account: createAccount()
and openAccount(). The createAccount() method instantiates a new account ❷
with the user's name, a starting amount, and a password passed in for the
new account. The openAccount() method asks the user questions to obtain
these three pieces of information ❸ and calls the createAccount() method
within the same class.

Having one method call another method in the same class is common. But the called method doesn't know whether it was called from inside or outside the class; it only knows that the first argument is the object on which it should run. Therefore, the call to the method must start with self., because self always refers to the current object. Generically, to call from one method to another method in the same class we need to write:

```
def myMethod(self, <other optional parameters>):
    ...
    self.methodInSameClass(<any needed arguments>)
```

After collecting information from the user for openAccount(), we have this line ❹:

```
userAccountNumber = self.createAccount(userName, userStartingAmount, userPassword)
```

Here, openAccount() calls createAccount() from the same class to create the account. The createAccount() method runs, instantiates an Account object, and returns an account number to openAccount(), which returns that account number back to the user.

Finally, the new method closeAccount() allows the user to close an existing account ❺. This is an extra piece of functionality we'll offer from our main code.

Our Bank class represents an abstract view of a bank rather than the physical brick-and-mortar object. This is another good example of a class that does not represent a physical structure.

## Main Code That Creates an Object Manager Object

The main code that creates and makes calls to the Bank object is shown in Listing 4-8.

### File: BankOOP5_SeparateBankClass/Main_Bank_Version5.py

```
# Main program for controlling a Bank made up of Accounts

# Bring in all the code of the Bank class
from Bank import *

# Create an instance of the Bank
oBank = Bank()

# Main code
# Create two test accounts
joesAccountNumber = oBank.createAccount('Joe', 100, 'JoesPassword')
print("Joe's account number is:", joesAccountNumber)

marysAccountNumber = oBank.createAccount('Mary', 12345, 'MarysPassword')
print("Mary's account number is:", marysAccountNumber)

while True:
    print()
```

```
    print('To get an account balance, press b')
    print('To close an account, press c')
    print('To make a deposit, press d')
    print('To open a new account, press o')
    print('To quit, press q')
    print('To show all accounts, press s')
    print('To make a withdrawal, press w ')
    print()

❶  action = input('What do you want to do? ')
    action = action.lower()
    action = action[0]  # grab the first letter
    print()

❷  if action == 'b':
        oBank.balance()

❸  elif action == 'c':
        oBank.closeAccount()

    elif action == 'd':
        oBank.deposit()

    elif action == 'o':
        oBank.openAccount()

    elif action == 's':
        oBank.show()

    elif action == 'q':
        break

    elif action == 'w':
        oBank.withdraw()

    else:
        print('Sorry, that was not a valid action. Please try again.')

print('Done')
```

*Listing 4-8: The main code that creates a Bank object and makes calls to it*

Notice how the code in Listing 4-8 presents the top-level menuing system. It asks the user for an action ❶, then calls an appropriate method in the Bank object to do the work ❷. You could easily extend the Bank object to handle some additional queries, like asking for the bank's hours, or address, or phone number. That data could simply be kept as additional instance variables inside the Bank object. The Bank would answer those questions without needing to communicate with any Account object.

When a close request is made ❸, the main code calls the closeAccount() method of the Bank object to close the account. The Bank object removes the specific account from its dictionary of accounts using a line like this:

```
del self.accountsDict[userAccountNumber]
```

Recall that our definition of an object is data, plus code that acts on that data, over time. The ability to delete an object demonstrates the third part of our definition of an object. We can create an object (in this case an Account object) whenever we want, not just when a program starts. In this program, we create a new Account object whenever a user decides to open an account. Our code can use that object by calling its methods. We can also delete an object at any time, in this case, when a user chooses to close their account. This is an example of how an object (like an Account object) has a life span, from whenever it is created it to whenever it is deleted.

## Better Error Handling with Exceptions

So far in our Account class, if a method detects an error (for example, if the user deposits a negative amount, enters an incorrect password, withdraws a negative amount, and so on) our placeholder solution is to return None as a signal that something went wrong. In this section, we'll discuss a better way of handling errors by using try/except blocks and raising exceptions.

### *try and except*

When a runtime error or abnormal condition occurs in a function or method from the Python Standard Library, that function or method signals the error by raising an exception (sometimes referred to as *throwing* or *generating* an exception). We can detect and react to exceptions using the try/except construct. Here is the general form:

```
try:
    # some code that may cause an error (raise an exception)
except <some exception name>:   # if an exception happens
    # some code to handle the exception
```

If the code inside the try block works correctly and does not generate an exception, the except clause is skipped, and execution continues after the except block. However, if the code in the try block results in an exception, control is passed to the except statement. If the exception matches the exception (or one of multiple exceptions) listed in the except statement, control is transferred to the code of the except clause. This is often referred to as *catching* the exception. That indented block typically contains code to report and/or recover from the error.

Here is a simple example where we ask for a number from the user and attempt to convert it to an integer:

```
age = input('Please enter your age: ')
try:  # attempt to convert to integer
    age = int(age)
except ValueError:  # if an exception is raised trying to convert
    print('Sorry, that was not a valid number')
```

Calls to the Python Standard Library can generate standard exceptions such as TypeError, ValueError, NameError, ZeroDivisionError, and so on. In this example, if the user enters letters or a floating-point number, the built-in int() function raises a ValueError exception, and control is transferred to the code in the except block.

## The raise Statement and Custom Exceptions

If your code detects a runtime error condition, you can use the raise statement to signal an exception. There are many forms of the raise statement, but the standard approach is to use this syntax:

```
raise <ExceptionName>('<Any string to describe the error>')
```

For the <ExceptionName>, you have three options. First, if there is a standard exception that matches the error you have detected (TypeError, ValueError, NameError, ZeroDivisionError, and so on), it's fine to use that. You can also add your own description string:

```
raise ValueError('You need to specify an integer')
```

Second, you can use the generic Exception exception:

```
raise Exception('The amount cannot be a floating-point number')
```

However, this is generally frowned upon because the standard practice is to write except statements to look for exceptions by name, and this does not provide a specific name.

A third choice, and perhaps the best, is to create your own custom exception. This is easy to do, but involves a technique called inheritance (which we will discuss at length in Chapter 10). Here is all you need to create your own exception:

```
# Define a custom exception
class <CustomExceptionName>(Exception):
    pass
```

You supply a unique name for your exception. You can then raise your custom exception in your code. Creating your own exceptions means you can explicitly check for these exceptions by name in a higher level of your code. In the next section, we'll rewrite the code of our bank example so that we raise a custom exception in our Bank and Account classes and check for and report the error in the main code. The main code will report the error but allow the program to continue running.

In the typical case, the raise statement causes the current function or method to exit and transfers control back to the caller. If the caller contains an except clause that catches the exception, execution continues inside that except clause. Otherwise, that function or method exits. This process is repeated until an except clause catches the exception. Control is transferred back through the sequence of calls, and if no except clause catches the exception, the program quits and Python displays the error.

## Using Exceptions in Our Bank Program

We can now rewrite all three levels of our program (main, Bank, and Account) to signal errors with raise statements and to handle errors using try/except blocks.

### Account Class with Exceptions

Listing 4-9 is a new version of the Account class rewritten to use exceptions and optimized so that no code is repeated. We start by defining a custom AbortTransaction exception, which will be raised if we discover some error while a user is attempting to do a transaction in our bank.

**File: BankOOP6_UsingExceptions/Account.py (modified to work with upcoming Bank.py)**

```
# Account class
# Errors indicated by "raise" statements

# Define a custom exception
class AbortTransaction(Exception): ❶
    '''raise this exception to abort a bank transaction'''
    pass

class Account():
    def __init__(self, name, balance, password):
        self.name = name
        self.balance = self.validateAmount(balance) ❷
        self.password = password

    def validateAmount(self, amount):
        try:
            amount = int(amount)
        except ValueError:
            raise AbortTransaction('Amount must be an integer') ❸
        if amount <= 0:
            raise AbortTransaction('Amount must be positive') ❹
        return amount

    def checkPasswordMatch(self, password): ❺
        if password != self.password:
            raise AbortTransaction('Incorrect password for this account')

    def deposit(self, amountToDeposit): ❻
        amountToDeposit = self.validateAmount(amountToDeposit)
        self.balance = self.balance + amountToDeposit
        return self.balance

    def getBalance(self):
```

```
        return self.balance

    def withdraw(self, amountToWithdraw):  ❼
        amountToWithdraw = self.validateAmount(amountToWithdraw)
        if amountToWithdraw > self.balance:
            raise AbortTransaction('You cannot withdraw more than you have in your account')
        self.balance = self.balance - amountToWithdraw
        return self.balance

    # Added for debugging
    def show(self):
        print('        Name:', self.name)
        print('        Balance:', self.balance)
        print('        Password:', self.password)
```

*Listing 4-9: A modified Account class that raises exceptions*

We start by defining our custom AbortTransaction exception ❶ so we can use it in this class and in other code that imports this class.

In the __init__() method of the Account class, we ensure that the amount provided as the starting balance is valid by calling validateAmount() ❷. This method uses a try/except block to ensure that the starting amount can successfully be converted to an integer. If the call to int() fails, it raises a ValueError exception, which is caught in the except clause. Rather than just allowing the generic ValueError to be returned to the caller, the code of this except block ❸ executes a raise statement, raising our AbortTransaction exception, and includes a more meaningful error message string. If the conversion to an integer succeeds, we perform another test. If the user gave a negative amount, we also raise the AbortTransaction exception ❹, but with a different error message string.

The checkPasswordMatch() method ❺ is called by methods in the Bank object to check if the password supplied by the user matches the password saved in the Account. If not, we execute another raise statement with the same exception, but we supply a more descriptive error message string.

This allows the code of deposit() ❻ and withdraw() ❼ to be simplified, because these methods assume that the amount has been validated and the password verified before they are invoked. There is an additional check in withdraw() to ensure that the user is not trying to withdraw more money than is in the account; if so, we raise the AbortTransaction exception with an appropriate description.

Since there is no code in this class to handle an AbortTransaction exception, any time one is raised, control is passed back to the caller. If the caller has no code to handle the exception, then control is passed back to the previous caller, and so on up the stack of calls. As we'll see, our main code will handle this exception.

## Optimized Bank Class

The full Bank class code is available for download. In Listing 4-10 I show some sample methods that demonstrate try/except techniques with calls to methods in the previously updated Account class.

## File: BankOOP6_UsingExceptions/Bank.py (modified to work with previous Account.py)

```
# Bank that manages a dictionary of Account objects

from Account import *

class Bank():
    def __init__(self, hours, address, phone): ❶
        self.accountsDict = {}
        self.nextAccountNumber = 0
        self.hours = hours
        self.address = address
        self.phone = phone

    def askForValidAccountNumber(self): ❷
        accountNumber = input('What is your account number? ')
        try: ❸
            accountNumber = int(accountNumber)
        except ValueError:
            raise AbortTransaction('The account number must be an integer')
        if accountNumber not in self.accountsDict:
            raise AbortTransaction('There is no account ' + str(accountNumber))
        return accountNumber

    def getUsersAccount(self): ❹
        accountNumber = self.askForValidAccountNumber()
        oAccount = self.accountsDict[accountNumber]
        self.askForValidPassword(oAccount)
        return oAccount

    --- snipped additional methods ---

    def deposit(self): ❺
        print('*** Deposit ***')
        oAccount = self.getUsersAccount()
        depositAmount = input('Please enter amount to deposit: ')
        theBalance = oAccount.deposit(depositAmount)
        print('Deposited:', depositAmount)
        print('Your new balance is:', theBalance)

    def withdraw(self): ❻
        print('*** Withdraw ***')
        oAccount = self.getUsersAccount()
        userAmount = input('Please enter the amount to withdraw: ')
        theBalance = oAccount.withdraw(userAmount)
        print('Withdrew:', userAmount)
        print('Your new balance is:', theBalance)

    def getInfo(self): ❼
        print('Hours:', self.hours)
        print('Address:', self.address)
        print('Phone:', self.phone)
        print('We currently have', len(self.accountsDict), 'account(s) open.')
```

```
# Special method for Bank administrator only
def show(self):
    print('*** Show ***')
    print('(This would typically require an admin password)')
    for userAccountNumber in self.accountsDict:
        oAccount = self.accountsDict[userAccountNumber]
        print('Account:', userAccountNumber)
        oAccount.show()
        print()
```

*Listing 4-10: The modified Bank class*

The Bank class starts with the __init__() method ❶ that saves all relevant information in instance variables.

The new askForValidAccountNumber() ❷ method is called from a number of other methods to ask the user for an account number and attempts to verify the given number. First it has a try/except block ❸ to ensure that the number is an integer. If it isn't, the except block detects the error as a ValueError exception but reports the error more clearly by raising a custom AbortTransaction exception with a descriptive message. Next, it checks to ensure that the given account number is one that the bank knows about. If not, it also raises an AbortTransaction exception, but it gives a different error message string.

The new getUsersAccount() method ❹ first calls the previous askForValid AccountNumber(), then uses the account number to find the appropriate Account object. Notice that there is no try/except in this method. If an exception is raised in askForValidAccountNumber() (or in a lower level), this method will immediatcly return to its caller.

The deposit() ❺ and withdraw() ❻ methods call getUsersAccount() in the same class. Similarly, if their call to getUsersAccount() raises an exception, the method will exit and pass the exception up the chain to the caller. If all tests pass, the code of deposit() and withdraw() calls similarly named methods in the specified Account object to perform the actual transaction.

The getInfo() ❼ method reports information about the bank (hours, address, phone) and doesn't access any individual account.

## Main Code That Handles Exceptions

Listing 4-11 shows the updated main code, rewritten to handle a custom exception. This is where any errors that occur are reported to the user.

**File: BankOOP6_UsingException/Main_Bank_Version6.py**

```
# Main program for controlling a Bank made up of Accounts
from Bank import *

# Create an instance of the Bank
❶ oBank = Bank('9 to 5', '123 Main Street, Anytown, USA', '(650) 555-1212')

# Main code
```

```
❷ while True:
       print()
       print('To get an account balance, press b')
       print('To close an account, press c')
       print('To make a deposit, press d')
       print('To get bank information, press i')
       print('To open a new account, press o')
       print('To quit, press q')
       print('To show all accounts, press s')
       print('To make a withdrawal, press w')
       print()

       action = input('What do you want to do? ')
       action = action.lower()
       action = action[0]   # grab the first letter
       print()

❸      try:
           if action == 'b':
               oBank.balance()
           elif action == 'c':
               oBank.closeAccount()
           elif action == 'd':
               oBank.deposit()
           elif action == 'i':
               oBank.getInfo()
           elif action == 'o':
               oBank.openAccount()
           elif action == 'q':
               break
           elif action == 's':
               oBank.show()
           elif action == 'w':
               oBank.withdraw()
❹      except AbortTransaction as error:
           # Print out the text of the error message
           print(error)

   print('Done')
```

*Listing 4-11: The main code that handles errors with try/except*

The main code starts by creating a single Bank object ❶. Then, in a loop, it presents a top-level menu to the user and asks them what action they wish to perform ❷. It calls an appropriate method for each command.

The important thing in this listing is that we have added a try block around all the calls to methods with the oBank object ❸. That way, if any method call raises an AbortTransaction exception, control will be transferred to the except statement ❹.

Exceptions are objects. In the except clause, we handle the AbortTransaction exception that was raised at any lower level. We assign the value of the exception to the variable error. When we print that variable, the user will see the associated error message. Since the exception was handled in the except clause, the program continues running, and the user is asked what they wish to do.

## Calling the Same Method on a List of Objects

Unlike in our bank example, in cases where individual objects do not need to be uniquely identified, using a list of objects works extremely well. Let's say you're coding a game and you need to have some number of bad guys, spaceships, bullets, zombies, or whatever else. Each such object will typically have some data it remembers and some actions it can perform. As long as each object does not require a unique identifier, the standard way to handle this is to create many instances of the object from the class and put all the objects into a list:

```python
objectList = []  # start off with an empty list
for i in range(nObjects):
    oNewObject = MyClass()   # create a new instance
    objectList.append(oNewObject)  # store the object in the list
```

In our game, we represent a world as a large grid, like a spreadsheet. We want monsters placed at random locations in the grid. Listing 4-12 shows the start of a Monster class with its __init__() method and a move() method. When a Monster is instantiated, it is told the number of rows and columns in the grid and the maximum speed, and it chooses a random starting location and speed.

**File: MonsterExample.py**

```python
import random

class Monster()
    def __init__(self, nRows, nCols, maxSpeed):
        self.nRows = nRows  # save away
        self.nCols = nCols  # save away
        self.myRow = random.randrange(self.nRows) # chooses a random row
        self.myCol = random.randrange(self.nCols) # chooses a random col
        self.mySpeedX = random.randrange(-maxSpeed, maxSpeed + 1) # chooses an X speed
        self.mySpeedY = random.randrange(-maxSpeed, maxSpeed + 1) # chooses a Y speed
        # Set other instance variables like health, power, etc.

    def move(self):
        self.myRow = (self.myRow + self.mySpeedY) %  self.nRows
        self.myCol = (self.myCol + self.mySpeedX) % self.nCols
```

*Listing 4-12: A Monster class that can be used to instantiate many Monsters*

With this `Monster` class, we can create a list of `Monster` objects like this:

```
N_MONSTERS = 20
N_ROWS = 100    # could be any size
N_COLS = 200    # could be any size
MAX_SPEED = 4
monsterList = []  # start with an empty list
for i in range(N_MONSTERS):
    oMonster = Monster(N_ROWS, N_COLS, MAX_SPEED)  # create a Monster
    monsterList.append(oMonster)  # add the Monster to our list
```

This loop will instantiate 20 `Monster`s, and each will know its own starting location in the grid and its individual speed. Once you have a list of objects, later in the program when you want each object to do the same action, you can write a simple loop where you call the same method of each object in the list:

```
for objectVariable in objectVariablesList:
    objectVariable.someMethod()
```

For example, if we want each of our `Monster` objects to move, we could use a loop like this:

```
for oMonster in monsterList:
    oMonster.move()
```

Since each `Monster` object remembers its location and speed, in the `move()` method, each `Monster` can move to and remember its new location.

This technique of building a list of objects and calling the same method of all objects in the list is extremely useful, and it's a standard approach to dealing with a collection of similar objects. We will use this approach quite often when we get to building games using pygame later.

## Interface vs. Implementation

Our earlier `Account` class seems to have methods and instance variables that work well. When you're confident your code is working well, you no longer have to be concerned with the details within the class. When a class does what you want it to do, all you need to remember is what methods are available in the class. There are two different ways to look at a class: by focusing on what it is capable of doing (the *interface*) and how it works internally (the *implementation*).

| | |
|---|---|
| **interface** | The collection of methods a class provides (and the parameters that each method expects). The interface shows *what* an object created from the class can do. |
| **implementation** | The actual code of the class, which shows *how* an object does what it does. |

If you are the creator or maintainer of a class, you need to fully understand the implementation—the code of all of the methods and how they work together to affect the instance variables. If you are purely writing code to *use* a class, you only need to concern yourself with the interface—the different methods that are available in the class, the values that need to be passed into each, and any value(s) that are returned from the methods. If you are coding on your own (as a "one-person team"), then you will be both the implementer of a class and the user of its interface.

As long as the interface of a class does not change, the class's implementation can change at any time. That is, if you find that a method can be implemented in a faster or more efficient way, changing the relevant code inside the class will not have any bad side effects on any other part of the program.

## Summary

An object manager object is an object that manages other objects. It does this by having one or more instance variables that are lists or dictionaries made up of other objects. The object manager can call methods of any specific object or of all managed objects. This technique gives full control of all managed objects to the object manager alone.

When you encounter an error in a method or function, you can raise an exception. The raise statement returns control to the caller. The caller can detect a potential error by placing the call in a try block, and it can react to any such error using an except block.

The interface of a class is the documentation of all the methods and related parameters in the class. The implementation is the actual code of the class. What you need to know depends on your role. The writer/maintainer of a class needs to understand the details of the code, whereas anyone who uses the class only needs to understand the interface that the class provides.

# PART II

## GRAPHICAL USER
## INTERFACES WITH PYGAME

These chapters introduce you to *pygame,* an external package that adds functionality common to GUI programs. Pygame allows you to write Python programs that have windows, respond to the mouse and keyboard, play sounds, and more.

Chapter 5 gives you a basic understanding of how pygame works and provides a standard template for building pygame-based programs. We'll build a few simple programs first, create a program that controls an image with the keyboard, then we'll build a ball-bouncing program.

Chapter 6 explains how pygame can best be used as an object-oriented framework. You'll see how to rewrite the ball-bouncing program using object-oriented techniques, and develop simple buttons and text input fields.

Chapter 7 describes the pygwidgets module, which contains full implementations of many standard user interface widgets like buttons, input and output fields, radio buttons, checkboxes, and more, all using object-oriented programming. All the code is available for you so that you can use it to build your own applications. I'll provide several examples.

# 5

## INTRODUCTION TO PYGAME

The Python language was designed to handle text input and text output. It provides the ability to get text from and send text to the user, a file, and the internet. The core language, however, has no way of dealing with more modern concepts such as windows, mouse clicks, sounds, and so on. So, what if you want to use Python to create something more state-of-the-art than a text-based program? In this chapter I'll introduce *pygame*, a free open source external package that was designed to extend Python to allow programmers to build game programs. You can also use pygame to build other kinds of interactive programs with a graphical user interface (GUI). It adds the ability to create windows, show images, recognize mouse movements and clicks, play sounds, and more. In short, it allows Python programmers to build the types of games and applications that current computer users have become familiar with.

It is not my intent to turn you all into game programmers—even though that might be a fun outcome. Rather, I'll use the pygame environment to make certain object-oriented programming techniques clearer and more visual. By working with pygame to make objects visible in a window and dealing with a user interacting with those objects, you should gain a deeper understanding of how to effectively use OOP techniques.

This chapter provides a general introduction to pygame, so most of the information and examples in this chapter will use procedural coding. Starting with the next chapter, I will explain how to use OOP effectively with pygame.

## Installing Pygame

Pygame is a free downloadable package. We'll use the package manager *pip* (short for *pip installs packages*) to install Python packages. As mentioned in the Introduction, I am assuming that you have installed the official version of Python from *python.org*. The pip program is included as part of that download, so you should already have it installed.

Unlike a standard application, you must run pip from the command line. On a Mac, start the Terminal application (located in the *Utilities* subfolder inside the *Applications* folder). On a Windows system, click the Windows icon, type **cmd**, and press ENTER.

**NOTE**    *This book was not tested with Linux systems. However, most, if not all, of the content should work with minimal tweaking. To install pygame on a Linux distribution, open a terminal in whatever way you're used to.*

Enter the following commands at the command line:

```
python3 -m pip install -U pip --user
python3 -m pip install -U pygame --user
```

The first command ensures that you have the latest version of the pip program. The second line installs the most recent version of pygame.

If you have any problems installing pygame, consult the pygame documentation at *https://www.pygame.org/wiki/GettingStarted*. To test that pygame has been installed correctly, open IDLE (the development environment that is bundled with the default implementation of Python), and in the shell window enter:

```
import pygame
```

If you see a message saying something like "Hello from the pygame community" or if you get no message at all, then pygame has been installed correctly. The lack of an error message indicates that Python has been able to find and load the pygame package and it's ready to use. If you would like to see a sample game using pygame, enter the following command (which starts a version of *Space Invaders*):

```
python3 -m pygame.examples.aliens
```

Before we get into using pygame, I need to explain two important concepts. First, I'll explain how individual pixels are addressed in programs that use a GUI. Then, I'll discuss event-driven programs and how they differ from typical text-based programs. After that, we'll code a few programs that demonstrate key pygame features.

## Window Details

A computer screen is made up of a large number of rows and columns of small dots called *pixels* (from the words *picture element*). A user interacts with a GUI program through one or more windows; each window is a rectangular portion of the screen. Programs can control the color of any individual pixel in their window(s). If you're running multiple GUI programs, each program is typically displayed in its own window. In this section, I'll discuss how you address and alter individual pixels in a window. These concepts are independent of Python; they are common to all computers and are used in all programming languages.

### The Window Coordinate System

You are probably familiar with Cartesian coordinates in a grid like Figure 5-1.

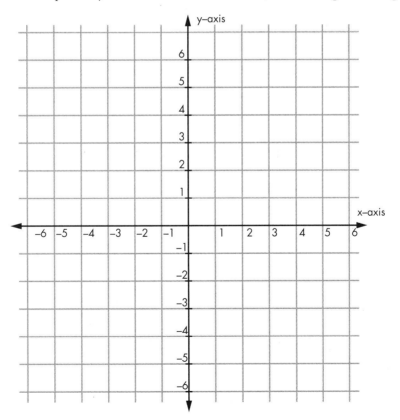

Figure 5-1: The standard Cartesian coordinate system

Any point in a Cartesian grid can be located by specifying its x- and y-coordinates (in that order). The origin is the point specified as (0, 0) and is found in the center of the grid.

Computer window coordinates work in a similar way (Figure 5-2).

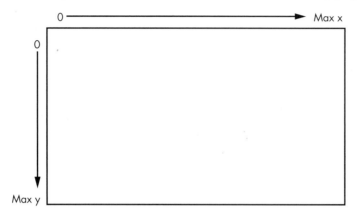

Figure 5-2: A computer window's coordinate system

However, there are a few key differences:

1. The origin (0, 0) point is in the upper-left corner of the window.
2. The y-axis is reversed so that y values start at zero at the top of the window and increase as you go down.
3. The x and y values are always integers. Each (x, y) pair specifies a single pixel in the window. These values are always specified as relative to the upper-left corner of the window, not the screen. That way, the user can move the window anywhere on the screen without affecting the coordinates of the elements of the program displayed in the window.

The full computer screen has its own set of (x, y) coordinates for every pixel and uses the same type of coordinate system, but programs rarely, if ever, need to deal with screen coordinates.

When we write a pygame application, we need to specify the width and height of the window we want to create. Within the window, we can address any pixel using its x- and y-coordinates, as shown in Figure 5-3.

Figure 5-3 shows a black pixel at position (3, 5). That is an x-value of 3 (note that this is actually the fourth column, since coordinates start at 0) and a y value of 5 (actually the sixth row). Each pixel in a window is commonly referred to as a *point*. To reference a point in a window, you would typically use a Python tuple. For example, you might have an assignment statement like this, with the x value first:

```
pixelLocation = (3, 5)
```

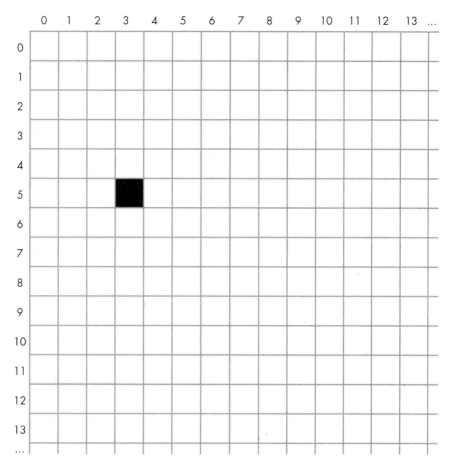

*Figure 5-3: A single point (a single pixel) in a computer window*

To show an image in a window, we need to specify the coordinates of its starting point—always the upper-left corner of the image—as an (x, y) pair, as in Figure 5-4, where we draw the image at location (3, 5).

When working with an image, you'll often need to deal with the *bounding rectangle*, which is the smallest rectangle that can be made that completely surrounds all pixels of the image. A rectangle is represented in pygame by a set of four values: x, y, width, height. The rectangle for the image in Figure 5-4 has values of 3, 5, 11, 7. I'll show you how to use a rectangle like this in an upcoming example program. Even if your image is not rectangular (for example, if it's a circle or an ellipse), you still have to consider its bounding rectangle for positioning and collision detection.

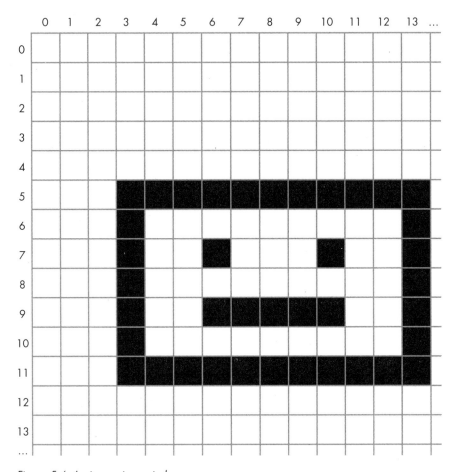

*Figure 5-4: An image in a window*

## Pixel Colors

Let's explore how colors are represented on the computer screen. If you have experience with a graphics program like Photoshop, you probably already know how this works, but you may want a quick refresher anyway.

Each pixel on the screen is made up of a combination of three colors: red, green, and blue, often referred to as *RGB*. The color displayed in any pixel is composed of some amount of red, green, and blue, where the amount of each is specified as a value from 0, meaning none, to 255, meaning full intensity. Therefore, there are $256 \times 256 \times 256$ possible combinations, or 16,777,216 (often referred to as just "16 million") possible colors, for each pixel.

Colors in pygame are given as RGB values, and we write them as Python tuples of three numbers. Here is how we create constants for the main colors:

```
RED = (255, 0, 0)    # full red, no green, no blue
GREEN = (0, 255, 0)  # no red, full green, no blue
BLUE = (0, 0, 255)   # no red, no green, full blue
```

Here are the definitions of a few more colors. You can create a color using any combination of three numbers between 0 and 255:

```
BLACK = (0, 0, 0)    # no red, no green, no blue
WHITE = (255, 255, 255)  # full red, full green, full blue
DARK_GRAY = (75, 75, 75)
MEDIUM_GRAY = (128, 128, 128)
LIGHT_GRAY = (175, 175, 175)
TEAL = (0, 128, 128)  # no red, half-strength green, half-strength blue
YELLOW = (255, 255, 0)
PURPLE = (128, 0, 128)
```

In pygame, you'll need to specify colors when you want to fill the background of a window, draw a shape in a color, draw text in a color, and so on. Defining colors up front as tuple constants makes them very easy to spot later in code.

# Event-Driven Programs

In most of the programs in the book so far, the main code has lived in a while loop. The program stops at a call to the built-in input() function and waits for some user input to work on. Program output is typically handled using calls to print().

In interactive GUI programs, this model no longer works. GUIs introduce a new model of computing known as the *event-driven* model. Event-driven programs don't rely on input() and print(); instead, the user interacts with elements in a window at will using a keyboard and/or mouse or other pointing device. They may be able to click various buttons or icons, make selections from menus, provide input in text fields, or give commands via clicks or key presses to control some avatar in the window.

**NOTE** *Calls to print() can still be highly useful for debugging, when used to write out intermediate results.*

Central to event-driven programming is the concept of an *event*. Events are difficult to define and are best described with examples, such as a mouse click and a key press (each of which is actually made up of two events: mouse down and mouse up and key down and key up, respectively). Here is my working definition.

**event**     Something that happens while your program is running that your program wants to or needs to respond to. Most events are generated by user actions.

An event-driven GUI program runs constantly in an infinite loop. Each time through the loop, the program checks for any new events it needs to react to and executes appropriate code to handle those events. Also, each time through the loop, the program needs to redraw all the elements in the window to update what the user sees.

For example, say we have a simple GUI program that displays two buttons: Bark and Meow. When clicked, the Bark button plays a sound of a dog barking and the Meow button plays a sound of a cat meowing (Figure 5-5).

Figure 5-5: A simple program
with two buttons

The user can click these buttons in any order and at any time. To handle the user's actions, the program runs in a loop and constantly checks to see if either button has been clicked. When it receives a mouse down event on a button, the program remembers that the button has been clicked and draws the depressed image of that button. When it receives a mouse up event on the button, it remembers the new state and redraws the button with its original appearance, and it plays the appropriate sound. Because the main loop runs so quickly, the user perceives that the sound plays immediately after they click the button. Each time through the loop, the program redraws both buttons with an image matching each button's current state.

## Using Pygame

At first, pygame may seem like an overwhelmingly large package with many different calls available. Although it is large, there's actually not a lot that you need to understand to get a small program up and running. To introduce pygame, I'll first give you a template that you can use for all pygame programs you create. Then I'll build on that template, adding key pieces of functionality little by little.

In the following sections, I'll show you how to:

- Bring up a blank window.
- Show an image.
- Detect a mouse click.
- Detect both single and continuous key presses.
- Create a simple animation.
- Play sound effects and background sounds.
- Draw shapes.

In the next chapter, we'll continue the discussion of pygame and you'll see how to:

- Animate many objects.
- Build and react to a button.
- Create a text display field.

## Bringing Up a Blank Window

As I said earlier, pygame programs run constantly in a loop, checking for events. It might help to think of your program as an animation, where each pass through the main loop is one frame. The user may click on something during any frame, and your program must not only respond to that input but also keep track of everything it needs to draw in the window. For instance, in one example program later in this chapter, we'll move a ball across the window so in each frame the ball is drawn in a slightly different position.

Listing 5-1 is a generic template that you can use as a starting point for all your pygame programs. This program opens a window and paints the entire contents black. The only thing the user can do is click the close button to quit the program.

### File: PygameDemo0_WindowOnly/PygameWindowOnly.py

```
# pygame demo 0 - window only

# 1 - Import packages
import pygame
from pygame.locals import *
import sys

# 2 - Define constants
BLACK = (0, 0, 0)
WINDOW_WIDTH = 640
WINDOW_HEIGHT = 480
FRAMES_PER_SECOND = 30

# 3 - Initialize the world
pygame.init()
window = pygame.display.set_mode((WINDOW_WIDTH, WINDOW_HEIGHT))
clock = pygame.time.Clock()

# 4 - Load assets: image(s), sound(s), etc.

# 5 - Initialize variables

# 6 - Loop forever
while True:

    # 7 - Check for and handle events
    for event in pygame.event.get():
        # Clicked the close button? Quit pygame and end the program
        if event.type == pygame.QUIT:
            pygame.quit()
            sys.exit()

    # 8 - Do any "per frame" actions

    # 9 - Clear the window
```

```
window.fill(BLACK)

# 10 - Draw all window elements

# 11 - Update the window
pygame.display.update()

# 12 - Slow things down a bit
clock.tick(FRAMES_PER_SECOND)
```

*Listing 5-1: A template for creating pygame programs*

Let's walk through the different parts of this template:

1. Import packages.

   The template starts with the `import` statements. We first import the pygame package itself, then some constants defined inside pygame that we'll use later. The last import is the sys package, which we'll use to quit our program.

2. Define constants.

   We next define any constants for our program. First we define the RGB value for `BLACK`, which we will use to paint the background of our window. Then we define constants for the width and height of our window in pixels and a constant for the refresh rate for our program. This number defines the maximum number of times the program will loop (and therefore redraw the window) per second. Our value of 30 is fairly typical. If the amount of work done in our main loop is excessive, the program might run slower than this value, but it will never run faster. A refresh rate that's too high might cause the program to run too fast. In our ball example, this means the ball might bounce around the window faster than intended.

3. Initialize the pygame environment.

   In this section, we call a function that tells pygame to initialize itself. We then ask pygame to create a window for our program with the `pygame.display.set_mode()` function and pass in the desired width and height of the window. Finally, we call another pygame function to create a clock object, which will be used at the bottom of our main loop to maintain our maximum frame rate.

4. Load assets: image(s), sound(s), and so on.

   This is a placeholder section, into which we will eventually add code to load external images, sounds, and so on from the disk for use in our program. In this basic program we're not using any external assets, so this section is empty for now.

5. Initialize variables.

   Here we will eventually initialize any variables that our program will use. Currently we have none, so we have no code here.

6. Loop forever.

Here we start our main loop. This is a simple `while True` infinite loop. Again, you can think of each iteration through the main loop as one frame in an animation.

7. Check for and handle events; commonly referred to as the *event loop*.

In this section, we call `pygame.event.get()` to get a list of the events that happened since the last time we checked (the last time the main loop ran), then iterate through the list of events. Each event reported to the program is an object, and every event object has a type. If no event has happened, this section is skipped over.

In this minimal program, where the only action a user can take is to close the window, the only event type we check for is the constant `pygame.QUIT`, generated by pygame when the user clicks the close button. If we find this event, we tell pygame to quit, which frees up any resources it was using. Then we quit our program.

8. Do any "per frame" actions.

In this section we'll eventually put any code that needs to run in every frame. This might involve moving things in the window or checking for collisions between elements. In this minimal program, we have nothing to do here.

9. Clear the window.

On each iteration through the main loop, our program must redraw everything in the window, which means we need to clear it first. The simplest approach is to just fill the window with a color, which we do here with a call to `window.fill()`, specifying a black background. We could also draw a background picture, but we'll hold off on that for now.

10. Draw all window elements.

Here we'll place code to draw everything we want to show in our window. In this sample program there is nothing to draw.

In real programs, things are drawn in the order they appear in the code, in layers from backmost to frontmost. For example, assume we want to draw two partially overlapping circles, A and B. If we draw A first, A will appear behind B, and portions of A will be obscured by B. If we draw B first and then A, the opposite happens, and we see A in front of B. This is a natural mapping equivalent to the layers in graphics programs such as Photoshop.

11. Update the window.

This line tells pygame to take all the drawing we've included and show it in the window. Pygame actually does all the drawing in steps 8, 9, and 10 in an off-screen buffer. When you tell pygame to update, it takes the contents of this off-screen buffer and puts them in the real window.

12. Slow things down a bit.

Computers are very fast, and if the loop continued to the next iteration right away without pausing, the program might run faster than the designated frame rate. The line in this section tells pygame to wait until a given amount of time has elapsed in order to make the frames of our program run at the frame rate that we specified. This is important to ensure the program runs at a consistent rate, independent of the speed of the computer on which it's running.

When you run this program, the program just puts up a blank window filled with black. To end the program, click on the close button in the title bar.

## Drawing an Image

Let's draw something in the window. There are two parts to showing a graphic image: first we load the image into the computer's memory, then we display the image in the application window.

With pygame, all images (and sounds) need to be kept in files external to your code. Pygame supports many standard graphic file formats, including *.png*, *.jpg*, and *.gif*. In this program we'll load a picture of a ball from the file *ball.png*. As a reminder, the code and assets associated with all the major listings in this book are available for download at *https://www.nostarch.com/objectorientedpython/* and *https://github.com/IrvKalb/Object-Oriented-Python-Code/*.

While we only need one graphic file in this program, it's a good idea to use a consistent approach to handling graphic and sound files, so I'll lay one out for you here. First, create a project folder. Place your main program in that folder, along with any related files containing Python classes and functions. Then, inside the project folder, create an *images* folder into which you'll place any image files you want to use in your program. Also create a *sounds* folder and place any sound files you want to use there. Figure 5-6 shows the suggested structure. All of the example programs in this book will use this project folder layout.

Figure 5-6: Suggested project folder hierarchy

A *path* (also called a *pathname*) is a string that uniquely identifies the location of a file or folder on a computer. To load a graphic or sound file into your program, you must specify the path to the file. There are two types of paths: relative and absolute.

A *relative path* is a relative to the current folder, often called the *current working directory*. When you run a program using an IDE such as IDLE or

PyCharm, it sets the current folder to the one containing your main Python program so you can use relative paths with ease. In this book, I will assume you're using an IDE and will represent all paths as relative paths.

The relative path for a graphic file (for example, *ball.png*) in the same folder as your main Python file would be just the filename as a string (for example, 'ball.png'). Using the suggested project structure, the relative path would be 'images/ball.png'.

This says that inside the project folder will be another folder named *images*, and inside that folder is a file named *ball.png*. In path strings, folder names are separated by the slash character.

However, if you expect to run your program from the command line, then you need to construct absolute paths for all files. An *absolute path* is one that starts from the root of the filesystem and includes the full hierarchy of folders to your file. To build an absolute path to any file, you can use code like this, which builds an absolute path string to the *ball.png* file in the *images* folder inside the project folder:

```
from pathlib import Path

# Place this in section #2, defining a constant
BASE_PATH = Path(__file__).resolve().parent

# Build a path to the file in the images folder
pathToBall = BASE_PATH / 'images/ball.png'
```

Now we'll create the code of the ball program, starting with the earlier 12-step template and adding just two new lines of code, as shown in Listing 5-2.

### File: PygameDemo1_OneImage/PygameOneImage.py

```
# pygame demo 1 - draw one image

--- snip ---
# 3 - Initialize the world
pygame.init()
window = pygame.display.set_mode((WINDOW_WIDTH, WINDOW_HEIGHT))
clock = pygame.time.Clock()

# 4 - Load assets: image(s), sound(s), etc.
❶ ballImage = pygame.image.load('images/ball.png')

# 5 - Initialize variables

--- snip ---

    # 10 - Draw all window elements
    # draw ball at position 100 across (x) and 200 down (y)
  ❷ window.blit(ballImage, (100, 200))

    # 11 - Update the window
```

```
    pygame.display.update()

    # 12 - Slow things down a bit
    clock.tick(FRAMES_PER_SECOND)   # make pygame wait
```

*Listing 5-2: Load one image and draw it in every frame.*

First, we tell pygame to find the file containing the image of the ball and load that image into memory ❶. The variable ballImage now refers to the image of the ball. Notice that this assignment statement is only executed once, before the main loop starts.

**NOTE**    *In the official documentation of pygame, every image, including the application window, is known as a* surface. *I'll use more specific terms: I will refer to the application window simply as a* window *and to any picture loaded from an external file as an* image. *I reserve the term* surface *for any picture drawn on the fly.*

We then tell the program to draw the ball ❷ every time we go through the main loop. We specify the location representing the position to place the upper-left corner of the image's bounding rectangle, typically as a tuple of x- and y-coordinates.

The function name blit() is a very old reference to the words *bit block transfer,* but in this context it really just means "draw." Since the program loaded the ball image earlier, pygame knows how big the image is, so we just need to tell it where to draw the ball. In Listing 5-2, we give an x value of 100 and a y value of 200.

When you run the program, on each iteration through the loop (30 times per second) every pixel in the window is set to black, then the ball is drawn over the background. From the user's point of view, it looks like nothing is happening—the ball just stays in one spot with the upper-left corner of its bounding rectangle at location (100, 200).

## Detecting a Mouse Click

Next, we'll allow our program to detect and react to a mouse click. The user will be able to click on the ball to make it appear somewhere else in the window. When the program detects a mouse click on the ball, it randomly picks new coordinates and draws the ball at that new location. Instead of using hardcoded coordinates of (100, 200), we'll create two variables, ballX and ballY, and refer to the coordinates of the ball in the window as the tuple (ballX, ballY). Listing 5-3 provides the code.

### File: PygameDemo2_ImageClickAndMove/PygameImageClickAndMove.py

```
# pygame demo 2 - one image, click and move

# 1 - Import packages
import pygame
from pygame.locals import *
import sys
```

```
❶ import random

   # 2 - Define constants
   BLACK = (0, 0, 0)
   WINDOW_WIDTH = 640
   WINDOW_HEIGHT = 480
   FRAMES_PER_SECOND = 30
❷ BALL_WIDTH_HEIGHT = 100
   MAX_WIDTH = WINDOW_WIDTH - BALL_WIDTH_HEIGHT
   MAX_HEIGHT = WINDOW_HEIGHT - BALL_WIDTH_HEIGHT

   # 3 - Initialize the world
   pygame.init()
   window = pygame.display.set_mode((WINDOW_WIDTH, WINDOW_HEIGHT))
   clock = pygame.time.Clock()

   # 4 - Load assets: image(s), sound(s), etc.
   ballImage = pygame.image.load('images/ball.png')

   # 5 - Initialize variables
❸ ballX = random.randrange(MAX_WIDTH)
   ballY = random.randrange(MAX_HEIGHT)
❹ ballRect = pygame.Rect(ballX, ballY, BALL_WIDTH_HEIGHT, BALL_WIDTH_HEIGHT)

   # 6 - Loop forever
   while True:

       # 7 - Check for and handle events
       for event in pygame.event.get():
           # Clicked the close button? Quit pygame and end the program
           if event.type == pygame.QUIT:
               pygame.quit()
               sys.exit()

           # See if user clicked
❺      if event.type == pygame.MOUSEBUTTONUP:
               # mouseX, mouseY = event.pos  # Could do this if we needed it

               # Check if the click was in the rect of the ball
               # If so, choose a random new location
❻          if ballRect.collidepoint(event.pos):
                   ballX = random.randrange(MAX_WIDTH)
                   ballY = random.randrange(MAX_HEIGHT)
                   ballRect = pygame.Rect(ballX, ballY, BALL_WIDTH_HEIGHT,
                                          BALL_WIDTH_HEIGHT)

       # 8  Do any "per frame" actions

       # 9 - Clear the window
       window.fill(BLACK)

       # 10 - Draw all window elements
       # Draw the ball at the randomized location
❼  window.blit(ballImage, (ballX, ballY))
```

```
# 11 - Update the window
pygame.display.update()

# 12 - Slow things down a bit
clock.tick(FRAMES_PER_SECOND)   # make pygame wait
```

*Listing 5-3: Detecting a mouse click and acting on it*

Since we need to generate random numbers for the ball coordinates, we import the random package ❶.

We then add a new constant to define the height and width of our image as 100 pixels ❷. We also create two more constants to limit the maximum width and height coordinates. By using these constants rather than the size of the window, we ensure that our ball image will always appear fully within the window (remember that when we refer to the location of an image, we are specifying the position of its upper-left corner). We use those constants to choose random values for the starting x- and y-coordinates for our ball ❸.

Next, we call pygame.Rect() to create a rectangle ❹. Defining a rectangle requires four parameters—an x-coordinate, a y-coordinate, a width, and a height, in that order:

```
<rectObject> = pygame.Rect(<x>, <y>, <width>, <height>)
```

This returns a pygame rectangle object, or rect. We'll use the rectangle of the ball in the processing of events.

We also add code to check if the user clicked the mouse. As mentioned, a mouse click is actually made up of two different events: a mouse down event and a mouse up event. Since the mouse up event is typically used to signal activation, we'll only look for that event here. This event is signaled by a new event.type value of pygame.MOUSEBUTTONUP ❺. When we find that a mouse up event has occurred, we'll then check to see if the location where the user clicked was inside the current rectangle of the ball.

When pygame detects that an event has happened, it builds an event object containing a lot of data. In this case, we only care about the x- and y-coordinates where the event happened. We retrieve the (x, y) position of the click using event.pos, which provides a tuple of two values.

**NOTE**    *If we need to separate the x- and y-coordinates of the click, we can unpack the tuple and store the values into two variables like this:*

```
mouseX, mouseY = event.pos
```

Now we check to see if the event happened inside the rectangle of the ball using collidepoint() ❻, whose syntax is:

```
<booleanVariable> = <someRectangle>.collidepoint(<someXYLocation>)
```

The method returns a Boolean True if the given point is inside the rectangle. If the user has clicked the ball, we randomly select new values for ballX and ballY. We use those values to create a new rectangle for the ball at the new random location.

The only change here is that we always draw the ball at the location given by the tuple (ballX, ballY) ❼. The effect is that whenever the user clicks inside the rectangle of the ball, the ball appears to move to some new random spot in the window.

## Handling the Keyboard

The next step is to allow the user to control some aspect of the program through the keyboard. There are two different ways to handle user keyboard interactions: as individual key presses, and when a user holds down a key to indicate that an action should happen for as long as that key is down (known as *continuous mode*).

### Recognizing Individual Key Presses

Like the mouse clicks, each key press generates two events: key down and key up. The two events have different event types: pygame.KEYDOWN and pygame.KEYUP.

Listing 5-4 shows a small sample program that allows the user to move the ball image in the window using the keyboard. The program also shows a target rectangle in the window. The user's goal is to move the ball image so that it overlaps with the target image.

### File: PygameDemo3_MoveByKeyboard/PygameMoveByKeyboardOncePerKey.py

```
# pygame demo 3(a) - one image, move by keyboard

# 1 - Import packages
import pygame
from pygame.locals import *
import sys
import random

# 2 - Define constants
BLACK = (0, 0, 0)
WINDOW_WIDTH = 640
WINDOW_HEIGHT = 480
FRAMES_PER_SECOND = 30
BALL_WIDTH_HEIGHT = 100
MAX_WIDTH = WINDOW_WIDTH - BALL_WIDTH_HEIGHT
MAX_HEIGHT = WINDOW_HEIGHT - BALL_WIDTH_HEIGHT
❶ TARGET_X = 400
TARGET_Y = 320
TARGET_WIDTH_HEIGHT = 120
N_PIXELS_TO_MOVE = 3

# 3 - Initialize the world
pygame.init()
```

```
window = pygame.display.set_mode((WINDOW_WIDTH, WINDOW_HEIGHT))
clock = pygame.time.Clock()

# 4 - Load assets: image(s), sound(s), etc.
ballImage = pygame.image.load('images/ball.png')
❷ targetImage = pygame.image.load('images/target.jpg')

# 5 - Initialize variables
ballX = random.randrange(MAX_WIDTH)
ballY = random.randrange(MAX_HEIGHT)
targetRect = pygame.Rect(TARGET_X, TARGET_Y, TARGET_WIDTH_HEIGHT, TARGET_
WIDTH_HEIGHT)

# 6 - Loop forever
while True:

    # 7 - Check for and handle events
    for event in pygame.event.get():
        # Clicked the close button? Quit pygame and end the program
        if event.type == pygame.QUIT:
            pygame.quit()
            sys.exit()

        # See if the user pressed a key
    ❸ elif event.type == pygame.KEYDOWN:
            if event.key == pygame.K_LEFT:
                ballX = ballX - N_PIXELS_TO_MOVE
            elif event.key == pygame.K_RIGHT:
                ballX = ballX + N_PIXELS_TO_MOVE
            elif event.key == pygame.K_UP:
                ballY = ballY - N_PIXELS_TO_MOVE
            elif event.key == pygame.K_DOWN:
                ballY = ballY + N_PIXELS_TO_MOVE

    # 8  Do any "per frame" actions
    # Check if the ball is colliding with the target
❹ ballRect = pygame.Rect(ballX, ballY,
                          BALL_WIDTH_HEIGHT, BALL_WIDTH_HEIGHT)
❺ if ballRect.colliderect(targetRect):
        print('Ball is touching the target')

    # 9 - Clear the window
    window.fill(BLACK)

    # 10 - Draw all window elements
❻ window.blit(targetImage, (TARGET_X, TARGET_Y))  # draw the target
    window.blit(ballImage, (ballX, ballY))  # draw the ball

    # 11 - Update the window
    pygame.display.update()

    # 12 - Slow things down a bit
    clock.tick(FRAMES_PER_SECOND)  # make pygame wait
```

*Listing 5-4: Detecting and acting on single key presses*

First we add a few new constants ❶ to define the x- and y-coordinates of the upper-left corner of the target rectangle and the width and height of the target. We then load the image of the target rectangle ❷.

In the loop where we look for for events, we add a test for a key press by checking for an event of type `pygame.KEYDOWN` ❸. If a key down event is detected, we look into the event to find out what key was pressed. Each key has an associated constant in pygame, so here we check if the user has pressed the left, up, down, or right arrow. For each of these keys, we modify the value of the ball's x- or y-coordinate appropriately by a small number of pixels.

Next we create a pygame rect object for the ball based on its x- and y-coordinates and its height and width ❹. We can check to see if two rectangles overlap with the following call:

```
<booleanVariable> = <rect1>.colliderect(<rect2>)
```

This call compares two rectangles and returns `True` if they overlap at all or `False` if they don't. We compare the ball rectangle with the target rectangle ❺, and if they overlap, the program prints "Ball is touching the target" to the shell window.

The last change is where we draw both the target and the ball. The target is drawn first so that when the two overlap, the ball appears over the target ❻.

When the program is run, if the rectangle of the ball overlaps the rectangle of the target, the message is written to the shell window. If you move the ball away from the target, the message stops being written out.

## Dealing with Repeating Keys in Continuous Mode

The second way to handle keyboard interactions in pygame is to *poll* the keyboard. This involves asking pygame for a list representing which keys are currently down in every frame using the following call:

```
<aTuple> = pygame.key.get_pressed()
```

This call returns a tuple of 0s and 1s representing the state of each key: 0 if the key is up, 1 if the key is down. You can then use constants defined within pygame as an index into the returned tuple to see if a *particular* key is down. For example, the following lines can be used to determine the state of the A key:

```
keyPressedTuple = pygame.key.get_pressed()
# Now use a constant to get the appropriate element of the tuple
aIsDown = keyPressedTuple[pygame.K_a]
```

The full listing of constants representing all keys defined in pygame can be found at *https://www.pygame.org/docs/ref/key.html*.

The code in Listing 5-5 shows how we can use this technique to move an image continuously rather than once per key press. In this version, we move the keyboard handling from section #7 to section #8. The rest of the code is identical to the previous version in Listing 5-4.

**File: PygameDemo3_MoveByKeyboard/PygameMoveByKeyboardContinuous.py**

```
# pygame demo 3(b) - one image, continuous mode, move as long as a key is down

--- snip ---
    # 7 - Check for and handle events
    for event in pygame.event.get():
        # Clicked the close button? Quit pygame and end the program
        if event.type == pygame.QUIT:
            pygame.quit()
            sys.exit()

    # 8 - Do any "per frame" actions
    # Check for user pressing keys
❶ keyPressedTuple = pygame.key.get_pressed()

    if keyPressedTuple[pygame.K_LEFT]:  # moving left
        ballX = ballX - N_PIXELS_TO_MOVE

    if keyPressedTuple[pygame.K_RIGHT]:  # moving right
        ballX = ballX + N_PIXELS_TO_MOVE

    if keyPressedTuple[pygame.K_UP]:  # moving up
        ballY = ballY - N_PIXELS_TO_MOVE

    if keyPressedTuple[pygame.K_DOWN]:  # moving down
        ballY = ballY + N_PIXELS_TO_MOVE

    # Check if the ball is colliding with the target
    ballRect = pygame.Rect(ballX, ballY,
                            BALL_WIDTH_HEIGHT, BALL_WIDTH_HEIGHT)
    if ballRect.colliderect(targetRect):
        print('Ball is touching the target')
--- snip ---
```

*Listing 5-5: Handling keys being held down*

The keyboard-handling code in Listing 5-5 does not rely on events, so we place the new code outside of the for loop that iterates through all events returned by pygame ❶.

Because we are doing this check in every frame, the movement of the ball will appear to be continuous as long as the user holds down a key. For example, if the user presses and holds the right arrow key, this code will add 3 to the value of the ballX coordinate in every frame, and the user will see the ball moving smoothly to the right. When they stop pressing the key, the movement stops.

The other change is that this approach allows you to check for multiple keys being down at the same time. For example, if the user presses and holds the left and down arrow keys, the ball will move diagonally down and to the left. You can check for as many keys being held down as you wish. However, the number of *simultaneous* key presses that can be detected is limited by the operating system, the keyboard hardware, and many other factors. The typical limit is around four keys, but your mileage may vary.

## Creating a Location-Based Animation

Next, we'll build a location-based animation. This code will allow us to move an image diagonally and then have it appear to bounce off the edges of the window. This was a favorite technique of screensavers on old CRT-based monitors, to avoid burning in a static image.

We'll change the location of our image slightly in every frame. We'll also check if the result of that movement would place any part of the image outside one of the window boundaries and, if so, reverse the movement in that direction. For example, if the image was moving down and would cross the bottom of the window, we would reverse the direction and make the image start moving up.

We'll again use the same starting template. Listing 5-6 gives the full source code.

**File: PygameDemo4_OneBallBounce/PygameOneBallBounceXY.py**

```
# pygame demo 4(d) - one image, bounce around the window using (x, y) coords

# 1 - Import packages
import pygame
from pygame.locals import *
import sys
import random

# 2 - Define constants
BLACK = (0, 0, 0)
WINDOW_WIDTH = 640
WINDOW_HEIGHT = 480
FRAMES_PER_SECOND = 30
BALL_WIDTH_HEIGHT = 100
N_PIXELS_PER_FRAME = 3

# 3 - Initialize the world
pygame.init()
window = pygame.display.set_mode((WINDOW_WIDTH, WINDOW_HEIGHT))
clock = pygame.time.Clock()

# 4 - Load assets: image(s), sound(s), etc.
ballImage = pygame.image.load('images/ball.png')

# 5 - Initialize variables
```

```
   MAX_WIDTH = WINDOW_WIDTH - BALL_WIDTH_HEIGHT
   MAX_HEIGHT = WINDOW_HEIGHT - BALL_WIDTH_HEIGHT
❶ ballX = random.randrange(MAX_WIDTH)
   ballY = random.randrange(MAX_HEIGHT)
   xSpeed = N_PIXELS_PER_FRAME
   ySpeed = N_PIXELS_PER_FRAME

   # 6 - Loop forever
   while True:

       # 7 - Check for and handle events
       for event in pygame.event.get():
           # Clicked the close button? Quit pygame and end the program
           if event.type == pygame.QUIT:
               pygame.quit()
               sys.exit()

       # 8 - Do any "per frame" actions
❷      if (ballX < 0) or (ballX >= MAX_WIDTH):
           xSpeed = -xSpeed  # reverse X direction

       if (ballY < 0) or (ballY >= MAX_HEIGHT):
           ySpeed = -ySpeed  # reverse Y direction

       # Update the ball's location, using the speed in two directions
❸      ballX = ballX + xSpeed
       ballY = ballY + ySpeed

       # 9 - Clear the window before drawing it again
       window.fill(BLACK)

       # 10 - Draw the window elements
       window.blit(ballImage, (ballX, ballY))

       # 11 - Update the window
       pygame.display.update()

       # 12 - Slow things down a bit
       clock.tick(FRAMES_PER_SECOND)
```

*Listing 5-6: A location-based animation, bouncing a ball around the window*

We start by creating and initializing the two variables xSpeed and ySpeed ❶, which determine how far and in what direction the image should move in each frame. We initialize both variables to the number of pixels to move per frame (3), so the image will start by moving three pixels to the right (the positive x direction) and three pixels down (the positive y direction).

In the key part of the program, we handle the x- and y-coordinates separately ❷. First, we check to see if the x-coordinate of the ball is less than zero, meaning that part of the image is off the left edge, or past the MAX_WIDTH pixel and so effectively off the right edge. If either of these is the case, we reverse the sign of the speed in the x direction, meaning it will go in the opposite direction. For example, if the ball was moving to the right and went off the right edge, we would change the value of xSpeed from 3 to –3 to cause the ball to start moving to the left, and vice versa.

Then we do a similar check for the y-coordinate to make the ball bounce off the top or bottom edge, as needed.

Finally, we update the position of the ball by adding the xSpeed to the ballX coordinate and adding the ySpeed to the ballY coordinate ❸. This positions the ball at a new location on both axes.

At the bottom of the main loop, we draw the ball. Since we're updating the values of ballX and ballY in every frame, the ball appears to animate smoothly. Try it out. Whenever the ball reaches any edge, it seems to bounce off.

### Using Pygame rects

Next I'll present a different way to achieve the same result. Rather than keeping track of the current x- and y-coordinates of the ball in separate variables, we'll use the rect of the ball, update the rect every frame, and check if performing the update would cause any part of the rect to move outside an edge of the window. This results in fewer variables, and because we'll start by making a call to get the rect of an image, it will work with images of any size.

When you create a rect object, in addition to remembering the left, top, width, and height as attributes of the rectangle, that object also calculates and maintains a number of other attributes for you. You can access any of these attributes directly by name using *dot syntax*, as shown in Table 5-1. (I'll provide more detail on this in Chapter 8.)

**Table 5-1:** Direct Access to Attributes of a rect

| Attribute | Description |
| --- | --- |
| `<rect>.x` | The x-coordinate of the left edge of the rect |
| `<rect>.y` | The y-coordinate of the top edge of the rect |
| `<rect>.left` | The x-coordinate of the left edge of the rect (same as `<rect>.x`) |
| `<rect>.top` | The y-coordinate of the top edge of the rect (same as `<rect>.y`) |
| `<rect>.right` | The x-coordinate of the right edge of the rect |
| `<rect>.bottom` | The y-coordinate of the bottom edge of the rect |
| `<rect>.topleft` | A two-integer tuple: the coordinates of the upper-left corner of the rect |
| `<rect>.bottomleft` | A two-integer tuple: the coordinates of the lower-left corner of the rect |
| `<rect>.topright` | A two-integer tuple: the coordinates of the upper-right corner of the rect |
| `<rect>.bottomright` | A two-integer tuple: the coordinates of the lower-right corner of the rect |

*(continued)*

**Table 5-1:** Direct Access to Attributes of a rect *(continued)*

| Attribute | Description |
|---|---|
| *<rect>*.midtop | A two-integer tuple: the coordinates of the midpoint of the top edge of the rect |
| *<rect>*.midleft | A two-integer tuple: the coordinates of the midpoint of the left edge of the rect |
| *<rect>*.midbottom | A two-integer tuple: the coordinates of the midpoint of the bottom edge of the rect |
| *<rect>*.midright | A two-integer tuple: the coordinates of the midpoint of the right edge of the rect |
| *<rect>*.center | A two-integer tuple: the coordinates at the center of the rect |
| *<rect>*.centerx | The x-coordinate of the center of the width of the rect |
| *<rect>*.centery | The y-coordinate of the center of the height of the rect |
| *<rect>*.size | A two-integer tuple: the (width, height) of the rect |
| *<rect>*.width | The width of the rect |
| *<rect>*.height | The height of the rect |
| *<rect>*.w | The width of the rect (same as *<rect>*.width) |
| *<rect>*.h | The height of the rect (same as *<rect>*.height) |

A pygame rect also can be thought of, and accessed as, a list of four elements. Specifically, you can use an index to get or set any individual part of a rect. For instance, using the ballRect, the individual elements can be accessed as:

- ballRect[0] is the x value (but you could also use ballRect.left)
- ballRect[1] is the y value (but you could also use ballRect.top)
- ballRect[2] is the width (but you could also use ballRect.width)
- ballRect[3] is the height (but you could also use ballRect.height)

Listing 5-7 is an alternative version of our bouncing ball program that maintains all the information about the ball in a rectangle object.

### File: PygameDemo4_OneBallBounce/PygameOneBallBounceRects.py

```
# pygame demo 4(b) - one image, bounce around the window using rects

# 1 - Import packages
import pygame
from pygame.locals import *
import sys
import random

# 2 - Define constants
BLACK = (0, 0, 0)
WINDOW_WIDTH = 640
WINDOW_HEIGHT = 480
```

```
FRAMES_PER_SECOND = 30
N_PIXELS_PER_FRAME = 3

# 3 - Initialize the world
pygame.init()
window = pygame.display.set_mode((WINDOW_WIDTH, WINDOW_HEIGHT))
clock = pygame.time.Clock()

# 4 - Load assets: image(s), sound(s), etc.
ballImage = pygame.image.load('images/ball.png')

# 5 - Initialize variables
❶ ballRect = ballImage.get_rect()
MAX_WIDTH = WINDOW_WIDTH - ballRect.width
MAX_HEIGHT = WINDOW_HEIGHT - ballRect.height
ballRect.left = random.randrange(MAX_WIDTH)
ballRect.top = random.randrange(MAX_HEIGHT)
xSpeed = N_PIXELS_PER_FRAME
ySpeed = N_PIXELS_PER_FRAME

# 6 - Loop forever
while True:

    # 7 - Check for and handle events
    for event in pygame.event.get():
        # Clicked the close button? Quit pygame and end the program
        if event.type == pygame.QUIT:
            pygame.quit()
            sys.exit()

    # 8 - Do any "per frame" actions
❷   if (ballRect.left < 0) or (ballRect.right >= WINDOW_WIDTH):
        xSpeed = -xSpeed  # reverse X direction

    if (ballRect.top < 0) or (ballRect.bottom >= WINDOW_HEIGHT):
        ySpeed = -ySpeed  # reverse Y direction

    # Update the ball's rectangle using the speed in two directions
    ballRect.left = ballRect.left + xSpeed
    ballRect.top = ballRect.top + ySpeed

    # 9 - Clear the window before drawing it again
    window.fill(BLACK)

    # 10 - Draw the window elements
❸   window.blit(ballImage, ballRect)

    # 11 - Update the window
    pygame.display.update()

    # 12 - Slow things down a bit
    clock.tick(FRAMES_PER_SECOND)
```

*Listing 5-7: A location-based animation, bouncing a ball around the window, using rects*

This approach of using a rect object is neither better nor worse than using separate variables. The resulting program works exactly the same as the original. The important lesson here is how you can use and manipulate attributes of a rect object.

After loading the image of the ball, we call the get_rect() method ❶ to get the bounding rectangle of the image. That call returns a rect object, which we store into a variable called ballRect. We use ballRect.width and ballRect.height to get direct access to the width and height of the ball image. (In the previous version, we used a constant of 100 for the width and the height.) Getting these values from the image that was loaded makes our code much more adaptable because it means we can use a graphic of any size.

The code also uses the attributes of the rectangle rather than using separate variables for checking if any part of the ball's rectangle goes over an edge. We can use ballRect.left and ballRect.right to see if the ballRect is off the left or right edges ❷. We do a similar test with ballRect.top and ballRect.bottom. Rather than updating individual x- and y-coordinate variables, we update the left and top of the ballRect.

The other subtle but important change is in the call to draw the ball ❸. The second argument in the call to blit() can be either an (x, y) tuple or a rect. The code inside blit() uses the left and top position in the rect as the x- and y-coordinates.

# Playing Sounds

There are two types of sounds that you might want to play in your programs: short sound effects and background music.

## Playing Sound Effects

All sound effects must live in external files and must be in either *.wav* or *.ogg* format. Playing a relatively short sound effect consists of two steps: load the sound from an external sound file once; then at the appropriate time(s) play your sound.

To load a sound effect into memory, you use a line like this:

```
<soundVariable> = pygame.mixer.Sound(<path to sound file>)
```

To play the sound effect, you only need to call its play() method:

```
<soundVariable>.play()
```

We'll modify Listing 5-7 to add a "boing" sound effect whenever the ball bounces off a side of the window. There is a *sounds* folder in the project folder at the same level as the main program. Right after loading the ball image, we load the sound file by adding this code:

```
# 4 - Load assets: image(s), sound(s), etc.
ballImage = pygame.image.load('images/ball.png')
bounceSound = pygame.mixer.Sound('sounds/boing.wav')
```

To play the "boing" sound effect whenever we change either the horizontal or vertical direction of the ball, we modify section #8 to look like this:

```
# 8 - Do any "per frame" actions
    if (ballRect.left < 0) or (ballRect.right >= WINDOW_WIDTH):
        xSpeed = -xSpeed  # reverse X direction
        bounceSound.play()

    if (ballRect.top < 0) or (ballRect.bottom >= WINDOW_HEIGHT):
        ySpeed = -ySpeed  # reverse Y direction
        bounceSound.play()
```

When you find a condition that should play a sound effect, you add a call to the play() method of the sound. There are many more options for controlling sound effects; you can find details in the official documentation at *https://www.pygame.org/docs/ref/mixer.html*.

## Playing Background Music

Playing background music involves two lines of code using calls to the pygame.mixer.music module. First, you need this to load the sound file into memory:

```
pygame.mixer.music.load(<path to sound file>)
```

The *<path to sound file>* is a path string where the sound file can be found. You can use *.mp3* files, which seem to work best, as well as *.wav* or *.ogg* files. When you want to start the music playing, you need to make this call:

```
pygame.mixer.music.play(<number of loops>, <starting position>)
```

To play some background music repeatedly, you can pass in a -1 for *<number of loops>* to run the music forever. The *<starting position>* is typically set to 0 to indicate that you want to play the sound from the beginning.

There is a downloadable, modified version of the bouncing ball program that properly loads the sound effect and background music files and starts the background sound playing. The only changes are in section #4, as shown here.

### File: PygameDemo4_OneBallBounce/PyGameOneBallBounceWithSound.py

```
# 4 - Load assets: image(s), sound(s), etc.
ballImage = pygame.image.load('images/ball.png')
bounceSound = pygame.mixer.Sound('sounds/boing.wav')
pygame.mixer.music.load('sounds/background.mp3')
pygame.mixer.music.play(-1, 0.0)
```

Pygame allows for much more intricate handling of background sounds. You can find the full documentation at *https://www.pygame.org/docs/ref/music.html#module-pygame.mixer.music*.

*In order to make future examples more clearly focused on OOP, I'll leave out calls to play sound effects and background music. But adding sounds greatly enhances the user experience of a game, and I strongly encourage including them.*

## Drawing Shapes

Pygame offers a number of built-in functions that allow you to draw certain shapes known as *primitives*, which include lines, circles, ellipses, arcs, polygons, and rectangles. Table 5-2 provides a list of these functions. Note that there are two calls that draw *anti-aliased* lines. These are lines that include blended colors at the edges to make the lines look smooth and less jagged. There are two key advantages to using these drawing functions: they execute extremely quickly, and they allow you to draw simple shapes without having to create or load images from external files.

**Table 5-2:** Functions for Drawing Shapes

| Function | Description |
| --- | --- |
| pygame.draw.aaline() | Draws an anti-aliased line |
| pygame.draw.aalines() | Draws a series of anti-aliased lines |
| pygame.draw.arc() | Draws an arc |
| pygame.draw.circle() | Draws a circle |
| pygame.draw.ellipse() | Draws an ellipse |
| pygame.draw.line() | Draws a line |
| pygame.draw.lines() | Draws a series of lines |
| pygame.draw.polygon() | Draws a polygon |
| pygame.draw.rect() | Draws a rectangle |

Figure 5-7 shows the output of a sample program that demonstrates calls to these primitive drawing functions.

Listing 5-8 is the code of the sample program, using the same 12-step template that produced the output in Figure 5-7.

### File: PygameDemo5_DrawingShapes.py

```
# pygame demo 5 - drawing

--- snip ---
while True:

    # 7 - Check for and handle events
    for event in pygame.event.get():
        # Clicked the close button? Quit pygame and end the program
        if event.type == pygame.QUIT:
            pygame.quit()
            sys.exit()
```

```
# 8 - Do any "per frame" actions

# 9 - Clear the window
window.fill(GRAY)

❶ # 10 - Draw all window elements
# Draw a box
pygame.draw.line(window, BLUE, (20, 20), (60, 20), 4)  # top
pygame.draw.line(window, BLUE, (20, 20), (20, 60), 4)  # left
pygame.draw.line(window, BLUE, (20, 60), (60, 60), 4)  # right
pygame.draw.line(window, BLUE, (60, 20), (60, 60), 4)  # bottom
# Draw an X in the box
pygame.draw.line(window, BLUE, (20, 20), (60, 60), 1)
pygame.draw.line(window, BLUE, (20, 60), (60, 20), 1)

# Draw a filled circle and an empty circle
pygame.draw.circle(window, GREEN, (250, 50), 30, 0)  # filled
pygame.draw.circle(window, GREEN, (400, 50), 30, 2)  # 2 pixel edge

# Draw a filled rectangle and an empty rectangle
pygame.draw.rect(window, RED, (250, 150, 100, 50), 0)  # filled
pygame.draw.rect(window, RED, (400, 150, 100, 50), 1)  # 1 pixel edge

# Draw a filled ellipse and an empty ellipse
pygame.draw.ellipse(window, YELLOW, (250, 250, 80, 40), 0)  # filled
pygame.draw.ellipse(window, YELLOW, (400, 250, 80, 40), 2)  # 2 pixel edge

# Draw a six-sided polygon
pygame.draw.polygon(window, TEAL, ((240, 350), (350, 350),
                                   (410, 410), (350, 470),
                                   (240, 470), (170, 410)))

# Draw an arc
pygame.draw.arc(window, BLUE, (20, 400, 100, 100), 0, 2, 5)

# Draw anti-aliased lines: a single line, then a list of points
pygame.draw.aaline(window, RED, (500, 400), (540, 470), 1)
pygame.draw.aalines(window, BLUE, True,
                ((580, 400), (587, 450),
                 (595, 460), (600, 444)), 1)

# 11 - Update the window
pygame.display.update()

# 12 - Slow things down a bit
clock.tick(FRAMES_PER_SECOND)  # make pygame wait
```

*Listing 5-8: A program to demonstrate calls to primitive drawing functions in pygame*

The drawing of all the primitives occurs in section #10 ❶. We make calls to pygame's drawing functions to draw a box with two diagonals, filled and empty circles, filled and empty rectangles, filled and empty ovals, a six-sided polygon, an arc, and two anti-aliased lines.

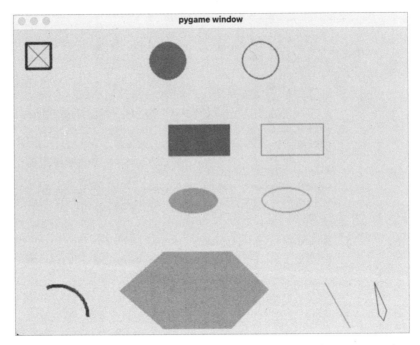

Figure 5-7: A sample program that demonstrates using calls to draw primitive shapes

## Reference for Primitive Shapes

For your reference, here is the documentation for the pygame methods to draw these primitives. In all of the following, the color argument expects you to pass in a tuple of RGB values:

**Anti-aliased line**

```
pygame.draw.aaline(window, color, startpos, endpos, blend=True)
```

Draws an anti-aliased line in the window. If blend is True, the shades will be blended with existing pixel shades instead of overwriting pixels.

**Anti-aliased lines**

```
pygame.draw.aalines(window, color, closed, points, blend=True)
```

Draws a sequence of anti-aliased lines in the window. The closed argument is a simple Boolean; if it's True, a line will be drawn between the first and last points to complete the shape. The points argument is a list or tuple of (x, y) coordinates to be connected by line segments (there must be at least two). The Boolean blend argument, if set to True, will blend the shades with existing pixel shades instead of overwriting them.

## Arc

```
pygame.draw.arc(window, color, rect, angle_start, angle_stop, width=0)
```

Draws an arc in the window. The arc will fit inside the given rect. The two angle arguments are the initial and final angles (in radians, with zero on the right). The width argument is the thickness to draw the outer edge.

## Circle

```
pygame.draw.circle(window, color, pos, radius, width=0)
```

Draws a circle in the window. The pos is the center of the circle, and radius is the radius. The width argument is the thickness to draw the outer edge. If width is 0, then the circle will be filled.

## Ellipse

```
pygame.draw.ellipse(window, color, rect, width=0)
```

Draws an ellipse in the window. The given rect is the area that the ellipse will fill. The width argument is the thickness to draw the outer edge. If width is 0, then the ellipse will be filled.

## Line

```
pygame.draw.line(window, color, startpos, endpos, width=1)
```

Draws a line in a window. The width argument is the thickness of the line.

## Lines

```
pygame.draw.lines(window, color, closed, points, width=1)
```

Draws a sequence of lines in the window. The closed argument is a simple Boolean; if it's True, a line will be drawn between the first and last points to complete the shape. The points argument is a list or tuple of (x, y) coordinates to be connected by line segments (there must be at least two). The width argument is the thickness of the line. Note that specifying a line width wider than 1 does not fill in the gaps between the lines. Therefore, wide lines and sharp corners won't be joined seamlessly.

## Polygon

```
pygame.draw.polygon(window, color, pointslist, width=0)
```

Draws a polygon in the window. The pointslist specifies the vertices of the polygon. The width argument is the thickness to draw the outer edge. If width is 0, then the polygon will be filled.

### Rectangle

```
pygame.draw.rect(window, color, rect, width=0)
```

Draws a rectangle in the window. The rect is the area of the rectangle. The width argument is the thickness to draw the outer edge. If width is 0, then the rectangle will be filled.

**NOTE** *For additional information, see* http://www.pygame.org/docs/ref/draw.html.

The set of primitive calls allows you the flexibility to draw any shapes you wish. Again, the order in which you make calls is important. Think of the order of your calls as layers; elements that are drawn early can be overlaid by later calls to any other drawing primitive function.

## Summary

In this chapter I introduced the basics of pygame. You installed pygame on your computer, then learned about the model of event-driven programming and the use of events, which is very different from coding text-based programs. I explained the coordinate system of pixels in a window and the way that colors are represented in code.

To start right at the beginning with pygame, I introduced a 12-section template that does nothing but bring up a window and can be used to build any pygame-based program. Using that framework, we then built sample programs that showed how to draw an image in the window (using blit()), how to detect mouse events, and how to handle keyboard input. The next demonstration explained how to build a location-based animation.

Rectangles are highly important in pygame, so I covered how the attributes of a rect object can be used. I also provided some example code to show how to play sound effects and background music to enhance the user's enjoyment of your programs. Finally, I introduced how to use pygame methods to draw primitive shapes in a window.

While I have introduced many concepts within pygame, almost everything I showed in this chapter has essentially been procedural. The rect object is an example of object-oriented code built directly into pygame. In the next chapter, I'll show how to use OOP in code to use pygame more effectively.

# 6

## OBJECT-ORIENTED PYGAME

In this chapter I'll demonstrate how you can use OOP techniques effectively within the pygame framework. We'll start off with an example of procedural code, then split that code into a single class and some main code that calls the methods of that class. After that, we'll build two classes, SimpleButton and SimpleText, that implement basic user interface widgets: a button and a field for displaying text. I'll also introduce the concept of a callback.

### Building the Screensaver Ball with OOP Pygame

In Chapter 5, we created an old-school screensaver where a ball bounced around inside a window (Listing 5-6, if you need to refresh your memory).

That code works, but the data for the ball and the code to manipulate the ball are intertwined, meaning there's a lot of initialization code, and the code to update and draw the ball are embedded in the 12-step framework.

A more modular approach is to split the code into a Ball class and a main program that instantiates a Ball object and makes calls to its methods. In this section we'll make this split, and I'll show you how to create multiple balls from the Ball class.

## Creating a Ball Class

We'll start by extracting all code relating to the ball from the main program and moving it into a separate Ball class. Looking at the original code, we can see that the sections that deal with the ball are:

- Section #4, which loads the image of the ball
- Section #5, which creates and initializes all the variables that have something to do with the ball
- Section #8, which includes code for moving the ball, detecting an edge bounce, and changing speed and direction
- Section #10, which draws the ball

From this we can conclude that our Ball class will require the following methods:

**create()** Loads an image, sets a location, and initializes all instance variables

**update()** Changes the location of the ball in every frame, based on the x speed and y speed of the ball

**draw()** Draws the ball in the window

The first step is to create a project folder, in which you need a *Ball.py* for the new Ball class, the main code file *Main_BallBounce.py*, and an *images* folder containing the *ball.png* image file.

Listing 6-1 shows the code of the new Ball class.

### File: PygameDemo6_BallBounceObjectOriented/Ball.py

```python
import pygame
from pygame.locals import *
import random

# Ball class
class Ball():

❶   def __init__(self, window, windowWidth, windowHeight):
        self.window = window  # remember the window, so we can draw later
        self.windowWidth = windowWidth
        self.windowHeight = windowHeight
```

```
❷ self.image = pygame.image.load('images/ball.png')
    # A rect is made up of [x, y, width, height]
    ballRect = self.image.get_rect()
    self.width = ballRect.width
    self.height = ballRect.height
    self.maxWidth = windowWidth - self.width
    self.maxHeight = windowHeight - self.height

    # Pick a random starting position
❸ self.x = random.randrange(0, self.maxWidth)
    self.y = random.randrange(0, self.maxHeight)

    # Choose a random speed between -4 and 4, but not zero,
    # in both the x and y directions
❹ speedsList = [-4, -3, -2, -1, 1, 2, 3, 4]
    self.xSpeed = random.choice(speedsList)
    self.ySpeed = random.choice(speedsList)

❺ def update(self):
    # Check for hitting a wall. If so, change that direction.
    if (self.x < 0) or (self.x >= self.maxWidth):
        self.xSpeed = -self.xSpeed

    if (self.y < 0) or (self.y >= self.maxHeight):
        self.ySpeed = -self.ySpeed

    # Update the Ball's x and y, using the speed in two directions
    self.x = self.x + self.xSpeed
    self.y = self.y + self.ySpeed

❻ def draw(self):
    self.window.blit(self.image, (self.x, self.y))
```

*Listing 6-1: The new Ball class*

When we instantiate a Ball object, the __init__() method receives three pieces of data: the window to draw into, the width of the window, and the height of the window ❶. We save the window variable into the instance variable self.window so that we can use it later in the draw() method, and we do the same with the self.windowHeight and self.windowWidth instance variables. We then load the image of the ball using the path to the file and get the rect of that ball image ❷. We need the rect to calculate the maximum values for x and y so that the ball will always fully appear in the window. Next, we pick a randomized starting location for the ball ❸. Finally, we set the speed in the x and y directions to a random value between −4 and 4 (but not 0), representing the number of pixels to move per frame ❹. Because of these numbers, the ball may move differently each time we run the program. All these values are saved in instance variables to be used by other methods.

In the main program, we'll call the update() method in each frame of the main loop, so this is where we place the code that checks for the ball hitting any border of the window ❺. If it does hit an edge, we reverse the speed in that direction and modify the x- and y-coordinates (self.x and self.y) by the current speed in the x and y directions.

We'll also call the draw() method, which simply calls blit() to draw the ball at its current x- and y-coordinates ❻, in every frame of the main loop.

## Using the Ball Class

Now all functionality associated with a ball has been placed in the Ball class code. All the main program needs to do is create the ball, then call its update() and draw() methods in every frame. Listing 6-2 shows the greatly simplified code of the main program.

### File: PygameDemo6_BallBounceObjectOriented/Main_BallBounce.py

```
# pygame demo 6(a) - using the Ball class, bounce one ball

# 1 - Import packages
import pygame
from pygame.locals import *
import sys
import random
❶ from Ball import *   # bring in the Ball class code

# 2 - Define constants
BLACK = (0, 0, 0)
WINDOW_WIDTH = 640
WINDOW_HEIGHT = 480
FRAMES_PER_SECOND = 30

# 3 - Initialize the world
pygame.init()
window = pygame.display.set_mode((WINDOW_WIDTH, WINDOW_HEIGHT))
clock = pygame.time.Clock()

# 4 - Load assets: image(s), sound(s), etc.

# 5 - Initialize variables
❷ oBall = Ball(window, WINDOW_WIDTH, WINDOW_HEIGHT)

# 6 - Loop forever
while True:

    # 7 - Check for and handle events
    for event in pygame.event.get():
        if event.type == pygame.QUIT:
            pygame.quit()
            sys.exit()

    # 8 - Do any "per frame" actions
❸   oBall.update()   # tell the Ball to update itself
```

```
    # 9 - Clear the window before drawing it again
    window.fill(BLACK)

    # 10 - Draw the window elements
❹ oBall.draw()   # tell the Ball to draw itself

    # 11 - Update the window
    pygame.display.update()

    # 12 - Slow things down a bit
    clock.tick(FRAMES_PER_SECOND)
```

*Listing 6-2: The new main program that instantiates a Ball and makes calls to its methods*

If you compare this new main program with the original code in Listing 5-6, you'll see that it's much simpler and clearer. We use an import statement to bring in the Ball class code ❶. We create a Ball object, passing in the window that we created and the width and height of that window ❷, and we save the resulting Ball object in a variable named oBall.

The responsibility of moving the ball is now in the Ball class code, so here we only need to call the update() method of the oBall object ❸. Since the Ball object knows how big the window is, how big the image of the ball is, and the location and speed of the ball, it can do all the calculations it needs to do to move the ball and bounce it off the walls.

The main code calls the draw() method of the oBall object ❹, but the actual drawing is done in the oBall object.

## Creating Many Ball Objects

Now let's make a slight but important modification to the main program to create multiple Ball objects. This is one of the real powers of object orientation: to create three balls, we only have to instantiate three Ball objects from the Ball class. Here we'll use a basic approach and build a list of Ball objects. In each frame, we'll iterate through the list of Ball objects, tell each one to update its location, then iterate again to tell each one to draw itself. Listing 6-3 shows a modified main program that creates and updates three Ball objects.

**File: PygameDemo6_BallBounceObjectOriented/Main_BallBounceManyBalls.py**

```
# pygame demo 6(b) - using the Ball class, bounce many balls

--- snip ---
N_BALLS = 3
--- snip ---

# 5 - Initialize variables
❶ ballList = []
  for oBall in range(0, N_BALLS):
      # Each time through the loop, create a Ball object
      oBall = Ball(window, WINDOW_WIDTH, WINDOW_HEIGHT)
```

```
        ballList.append(oBall)  # append the new Ball to the list of Balls

    # 6 - Loop forever
    while True:

        --- snip ---

        # 8 - Do any "per frame" actions
    ❷ for oBall in ballList:
            oBall.update()  # tell each Ball to update itself

        # 9 - Clear the window before drawing it again
        window.fill(BLACK)

        # 10 - Draw the window elements
    ❸ for oBall in ballList:
            oBall.draw()    # tell each Ball to draw itself

        # 11 - Update the window
        pygame.display.update()

        # 12 - Slow things down a bit
        clock.tick(FRAMES_PER_SECOND)
```

*Listing 6-3: Creating, moving, and displaying three balls*

We start with an empty list of Ball objects ❶. Then we have a loop that creates three Ball objects, each of which we append to our list of Ball objects, ballList. Each Ball object chooses and remembers a randomized starting location and a randomized speed in both the x and y directions.

Inside the main loop, we iterate through all the Ball objects and tell each one to update itself ❷, changing the x- and y-coordinates of each Ball object to a new location. We then iterate through the list again, calling the draw() method of each Ball object ❸.

When we run the program, we see three balls, each starting at a randomized location and each moving with a randomized x and y speed. Each ball bounces correctly off the boundaries of the window.

Using this object-oriented approach, we made no changes to the Ball class, but just changed our main program to now manage a list of Ball objects instead of a single Ball object. This is a common, and very positive, side effect of OOP code: well-written classes can often be reused without change.

## Creating Many, Many Ball Objects

We can change the value of the constant N_BALLS from 3 to some much larger value, like 300, to quickly create that many balls (Figure 6-1). By changing just a single constant, we make a major change to the behavior of the program. Each ball maintains its own speed and location and draws itself.

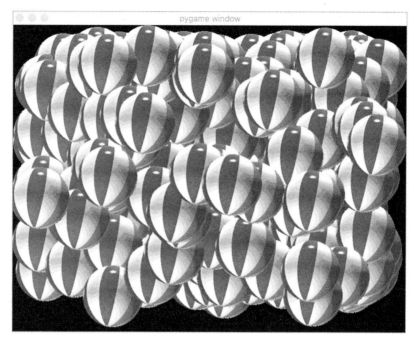

*Figure 6-1: Creating, updating, and drawing 300 Ball objects*

The fact that we can instantiate any number of objects from a single script will be vital not only in defining game objects like spaceships, zombies, bullets, treasures, and so on, but also in building GUI controls such as buttons, checkboxes, text input fields, and text outputs.

## Building a Reusable Object-Oriented Button

The simple button is one of the most recognizable elements of a graphical user interface. The standard behavior of a button consists of the user using their mouse to click down on the button image and then releasing it.

Buttons typically consist of at least two images: one to represent the *up* or normal state of the button and another to represent the *down* or pressed state of the button. The sequence of a click can be broken down into the following steps:

1. User moves the mouse pointer over the button
2. User presses the mouse button down
3. Program reacts by changing the image to the down state
4. User releases the mouse button
5. Program reacts by showing the up image of the button
6. Program performs some action based on the button click

Good GUIs also allow the user to click down on a button, temporarily roll off the button, changing the button to the up state, and then, with the mouse button still down, roll back over the image so the button changes back to the down image. If the user clicks down on a button but then rolls the mouse off and lifts up on the mouse button, that is not considered a click. This means the program takes action only when the user presses down and releases while the mouse is positioned over the image of a button.

## Building a Button Class

The button behavior should be common and consistent for all buttons used in a GUI, so we'll build a class that takes care of the behavior details. Once we've built a simple button class, we can instantiate any number of buttons and they'll all work exactly the same way.

Let's consider what behaviors our button class must support. We'll need methods to:

- Load the images of the up and down states, then initialize any instance variables needed to track the button's state.
- Tell the button about all events that the main program has detected and check whether there are any that the button needs to react to.
- Draw the current image representing the button.

Listing 6-4 presents the code of a SimpleButton class. (We'll build a more complicated button class in Chapter 7.) This class has three methods, __init__(), handleEvent(), and draw(), that implement the behaviors mentioned. The code of the handleEvent() method does get a little tricky, but once you have it working, it's incredibly easy to use. Feel free to work your way through it, but know that the implementation of the code is not that relevant. The important thing here is to understand the purpose and usage of the different methods.

### File: PygameDemo7_SimpleButton/SimpleButton.py

```
# SimpleButton class
#
# Uses a "state machine" approach
#

import pygame
from pygame.locals import *

class SimpleButton():
    # Used to track the state of the button
    STATE_IDLE = 'idle' # button is up, mouse not over button
    STATE_ARMED = 'armed' # button is down, mouse over button
    STATE_DISARMED = 'disarmed' # clicked down on button, rolled off

    def __init__(self, window, loc, up, down): ❶
        self.window = window
        self.loc = loc
        self.surfaceUp = pygame.image.load(up)
```

```
        self.surfaceDown = pygame.image.load(down)

        # Get the rect of the button (used to see if the mouse is over the button)
        self.rect = self.surfaceUp.get_rect()
        self.rect[0] = loc[0]
        self.rect[1] = loc[1]

        self.state = SimpleButton.STATE_IDLE

    def handleEvent(self, eventObj): ❷
        # This method will return True if user clicks the button.
        # Normally returns False.

        if eventObj.type not in (MOUSEMOTION, MOUSEBUTTONUP, MOUSEBUTTONDOWN): ❸
            # The button only cares about mouse-related events
            return False

        eventPointInButtonRect = self.rect.collidepoint(eventObj.pos)

        if self.state == SimpleButton.STATE_IDLE:
            if (eventObj.type == MOUSEBUTTONDOWN) and eventPointInButtonRect:
                self.state = SimpleButton.STATE_ARMED

        elif self.state == SimpleButton.STATE_ARMED:
            if (eventObj.type == MOUSEBUTTONUP) and eventPointInButtonRect:
                self.state = SimpleButton.STATE_IDLE
                return True  # clicked!

            if (eventObj.type == MOUSEMOTION) and (not eventPointInButtonRect):
                self.state = SimpleButton.STATE_DISARMED

        elif self.state == SimpleButton.STATE_DISARMED:
            if eventPointInButtonRect:
                self.state = SimpleButton.STATE_ARMED
            elif eventObj.type == MOUSEBUTTONUP:
                self.state = SimpleButton.STATE_IDLE

        return False

    def draw(self): ❹
        # Draw the button's current appearance to the window
        if self.state == SimpleButton.STATE_ARMED:
            self.window.blit(self.surfaceDown, self.loc)

        else:  # IDLE or DISARMED
            self.window.blit(self.surfaceUp, self.loc)
```

Listing 6-4: The SimpleButton class

The __init__() method begins by saving all values passed in into instance variables ❶ to use in other methods. It then initializes a few more instance variables.

Whenever the main program detects any event, it calls the handleEvent() method ❷. This method first checks that the event is one of MOUSEMOTION,

MOUSEBUTTONUP, or MOUSEBUTTONDOWN ❸. The rest of the method is implemented as a *state machine*, a technique that I will go into more detail about in Chapter 15. The code is a little complicated, and you should feel free to study how it works, but for now note that it uses the instance variable self.state (over the course of multiple calls) to detect if the user has clicked on the button. The handleEvent() method returns True when the user completes a mouse click by pressing down on the button, then later releasing on the same button. In all other cases, handleEvent() returns False.

Finally, the draw() method uses the state of the object's instance variable self.state to decide which image (up or down) to draw ❹.

## Main Code Using a SimpleButton

To use a SimpleButton in the main code, we first instantiate one from the SimpleButton class before the main loop starts with a line like this:

```
oButton = SimpleButton(window, (150, 30),
                       'images/buttonUp.png',
                       'images/buttonDown.png')
```

This line creates a SimpleButton object, specifying a location to draw it (as usual, the coordinates are for the top-left corner of the bounding rectangle) and providing the paths to both the up and down images of the button. In the main loop, any time any event happens we need to call the handleEvent() method to see if the user has clicked the button. If the user clicks the button, the program should perform some action. Also in the main loop, we need to call the draw() method to make the button show in the window.

We'll build a small test program, which will generate a user interface like Figure 6-2, to incorporate one instance of a SimpleButton.

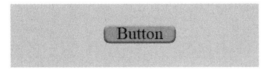

Figure 6-2: The user interface of a program with a single instance of a SimpleButton

Whenever the user completes a click on the button, the program outputs a line of text in the shell saying that the button has been clicked. Listing 6-5 contains the main program code.

### File: PygameDemo7_SimpleButton/Main_SimpleButton.py

```
# Pygame demo 7 - SimpleButton test

--- snip ---
# 5 - Initialize variables
# Create an instance of a SimpleButton
```

```
❶ oButton = SimpleButton(window, (150, 30),
                         'images/buttonUp.png',
                         'images/buttonDown.png')

# 6 - Loop forever
while True:

    # 7 - Check for and handle events
    for event in pygame.event.get():
        if event.type == pygame.QUIT:
            pygame.quit()
            sys.exit()

        # Pass the event to the button, see if it has been clicked on
❷       if oButton.handleEvent(event):
❸           print('User has clicked the button')

    # 8 - Do any "per frame" actions

    # 9 - Clear the window
    window.fill(GRAY)

    # 10 - Draw all window elements
❹   oButton.draw() # draw the button

    # 11 - Update the window
    pygame.display.update()

    # 12 - Slow things down a bit
    clock.tick(FRAMES_PER_SECOND)
```

*Listing 6-5: The main program that creates and reacts to a SimpleButton*

Again, we start with the standard pygame template from Chapter 5. Before the main loop, we create an instance of our SimpleButton ❶, specifying a window to draw into, a location, a path to the up image, and a path to the down image.

Every time through the main loop, we need to react to events detected in the main program. To implement this, we call the SimpleButton class's handleEvent() method ❷ and pass in the event from the main program.

The handleEvent() method tracks all of the user's actions on the button (pressing down, releasing, rolling off, rolling back on). When handleEvent() returns True, indicating that a click has occurred, we perform the action associated with clicking that button. Here, we just print a message ❸.

Finally we call the button's draw() method ❹ to draw an image to represent the appropriate state of the button (up or down).

### Creating a Program with Multiple Buttons

With our SimpleButton class, we can instantiate as many buttons as we wish. For example, we can modify our main program to incorporate three SimpleButton instances, as shown in Figure 6-3.

Figure 6-3: The main program with three SimpleButton objects

We don't need to make any changes to the SimpleButton class file to do this. We simply modify our main code to instantiate three SimpleButton objects instead of one.

### File: PygameDemo7_SimpleButton/Main_SimpleButton3Buttons.py

```
oButtonA = SimpleButton(window, (25, 30),
                        'images/buttonAUp.png',
                        'images/buttonADown.png')
oButtonB = SimpleButton(window, (150, 30),
                        'images/buttonBUp.png',
                        'images/buttonBDown.png')
oButtonC = SimpleButton(window, (275, 30),
                        'images/buttonCUp.png',
                        'images/buttonCDown.png')
```

We now need to call the handleEvent() method of all three buttons:

```
# Pass the event to each button, see if one has been clicked
if oButtonA.handleEvent(event):
    print('User clicked button A.')
elif oButtonB.handleEvent(event):
    print('User clicked button B.')
elif oButtonC.handleEvent(event):
    print('User clicked button C.')
```

Finally, we tell each button to draw itself:

```
oButtonA.draw()
oButtonB.draw()
oButtonC.draw()
```

When you run the program, you'll see a window with three buttons. Clicking any of the buttons prints a message showing the name of the button that was clicked.

The key idea here is that since we are using three instances of the same SimpleButton class, the behavior of each button will be identical. An important benefit of this approach is that any change to the code in the SimpleButton class will affect all buttons instantiated from the class. The main program does not need to worry about any details of the inner workings of the button code, needing only to call the handleEvent() method of each button in the main loop. Each button will return True or False to say that it has or has not been clicked.

# Building a Reusable Object-Oriented Text Display

There are two different types of text in a pygame program: display text and input text. Display text is output from your program, equivalent to a call to the print() function, except it's displayed in a pygame window. Input text is string input from the user, equivalent to a call to input(). In this section, I'll discuss display text. We'll look at how to deal with input text in the next chapter.

## Steps to Display Text

Displaying text in a window is a fairly complicated process in pygame because it's not simply displayed as a string in the shell, but requires you to choose a location, fonts and sizes, and other attributes. For example, you might use code like the following:

```
pygame.font.init()

myFont = pygame.font.SysFont('Comic Sans MS', 30)
textSurface = myfont.render('Some text', True, (0, 0, 0))
window.blit(textSurface, (10, 10))
```

We start by initializing the font system within pygame; we do this before the main loop starts. Then we tell pygame to load a particular font from the system by name. Here, we request Comic Sans with a font size of 30.

The next step is the key one: we use that font to *render* our text, which creates a graphical image of the text, called a *surface* in pygame. We supply the text we want to output, a Boolean that says whether we want our text to be anti-aliased, and a color in RGB format. Here, (0, 0, 0) indicates that we want our text to be black. Finally, using blit(), we draw the image of the text into the window at some (x, y) location.

This code works well to show the provided text in the window at the given location. However, if the text doesn't change, there will be a lot of wasted work done re-creating the textSurface on each iteration through the main loop. There are also a lot of details to remember, and you must get them all correct to draw the text properly. We can hide most of this complexity by building a class.

## Creating a SimpleText Class

The idea is to build a set of methods that take care of font loading and text rendering in pygame, meaning we no longer have to remember the details of the implementation. Listing 6-6 contains a new class called SimpleText that does this work.

### File: PygameDemo8_SimpleTextDisplay/SimpleText.py

```
# SimpleText class

import pygame
from pygame.locals import *
```

```
class SimpleText():
❶ def __init__(self, window, loc, value, textColor):
❷     pygame.font.init()
      self.window = window
      self.loc = loc
❸     self.font = pygame.font.SysFont(None, 30)
      self.textColor = textColor
      self.text = None # so that the call to setText below will
                       # force the creation of the text image
      self.setValue(value) # set the initial text for drawing

❹ def setValue(self, newText):
      if self.text == newText:
          return  # nothing to change

      self.text = newText  # save the new text
      self.textSurface = self.font.render(self.text, True, self.textColor)

❺ def draw(self):
      self.window.blit(self.textSurface, self.loc)
```

*Listing 6-6: The* SimpleText *class for displaying text*

You can think of a SimpleText object as a field in the window where you want text to be displayed. You can use one to display unchanging label text or to display text that changes throughout a program.

The SimpleText class has only three methods. The __init__() method ❶ expects the window to draw into, the location at which to draw the text in the window, any initial text you want to see displayed in the field, and a text color. Calling pygame.font.init() ❷ starts up pygame's font system. The call in the first instantiated SimpleText object actually does the initialization; any additional SimpleText objects will also make this call, but since fonts have already been initialized, the call returns immediately. We create a new Font object with pygame.font.SysFont() ❸. Rather than providing a specific font name, None indicates that we will use whatever the standard system font is.

The setValue() method renders an image of the text to display and saves that image in the self.textSurface instance variable ❹. As the program runs, any time you want to change the text that's displayed, you call the setValue() method, passing in the new text to display. The setValue() method has an optimization, too: it remembers the last text that it rendered, and before doing anything else, it checks if the new text is the same as the previous text. If the text has not changed, there is nothing to do and the method just returns. If there is new text, it renders the new text into a surface to be drawn.

The draw() method ❺ draws the image contained in the self.textSurface instance variable into the window at the given location. This method should be called in every frame.

There are multiple advantages to this approach:

• The class hides all the details of pygame's rendering of text, so the user of this class never needs to know what pygame-specific calls are needed to show text.

- Each `SimpleText` object remembers the window that it draws into, the location where the text should be placed, and the text color. Therefore, you only need to specify these values once, when you instantiate a `SimpleText` object, typically before the main loop starts.

- Each `SimpleText` object is also optimized to remember both the text that it was last told to draw and the image (`self.textSurface`) that it made from the current text. It only needs to render a new surface when the text changes.

- To show multiple pieces of text in a window, you only need to instantiate multiple `SimpleText` objects. This is a key concept of object-oriented programming.

## Demo Ball with SimpleText and SimpleButton

To cap this off, we'll modify Listing 6-2 to use the `SimpleText` and `SimpleButton` classes. The updated program in Listing 6-7 keeps track of the number of times it goes through the main loop and reports that information at the top of the window. Clicking the Restart button resets the counter.

### File: PygameDemo8_SimpleTextDisplay/Main_BallTextAndButton.py

```
# pygame demo 8 - SimpleText, SimpleButton, and Ball

# 1 - Import packages
import pygame
from pygame.locals import *
import sys
import random
❶ from Ball import *  # bring in the Ball class code
from SimpleText import *
from SimpleButton import *

# 2 - Define constants
BLACK = (0, 0, 0)
WHITE = (255, 255, 255)
WINDOW_WIDTH = 640
WINDOW_HEIGHT = 480
FRAMES_PER_SECOND = 30

# 3 - Initialize the world
pygame.init()
window = pygame.display.set_mode((WINDOW_WIDTH, WINDOW_HEIGHT))
clock = pygame.time.Clock()

# 4 - Load assets: image(s), sound(s), etc.

# 5 - Initialize variables
❷ oBall = Ball(window, WINDOW_WIDTH, WINDOW_HEIGHT)
oFrameCountLabel = SimpleText(window, (60, 20),
                    'Program has run through this many loops: ', WHITE)
```

```
oFrameCountDisplay = SimpleText(window, (500, 20), '', WHITE)
oRestartButton = SimpleButton(window, (280, 60),
                      'images/restartUp.png', 'images/restartDown.png')
frameCounter = 0

# 6 - Loop forever
while True:

    # 7 - Check for and handle events
    for event in pygame.event.get():
        if event.type == pygame.QUIT:
            pygame.quit()
            sys.exit()

    ❸ if oRestartButton.handleEvent(event):
            frameCounter = 0  # clicked button, reset counter

    # 8 - Do any "per frame" actions
❹ oBall.update()  # tell the ball to update itself
    frameCounter = frameCounter + 1  # increment each frame
❺ oFrameCountDisplay.setValue(str(frameCounter))

    # 9 - Clear the window before drawing it again
    window.fill(BLACK)

    # 10 - Draw the window elements
❻ oBall.draw()  # tell the ball to draw itself
    oFrameCountLabel.draw()
    oFrameCountDisplay.draw()
    oRestartButton.draw()

    # 11 - Update the window
    pygame.display.update()

    # 12 - Slow things down a bit
    clock.tick(FRAMES_PER_SECOND)
```

*Listing 6-7: An example main program to show* Ball, SimpleText, *and* SimpleButton

At the top of the program, we import the code of the Ball, SimpleText, and SimpleButton classes ❶. Before our main loop starts, we create an instance of the Ball ❷, two instances of the SimpleText class (oFrameCountLabel for the unchanging message label and oFrameCountDisplay for the changing display of frames), and an instance of the SimpleButton class that we store in oRestartButton. We also initialize a variable frameCounter to zero, which we will increment every time through the main loop.

In the main loop, we check if the user pressed the Restart button ❸. If True, we reset the frame counter.

We tell the ball to update its position ❹. We increment the frame counter, then call the setValue() method of the text field to show the new count of frames ❺. Finally, we tell the ball to draw itself tell the text fields to draw themselves, and tell the Restart button to draw itself, by calling the draw() method of each object ❻.

In the instantiation of the SimpleText objects, the last argument is a text color, and we specified that the objects should be rendered in WHITE so they can be seen against a BLACK background. In the next chapter, I'll show how to expand the SimpleText class to incorporate more attributes, without complicating the interface of the class. We'll build a more full-featured text object that has reasonable default values for each of these attributes, but allows you to override those defaults.

## Interface vs. Implementation

The SimpleButton and SimpleText examples bring up the important topic of interface versus implementation. As mentioned in Chapter 4, the interface refers to how something is used, while the implementation refers to how something works (internally).

In an OOP environment, the interface is the set of methods in a class and their related parameters—also known as the *application programming interface (API)*. The implementation is the actual code of all the methods in the class.

An external package such as pygame will most likely come with documentation of the API that explains the calls that are available and the arguments you are expected to pass with each call. The full pygame API documentation is available at *https://www.pygame.org/docs/*.

When you write code that makes calls to pygame, you don't need to worry about the implementation of the methods you are using. For example, when you make a call to blit() to draw image, you really don't care *how* blit() does what it does; you just need to know *what* the call does and what arguments need to be passed in. On the other side, you can trust that the implementer(s) who wrote the blit() method have thought extensively about how to make blit() work most efficiently.

In the programming world, we often wear two hats as both the implementer and the application developer, so we need to make an effort to design APIs that not only make sense in the current situation, but also are general enough to be used by future programs of our own and by programs written by other people. Our SimpleButton and SimpleText classes are good examples, as they are written in a general way so that they can be reused easily. I'll talk more about interface versus implementation in Chapter 8, when we look at encapsulation.

## Callbacks

When using a SimpleButton object, we handle checking for and reacting to a button click like this:

```
if oButton.handleEvent(event):
    print('The button was clicked')
```

This approach to handling events works well with the `SimpleButton` class. However, some other Python packages and many other programming languages handle events in a different way: with a *callback*.

---

**callback**    A function or method of an object that is called when a particular action, event, or condition happens.

---

An easy way to understand this is to think about the 1984 hit movie *Ghostbusters*. The tagline for the movie is "Who you gonna call?" In the movie, the Ghostbusters ran an ad on TV that told people that if they saw a ghost (that's the event to look for), they should call the Ghostbusters (the callback) to get rid of it. Upon receiving the call, the Ghostbusters take the appropriate actions to eliminate the ghost.

As an example, consider a button object that is initialized to have a callback. When the user clicks the button, the button will call the callback function or method. That function or method executes whatever code is needed to react to the button click.

## Creating a Callback

To set up a callback, when you create an object or call one of an object's methods, you pass the name of a function or a method of an object to be called. As an example, there is a standard GUI package for Python called tkinter. The code needed to create a button with this package is very different from what I have shown—here's an example:

```python
import tkinter

def myFunction():
    print('myCallBackFunction was called')

oButton = tkinter.Button(text='Click me', command=myFunction)
```

When you create a button with tkinter, you must pass in a function (or a method of an object), which will be called back when the user clicks the button. Here, we are passing myFunction as the function to be called back. (This call is using keyword parameters, which will be discussed at length in Chapter 7.) The tkinter button remembers that function as the callback, and when the user clicks the resulting button, it calls the function myFunction().

You can also use a callback when you initiate some action that may take some time. Instead of waiting for the action to finish and causing the program appear to freeze for a period of time, you provide a callback to be called when the action is completed. For example, imagine that you want to make a request across the internet. Rather than making a call and waiting for that call to return data, which may take a long time, there are packages that allow you to use the approach of making the call and setting a callback. That way, the program can continue running, and the user is not locked out of it. This often involves multiple Python threads and is beyond the scope of this book, but the technique of using a callback is the general way that it is done.

## Using a Callback with SimpleButton

To demonstrate this concept, we'll make a minor modification to the SimpleButton class to allow it to accept a callback. As an additional optional parameter, the caller can provide a function or method of an object to be called back when a click on a SimpleButton object happens. Each instance of SimpleButton remembers the callback in an instance variable. When the user completes a click, the instance of SimpleButton calls the callback.

The main program in Listing 6-8 creates three instances of the SimpleButton class, each of which handles the button click in a different way. The first button, oButtonA, provides no callback; oButtonB provides a callback to a function; and oButtonC specifies a callback to a method of an object.

**File: PygameDemo9_SimpleButtonWithCallback/Main_SimpleButtonCallback.py**

```
#  pygame demo 9 - 3-button test with callbacks

# 1 - Import packages
import pygame
from pygame.locals import *
from SimpleButton import *
import sys

# #2 - Define constants
GRAY = (200, 200, 200)
WINDOW_WIDTH = 400
WINDOW_HEIGHT = 100
FRAMES_PER_SECOND = 30

# Define a function to be used as a "callback"
def myCallBackFunction(): ❶
    print('User pressed Button B, called myCallBackFunction')

# Define a class with a method to be used as a "callback"
class CallBackTest(): ❷
--- snipped any other methods in this class ---

    def myMethod(self):
        print('User pressed ButtonC, called myMethod of the CallBackTest object')

# 3 - Initialize the world
pygame.init()
window = pygame.display.set_mode((WINDOW_WIDTH, WINDOW_HEIGHT))
clock = pygame.time.Clock()

# 4 - Load assets: image(s), sound(s), etc.

# 5 - Initialize variables
```

```
oCallBackTest = CallBackTest() ❸
# Create instances of SimpleButton
# No call back
oButtonA = SimpleButton(window, (25, 30), ❹
                        'images/buttonAUp.png',
                        'images/buttonADown.png')
# Specifying a function to call back
oButtonB = SimpleButton(window, (150, 30),
                        'images/buttonBUp.png',
                        'images/buttonBDown.png',
                        callBack=myCallBackFunction)
# Specifying a method of an object to call back
oButtonC = SimpleButton(window, (275, 30),
                        'images/buttonCUp.png',
                        'images/buttonCDown.png',
                        callBack=oCallBackTest.myMethod)

counter = 0

# 6 - Loop forever
while True:

    # 7 - Check for and handle events
    for event in pygame.event.get():
        if event.type == pygame.QUIT:
            pygame.quit()
            sys.exit()

        # Pass the event to the button, see if it has been clicked on
        if oButtonA.handleEvent(event): ❺
            print('User pressed button A, handled in the main loop')

        # oButtonB and oButtonC have callbacks,
        # no need to check result of these calls
        oButtonB.handleEvent(event) ❻

        oButtonC.handleEvent(event) ❼

    # 8 - Do any "per frame" actions
    counter = counter + 1

    # 9 - Clear the window
    window.fill(GRAY)

    # 10 - Draw all window elements
    oButtonA.draw()
    oButtonB.draw()
    oButtonC.draw()

    # 11 - Update the window
    pygame.display.update()

    # 12 - Slow things down a bit
    clock.tick(FRAMES_PER_SECOND)  # make pygame wait
```

*Listing 6-8: A version of the main program that handles button clicks three different ways*

We start with a simple function, myCallBackFunction() ❶, that just prints a message to announce that it has been called. Next, we have a CallBackTest class that contains the method myMethod() ❷, which prints its own message to announce that it's been called. We create an oCallBackTest object from the CallBackTest class ❸. We need this object so we can set up a callback to oCallBack.myMethod().

Then we create three SimpleButton objects, each using a different approach ❹. The first, oButtonA, has no callback. The second, oButtonB, sets its callback to the function myCallBackFunction(). The third, oButtonC, sets its callback to oCallBack.myMethod().

In the main loop, we check for the user clicking on any of the three buttons by calling the handleEvent() method of each button. Since oButtonA has no callback, we must check if the value returned is True ❺ and, if so, perform an action. When oButtonB is clicked ❻, the myCallBackFunction() function will be called and will print its message. When oButtonC is clicked ❼, the myMethod() method of the oCallBackTest object will be called and will print its message.

Some programmers prefer using a callback approach, because the target to be called is set up when you create the object. It's important to understand this technique, especially if you are using a package that requires it. However, I will use the original approach of checking for the value returned by a call to handleEvent() in all my demonstration code.

## Summary

In this chapter, I showed how you can start with a procedural program and extract related code to build a class. We created a Ball class to demonstrate this, then modified the main code of our demo program from the previous chapter to call methods of the class to tell the Ball object *what* to do, without worrying about *how* it achieves the outcome. With all the related code in a separate class, it's easy to create a list of objects and instantiate and manage as many objects as we want to.

We then built a SimpleButton class and a SimpleText class that hide complexity inside their implementation and create highly reusable code. In the next chapter, I'll build on these classes to develop "professional-strength" button and text display classes.

Finally, I introduced the concept of a callback, where you pass in a function or method in a call to an object. The callback is later called back when an event happens or an action completes.

# 7

## PYGAME GUI WIDGETS

Pygame allows programmers to take the text-based language of Python and use it to build GUI-based programs. Windows, pointing devices, clicking, dragging, and sounds have all become standard parts of our experience using computers. Unfortunately, the pygame package doesn't come with built-in basic user interface elements, so we need to build them ourselves. We'll do so with `pygwidgets`, a library of GUI widgets.

This chapter explains how standard widgets such as images, buttons, and input or output fields can be built as classes and how client code uses them. Building each element as a class allows programmers to incorporate multiple instances of each element when creating a GUI. Before we get started building these GUI widgets, however, I first need to discuss one more Python feature: passing data in a call to a function or method.

## Passing Arguments into a Function or Method

The arguments in a call to a function and the parameters defined in the function have a one-to-one relationship, so that the value of the first argument is given to the first parameter, the value of the second argument is given to the second parameter, and so on.

Figure 7-1, duplicated from Chapter 3, shows that the same is true when you make a call to a method of an object. We can see that the first parameter, which is always self, is set to the object in the call.

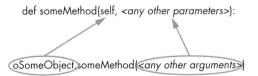

Figure 7-1: How arguments passed into a method match up with its parameters

However, Python (and some other languages) allows you to make some of the arguments optional. If an optional argument isn't provided in a call, we can provide a default value to use in the function or method instead. I'll explain by means of a real-world analogy.

If you order a hamburger at a Burger King restaurant, your burger will come with ketchup, mustard, and pickles. But Burger King is famous for saying, "You can have it your way." If you want some other combination of condiments, you must say what you want (or don't want) when you make your order.

We'll start by writing an orderBurgers() function that simulates making a burger order in the regular way we've been defining functions, without implementing default values:

```
def orderBurgers(nBurgers, ketchup, mustard, pickles):
```

You must specify the number of hamburgers you want to order, but ideally, if you want the defaults of True for adding ketchup, mustard, and pickles, you shouldn't need to pass in any more arguments. So, to order two hamburgers with the standard defaults, you might think your call should look like this:

```
orderBurgers(2)  # with ketchup, mustard, and pickles
```

However, in Python, this will trigger an error because there is a mismatch between the number of arguments in the call and the number of parameters specified in the function:

```
TypeError: orderBurgers() missing 3 required positional arguments: 'ketchup',
'mustard', and 'pickles'
```

Let's see how Python allows us to set up optional parameters that can be given default values if nothing is specified.

## Positional and Keyword Parameters

Python has two different types of parameters: positional parameters and keyword parameters. *Positional parameters* are the type that we're already familiar with, where each argument in a call has a matching parameter in the function or method definition.

A *keyword parameter* allows you to specify a default value. You write a keyword parameter as a variable name, an equal sign, and a default value, like this:

```
def someFunction(<keywordParameter>=<default value>):
```

You can have multiple keyword parameters, each with a name and a default value.

A function or method can have both positional parameters and keyword parameters, in which case you must specify all positional parameters *before* any keyword parameters:

```
def someOtherFunction(positionalParam1, positionalParam2, ...
        <keywordParameter1>=<default value 1>,
        <keywordParameter2>=<default value 2>, ...):
```

Let's rewrite orderBurgers() to use one positional parameter and three keyword parameters with default values, like this:

```
def orderBurgers(nBurgers, ketchup=True, mustard=True, pickles=True):
```

When we make a call to this function, nBurgers is a positional parameter and therefore must be specified as an argument in every call. The other three are keyword parameters. If no values are passed for ketchup, mustard, and pickles, the function will use the default value of True for each of those parameter variables. Now we can order two burgers with all the condiments like this:

```
orderBurgers(2)
```

If we want something other than a default value, we can specify the name of the keyword parameter and a different value in our call. For example, if we only want ketchup on our two burgers, we can make the call this way:

```
orderBurgers(2, mustard=False, pickles=False)
```

When the function runs, the values of the mustard and pickles variables are set to False. Since we did not specify a value for ketchup, it is given the default of True.

You can also make the call specifying all arguments positionally, including those written as keyword parameters. Python will use the ordering of your arguments to assign each parameter the correct value:

```
orderBurgers(2, True, False, False)
```

In this call, we are again specifying two burgers with ketchup, no mustard, and no pickles.

## Additional Notes on Keyword Parameters

Let's quickly go over a few conventions and tips for using keyword parameters. As a Python convention, when you use keyword parameters and keywords with arguments, the equal sign between the keyword and the value should *not* have spaces around it, to show that these are not typical assignment statements. These lines are properly formatted:

```
def orderBurgers(nBurgers, ketchup=True, mustard=True, pickles=True):

orderBurgers(2, mustard=False)
```

These lines will also work fine, but they don't follow the formatting convention and are less readable:

```
def orderBurgers(nBurgers, ketchup = True, mustard = True, pickles = True):

orderBurgers(2, mustard = False)
```

When calling a function that has both positional parameters and keyword parameters, you must provide values for all the positional parameters first, before any optional keyword parameters.

Keyword arguments in calls can be specified in any order. Calls to our orderBurgers() function could be made in various ways, such as:

```
orderBurgers(2, mustard=False, pickles=False)  # only ketchup
```

or:

```
orderBurgers(2, pickles=False, mustard=False, ketchup=False)  # plain
```

All keyword parameters will be given the appropriate values, independent of the order of the arguments.

While all the default values in the orderBurgers() example were Boolean values, a keyword parameter can have a default value of any data type. For example, we could write a function to allow a customer to make an ice cream order like this:

```
def orderIceCream(flavor, nScoops=1, coneOrCup='cone', sprinkles=False):
```

The caller must specify a flavor, but by default will get one scoop in a cone with no sprinkles. The caller could override these defaults with different keyword values.

## Using None as a Default Value

It's sometimes helpful to know whether the caller passed in a value for a keyword parameter or not. For this example, the caller orders a pizza. At a minimum, the caller must specify a size. The second parameter will be a style that defaults to 'regular' but could be 'deepdish'. As a third parameter, the caller can optionally pass in a single desired topping. If the caller wants a topping, we must charge them extra.

In Listing 7-1, we'll use a positional parameter for the size and keyword parameters for the style and topping. The default for style is the string 'regular'. Since the topping choice is optional, we'll use the special Python value of None as the default, but the caller may pass in the topping of their choice.

### File: OrderPizzaWithNone.py

```python
def orderPizza(size, style='regular', topping=None):
    # Do some calculations based on the size and style
    # Check if a topping was specified
    PRICE_OF_TOPPING = 1.50  # price for any topping

    if size == 'small':
        price = 10.00
    elif size == 'medium':
        price = 14.00
    else: # large
        price = 18.00

    if style == 'deepdish':
        price = price + 2.00 # charge extra for deepdish

    line = 'You have ordered a ' + size + ' ' + style + ' pizza with '
❶ if topping is None:  # check if no topping was passed in
        print(line + 'no topping')
    else:
        print(line + topping)
        price = price + PRICE_OF_TOPPING

    print('The price is $', price)
    print()

# You could order a pizza in the following ways:
❷ orderPizza('large')   # large, defaults to regular, no topping

orderPizza('large', style='regular')  # same as above

❸ orderPizza('medium', style='deepdish', topping='mushrooms')

orderPizza('small', topping='mushrooms') # style defaults to regular
```

*Listing 7-1: A function with a keyword parameter defaulting to None*

The first and second calls would be seen as the same, with the value of the variable topping set to None ❷. In the third and fourth calls, the value of topping is set to 'mushrooms' ❸. Because 'mushrooms' is not None, in these calls the code would add in an extra charge for a topping on the pizzas ❶.

Using None as a default value for a keyword parameter gives you a way to see if the caller provided a value in the call. This may be a very subtle use of keyword parameters, but it will be very useful in our upcoming discussion.

### Choosing Keywords and Default Values

Using default values makes calling functions and methods simpler, but there is a downside. Your choice of each keyword for keyword parameters is very important. Once programmers start making calls that override default values, it's very difficult to change the name of a keyword parameter because that name must be changed in *all* calls to the function or method in lockstep. Otherwise, code that was working will break. For more widely distributed code, this can potentially cause a great deal of pain to programmers using your code. Bottom line, don't change the name of a keyword parameter unless it is absolutely necessary. So, choose wisely!

It's also very important to use default values that should suit the widest possible range of users. (On a personal note, I *hate* mustard! Whenever I go to Burger King, I have to remember to specify no mustard or I'll get what I consider to be an inedible hamburger. I think they made a bad default choice.)

### Default Values in GUI Widgets

In the next section, I'll present a collection of classes that you can use to easily create GUI elements such as buttons and text fields within pygame. These classes will each be initialized using a few positional parameters but will also have assorted optional keyword parameters, all with reasonable defaults to allow programmers to create GUI widgets by specifying only a few positional arguments. More precise control can be obtained by specifying values to overwrite the default values of keyword parameters.

For an in-depth example, we'll look at a widget to display text in the application's window. Text can be shown in a variety of fonts, font sizes, colors, background colors, and so on. We'll build a DisplayText class that will have default values for all of these attributes but will give client code the option of specifying different values.

## The pygwidgets Package

The rest of this chapter will focus on the pygwidgets (pronounced "pig wijits") package, which was written with two goals in mind:

1. To demonstrate many different object-oriented programming techniques
2. To allow programmers to easily create and use GUI widgets in pygame programs

The pygwidgets package contains the following classes:

**TextButton**

Button built with standard art, using a text string

**CustomButton**

Button with custom artwork

**TextCheckBox**

Checkbox with standard art, built from a text string

**CustomCheckBox**

Checkbox with custom artwork

**TextRadioButton**

Radio buttons with standard art, built from a text string

**CustomRadioButton**

Radio buttons with custom artwork

**DisplayText**

Field used to display output text

**InputText**

Field where the user can type text

**Dragger**

Allows the user to drag an image

**Image**

Displays an image at a location

**ImageCollection**

Displays one of a collection of images at a location

**Animation**

Displays a sequence of images

**SpriteSheetAnimation**

Displays a sequence of images from a single larger image

## Setting Up

To install `pygwidgets`, open the command line and enter the following:

```
python3 -m pip install -U pip --user
python3 -m pip install -U pygwidgets --user
```

These commands download and install the latest version of `pygwidgets` from the Python Package Index (PyPI). It is placed into a folder (named *site-packages*) that is available to all your Python programs. Once installed, you can use `pygwidgets` by including the following statement at the beginning of your programs:

```
import pygwidgets
```

This imports the entire package. After importing, you can instantiate objects from its classes and call the methods of those objects.

The most current documentation of `pygwidgets` is at *https://pygwidgets .readthedocs.io/en/latest/*. If you'd like to view the source code for the package, it's available via my GitHub repository at *https://github.com/IrvKalb/pygwidgets/*.

## Overall Design Approach

As shown in Chapter 5, one of the first things you do in every pygame program is to define the window of the application. The following line creates an application window and saves a reference to it in a variable named `window`:

```
window = pygame.display.set_mode((WINDOW_WIDTH, WINDOW_HEIGHT))
```

As we will soon see, whenever we instantiate any widget, we will need to pass in the `window` variable so the widget can draw itself in the application's window.

Most widgets in `pygwidgets` work in a similar way, typically involving these three steps:

1. Before the main `while` loop starts, create an instance of the widget, passing in any initialization arguments.
2. In the main loop, whenever any event happens, call the `handleEvent()` method of the widget (passing in the event object).
3. At the bottom of the main loop, call the `draw()` method of the widget.

Step 1 in using any widget is to instantiate one with a line like this:

```
oWidget = pygwidgets.<SomeWidgetClass>(window, loc, <other arguments as needed>)
```

The first argument is always the window of the application. The second argument is always the location in the window at which to display the widget, given as a tuple: `(x, y)`.

Step 2 is to handle any event that could affect the widget by calling the object's `handleEvent()` method inside the event loop. If any event (like a mouse click or button press) happens and the widget handles the event, this call will return `True`. The code at the top of the main `while` loop generally looks like this:

```
while True:
    for event in pygame.event.get():
        if event.type == pygame.QUIT:
            pygame.quit()
            sys.exit()

        if oWidget.handleEvent(event):
            # The user has done something to oWidget that we should respond to
            # Add code here
```

Step 3 is to add a line near the bottom of the `while` loop to call the `draw()` method of the widget, to make it appear it in the window:

```
oWidget.draw()
```

Since we specified the window to draw into, the location, and any details that affect the appearance of the widget in step 1, we don't pass anything in the call to draw().

## Adding an Image

Our first example will be the simplest widget: we'll use the Image class to display an image in a window. When you instantiate an Image object, the only required arguments are the window, the location in the window to draw the image, and the path to the image file. Create the Image object before the main loop starts, like so:

```
oImage = pygwidgets.Image(window, (100, 200), 'images/SomeImage.png')
```

The path used here assumes that the project folder containing the main program also contains a folder named *images*, inside which is the *SomeImage.png* file. Then, in the main loop you just need to call the object's draw() method:

```
oImage.draw()
```

The draw() method of the Image class contains a call to blit() to actually draw the image, so you never need to call blit() directly. To move the image, you can call its setLoc() method (short for set location), specifying the new x- and y-coordinates as a tuple:

```
oImage.setLoc((newX, newY))
```

The next time the image is drawn, it will show up at the new coordinates. The documentation lists many additional methods that you can call to flip, rotate, scale, get the image's location and rectangle, and so on.

---

### THE SPRITE MODULE

Pygame has a built-in module to show images in a window, called the *sprite module*. Such images are called *sprites*. The sprite module provides a Sprite class for handling individual sprites and a Group class for handling multiple Sprite objects. Together, these classes provide excellent functionality, and if you intend to do heavy-duty pygame programming, it is probably worth your time to look into them. However, in order to explain the underlying OOP concepts, I have chosen not to use those classes. Instead, I will proceed with general GUI elements so that they can be used in any environment and language. If you want to learn more about the sprite module, see the tutorial at *https://www.pygame.org/docs/tut/SpriteIntro.html*.

---

## Adding Buttons, Checkboxes, and Radio Buttons

When you instantiate a button, checkbox, or radio button widget in pygwidgets, you have two options: instantiate a text version that draws its own art and adds a text label based on a string you pass in, or instantiate a custom version where you supply the art. Table 7-1 shows the different button classes that are available.

**Table 7-1:** Text and Custom Button Classes in pygwidgets

|  | Text version (builds art on the fly) | Custom version (uses your artwork) |
| --- | --- | --- |
| Button | TextButton | CustomButton |
| Checkbox | TextCheckBox | CustomCheckBox |
| Radio button | TextRadioButton | CustomRadioButton |

The differences between the text and custom versions of these classes are only relevant during instantiation. Once you create an object from a text or custom button class, all the remaining methods of the pair of classes are identical. To make this clear, let's take a look at the TextButton and CustomButton classes.

### TextButtons

Here is the actual definition of the __init__() method of the TextButton class in pygwidgets:

```
def __init__(self, window, loc, text,
            width=None,
            height=40,
            textColor=PYGWIDGETS_BLACK,
            upColor=PYGWIDGETS_NORMAL_GRAY,
            overColor=PYGWIDGETS_OVER_GRAY,
            downColor=PYGWIDGETS_DOWN_GRAY,
            fontName=DEFAULT_FONT_NAME,
            fontSize=DEFAULT_FONT_SIZE,
            soundOnClick=None,
            enterToActivate=False,
            callback=None
            nickname=None):
```

However, rather than reading through the code of a class, a programmer will typically refer to its documentation. As mentioned earlier, you can find the complete documentation for pygwidgets at *https://pygwidgets.readthedocs.io/en/latest/*.

You can also view documentation of a class by calling the built-in help() function in the Python shell like so:

```
>>> help(pygwidgets.TextButton)
```

When you create an instance of a `TextButton`, you are only required to pass in the window, the location in the window, and the text to be shown on the button. If you only specify these positional parameters, your button will use reasonable defaults for the width and height, the background colors for the four states of the button (different shades of gray), the font, and the font size. By default, no sound effect will be played when the user clicks on the button.

The code to create a `TextButton` using all the defaults looks like this:

```
oButton = pygwidgets.TextButton(window, (50, 50), 'Text Button')
```

The code in the `__init__()` method of the `TextButton` class uses the pygame drawing methods to construct its own art for all four states (up, down, over, and disabled). The preceding line creates an "up" version of a button that looks like Figure 7-2.

Figure 7-2: A TextButton
using defaults

You can override any or all of the default parameters with keyword values like so:

```
oButton = pygwidgets.TextButton(window, (50, 50), 'Text Button',
                                width=200,
                                height=30,
                                textColor=(255, 255, 128),
                                upColor=(128, 0, 0),
                                fontName='Courier',
                                fontSize=14,
                                soundOnClick='sounds/blip.wav',
                                enterToActivate=True)
```

This instantiation will create a button that looks like Figure 7-3.

Text Button

Figure 7-3: A TextButton using keyword
arguments for font, size, colors, and so on

The image-switching behavior of these two buttons would work exactly the same way; the only differences would be in the appearance of the images.

## CustomButtons

The `CustomButton` class allows you to use your own art for a button. To instantiate a `CustomButton`, you need only pass in a window, a location, and a path to the image of the up state of the button. Here is an example:

```
restartButton = pygwidgets.CustomButton(window, (100, 430),
                                'images/RestartButtonUp.png')
```

The down, over, and disabled states are optional keyword arguments, and for any of these where no value is passed in, CustomButton will use a copy of the up image. It's more typical (and strongly suggested) to pass in paths for the optional images, like so:

```
restartButton = pygwidgets.CustomButton(window, (100, 430),
                    'images/RestartButtonUp.png',
                    down='images/RestartButtonDown.png',
                    over='images/RestartButtonOver.png',
                    disabled='images/RestartButtonDisabled.png',
                    soundOnClick='sounds/blip.wav',
                    nickname='restart')
```

Here we also specified a sound effect that should be played when the user clicks the button, and we provided an internal nickname we can use later.

### Using Buttons

After instantiation, here's some typical code to use a button object, oButton, independent of it being a TextButton or a CustomButton:

```
while True:
    for event in pygame.event.get():
        if event.type == pygame.QUIT:
            pygame.quit()
            sys.exit()

        if oButton.handleEvent(event):
            # User has clicked this button
            <Any code you want to run here when the button is clicked>
--- snip ---
        oButton.draw()  # at the bottom of the while loop, tell it to draw
```

Every time we detect an event, we need to call the handleEvent() method of the button to allow it to react to the user's actions. This call normally returns False but will return True when the user completes a click on the button. At the bottom of the main while loop, we need to call the draw() method of the button to allow it to draw itself.

## Text Output and Input

As we saw in Chapter 6, handling text input and output in pygame is tricky, but here I'll introduce new classes for a text display field and an input text field. Both of these classes have minimal required (positional) parameters, and they have reasonable defaults for other attributes (font, font size, color, and so on) that are easily overridden.

### Text Output

The pygwidgets package contains a DisplayText class for showing text that is a more full-featured version of the SimpleText class from Chapter 6. When you instantiate a `DisplayText` field, the only required arguments are the window and the location. The first keyword parameter is value, which may be specified with a string as starting text to be shown in the field. This is typically used for a default end user value or for text that never changes, like a label or instructions. Since value is the first keyword parameter, it can be given as either a positional or a keyword argument. For example, this:

```
oTextField = pygwidgets.DisplayText(window, (10, 400), 'Hello World')
```

will work the same way as this:

```
oTextField = pygwidgets.DisplayText(window, (10, 400), value='Hello World')
```

You can also customize the look of the output text by specifying any or all of the optional keyword parameters. For example:

```
oTextField = pygwidgets.DisplayText(window, (10, 400),
                                    value='Some title text',
                                    fontName='Courier',
                                    fontSize=40,
                                    width=150,
                                    justified='center',
                                    textColor=(255, 255, 0))
```

The `DisplayText` class has a number of additional methods, the most important of which is setValue(), which you call to change the text drawn in the field:

```
oTextField.setValue('Any new text you want to see')
```

At the bottom of the main while loop, you need to call the object's draw() method:

```
oTextField.draw()
```

And of course, you can create as many `DisplayText` objects as you wish, each displaying different text and each with its own font, size, color, and so on.

## Text Input

In a typical text-based Python program, to get input from the user you would make a call to the input() function, which stops the program until the user enters text in the shell window. But in the world of event-driven GUI programs, the main loop never stops. Therefore, we must use a different approach.

For text input from the user, a GUI program typically presents a field that the user can type in. An input field must deal with all keyboard keys, some of which show while others are used for editing or cursor movement within the field. It must also allow for the user holding down a key to repeat it. The pygwidgets `InputText` class provides all this functionality.

The only required arguments to instantiate an `InputText` object are the window and a location:

```
oInputField = pygwidgets.InputText(window, (10, 100))
```

However, you can customize the text attributes of an `InputText` object by specifying optional keyword arguments:

```
oInputField = pygwidgets.InputText(window, (10, 400),
                                   value='Starting Text',
                                   fontName='Helvetica',
                                   fontSize=40,
                                   width=150,
                                   textColor=(255, 255, 0))
```

After instantiating an `InputText` field, the typical code in the main loop would look like this:

```
while True:
    for event in pygame.event.get():
        if event.type == pygame.QUIT:
            pygame.quit()
            sys.exit()

        if oInputField.handleEvent(event):
            # User has pressed Enter or Return
            userText = oInputField.getValue()  # get the text the user entered
            <Any code you want to run using the user's input>
--- snip ---
    oInputField.draw()  # at the bottom of the main while loop
```

For every event, we need to call the `handleEvent()` method of the `InputText` field to allow it to react to keystrokes and mouse clicks. This call normally returns `False`, but when the user presses ENTER or RETURN, it returns `True`. We can then retrieve the text that the user entered by calling the `getValue()` method of the object.

At the bottom of the main `while` loop, we need to call the `draw()` method to allow the field to draw itself.

If a window contains multiple input fields, key presses are handled by the field with current keyboard focus, which is changed when a user clicks in a different field. If you want to allow a field to have initial keyboard focus, then you can set the `initialFocus` keyword parameter to `True` in the `InputText` object of your choice when you create that object. Further, if you have multiple `InputText` fields in a window, a typical user interface design approach is to include an OK or Submit button. When this button is clicked, you could then call the `getValue()` method of each field.

**NOTE** *At the time of writing, the* InputText *class does not handle highlighting multiple characters by dragging the mouse. If this functionality is added in a later version, no change will be required to programs that use* InputText *because the code will be entirely within that class. Any new behavior will be supported automatically in all* InputText *objects.*

## Other pygwidgets Classes

As you saw at the beginning of this section, pygwidgets contains a number of other classes.

The ImageCollection class allows you to show any single image from a collection of images. For example, suppose you have images of a character facing front, left, back, and right. To represent all the potential images, you can build a dictionary like this:

```
imageDict = {'front':'images/front.png', 'left':'images/left.png',
             'back':'images/back.png', 'right':'images/right.png'}
```

You can then create an ImageCollection object, specifying this dictionary and the key of the image you want to start with. To change to a different image, you call the replace() method and pass in a different key. Calling the draw() method at the bottom of the loop always shows the current image.

The Dragger class displays a single image but allows the user to drag the image anywhere in the window. You must call its handleEvent() method in the event loop. When the user finishes dragging, handleEvent() returns True, and you can call the Dragger object's getMouseUpLoc() method to get the location where the user released the mouse button.

The Animation and SpriteSheetAnimation classes handle building and showing an animation. Both require a set of images to iterate through. The Animation class gets the images from individual files, while the SpriteSheetAnimation class requires a single image with evenly spaced internal images. We'll explore these classes more fully in Chapter 14.

## pygwidgets Example Program

Figure 7-4 shows a screenshot of a sample program that demonstrates objects instantiated from many of the classes in pygwidgets, including Image, DisplayText, InputText, TextButton, CustomButton, TextRadioButton, CustomRadioButton, TextCheckBox, CustomCheckBox, ImageCollection, and Dragger.

The source of this example program can be found in the *pygwidgets_test* folder in my GitHub repository, *https://github.com/IrvKalb/pygwidgets/*.

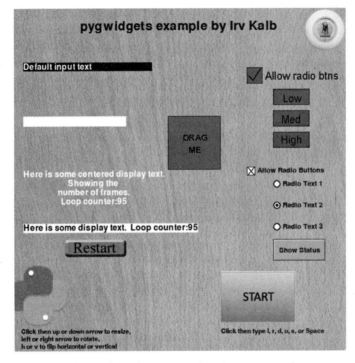

Figure 7-4: The window of a program that demonstrates objects instantiated from a variety of pygwidgets classes

## The Importance of a Consistent API

One final note about building an API for a set of classes: whenever possible, it's a very good idea to build consistency into the parameters of methods in different, but similar, classes. As a good example, the first two parameters to the __init__() method of every class in pygwidgets are window and loc, in that order. If these had been in a different order in some calls, using the package as a whole would be much more difficult.

Additionally, if different classes implement the same functionality, it's a good idea to use the same method names. For example, many of the classes in pygwidgets have a method named setValue() and another named getValue(). I'll talk more about why this type of consistency is so important in the next two chapters.

## Summary

This chapter provided an introduction to the object-oriented pygwidgets package of graphical user interface widgets. We began by discussing default values for parameters in methods, and I explained that a keyword parameter allows for a default value to be used if no matching argument value is specified in a call.

I then introduced you to the pygwidgets module, which contains a number of prebuilt GUI widget classes, and showed you how to use several of these. Finally, I showed a sample program that provides examples of most of these widgets.

There are two key advantages to writing classes like those in pygwidgets. First, classes can hide complexity in methods. Once you have your class working correctly, you never have to worry about the internal details again. Second, you can reuse the code by creating as many instances of a class as you need. Your classes can provide basic functionality by including keyword parameters with well-chosen default values. However, the default values can easily be overwritten to allow for customization.

You can publish the interfaces of your classes for other programmers (and yourself) to take advantage of in different projects. Good documentation and consistency go a long way toward making these types of classes highly usable.

# PART III

## ENCAPSULATION, POLYMORPHISM, AND INHERITANCE

The three main tenets of object-oriented programming are encapsulation, polymorphism, and inheritance. The next three chapters will explain each of these in turn, describing the underlying concepts and showing examples of how they are implemented in Python. In order for a programming language to call itself an OOP language, it must support all three of these central requirements. (If you're ever asked in an interview about the requirements for a language to be object-oriented, here's an easy way to remember them: it's as easy as PIE!)

Chapter 8 explains encapsulation: hiding the details and keeping everything in one place.

Chapter 9 discusses polymorphism: how multiple classes can have methods with the same names.

Chapter 10 covers inheritance: building on code that already exists.

Finally, Chapter 11 goes into detail on a number of topics (mostly dealing with memory management) that do not logically fit into the previous three chapters but are useful and important to OOP.

# 8

## ENCAPSULATION

The first of the three main tenets of object-oriented programming is *encapsulation*. This word might conjure up an image of a space capsule, a cell wall, or a medicine gelcap, where the precious cargo inside is protected from the outside environment. In programming, encapsulation has a similar but even more detailed meaning: hiding internal details of state and behavior from any external code and having all code in one place.

In this chapter, we'll see how encapsulation works with functions, then with methods of objects. I'll discuss different interpretations of encapsulation: using direct access versus using getters and setters. I'll show how Python allows you to mark an instance variable as private, indicating that it should not be accessed by code external to a class, and I'll touch on the Python property decorator. Finally, I'll discuss the concept of abstraction in the design of classes.

## Encapsulation with Functions

Functions are a prime example of encapsulation because when you call a function, you generally don't care *how* the function works internally. A well-written function contains a series of steps that make up a larger single task, which you do care about. The name of the function should describe the action that its code embodies. Consider the built-in len() function from the Python Standard Library, used to find the number of characters in a string or elements in a list. You pass in a string or list, and it returns the count. When you write code that calls this function, you don't care how len() does what it does. You don't stop to think about whether the code of the function contains two lines or two thousand lines, whether it uses one local variable or a hundred. You just need to know what argument to pass in and how to use the result that's returned.

The same is true of functions that you write, like this function that calculates and returns the average of a list of numbers:

```
def calculateAverage(numbersList):
    total = 0.0
    for number in numbersList:
        total = total + number
    nElements = len(numbersList)
    average = total / nElements
    return average
```

Once you've tested a function like this and found that it works, you no longer have to worry about the details of the implementation. You only need to know what argument(s) to send into the function and what it returns.

However, if one day you find that there is a much simpler or faster algorithm to calculate an average, you could rewrite the function in a new way. As long as the interface (the inputs and outputs) does not change, there is no need to change any calls to the function. This type of modularization makes the code more maintainable.

## Encapsulation with Objects

Unlike variables used in regular functions, instance variables in objects persist across different method calls. To keep the remaining discussion clear, I'll introduce a new term: *client*. (I don't want to use the term *user* here since that typically refers to the human user of the final program.)

**client**   Any software that creates an object from a class and makes calls to the methods of that object.

We must also consider the duality of *inside* versus *outside* an object or class. When you're working inside a class (writing the code of the methods in a class), you need to concern yourself with how the different methods of the class share the instance variables. You consider the efficiency of your algorithms. You think about what the interface should look like: what methods you should provide, what the parameters for each are, and what should be used as default values. In short, you are concerned with the design and implementation of the methods.

From the outside, as a client programmer, you need to know the interface of the class. You're concerned with what the class methods do, what arguments should be passed in, and what data is passed back from each method.

A class therefore provides encapsulation by:

- Hiding all details of implementation in its methods and instance variables
- Providing all the functionality a client needs from an object through its interface (the methods defined in the class)

### Objects Own Their Data

In object-oriented programming, we say that the data inside an object is *owned* by the object. OOP programmers generally agree that, as a good design principle, client code should only be concerned with the interface of a class and should not care about the implementation of the methods. Consider the example of a simple Person class in Listing 8-1.

```
class Person():

    def __init__(self, name, salary):
        self.name = name
        self.salary = salary
```

*Listing 8-1: Data ownership in the Person class*

The values of the instance variables self.name and self.salary are set whenever we instantiate new Person objects, like this:

```
oPerson1 = Person('Joe Schmoe', 90000)
oPerson2 = Person('Jane Smith', 99000)
```

Each Person object owns its own set of the two instance variables.

## Interpretations of Encapsulation

Here is where things get a little controversial. Different programmers have different views about the accessibility of an instance variable. Python provides for a loose interpretation of encapsulation by allowing direct access to instance variables using simple dot syntax. Client code can legally access an instance variable of an object by name using the syntax *<object>.<instanceVariableName>*.

However, a *strict* interpretation of encapsulation says that client software should never be able to retrieve or change the value of an instance variable directly. Instead, the only way that a client can retrieve or change a value held in an object is to use a method provided by the class for this purpose.

Let's look at both approaches.

## Direct Access and Why You Should Avoid It

As mentioned, Python does allow direct access to instance variables. Listing 8-2 instantiates the same two objects from the Person class in Listing 8-1 as in the previous section, but then accesses their self.salary instance variables directly.

**File: PersonGettersSettersAndDirectAccess/Main_PersonDirectAccess.py**

```
# Person example main program using direct access

from Person import *

oPerson1 = Person('Joe Schmoe', 90000)
oPerson2 = Person('Jane Smith', 99000)

# Get the values of the salary variable directly
❶ print(oPerson1.salary)
print(oPerson2.salary)

# Change the salary variable directly
❷ oPerson1.salary = 100000
oPerson2.salary = 111111

# Get the updated salaries and print again
print(oPerson1.salary)
print(oPerson2.salary)
```

*Listing 8-2: Example main code using direct access to an instance variable*

Python allows you to write code like this that reaches into an object to directly get ❶ and set ❷ any instance variable using standard dot syntax. Most Python programmers feel that this technique is perfectly acceptable. In fact, Guido van Rossum (the creator of Python) famously said in reference to this issue, "We are all adults here," meaning that programmers should know what they are doing, and the risks involved, when they attempt to access instance variables directly.

However, I strongly believe that directly accessing an instance variable of an object is an extremely dangerous practice, as it breaks the core idea of encapsulation. To illustrate why this is the case, let's take a look at a few example scenarios where direct access can be problematic.

### Changing the Name of an Instance Variable

The first problem with direct access is that changing the name of an instance variable will break any client code that uses the original name directly. This can happen when the developer of a class decides that the initial choice of the name of the variable was not optimal, for reasons such as the following:

- The name doesn't describe the data it represents clearly enough.
- The variable is a Boolean, and they want to swap what True and False represent by renaming the variable (for example, closed to open, allowed to disallowed, active to disabled).
- There was a spelling or capitalization mistake in the original name.
- The variable was originally a Boolean, but they later realize that they need to represent more than two values.

In any of these cases, if the developer changes the name of an instance variable in the class from self.*<originalName>* to self.*<newName>*, then any client software that uses the original name directly will break.

### Changing an Instance Variable into a Calculation

A second situation where direct access is problematic is when the code of a class needs to change to meet new requirements. Suppose that when writing a class, you use an instance variable to represent a piece of data, but the functionality changes so that you need an algorithm to compute a value instead. Take our Account class from Chapter 4, for example. To make our bank accounts more realistic, we might want to add an interest rate. You might think this is a simple matter of adding an instance variable for the interest rate named self.interestRate. Then, using the direct access approach, client software could access this value of an Account object using:

```
oAccount.interestRate
```

This would work, for a while. But later the bank might decide on a new policy—say that the interest rate will depend on the amount of money in the account. The interest rate might be calculated like this:

```
def calculateInterestRate(self):
    # Assuming self.balance has been set in another method
    if self.balance < 1000:
        self.interestRate = 1.0
    elif self.balance < 5000:
        self.interestRate = 1.5
    else:
        self.interestRate = 2.0
```

Rather than just relying on a single interest rate value in self.interestRate, the calculateInterestRate() method determines the current rate based on the account balance.

Any client software that directly accesses oAccount.interestRate and uses the value of the instance variable might then get an outdated value, depending on the last time calculateInterestRate() was called. And any client software that *sets* a new `interestRate` may find that the new value is mysteriously changed by some other code that calls `calculateInterestRate()` or when the bank account owner makes a deposit or withdrawal.

If, however, the interest calculation method was named `getInterestRate()` and client software called that instead, the interest rate would always be calculated on the fly and there would be no potential error.

## Validating Data

The third reason to avoid direct access when setting a value is that client code can too easily set an instance variable to an invalid value. A better approach is to call a method in the class, whose job is to set the value. As the developer, you can include validation code in that method to ensure that the value being set is appropriate. Consider the code in Listing 8-3, whose purpose is to manage the members of a club.

**File: ValidatingData_ClubExample/Club.py**

```
# Club class

class Club():

    def __init__(self, clubName, maxMembers):
        self.clubName = clubName ❶
        self.maxMembers = maxMembers
        self.membersList = []

    def addMember(self, name): ❷
        # Make sure that there is enough room left
        if len(self.membersList) < self.maxMembers:
            self.membersList.append(name)
            print('OK.', name, 'has been added to the', self.clubName, 'club')
        else:
            print('Sorry, but we cannot add', name, 'to the', self.clubName, 'club.')
            print('This club already has the maximum of', self.maxMembers, 'members.')

    def report(self): ❸
        print()
        print('Here are the', len(self.membersList), 'members of the', self.clubName,
            'club:')
        for name in self.membersList:
            print('   ' + name)
        print()
```

*Listing 8-3: An example of a* Club *class*

The `Club` code keeps track of the name of the club, the maximum number of members, and the list of members, all in instance variables ❶. Once instantiated, you can call methods to add a member to the club ❷ and to report the members of the club ❸. (We could easily add more methods to remove members, change names, and so on, but these two are good enough the make the point.)

Here is some test code that uses the Club class.

### File: ValidatingData_ClubExample/Main_Club.py

```
# Club example main program

from Club import *

# Create a club with at most 5 members
oProgrammingClub = Club('Programming', 5)

oProgrammingClub.addMember('Joe Schmoe')
oProgrammingClub.addMember('Cindy Lou Hoo')
oProgrammingClub.addMember('Dino Richmond')
oProgrammingClub.addMember('Susie Sweetness')
oProgrammingClub.addMember('Fred Farkle')
oProgrammingClub.report()
```

We create a Programming club that allows a maximum of five members and then we add five members. The code runs well and reports the members added to the club:

```
OK. Joe Schmoe has been added to the Programming club
OK. Cindy Lou Hoo has been added to the Programming club
OK. Dino Richmond has been added to the Programming club
OK. Susie Sweetness has been added to the Programming club
OK. Fred Farkle has been added to the Programming club
```

Now let's try to add a sixth member:

```
# Attempt to add additional member
oProgrammingClub.addMember('Iwanna Join')
```

This attempt to add a member is rejected, and we see an appropriate error message:

```
Sorry, but we cannot add Iwanna Join to the Programming club.
This club already has the maximum of 5 members.
```

The code of addMember() does all the validation needed to ensure that a call to add a new member works correctly or generates an error message. However, with direct access, a client could change the fundamental nature of the Club class. For example, a client could maliciously or accidentally change the maximum number of members:

```
oProgrammingClub.maxMembers = 300
```

Further, suppose you know that the Club class represents the members as a list, and you know the name of the instance variable that represents the members. In that case you can write client code to add to the list of members directly, without making the method call, like so:

```
oProgrammingClub.memberList.append('Iwanna Join')
```

This line would push the membership over the intended limit because it avoids the code that ensures that the request to add the member is valid.

Client code using direct access could even cause an error inside the Club object. For example, the instance variable self.maxMembers is intended to be an integer. Using direct access, client code could change its value to a string. Any subsequent call to addMember() would crash at the first line of that method, where it attempts to compare the length of the list of members against the maximum number of members, because Python cannot compare an integer to a string.

Allowing direct access to instance variables from outside an object can be dangerous, bypassing safeguards that were designed to protect the data of an object.

## Strict Interpretation with Getters and Setters

The strict approach to encapsulation says that client code *never* accesses an instance variable directly. If a class wants to allow client software to access the information held inside an object, the standard approach is to include a *getter* and a *setter* method in the class.

**getter**    A method that retrieves data from an object instantiated from a class.

**setter**    A method that assigns data into an object instantiated from a class.

Getter and setter methods are designed to allow writers of client software to get data from and set data in an object, without needing explicit knowledge of the implementation of a class—specifically, without having to know or use the name of any instance variable. The Person class code in Listing 8-1 has an instance variable self.salary. In Listing 8-4 we add a getter and a setter to the Person class to allow the caller to get and set the salary, without providing direct access to the Person's self.salary instance variable.

### File: PersonGettersSettersAndDirectAccess/Person.py

```
class Person():
    def __init__(self, name, salary):
        self.name = name
        self.salary = salary

    # Allow the caller to retrieve the salary
❶ def getSalary(self):
```

```
        return self.salary

    # Allow the caller to set a new salary
❷ def setSalary(self, salary):
        self.salary = salary
```

*Listing 8-4: An example of a Person class with a getter and a setter*

The get ❶ and set ❷ portions of these method names are not required but are used by convention. You generally follow these words with a description of the data being accessed, in this case Salary. While it is typical to use the name of the instance variable being accessed, this is also not a requirement.

Listing 8-5 shows some test code that instantiates two Person objects, then gets and sets their salaries using these getter and setter methods.

### File: PersonGettersSettersAndDirectAccess/Main_PersonGetterSetter.py

```
# Person example main program using getters and setters

from Person import *

❶ oPerson1 = Person('Joe Schmoe', 90000)
oPerson2 = Person('Jane Smith', 99000)

# Get the salaries using getter and print
❷ print(oPerson1.getSalary())
print(oPerson2.getSalary())

# Change the salaries using setter
❸ oPerson1.setSalary(100000)
oPerson2.setSalary(111111)

# Get the salaries and print again
print(oPerson1.getSalary())
print(oPerson2.getSalary())
```

*Listing 8-5: Example main code using getter and setter methods*

First we create two Person objects from the Person class ❶. Then we use the getter and setter methods to retrieve ❷ and change ❸ the salaries in the Person objects.

Getters and setters provide a formal way to get and set values in an object. They enforce a layer of protection that only allows access to instance variables if the class writer wants to allow it.

**NOTE**   *Some Python literature uses the terms* accessor *for a getter method and* mutator *for the setter method. These are just different names for the same things. I will use the more generic terms* getter *and* setter.

## Safe Direct Access

There are certain circumstances where it seems reasonable to access instance variables directly: when it is absolutely clear what the instance variable means, little or no validation of the data is needed, and there is no chance that the name will ever change. A good example of this is the Rect (rectangle) class in the pygame package. A rectangle in pygame is defined using four values—x, y, width, and height—like this:

```
oRectangle = pygame.Rect(10, 20, 300, 300)
```

After creating that rectangle object, using oRectangle.x, oRectangle.y, oRectangle.width, and oRectangle.height directly as variables seems acceptable.

# Making Instance Variables More Private

In Python, all instance variables are public (that is, can be accessed by code external to the class). But what if you want to allow access to some of your class's instance variables, but not all of them? Some OOP languages allow you to explicitly mark certain instance variables as public or private, but Python doesn't have those keywords. However, there are two ways that programmers who develop classes in Python can indicate that their instance variables and methods are intended to be private.

## Implicitly Private

To mark an instance variable as one that should never be accessed externally, by convention you start the name of your instance variable with one leading underscore:

```
self._name
self._socialSecurityNumber
self._dontTouchThis
```

Instance variables with names like these are intended to represent private data, and client software should never attempt to access them directly. The code may still work if the instance variables are accessed, but it is not guaranteed.

The same convention is used for method names:

```
def _internalMethod(self):

def _dontCallMeFromClientSoftware(self):
```

Again, this is only a convention; there is no enforcement. If any client software makes a call to a method with a name beginning with an underscore, Python will allow it, but there is a good chance that doing so will lead to unexpected errors.

## More Explicitly Private

Python does allow for a more explicit level of privatization. To disallow client software from directly accessing your data, you create an instance variable name that starts with two underscores.

Suppose we create a class named `PrivatePerson` with an instance variable `self.__privateData` that should never be accessed from outside an object:

```
# PrivatePerson class

class PrivatePerson():

    def __init__(self, name, privateData):
        self.name = name
    ❶ self.__privateData = privateData

    def getName(self):
        return self.name

    def setName(self, name):
        self.name = name
```

We can then create a `PrivatePerson` object, passing in some data that we wish to keep private ❶. Attempting to access the `__privateData` instance variable directly from client software, like this:

```
usersPrivateData = oPrivatePerson.__privateData
```

will generate an error:

```
AttributeError: 'PrivatePerson' object has no attribute '__privateData'
```

Similarly, if you create a method name that starts with two underscores, any attempt by client software to call the method will generate an error.

Python provides this ability by performing *name mangling*. Behind the scenes, Python changes any name that starts with two underscores by prepending it with an underscore and the name of the class, so `__<name>` becomes `_<className>__<name>`. For example, in the `PrivatePerson` class, Python will change `self.__privateData` to `self._PrivatePerson__privateData`. Therefore, if a client tries to use the name `oPrivatePerson.__privateData`, that name won't be recognized.

This is a subtle change designed as a deterrent to using direct access, but you should note that it doesn't absolutely guarantee privacy. If the client programmer knows how this works, they can still access the instance variable with `<object>._<className>__<name>` (or, in our example, `oPrivatePerson._PrivatePerson__privateData`).

# Decorators and @property

At a high level, a decorator is a method that takes another method as an argument and extends the way the original method works. (Decorators can also be functions that decorate functions or methods, but I'll concentrate on methods.) Decorators are an advanced topic and are generally beyond the scope of this book. However, there is a set of built-in decorators that provide a compromise between direct access and the use of getters and setters in a class.

A decorator is written as a line that starts with the @ symbol followed by a decorator name and is placed directly before the def statement of a method. This applies the decorator to a method to add to its behavior:

```
@<decorator>
def <someMethod>(self, <parameters>)
```

We'll use two built-in decorators and apply them to two methods in a class to implement a *property*.

| property | An attribute of a class that appears to client code to be an instance variable, but instead causes a method to be called when it is accessed. |
|---|---|

A property allows class developers to use indirection, the way that a magician uses misdirection—the audience thinks they are seeing one thing, while behind the scenes something very different is happening. When writing a class to use property decorators, the developer writes a getter and a setter method and adds a distinct built-in decorator to each one. The first method is a getter and is preceded with the built-in @property decorator. The name of the method defines a name of a property to be used by client code. The second method is a setter and is preceded with the @<name of the property>.setter decorator. Here is a minimal sample class:

```
class Example():
    def __init__(self, startingValue):
        self._x = startingValue

    @property
    def x(self):   # this is the decorated getter method
        return self._x

    @x.setter
    def x(self, value):   # this is the decorated setter method
        self._x = value
```

In the Example class, x is the name of the property. After the standard __init__() method, the unusual thing is that we have two methods that both have the same name: the name of the property. The first method is a getter, while the second is a setter. The setter method is optional, and if it's not present, the property will be read-only.

Given the `Example` class, here is some sample client code:

```
oExample = Example(10)
print(oExample.x)
oExample.x = 20
```

In this code we create an instance of the `Example` class, make a call to `print()`, and execute a simple assignment. From the client's point of view, this code is highly readable. When we write `oExample.x`, it looks like we are using direct access to an instance variable. However, when client code accesses the value of an object's property (on the right side of an assignment statement or as an argument in a call to a function or method), Python translates it into a call to the getter method of the object. When an object dot property appears on the left side of an assignment statement, Python calls the setter method. The getter and setter methods affect the real instance variable, `self._x`.

Here is a more realistic example that should help make this clear. Listing 8-6 shows a `Student` class that includes a property grade, properly decorated getter and setter methods, and a private instance variable __grade.

**File: PropertyDecorator/Student.py**

```
# Using a property to (indirectly) access data in an object

class Student():

    def __init__(self, name, startingGrade=0):
        self.__name = name
        self.grade = startingGrade  ❶

    @property  ❷
    def grade(self):  ❸
        return self.__grade

    @grade.setter  ❹
    def grade(self, newGrade):  ❺
        try:
            newGrade = int(newGrade)
        except (TypeError, ValueError) as e:
            raise type(e)('New grade: ' + str(newGrade) + ', is an invalid type.')
        if (newGrade < 0) or (newGrade > 100):
            raise ValueError('New grade: ' + str(newGrade) + ', must be between 0 and 100.')
        self.__grade = newGrade
```

*Listing 8-6: The Student class with property decorators*

The __init__() method has a little trick to it, so let's examine the other methods first. Notice we have two methods with the name grade(). Preceding the definition of the first grade() method, we add an @property decorator ❷. This defines the name grade as a property of any object created from this class. The first method ❸ is a getter that just returns the value of the current grade, kept in the private self.__grade instance variable, but could include any code that might be needed to calculate a value and return it.

Preceding the second grade() method is an @grade.setter decorator ❹. This second method ❺ accepts a new value as a parameter, does a number of checks to ensure that value is valid, then sets the new value into self.__grade.

The __init__() method first stores the student's name in an instance variable. The next line ❶ seems straightforward but is a little unusual. As we have seen, we typically store the values of parameters into instance variables. Therefore, we might be tempted to write this line as:

```
self.__grade = startingGrade
```

But instead, we are storing the starting grade into the property grade. Since grade is a property, Python translates this assignment statement into a call to the setter method ❺, which has the advantage of validating the input before storing the value in the instance variable self.__grade.

Listing 8-7 provides some test code that uses the Student class.

**File: PropertyDecorator/Main_Property.py**

```
# Main Student property example
❶ oStudent1= Student('Joe Schmoe')
  oStudent2= Student ('Jane Smith')

  # Get the students' grades using the 'grade' property and print
❷ print(oStudent1.grade)
  print(oStudent2.grade)
  print()

  # Set new values using the 'grade' property
❸ oStudent1.grade = 85
  oStudent2.grade = 92

❹ print(oStudent1.grade)
  print(oStudent2.grade)
```

*Listing 8-7: The main code that creates Student objects and accesses a property*

In the test code, we first create two Student objects ❶ and print the grade of each ❷. It looks like we're reaching into each object directly to get the grade values, but since grade is a property Python turns these lines into calls to the getter method and returns the value of the private instance variable self.__grade for each object.

We then set new grade values for each Student object ❸. Here it looks like we're setting values directly into each object's data, but again, because grade is a property, Python turns these lines into calls to the setter method. That method validates each value before doing the assignment. The test code ends by printing the new values of the grades ❹.

When we run the test code, we get this output, as we expect:

```
0
0

85
92
```

Using the @property and @<property_name>.setter decorators gives you the best of both the direct access and getter-and-setter worlds. Client software can be written in a way that *appears* to access instance variables directly, but as the class programmer, your decorated methods get and set the actual instance variables owned by the object and even allow for validation of inputs. This approach supports encapsulation because the client code is not accessing an instance variable directly.

While this technique is used by many professional Python developers, I personally find it a little ambiguous, because when I read other developers' code that uses this approach, it is not immediately apparent whether it's using direct accesses to instance variables or using properties that Python translates into calls to decorated methods. I prefer to use standard getter and setter methods and will use them in the rest of this book.

## Encapsulation in pygwidgets Classes

The definition of encapsulation at the start of this chapter focused on two areas: hiding internal details and having all related code in one place. All the classes in pygwidgets were designed with these considerations in mind. As examples, consider the TextButton and CustomButton classes.

The methods of these two classes encapsulate all the functionality of GUI buttons. While the source code of these classes is available, there is no need for a client programmer to look at it to use them effectively. There's also no need for client code to attempt to access any of their instance variables: all button functionality is available through calling the methods of these classes. This adheres to the strict interpretation of encapsulation, meaning that the *only* way that client software should access an object's data is by calling that object's methods. A client programmer can think of these classes as black boxes, since there is no reason to look at how they accomplish their tasks.

**NOTE** *A whole* black box testing *industry has developed around the idea of a test programmer being given a class to test without being allowed to see the code of the class. The tester is only supplied with documentation of the interfaces, and with that writes code that tests all the interfaces under many different cases to ensure that all methods work as described. The set of tests not only ensures that the code and documentation match, but is used again whenever code is added or modified in the class to ensure that the changes have not broken anything.*

# A Story from the Real World

A number of years ago, I was involved in the design and development of a very large educational project that was built in an environment called *Director* from Macromedia (later Adobe), using the object-oriented *Lingo* language. Director was designed to be extended through *XTRAs* that could add functionality, similar to the way plug-ins are added to browsers. These XTRAs were developed and sold by a number of third-party vendors. In the design, we planned on storing navigational and other course-related information in a database. I looked at all the different database XTRAs that were available and purchased a particular XTRA, which I'll call XTRA1.

Each XTRA came with documentation of its API, which showed how to make queries to the database using Structured Query Language (SQL). I decided to create a Database class that incorporated all the functionality of accessing the database using XTRA1's API. That way, all code that communicated with the XTRA directly was in the Database class. Figure 8-1 shows the overall architecture.

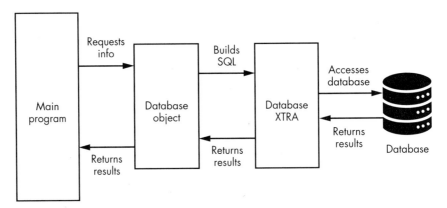

Figure 8-1: The architecture of accessing a database using an object and an XTRA

When the program started, it created a single instance of the Database class. The main code was a client of the Database object. Whenever the main code wanted information from the database, rather than formatting a SQL query itself, it called a method of the Database object, supplying details about what information it wanted. The methods in the Database object translated each request into a SQL query made to XTRA1 to get data from the database. That way, only the code of the Database object knew how to access the XTRA using its API.

The program worked well, and the customers enjoyed using the product. But every once in a while, we would run into errors in the data we got back from the database. I contacted the XTRA1 developer and gave many easily reproducible examples of the problems. Unfortunately, the developer never addressed these issues.

Because of the lack of response, we eventually decided to purchase a different database XTRA, XTRA2, to serve this purpose. XTRA2 worked in a similar way but had some subtle differences in how it was initialized and required some minor changes in the way that SQL queries were built.

Because the `Database` class encapsulated all the details of communicating with the XTRA, we were able to make all the necessary changes to work with XTRA2 only in the `Database` class. We did not change a single line in the main program (the client code).

In this case, I was both the `Database` class developer and the client software developer. If my client code had used the names of instance variables in the class, I would have had to crawl through the program, modifying each line of relevant code. Using encapsulation with a class saved me from countless hours of reworking and testing.

As a follow-up to the story, while XTRA2 worked well, that company eventually went out of business and I had to go through the same process again. Once again, because of encapsulation, only the code of the `Database` class was modified to work with XTRA3.

## Abstraction

Abstraction is another OOP concept closely related to encapsulation; many developers consider it to be the fourth tenet of OOP.

Whereas encapsulation is about implementation, hiding the details of the code and data that make up a class, *abstraction* is about the client's view of a class. It's about the perception of a class from the outside.

| | |
|---|---|
| **abstraction** | Handling complexity by hiding unnecessary details. |

Essentially, abstraction is a reminder to make sure that the user's view of a system is as simple as possible.

Abstraction is extremely common in consumer products. Many people use TVs, computers, microwave ovens, cars, and so on every day. We become comfortable with the user interface that these products extend to us. Through their controls, they provide an abstraction of their functionality. You press the accelerator pedal in a car to make it go forward. With a microwave, you set an amount of time and press Start to heat up some food. But few of us really know how these products work internally.

Here's an example of abstraction from the world of computer science. In programming, a *stack* is a mechanism for remembering data in a *last in, first out (LIFO)* order. Think of a pile of plates, where clean plates are added to the top and users take one from the top when they need a plate. A stack has two standard operations: push adds an item to the top of the stack, and pop removes the topmost item from the stack.

A stack is particularly useful whenever your program does any navigation because it can be used to leave a trail of breadcrumbs for finding your way back. This is how programming languages keep track of the execution of function and method calls in code: when you call a function or method, the return point is pushed onto a stack, and when the function or method returns, the place to return to is discovered by popping the most recent information off the top of the stack. In this way, code can make as many levels of calls as you need, and it always unwinds correctly.

As an abstraction, suppose a client program required the functionality of a stack that would be simple to create and would provide the ability to push and pop information. If this were written as a class, the client code would create a stack like this:

```
oStack = Stack()
```

A client would add information by calling a push() method like this:

```
oStack.push(<someData>)
```

And it would retrieve the most recent data by calling a pop() method like this:

```
<someVariable> = oStack.pop()
```

The client would not need to know or care how these methods were implemented or how the data was stored. The implementation of the Stack would be handled completely by the methods of the Stack.

While the client code could view a Stack class as a black box, writing such a class in Python is fairly trivial. Listing 8-8 shows how it could be implemented.

### File: Stack/Stack.py

```
# Stack class

class Stack():
    ''' Stack class implements a last in first out LIFO algorithm'''
    def __init__(self, startingStackAsList=None):
        if startingStackAsList is None:
          ❶ self.dataList = [ ]
        else:
            self.dataList = startingStackAsList[:] # make a copy

  ❷ def push(self, item):
        self.dataList.append(item)

  ❸ def pop(self):
        if len(self.dataList) == 0:
            raise IndexError
        element = self.dataList.pop()
        return element
```

```
❹ def peek(self):
      # Retrieve the top item, without removing it
      item = self.dataList[-1]
      return item

❺ def getSize(self):
      nElements = len(self.dataList)
      return nElements

❻ def show(self):
      # Show the stack in a vertical orientation
      print('Stack is:')
      for value in reversed(self.dataList):
          print('   ', value)
```

*Listing 8-8: A stack as a Python class*

The Stack class keeps track of all the data using a list instance variable named self.dataList ❶. The client doesn't need to know this level of detail, but push() ❷ just adds an item to the internal list using the Python append() operation, while pop() ❸ pops the last element from the internal list. Because it is easy to do, this implementation of the Stack class also implements three additional methods:

- peek() ❹ allows the caller to obtain the data at the top of the stack without removing it from the stack.

- getSize() ❺ returns the number of items on the stack.

- show() ❻ prints the contents of the stack in the way that the client thinks of a stack: the data is displayed vertically, with the most recent data pushed shown at the top. This can be helpful in debugging client code that involves multiple calls to push() and pop().

This was an extremely simple example, but as you gain more experience writing classes, your classes will typically become more complex. Along the way, you may find cleaner and more efficient ways of writing some methods and perhaps rewrite them. Because objects provide both encapsulation and abstraction, as the writer of a class, you should feel free to modify its code and data, as long as the published interfaces do not change. Changes to the implementation of methods should have no ill effects on client software but rather should allow you to make improvements without affecting any client code. In fact, if you find ways to make your code more efficient and publish a new version, client code may appear to speed up, with zero changes required to that code.

A property is an excellent example of abstraction. As you saw earlier, with properties the client programmer can use a syntax that makes their intent clear (to get and set a value in an object). The implementation in the methods that are called as a result can be much more complicated, but is totally hidden from the client code.

# Summary

Encapsulation is the first major tenet of object-oriented programming, allowing classes to hide their implementation and data from client code and ensuring that a class provides all the functionality that a client needs in a single place.

A key concept of OOP is that objects own their data, and that's why I recommend that you provide getter and setter methods if you want client code to access the data held in an instance variable. Python does allow direct access to instance variables using dot syntax, but I strongly encourage you to stay away from this syntax for the reasons laid out in this chapter.

There are conventions for marking instance variables and methods as private, using a leading underscore or double underscore depending on the level of privatization you require. As a compromise, Python also allows the use of the `@property` decorator. This makes it appear as if the client code is able to access an instance variable directly, while behind the scenes Python turns such references into calls to the decorated getter and setter methods in the class.

The `pygwidgets` package provides many good examples of encapsulation. As a client programmer, you see a class from the outside and work with the interfaces that the class provides. As a class designer, abstraction—handling complexity by hiding details—helps you design a good interface by considering the interface of the class from the client's point of view. However, in Python, you often have the source code available so that you can look at the implementation if you wish.

# 9

## POLYMORPHISM

This chapter is about the second major tenet of OOP: *polymorphism*. Its component parts are from the Greek: the prefix *poly* means "much" or "many," and *morphism* means "shape," "form," or "structure."

So, *polymorphism* essentially means *many forms*. I'm not talking about a *Star Trek*–style shape-shifting alien—in fact, it's quite the opposite. Rather than one thing taking on many shapes, polymorphism in OOP is about how multiple classes can have methods with the exact same names. This will eventually give us a highly intuitive way to act on a collection of objects, independent of what class each came from.

OOP programmers often use the term "send a message" when we talk about client code calling a method of an object. What the object should do when it receives the message is up to the object. With polymorphism, we can send the same message to multiple objects, and each object will react differently depending on what it's designed to do and the data available to it.

In this chapter, I'll discuss how this ability allows you to build packages of classes that are easily extensible and predictable. We'll also use polymorphism with operators to make the same operators perform different operations depending on the data types they are working with. Finally, I'll show you how to use the print() function to get valuable debugging information from objects.

## Sending Messages to Real-World Objects

Let's look at polymorphism in the real world, using cars as an example. All cars have an accelerator pedal. When the driver presses that pedal, they're sending the "accelerate" message to the car. The car they're driving could have an internal combustion engine or an electric motor, or be a hybrid. Each of these types of cars has its own implementation of what happens when it receives the accelerate message, and each behaves accordingly.

Polymorphism allows for easier adoption of new technology. If someone were to develop a nuclear-powered car, the user interface of the car would remain the same—the driver would still press the accelerator pedal to send the same message—but a very different mechanism would make the nuclear-powered car go faster.

As another real-world example, imagine you enter a large room with a bank of light switches that control a variety of different lights. Some of the bulbs are old-style incandescent bulbs, some are fluorescent, and some are newer LED bulbs. When you flip all the switches up, you are sending the "turn on" message to all the bulbs. The underlying mechanisms that cause incandescent, fluorescent, and LED bulbs to emit light are wildly different, but each achieves the user's intended goal.

## A Classic Example of Polymorphism in Programming

In terms of OOP, polymorphism is about how client code can call a method with the exact same name in different objects, and each object will do whatever it needs to do to implement the meaning of that method for that object.

The classic example of polymorphism is to consider code that represents different types of pets. Let's say you have a collection of dogs, cats, and birds, and each understands some basic commands. If you ask these pets to speak (that is, you send the "speak" message to each), the dogs will say "bark," the cats will say "meow," and the birds will say "tweet." Listing 9-1 shows how we might implement this in code.

### File: PetsPolymorphism.py

```
# Pets polymorphism
# Three classes, all with a different "speak" method

class Dog():
    def __init__(self, name):
        self.name = name
```

```
❶ def speak(self):
       print(self.name, 'says bark, bark, bark!')

   class Cat():
       def __init__(self, name):
           self.name = name

❷ def speak(self):
       print(self.name, 'says meeeooooow')

   class Bird():
       def __init__(self, name):
           self.name = name

❸ def speak(self):
       print(self.name, 'says tweet')

   oDog1 = Dog('Rover')
   oDog2 = Dog('Fido')
   oCat1 = Cat('Fluffy')
   oCat2 = Cat('Spike')
   oBird = Bird('Big Bird')

❹ petsList = [oDog1, oDog2, oCat1, oCat2, oBird]

   # Send the same message (call the same method) of all pets
   for oPet in petsList:
   ❺ oPet.speak()
```

*Listing 9-1: Sending the "speak" message to objects instantiated from different classes*

Each class has a speak() method, but the content of each method is different ❶ ❷ ❸. Each class does whatever it needs to do in its version of this method; the method name is the same, but it has different implementations.

To make things easy to deal with, we put all the pet objects into a list ❹. To make them all speak, we then loop through all the objects and send the same message by calling a method with the exact same name in each object ❺, without worrying about the type of the object.

## Example Using Pygame Shapes

Next, we'll look at a demonstration of polymorphism using pygame. In Chapter 5 we used pygame to draw primitive shapes such as rectangles, circles, polygons, ellipses, and lines. Here we'll build a demonstration program that will randomly create and draw different shapes in a window. The user can then click on any shape, and the program will report the type and area of the shape that was clicked. Because the shapes are randomly created, each time the program runs, the size, location, number, and position of the shapes will be different. Figure 9-1 shows some sample output from the demonstration program.

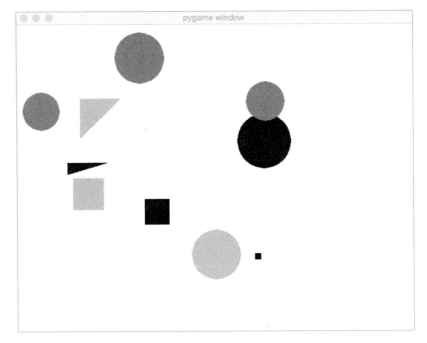

*Figure 9-1: A pygame-based example of using polymorphism to draw different shapes*

We'll implement the program with a class for each of three different shapes: Square, Circle, and Triangle. The key thing to note here is that all three shape classes contain methods with the same names, __init__(), draw(), getType(), getArea(), and clickedInside(), that perform the same tasks. However, the implementation of each method is different because each class deals with a different shape.

## The Square Shape Class

I'll start with the simplest shape. Listing 9-2 shows the code of the Square class.

**File: Shapes/Square.py**

```
# Square class

import pygame
import random

# Set up the colors
RED = (255, 0, 0)
GREEN = (0, 255, 0)
BLUE = (0, 0, 255)

class Square():
```

```
❶ def __init__(self, window, maxWidth, maxHeight):
      self.window = window
      self.widthAndHeight = random.randrange(10, 100)
      self.color = random.choice((RED, GREEN, BLUE))
      self.x = random.randrange(1, maxWidth - 100)
      self.y = random.randrange(25, maxHeight - 100)
      self.rect = pygame.Rect(self.x, self.y, self.widthAndHeight,
                              self.widthAndHeight)
      self.shapeType = 'Square'

❷ def clickedInside(self, mousePoint):
      clicked = self.rect.collidepoint(mousePoint)
      return clicked

❸ def getType(self):
      return self.shapeType

❹ def getArea(self):
      theArea = self.widthAndHeight * self.widthAndHeight
      return theArea

❺ def draw(self):
      pygame.draw.rect(self.window, self.color,
                       (self.x, self.y, self.widthAndHeight,
                        self.widthAndHeight))
```

*Listing 9-2: The Square class*

In the __init__() method ❶, we set up a number of instance variables to use in the methods of the class. That lets us keep the code of the methods very simple. Since the __init__() method saved the rectangle of the Square, the clickedInside() method ❷ just checks if the location of a mouse click was inside that rectangle, returning True or False.

The getType() method ❸ simply returns the information that the item clicked is a square. The getArea() method ❹ multiplies the width by the height and returns the resulting area. The draw(.) method ❺ uses pygame's draw.rect() to draw the shape in the randomly chosen color.

## The Circle and Triangle Shape Classes

Next, let's take a look at the code of the Circle and the Triangle classes. The important thing to notice is that these classes have methods with the same names as the Square class, but the code in these methods (especially clickedInside() and getArea()) is very different. Listing 9-3 shows the Circle class. Listing 9-4 shows the Triangle class that creates randomly sized right triangles whose edges are parallel to the x- and y-axes, with the right angle in the upper-left corner.

**File: Shapes/Circle.py**

```
# Circle class

import pygame
import random
import math

# Set up the colors
RED = (255, 0, 0)
GREEN = (0, 255, 0)
BLUE = (0, 0, 255)

class Circle():

    def __init__(self, window, maxWidth, maxHeight):
        self.window = window

        self.color = random.choice((RED, GREEN, BLUE))
        self.x = random.randrange(1, maxWidth - 100)
        self.y = random.randrange(25, maxHeight - 100)
        self.radius = random.randrange(10, 50)
        self.centerX = self.x + self.radius
        self.centerY = self.y + self.radius
        self.rect = pygame.Rect(self.x, self.y,
                                self.radius * 2, self.radius * 2)
        self.shapeType = 'Circle'

    def clickedInside(self, mousePoint):
        distance = math.sqrt(((mousePoint[0] - self.centerX) ** 2) +
                             ((mousePoint[1] - self.centerY) ** 2))
        if distance <= self.radius:
            return True
        else:
            return False

    def getArea(self):
        theArea = math.pi * (self.radius ** 2) squared
        return theArea

    def getType(self):
        return self.shapeType

    def draw(self):
        pygame.draw.circle(self.window, self.color,
                           (self.centerX, self.centerY),
                           self.radius, 0)
```

❶ `def clickedInside(self, mousePoint):`
❷ `def getArea(self):`
❸ `def draw(self):`

*Listing 9-3: The Circle class*

## File: Shapes/Triangle.py

```
# Triangle class

import pygame
import random

# Set up the colors
RED = (255, 0, 0)
GREEN = (0, 255, 0)
BLUE = (0, 0, 255)

class Triangle():

    def __init__(self, window, maxWidth, maxHeight):
        self.window = window
        self.width = random.randrange(10, 100)
        self.height = random.randrange(10, 100)
        self.triangleSlope = -1 * (self.height / self.width)

        self.color - random.choice((RED, GREEN, BLUE))
        self.x = random.randrange(1, maxWidth - 100)
        self.y = random.randrange(25, maxHeight - 100)
        self.rect = pygame.Rect(self.x, self.y,
                                self.width, self.height)
        self.shapeType = 'Triangle'

    def clickedInside(self, mousePoint):
        inRect = self.rect.collidepoint(mousePoint)
        if not inRect:
            return False

        # Do some math to see if the point is inside the triangle
        xOffset = mousePoint[0] - self.x
        yOffset = mousePoint[1] - self.y
        if xOffset == 0:
            return True

        # Calculate the slope (rise over run)
        pointSlopeFromYIntercept = (yOffset - self.height) / xOffset
        if pointSlopeFromYIntercept < self.triangleSlope:
            return True
        else:
            return False

    def getType(self):
        return self.shapeType

    def getArea(self):
        theArea = .5 * self.width * self.height
        return theArea
```

```
❻ def draw(self):
    pygame.draw.polygon(self.window, self.color,
                        ((self.x, self.y + self.height),
                        (self.x, self.y),
                        (self.x + self.width, self.y)))
```

*Listing 9-4: The Triangle class*

To understand the polymorphism at work here, let's look at the codeof the `clickedInside()` method for each shape. The `clickedInside()` method of the `Square` class was very simple: a check to see if the mouse click occurred inside the rectangle of the `Square`. The details of the calculations for `clickedInside()` in the `Circle` and `Triangle` classes are not particularly important, but they clearly are doing different calculations. The `clickedInside()` method of the `Circle` class ❶ only reports a click if the user clicks on a colored pixel of the shape. That is, it detects a click that is within the bounding rectangle of the circle, but the click must also be within the radius of the circle for it to count as a click. The `clickedInside()` method of the `Triangle` class ❹ must determine if the user has clicked on a pixel inside the colored triangular portion of the rectangle. The methods in all three classes accept a mouse click as a parameter and return either `True` or `False` as a result.

The `getArea()` ❷ ❺ and `draw()` methods ❸ ❻ of these classes have names that are identical to methods of the `Square` class, but they do different work internally. There's a different calculation for area, and they draw different shapes.

## The Main Program Creating Shapes

Listing 9-5 shows the source of the main program, which creates a list of randomly chosen shape objects.

**File: Shapes/Main_ShapesExample.py**

```
import pygame
import sys
from pygame.locals import *
from Square import *
from Circle import *
from Triangle import *
import pygwidgets

# Set up the constants
WHITE = (255, 255, 255)
WINDOW_WIDTH = 640
WINDOW_HEIGHT = 480
FRAMES_PER_SECOND = 30
N_SHAPES = 10

# Set up the window
pygame.init()
```

```
window = pygame.display.set_mode((WINDOW_WIDTH, WINDOW_HEIGHT), 0, 32)
clock = pygame.time.Clock()

shapesList = []
shapeClassesTuple = (Square, Circle, Triangle)
for i in range(0, N_SHAPES):  ❶
    randomlyChosenClass = random.choice(shapeClassesTuple)
    oShape = randomlyChosenClass (window, WINDOW_WIDTH, WINDOW_HEIGHT)
    shapesList.append(oShape)

oStatusLine = pygwidgets.DisplayText(window, (4,4),
                                     'Click on shapes', fontSize=28)

# Main loop
while True:
    for event in pygame.event.get():
        if event.type == QUIT:
            pygame.quit()
            sys.exit()

        if event.type == MOUSEBUTTONDOWN:  ❷
            # Reverse order to check last drawn shape first
            for oShape in reversed(shapesList):  ❸
                if oShape.clickedInside(event.pos):  ❹
                    area = oShape.getArea()  ❺
                    area = str(area)
                    theType = oShape.getType()
                    newText = 'Clicked on a ' + theType + ' whose area is ' + area
                    oStatusLine.setValue(newText)
                    break  # only deal with topmost shape

    # Tell each shape to draw itself
    window.fill(WHITE)
    for oShape in shapesList:
        oShape.draw()
    oStatusLine.draw()

    pygame.display.update()
    clock.tick(FRAMES_PER_SECOND)
```

*Listing 9-5: The main program that creates random shapes from three classes*

As we saw in Chapter 4, whenever we have a large number of objects to manage, the typical approach is to build a list of objects. So, before the main loop starts, the program first builds a list of shapes ❶ by randomly choosing among a circle, a square, and a triangle; creating an object of that type; and appending it to the list. Using this approach, we can then iterate over the list and call methods of the same name in every object in the list.

Inside the main loop, the program checks for the mouse down event ❷ that happens when the user clicks. Whenever the event is detected, the code iterates through the shapesList ❸ and calls the clickedInside() ❹ method for each shape. Because of polymorphism, it doesn't matter which class the object was instantiated from. Again, the key is that the implementation of the clickedInside() method can be different for different classes.

When any `clickedInside()` method returns `True` ❺, we call the `getArea()` then `getType()` methods of that object, without worrying about which type of object was clicked on.

Here is the output of a typical run, after clicking on a few of the different shapes:

```
Clicked on a Circle whose area is 5026.544
Clicked on a Square whose area is 1600
Clicked on a Triangle whose area is 1982.5
Clicked on a Square whose area is 1600
Clicked on a Square whose area is 100
Clicked on a Triangle whose area is 576.0
Clicked on a Circle whose area is 3019.06799
```

## Extending a Pattern

Building classes with commonly named methods creates a consistent pattern that allows us to easily extend the program. For example, to add the ability for our program to include ellipses, we would build an `Ellipse` class that implements the `getArea()`, `clickedInside()`, `draw()`, and `getType()` methods. (The code of the `clickedInside()` method might be mathematically complicated for an ellipse!)

Once we've written the code of the `Ellipse` class, the only change we need to make to the setup code is to add `Ellipse` to the tuple of shape classes to choose from. The code in the main loop that does the checking for clicks, gets the area of the shape, and so on will not need to change at all.

This example demonstrates two important features of polymorphism:

- Polymorphism extends the concept of abstraction discussed in Chapter 8 to a collection of classes. If multiple classes have the same interfaces for their methods, the client programmer can ignore the implementation of those methods in all the classes.

- Polymorphism can make client programming easier. If a client programmer is already familiar with the interfaces provided by one or more classes, then calling the methods of another polymorphic class should as be simple as following the pattern.

## pygwidgets Exhibits Polymorphism

All the classes in `pygwidgets` were designed to use polymorphism, and they all implement two common methods. The first is the `handleEvent()` method we first used in Chapter 6, which takes an event object as a parameter. Each class must contain its own code in this method to handle any event that pygame may generate. Each time through the main loop, client programs need to call the `handleEvent()` method for every instance of every object instantiated from `pygwidgets`.

Second is the `draw()` method, which draws images to the window. A typical drawing portion of a program that uses `pygwidgets` might look like this:

```
inputTextA.draw()
inputTextB.draw()
displayTextA.draw()
displayTextB.draw()
restartButton.draw()
checkBoxA.draw()
checkBoxB.draw()
radioCustom1.draw()
radioCustom2.draw()
radioCustom3.draw()
checkBoxC.draw()
radioDefault1.draw()
radioDefault2.draw()
radioDefault3.draw()
statusButton.draw()
```

From the client's point of view, each line just calls the `draw()` method and passes in nothing. From an internal point of view, the code to implement each of these methods is very different. The `draw()` method of the `TextButton` class is completely different from that of the `InputText` class, for instance.

Additionally, all widgets that manage a value contain a `setValue()` and optionally a `getValue()` method. For example, to get the text the user enters into an `InputText` widget, you call the `getValue()` getter method. Radio button and checkbox widgets also have a `getValue()` method to get their current values. To put new text into a `DisplayText` widget, you call the `setValue()` setter method, passing in the new text. Radio button and checkbox widgets can be set with a call to their `setValue()` method.

Polymorphism allows client programmers to feel comfortable with a collection of classes. When clients see a pattern, like using methods named `handleEvent()` and `draw()`, it makes it easy for them to predict how to use a new class in the same collection.

As of this writing, the `pygwidgets` package does not provide either a horizontal or a vertical `Slider` class widget to allow a user to easily select from a range of numbers. If I were to add these widgets, they would certainly contain the following: a `handleEvent()` method, where all user interaction would take place; a `getValue()` and a `setValue()` method to get and set a current value for the `Slider`; and a `draw()` method.

## Polymorphism for Operators

Python also exhibits polymorphism with operators. Consider the following example with the + operator:

```
value1 = 4
value2 = 5
result = value1 + value2
print(result)
```

which prints:

```
9
```

The + operator here clearly means "add" in a mathematic sense because both variables contain integer values. But now consider this second example:

```
value1 = 'Joe'
value2 = 'Schmoe'
result = value1 + value2
print(result)
```

which prints:

```
JoeSchmoe
```

The line `result = value1 + value2` is exactly the same as in the first example, but it performs a completely different operation. With string values, the + operator performs a string concatenation. The same operator was used, but a different action was performed.

This technique of having multiple meanings for an operator is commonly known as *operator overloading*. For some classes, the ability to overload operators adds highly useful features and greatly improves the readability of client code.

## Magic Methods

Python reserves method names with the unusual form of two underscores, some name, and two underscores for a particular purpose:

```
__<someName>__()
```

These are officially called *special methods* but are more commonly referred to by Python programmers as *magic methods*. Many of these are already defined, such as __init__(), which is called whenever you instantiate an object from a class, but all other names in this style are available for future expansion. These are known as "magic" methods because Python calls them behind the scenes whenever it detects an operator, a special function call, or some other special circumstance. They are not intended to be called by client code directly.

**NOTE** *Because the names of these magic methods are difficult to pronounce—for example, __init__() is read as "underscore underscore init underscore underscore"—Python programmers often refer to these as* dunder *methods (a shortened version of* double underscore*). This method would be referred to as "dunder init."*

Continuing with the previous examples, we'll look at how this works with the + operator. The built-in data types (integer, float, string, Boolean, and so on) are actually implemented as classes in Python. We can see this by testing with the built-in `isinstance()` function, which takes an object and a class and returns `True` if the object was instantiated from the class or `False` if not. These lines will both report `True`:

```
print(isinstance(123, int))
print(isinstance('some string', str))
```

The classes for the built-in data types contain a set of magic methods, including ones for the basic math operators. When Python detects the + operator with integers, it calls the magic method named __add__() in the built-in integer class, which performs integer addition. When Python sees the same operator used with strings, it calls the __add__() method in the string class, which performs string concatenation.

This mechanism is generalized so that when Python encounters a + operator when working with objects instantiated from your class, it will call the __add__() method if one is present in your class. Therefore, as the class developer, you can write code to invent a new meaning for this operator.

Each operator maps to a specific magic method name. While there are many types of magic methods, let's start with those related to the comparison operators.

## Comparison Operator Magic Methods

Consider our `Square` class from Listing 9-2. You want client software to be able to compare two `Square` objects to see if they are equal. It is up to you to decide what "equal" means when comparing objects. For instance, you might define it as two objects being the same color and at the same location and with the same size. As a simple example, we'll define two `Square` objects as equal if they just have the same side length. This is easily implemented by comparing the `self.heightAndWidth` instance variables of the two objects and returning a Boolean. You could write your own `equals()` method, and client software could then call it like this:

```
if oSquare1.equals(oSquare2):
```

This would work fine. However, it would be more natural for client software to use the standard == comparison operator:

```
if oSquare1 == oSquare2:
```

Written this way, Python translates the == operator into a call to a magic method of the first object. In this case, Python will attempt to call a magic method named __eq__() in the `Square` class. Table 9-1 shows the magic methods for all the comparison operators.

**Table 9-1:** Comparison Operator Symbols, Meanings, and Magic Method Names

| Symbol | Meaning | Magic method name |
|--------|---------|-------------------|
| == | Equal to | __eq__() |
| != | Not equal to | __ne__() |
| < | Less than | __lt__() |
| > | Greater than | __gt__() |
| <= | Less than or equal to | __le__() |
| >= | Greater than or equal to | __ge__() |

To allow the == comparison operator to check for equality between two Square objects, you would write a method like this in the Square class:

```
def __eq__(self, oOtherSquare):
    if not isinstance(oOtherSquare, Square):
        raise TypeError('Second object was not a Square')
    if self.heightAndWidth == oOtherSquare.heightAndWidth:
        return True  # match
    else:
        return False  # not a match
```

When Python detects an == comparison where the first object is a Square, it calls this method in the Square class. Since Python is a loosely typed language (it doesn't require you to define variable types), the second parameter could be of any data type. However, in order for the comparison to work correctly, the second parameter must also be a Square object. We perform a check using the isinstance() function, which works with programmer-defined classes the same way it works with built-in classes. If the second object is not a Square, we raise an exception.

We then compare the heightAndWidth of the current object (self) with the heightAndWidth of a second object (oOtherSquare). This is a case where using direct access to the instance variables of two objects is perfectly acceptable, because both objects are of the same type, and therefore they must contain the same instance variables.

## A Rectangle Class with Magic Methods

To expand, we'll build a program that draws a number of rectangle shapes using a Rectangle class. The user will be able to click on any two rectangles, and the program will report if the rectangles have the same area or if the area of the first one is larger or smaller than the area of the second rectangle. We'll use the ==, <, and > operators and expect the result to be a Boolean True or False for each comparison. Listing 9-6 contains the code of the Rectangle class, which implements magic methods for these operators.

## File: MagicMethods/Rectangle/Rectangle.py

```python
# Rectangle class

import pygame
import random

# Set up the colors
RED = (255, 0, 0)
GREEN = (0, 255, 0)
BLUE = (0, 0, 255)

class Rectangle():

    def __init__(self, window):
        self.window = window
        self.width = random.choice((20, 30, 40))
        self.height = random.choice((20, 30, 40))
        self.color = random.choice((RED, GREEN, BLUE))
        self.x = random.randrange(0, 400)
        self.y = random.randrange(0, 400)
        self.rect = pygame.Rect(self.x, self.y, self.width, self.height)
        self.area = self.width * self.height

    def clickedInside(self, mousePoint):
        clicked = self.rect.collidepoint(mousePoint)
        return clicked

    # Magic method called when you compare
    # two Rectangle objects with the == operator
    def __eq__ (self, oOtherRectangle):  ❶
        if not isinstance(oOtherRectangle, Rectangle):
            raise TypeError('Second object was not a Rectangle')
        if self.area == oOtherRectangle.area:
            return True
        else:
            return False

    # Magic method called when you compare
    # two Rectangle objects with the < operator
    def __lt__ (self, oOtherRectangle):  ❷
        if not isinstance(oOtherRectangle, Rectangle):
            raise TypeError('Second object was not a Rectangle')
        if self.area < oOtherRectangle.area:
            return True
        else:
            return False

    # Magic method called when you compare
    # two Rectangle objects with the > operator
    def __gt__ (self, oOtherRectangle):  ❸
        if not isinstance(oOtherRectangle, Rectangle):
            raise TypeError('Second object was not a Rectangle')
```

```
        if self.area > oOtherRectangle.area:
            return True
        else:
            return False

    def getArea(self):
        return self.area

    def draw(self):
        pygame.draw.rect(self.window, self.color, (self.x, self.y, self.width, self.height))
```

*Listing 9-6: The Rectangle class*

The methods _eq_() ❶, _lt_() ❷, and _gt_() ❸ allow client code to use standard comparison operators between Rectangle objects. To compare two rectangles for equality, you would write:

```
if oRectangle1 == oRectangle2:
```

When this line runs, the _eq_() method of the first object is called, and the second object is passed in as the second parameter. The function returns either True or False. Similarly, to compare for less than, you would write a line like this:

```
if oRectangle1 < oRectangle2:
```

The _lt_() method then checks for the area of the first rectangle being less than the area of the second rectangle. If client code used the > operator to compare two rectangles, the _gt_() method would be called.

## Main Program Using Magic Methods

Listing 9-7 shows the code of the main program that tests the magic methods.

**File: MagicMethods/Rectangle/Main_RectangleExample.py**

```
import pygame
import sys
from pygame.locals import *
from Rectangle import *

# Set up the constants
WHITE = (255, 255, 255)
WINDOW_WIDTH = 640
WINDOW_HEIGHT = 480
FRAMES_PER_SECOND = 30
N_RECTANGLES = 10
FIRST_RECTANGLE = 'first'
SECOND_RECTANGLE = 'second'

# Set up the window
pygame.init()
```

```
window = pygame.display.set_mode((WINDOW_WIDTH, WINDOW_HEIGHT), 0, 32)
clock = pygame.time.Clock()

rectanglesList = []
for i in range(0, N_RECTANGLES):
    oRectangle = Rectangle(window)
    rectanglesList.append(oRectangle)

whichRectangle = FIRST_RECTANGLE

# Main loop
while True:
    for event in pygame.event.get():
        if event.type == QUIT:
            pygame.quit()
            sys.exit()

        if event.type == MOUSEBUTTONDOWN:
            for oRectangle in rectanglesList:
                if oRectangle.clickedInside(event.pos):
                    print('Clicked on', whichRectangle, 'rectangle.')

                    if whichRectangle == FIRST_RECTANGLE:
                        oFirstRectangle = oRectangle ❶
                        whichRectangle = SECOND_RECTANGLE

                    elif whichRectangle == SECOND_RECTANGLE:
                        oSecondRectangle2 = oRectangle ❷
                        # User has chosen 2 rectangles, let's compare
                        if oFirstRectangle == oSecondRectangle: ❸
                            print('Rectangles are the same size.')
                        elif oFirstRectangle < oSecondRectangle: ❹
                            print('First rectangle is smaller than second rectangle.')
                        else:  # must be larger ❺
                            print('First rectangle is larger than second rectangle.')
                        whichRectangle = FIRST_RECTANGLE

    # Clear the window and draw all rectangles
    window.fill(WHITE)
    for oRectangle in rectanglesList: ❻
        oRectangle.draw()

    pygame.display.update()

    clock.tick(FRAMES_PER_SECOND)
```

*Listing 9-7: The main program that draws and then compares Rectangle objects*

The user of the program clicks on pairs of rectangles to compare their sizes. We store the selected rectangles in two variables ❶ ❷.

We check for equality using the == operator ❸, which resolves to calling the __eq__() method of the Rectangle class. If the rectangles are the same size, we print out an appropriate message. If not, we check if the first rectangle is smaller than the second using the < operator ❹, which results in a call to the __lt__() method. If this comparison is also not True, we print the message for the first being larger than the second ❺. We didn't need to use the > operator in this program; however, since other client code might implement size comparisons differently, we've included the __gt__() method for completeness.

Finally, we draw all the rectangles in our list ❻.

Because we included the magic methods __eq__(), __lt__(), and __gt__() in the Rectangle class, we were able to use the standard comparison operators in a highly intuitive and readable way.

Here is the output from clicking on a number of different rectangles:

```
Clicked on first rectangle.
Clicked on second rectangle.
Rectangles are the same size.
Clicked on first rectangle.
Clicked on second rectangle.
First rectangle is smaller than second rectangle.
Clicked on first rectangle.
Clicked on second rectangle.
First rectangle is larger than second rectangle.
```

## Math Operator Magic Methods

You can write additional magic methods to define what happens when client code uses the other arithmetic operators between objects instantiated from your class.

Table 9-2 shows the methods that are called for the basic arithmetic operators.

**Table 9-2:** Math Operator Symbols, Meanings, and Magic Method Names

| Symbol | Meaning | Magic method name |
|---|---|---|
| + | Addition | __add__() |
| - | Subtraction | __sub__() |
| * | Multiplication | __mul__() |
| / | Division (floating-point result) | __truediv__() |
| // | Integer division | __floordiv__() |
| % | Modulo | __mod__() |
| abs | Absolute value | __abs__() |

For example, to handle the + operator, you would implement a method in your class like this:

```
def __add__(self, oOther):
    # Your code here to determine what happens when code
    # attempts to add two of these objects.
```

A full list of all the magic or dunder methods can be found in the official documentation at *https://docs.python.org/3/reference/datamodel.html.*

## Vector Example

In math, a *vector* is an ordered pair of x and y values that is often represented on a graph as a directed line segment. In this section, we'll build a class that uses math operator magic methods to operate on vectors. There are a number of math operations that can be performed on vectors. Figure 9-2 shows an example of adding two vectors.

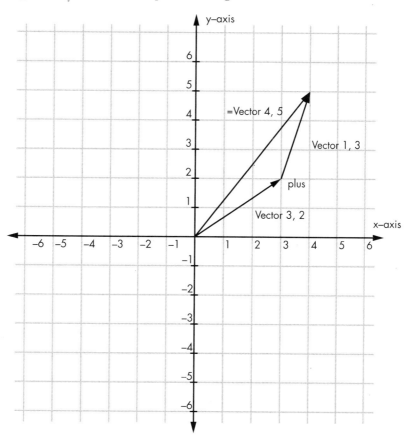

Figure 9-2: Vector addition in Cartesian coordinates

Adding two vectors results in a new vector whose x value is the sum of the x values of the two added vectors and whose y value is the sum of the y values of the two added vectors. In Figure 9-2, we add the vector (3, 2) and the vector (1, 3) to create a vector (4, 5).

Two vectors are considered equal if their x values are the same and their y values are the same. A vector's size is computed to be the hypotenuse of the right triangle with one side of length x and the second side of length y. We can use the Pythagorean theorem to compute the length and use the lengths to compare two vectors' sizes.

Listing 9-8 is a Vector class that illustrates the appropriate magic methods for doing math and comparisons between two Vector objects. (Each of these methods has additional code using a call to isinstance() to ensure that the second object is a Vector. These checks are included in the downloadable file, but I have omitted them here to save space.)

**File: MagicMethods/Vectors/Vector.py**

```
# Vector class

import math

class Vector():
    '''The Vector class represents two values as a vector,
        allows for many math calculations'''
    def __init__(self, x, y):
        self.x = x
        self.y = y

❶   def __add__(self, oOther):  # called for + operator
        return Vector(self.x + oOther.x, self.y + oOther.y)

    def __sub__(self, oOther):  # called for - operator
        return Vector(self.x - oOther.x, self.y - oOther.y)

❷   def __mul__(self, oOther):  # called for * operator
        # Special code to allow for multiplying by a vector or a scalar
        if isinstance(oOther, Vector):  # multiply two vectors
            return Vector((self.x * oOther.x), (self.y * oOther.y))
        elif isinstance(oOther, (int, float)):  # multiply by a scalar
            return Vector((self.x * oOther), (self.y * oOther))
        else:
            raise TypeError('Second value must be a vector or scalar')

    def __abs__(self):
        return math.sqrt((self.x ** 2) + (self.y ** 2))

    def __eq__(self, oOther):  # called for == operator
        return (self.x == oOther.x) and (self.y == oOther.y)

    def __ne__(self, oOther):  # called for != operator
        return not (self == oOther)  # calls __eq__ method

    def __lt__(self, oOther):  # called for < operator
        if abs(self) < abs(oOther):  # calls __abs__ method
            return True
        else:
            return False

    def __gt__(self, oOther):  # called for > operator
        if abs(self) > abs(oOther):  # calls __abs__ method
```

```
                return True
        else:
                return False
```

*Listing 9-8: The Vector class that implements a number of magic methods*

This class implements arithmetic and comparison operators as magic methods. Client code would use standard symbols for math and comparison between two Vector objects. For example, the addition of vectors in Figure 9-2 could be handled like this:

```
oVector1 = Vector(3, 2)
oVector2 = Vector(1, 3)
oNewVector = oVector1 + oVector2   # use the + operator to add vectors
```

When the third line runs, the __add__() method ❶is called to add the two Vector objects, resulting in the creation of a new Vector object. There is a special check in the __mul__() method ❷ that allows the * operator to either multiply two Vectors or multiply one Vector by a scalar value, depending on the type of the second value.

## Creating a String Representation of Values in an Object

A standard approach to debugging is to add calls to print() to write out the values of variables at certain points in your program:

```
print('My variable is', myVariable)
```

However, if you try to use print() to help you debug the contents of an object, the results are not particularly helpful. For example, here we create a Vector object and print it:

```
oVector = Vector(3, 4)
print('My vector is', oVector)
```

This is what is printed:

```
<Vector object at 0x10361b518>
```

This tells us that we have an object instantiated from the Vector class and shows the memory address of that object. However, in most cases, what we really want to know are the values of the instance variables in the object at that moment. Luckily, we can use magic methods for that.

There are two magic methods that can be useful in getting information (as strings) from an object:

• The __str__() method is used to create a string representation of an object that can be read easily by humans. If client code makes a call to the str() built-in function and passes in an object, Python will call the magic method __str__() if it is present in that class.

- The __repr__() method is used to create an unambiguous, possibly machine-readable string representation of the object. If client code makes a call to the repr() built-in function and passes in an object, Python will attempt to call the magic method __repr__() in that class, if present.

I'll show the __str__() method, as it's more generally used for simple debugging. When you call the print() function, Python calls the built-in str() function to convert each argument into a string. For any argument that does not have a __str__() method, this function formats a string that contains the type of the object, the words "object at," and the memory address, then returns the resulting string. That's why we see the earlier output containing the memory address.

Instead, you can write your own version of __str__() and have it produce whatever string you want to help debug the code of your class. The general approach is to build a string that contains the values of any instance variables that you want to see and return that string to be printed. For example, we can add the following method to the Vector class from Listing 9-8 to get information about any Vector object:

```python
class Vector():
    --- snipped all previous methods ---
    def __str__(self):
        return 'This vector has the value (' + str(self.x) + ', ' + str(self.y) + ')'
```

If you instantiate a Vector, you can then call the print() function and pass in a Vector object:

```python
oVector = Vector(10, 7)
print(oVector)
```

Rather than just printing the memory address of the Vector object, you will get a nicely formatted report of the values of the two instance variables contained in the object:

```
This vector has the value (10, 7)
```

The main code in Listing 9-9 creates a few Vector objects, does some vector math, and prints out the results of some Vector calculations.

### File: Vectors/Main_Vectors.py

```python
# Vector test code

from Vector import *

v1 = Vector(3, 4)
v2 = Vector(2, 2)
v3 = Vector(3, 4)
```

```
# These lines print Boolean or numeric values
print(v1 == v2)
print(v1 == v3)
print(v1 < v2)
print(v1 > v2)
print(abs(v1))
print(abs(v2))
print()

# These lines print Vectors (calls the __str__() method)
print('Vector 1:', v1)
print('Vector 2:', v2)
print('Vector 1 + Vector 2:', v1 + v2)
print('Vector 1 - Vector 2:', v1 - v2)
print('Vector 1 times Vector 2:', v1 * v2)
print('Vector 1 times 5:', v1 * 5)
```

*Listing 9-9: Sample main code that creates and compares Vectors, does math, and prints Vectors*

This generates the following output:

```
False
True
False
True
5.0
2.8284271247461903

Vector 1: This vector has the value (3, 4)
Vector 2: This vector has the value (2, 2)
Vector 1 + Vector 2: This vector has the value (5, 6)
Vector 1 - Vector 2: This vector has the value (1, 2)
Vector 1 times Vector 2: This vector has the value (6, 8)
Vector 1 times 5: This vector has the value (15, 20)
```

The first set of calls to print() output Boolean and numeric values, which result from calling math and comparison operator magic methods. In the second set, we print two Vector objects, then compute and print some new Vectors. Internally, the print() function first calls Python's str() function for each item to be printed; that results in a call to the Vector's __str__() magic method, which creates a formatted string with the relevant information.

# A Fraction Class with Magic Methods

Let's put some of these magic methods together in a more complex example. Listing 9-10 shows the code of a Fraction class. Each Fraction object is made up of a numerator (top part) and a denominator (bottom part). The class keeps track of a fraction by storing the separate parts in instance variables, along with the fraction's approximate decimal value. The methods allow the caller to get the reduced value of the fraction, print the fraction along with its floating-point value, compare two fractions for equality, and add two Fraction objects. (This code works with Python 3.9 and above.)

## File: MagicMethods/Fraction.py

```
# Fraction class

import math

class Fraction():
    def __init__(self, numerator, denominator): ❶
        if not isinstance(numerator, int):
            raise TypeError('Numerator', numerator, 'must be an integer')
        if not isinstance(denominator, int):
            raise TypeError('Denominator', denominator, 'must be an integer')
        self.numerator = numerator
        self.denominator = denominator

        # Use the math package to find the greatest common divisor
        greatestCommonDivisor = math.gcd(self.numerator, self.denominator)
        if greatestCommonDivisor > 1:
            self.numerator = self.numerator // greatestCommonDivisor
            self.denominator = self.denominator // greatestCommonDivisor
        self.value = self.numerator / self.denominator

        # Normalize the sign of the numerator and denominator
        self.numerator = int(math.copysign(1.0, self.value)) * abs(self.numerator)
        self.denominator = abs(self.denominator)

    def getValue(self): ❷
        return self.value

    def __str__(self): ❸
        '''Create a string representation of the fraction'''
        output = '  Fraction: ' + str(self.numerator) + '/' + \
                str(self.denominator) + '\n' + \
                '  Value: ' + str(self.value) + '\n'
        return output

    def __add__(self, oOtherFraction): ❹
        ''' Add two Fraction objects'''
        if not isinstance(oOtherFraction, Fraction):
            raise TypeError('Second value in attempt to add is not a Fraction')
        # Use the math package to find the least common multiple
        newDenominator = math.lcm(self.denominator, oOtherFraction.denominator)

        multiplicationFactor = newDenominator // self.denominator
        equivalentNumerator = self.numerator * multiplicationFactor

        otherMultiplicationFactor = newDenominator // oOtherFraction.denominator
        oOtherFractionEquivalentNumerator =
                oOtherFraction.numerator * otherMultiplicationFactor
```

```
        newNumerator = equivalentNumerator + oOtherFractionEquivalentNumerator

        oAddedFraction = Fraction(newNumerator, newDenominator)
        return oAddedFraction

    def __eq__(self, oOtherFraction): ❺
        '''Test for equality '''
        if not isinstance(oOtherFraction, Fraction):
            return False  # not comparing to a fraction
        if (self.numerator == oOtherFraction.numerator) and \
           (self.denominator == oOtherFraction.denominator):
            return True
        else:
            return False
```

*Listing 9-10: The Fraction class that implements a number of magic methods*

When you create a Fraction object, you pass in a numerator and a denominator ❶, and the __init__() method immediately calculates the reduced fraction and its floating-point value. At any time, client code can call the getValue() method to retrieve that value ❷. Client code can also call print() to print out the object, and Python will call the __str__() method to format a string to be printed ❸.

The client can add two different Fraction objects together with the + operator. When this happens, the __add__() method is called ❹. That method uses the math.lcd() (least common denominator) method to ensure that the resulting Fraction object has the smallest common denominator.

Finally, client code can use the == operator to check if two Fraction objects are equal. When you use this operator, the __eq__() method is called ❺, which checks the values of the two Fractions and returns True or False.

Here is some code that instantiates Fraction objects and tests the various magic methods:

```
# Test code

oFraction1 = Fraction(1, 3)  # create a Fraction object
oFraction2 = Fraction(2, 5)
print('Fraction1\n', oFraction1)  # print the object ... calls __str__
print('Fraction2\n', oFraction2)

oSumFraction = oFraction1 + oFraction2  # calls __add__
print('Sum is\n', oSumFraction)

print('Are fractions 1 and 2 equal?', (oFraction1 == oFraction2)) # expect False
print()

oFraction3 = Fraction(-20, 80)
oFraction4 = Fraction(4, -16)
print('Fraction3\n', oFraction3)
print('Fraction4\n', oFraction4)
print('Are fractions 3 and 4 equal?', (oFraction3 == oFraction4)) # expect True
print()
```

```
oFraction5 = Fraction(5, 2)
oFraction6 = Fraction(500, 200)
print('Sum of 5/2 and 500/2\n', oFraction5 + oFraction6)
```

When run, this code produces:

```
Fraction1
   Fraction: 1/3
   Value: 0.3333333333333333

Fraction2
   Fraction: 2/5
   Value: 0.4

Sum is
   Fraction: 11/15
   Value: 0.7333333333333333

Are fractions 1 and 2 equal? False

Fraction3
   Fraction: -1/4
   Value: -0.25

Fraction4
   Fraction: -1/4
   Value: -0.25

Are fractions 3 and 4 equal? True

Sum of 5/2 and 500/2
   Fraction: 5/1
   Value: 5.0
```

## Summary

This chapter was about the key OOP concept of polymorphism. Stated simply, polymorphism is the ability for multiple classes to implement methods with the same names. Each class contains specific code to do whatever needs to be done for objects instantiated from that class. As a demonstration program, I showed how you could create a number of different shape classes, each of which had an __init__(), getArea(), clickedInside(), and draw() method. The code of each version of these methods was specific to the type of the shape.

As you saw, there are two key advantages to using polymorphism. First, it extends the concept of abstraction to a collection of classes, allowing the client programmer to ignore the implementation. Second, it allows for a system of classes that work in similar ways, making a system predictable to client programmers.

I also discussed the idea of polymorphism in operators, explaining how the same operator could do different operations with different types of data. I showed how Python's magic methods are used to make this happen and how you can build methods to implement these operators in your own classes. To demonstrate the use of arithmetic and comparison operator magic methods, I showed a Vector class and a Fraction class. I also showed how you can use the __str__() method to help in debugging the content of an object.

# 10

## INHERITANCE

The third tenet of OOP is *inheritance*, which is a mechanism for deriving a new class from an existing class. Rather than starting from scratch and potentially duplicating code, inheritance allows a programmer to write code for a new class that extends or differentiates it from an existing class.

Let's begin with a real-world example that demonstrates what inheritance is basically about. You're attending culinary school. One of your lessons involves an exhaustive demonstration of making hamburgers. You learn everything that there is to know about the different cuts of meat, the grinding of the meat, the best types of buns, the best lettuce, tomato, and condiments—just about everything you could imagine. You also learn about the best way to cook the hamburger, how long to cook it, when and how often to flip it over, and so on.

The next lesson in the curriculum is about cheeseburgers. The instructor *could* start from scratch and go through all the material about hamburgers again. But instead, they assume that you've retained the knowledge from the previous lesson and so already know everything there is to know about creating a great hamburger. This lesson therefore focuses on what types of cheese to use, when to add it, how much to use, and so on.

The point of the story is that there is no need to "reinvent the wheel"; instead, you can simply add on to what you already know.

## Inheritance in Object-Oriented Programming

Inheritance in OOP is the ability to create a class that builds on (*extends*) an existing class. When creating large programs, you will often use classes that provide very useful general capabilities. You'll sometimes want to build a class that's similar to a class that already exists, but does some things slightly differently. Inheritance allows you to do just that, creating a new class that includes all the methods and instance variables of an existing class, but adds new and different functionality.

Inheritance is an extremely powerful concept. When classes are set up correctly, using inheritance can *seem* simple. However, being able to design classes to use it in a clear manner is a skill that's difficult to master. As an implementer, inheritance takes a great deal of practice to use properly and efficiently.

With inheritance, we talk about the relationship between two classes, typically referred to as the *base class* and *subclass*.

---

**Base class**    The class that is inherited from; it serves as a starting point for the subclass.

---

**Subclass**    The class that is doing the inheriting; it enhances the base class.

---

While these are the most common terms used to describe the two classes in Python, you may also hear them referred to in other ways, such as:

- *Superclass* and *subclass*
- *Base class* and *derived class*
- *Parent class* and *child class*

Figure 10-1 is a standard diagram that shows this relationship.

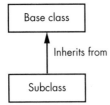

Figure 10-1: A subclass inherits from a base class.

A subclass inherits all of the methods and instance variables defined in a base class.

Figure 10-2 provides a different, perhaps more accurate, way to think of the relationship between the two classes.

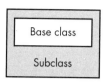

Figure 10-2: A base class is incorporated into a subclass.

As the implementer, you can think of the base class as being incorporated into the subclass. That is, the base class actually becomes part of the larger subclass. As a client of a subclass, you think about the subclass as a single unit and do not need to know that the base class is there at all.

When discussing inheritance, we often say there is an *is a* relationship between a subclass and a base class. For example, a student is a person, an orange is a fruit, a car is a vehicle, and so on. The subclass is a specialized version of the base class that inherits all the properties and behavior of the base class, but also provides additional details and functionality.

Most importantly, a subclass extends a base class in either or both of the following ways (which will be explained soon):

- A subclass can *redefine* a method that's defined in the base class. That is, a subclass can provide a method with same name as one in the base class but with different functionality. This is called *overriding* a method. When client code makes a call to an overridden method, the method in the subclass is called. (However, the code of the method in the subclass can still call the method of the same name in the base class.)

- A subclass can add new methods and instance variables that do not appear in the base class.

One way to think of a subclass is with the phrase *coding by difference.* Since the subclass inherits all the instance variables and methods of the base class, it does not need to repeat all of that code; the subclass only needs to contain code that differentiates it from the base class. The code of the subclass therefore only contains new instance variables (and their initialization), overriding methods, and/or new methods not found in the base class.

## Implementing Inheritance

The syntax of inheritance in Python is simple and elegant. The base class docs not need to *know* that it is being used as a base class. Only the subclass needs to indicate that it wants to inherit from a base class. Here is the general syntax:

```
class <BaseClassName>():
    # BaseClass methods

class <SubClassName>(<BaseClassName>):
    # SubClass methods
```

In the class statement of the subclass, within the parentheses you specify the name of the base class it should inherit from. In this case, we want the subclass <SubClassName> to inherit from the base class <BaseClassName>. (Programmers will often use the word *subclass* as a verb, as in "Let's subclass ClassA to build ClassB.") Here's an example with real class names:

```
class Widget():
    # Widget's methods

class WidgetWithFrills(Widget):
    # WidgetWithFrills's methods
```

The Widget class will provide general functionality. The WidgetWithFrills class will include everything from the Widget class and define any additional methods and instance variables it wants with more specific capabilities.

## Employee and Manager Example

I'll start with an extremely simple example to make the key concepts clear, then move on to some more practical examples.

### Base Class: Employee

Listing 10-1 defines a base class called Employee.

**File: EmployeeManagerInheritance/EmployeeManagerInheritance.py**

```
#   Employee Manager inheritance
#
# Define the Employee class, which we will use as a base class

class Employee():
    def __init__(self, name, title, ratePerHour=None):
        self.name = name
        self.title = title
        if ratePerHour is not None:
            ratePerHour = float(ratePerHour)
        self.ratePerHour = ratePerHour

    def getName(self):
        return self.name

    def getTitle(self):
```

```
            return self.title

    def payPerYear(self):
        # 52 weeks * 5 days a week * 8 hours per day
        pay = 52 * 5 * 8 * self.ratePerHour
        return pay
```

*Listing 10-1: The* Employee *class, which will be used as a base class*

The Employee class has the methods __init__(), getName(), getTitle(), and payPerYear(). It also has three instance variables, self.name, self.title, and self.ratePerHour, which are set in the __init__() method. We retrieve the name and title using getter methods. These employees are paid per hour, so self.payPerYear() does a calculation to determine the annual pay based on the hourly rate. Everything in this class should be familiar to you; there is nothing new here. You can instantiate an Employee object by itself, and it will work fine.

## Subclass: Manager

For the Manager class, we consider the differences between a manager and an employee: the manager is a salaried employee who has a number of direct reports. If this manager does a good job, they get a 10 percent bonus for the year. The Manager class can extend the Employee class, since the manager is an employee but has additional capabilities and responsibilities.

Listing 10-2 shows the code of our Manager class. It only needs to contain code that is different from the Employee class, so you'll see that it doesn't have a getName() or getTitle() method. Any calls to those methods with a Manager object will be handled by the methods in the Employee class.

**File: EmployeeManagerInheritance/EmployeeManagerInheritance.py**

```
  # Define a Manager subclass that inherits from Employee

❶ class Manager(Employee):
      def __init__(self, name, title, salary, reportsList=None):
❷         self.salary = float(salary)
          if reportsList is None:
              reportsList = []
          self.reportsList = reportsList
❸         super().__init__(name, title)

❹     def getReports(self):
          return self.reportsList

❺     def payPerYear(self, giveBonus=False):
          pay = self.salary
          if giveBonus:
              pay = pay + (.10 * self.salary)   # add a bonus of 10%
❻             print(self.name, 'gets a bonus for good work')
          return pay
```

*Listing 10-2: The* Manager *class, implemented as a subclass of the* Employee *class*

In the class statement ❶, you can see that this class inherits from the Employee class because Employee is inside the parentheses after the name Manager.

The \_\_init\_\_() method of the Employee class expects a name, a title, and an optional rate per hour. A manager is a salaried employee and manages a number of employees, so the \_\_init\_\_() method of the Manager class expects a name, a title, a salary, and a list of employees. Adhering to the principle of coding by difference, the \_\_init\_\_() method starts by initializing anything the \_\_init\_\_() method of the Employee class doesn't do. Therefore, we save the salary and reportsList in similarly named instance variables ❷.

Next we want to call the \_\_init\_\_() method of the Employee base class ❸. Here, I am calling the built-in function super(), which asks Python to figure out which class is the base class (often referred to as the *superclass*) and call that class's \_\_init\_\_() method. It also adjusts the arguments to include self as the first argument in this call. Therefore, you can think of this line as translating to:

```
Employee.__init__(self, name, title)
```

In fact, coding that line this way would work perfectly well; using the call to super() is simply a much cleaner way to write the call without having to specify the name of the base class.

The effect is that the new Manager class's \_\_init\_\_() method initializes the two instance variables (self.salary and self.reportsList) that are different from those in the Employee class, and the Employee class's \_\_init\_\_() method initializes the self.name and self.title instance variables that are common to any Employee or Manager object that is created. For a Manager who has a salary, self.ratePerHour is set to None.

**NOTE** *Older versions of Python required you to write this code in yet a third way, so you may see this in older programs and documentation:*

```
super(Employee, self).__init__(name, salary)
```

*This also does the exact same thing. However, the newer syntax with the simple call to super() is much easier to remember. Using super() also makes it less error-prone if you decide that you want to change the name of your base class.*

The Manager class has an added getter method, getReports() ❹, that allows client code to retrieve a list of Employees who report to the Manager. The payPerYear() method ❺ calculates and returns the Manager's pay.

Notice that both the Employee and the Manager classes have a method named payPerYear(). If you call the payPerYear() method using an instance of Employee, the Employee class's method will run and calculate the pay based on the hourly rate. If you call the payPerYear() method with an instance of Manager, the Manager class's method will run and do a different calculation. The payPerYear() method in the Manager class *overrides* the method by the same name in the base class. Overriding a method in a subclass specializes the subclass to differentiate it from the base class. The overriding method must have the exact same name as the method that it overrides (although it may have a different list of parameters). In the overriding method, you can:

- Completely replace the overridden method in the base class. We see this in the payPerYear() method of the Manager class.
- Do some work on its own and call the inherited or overridden method of the same name in the base class. We see this in the \_\_init\_\_() method of the Manager class.

The actual content of the overriding method depends on the situation. If the client makes a call to a method that does not exist in a subclass, the method call will be sent on to the base class. For example, notice that there is no method named getName() in the Manager class, but it does exist in the Employee base class. If a client calls getName() on an instance of Manager, that call is handled by the base class, Employee.

The payPerYear() method of the Manager class contains this code:

```
if giveBonus:
    pay = pay + (.10 * self.salary)  # add a bonus of 10%
  ❻ print(self.name, 'gets a bonus for good work')
```

The instance variable self.name was defined in the Employee class, but the Manager class has no previous mention of it. This demonstrates that instance variables defined in a base class are available for use in methods of a subclass. Here we are calculating the pay for a manager, which works correctly because payPerYear() has access to instance variables defined inside its own class (self.salary) *and* instance variables defined in the base class (printing using self.name ❻).

## Test Code

Let's test our Employee and Manager objects and call methods of each.

### File: EmployeeManagerInheritance/EmployeeManagerInheritance.py

```
# Create objects
oEmployee1 = Employee('Joe Schmoe', 'Pizza Maker', 16)
oEmployee2 = Employee('Chris Smith', 'Cashier', 14)
oManager = Manager('Sue Jones', 'Pizza Restaurant Manager',
                   55000, [oEmployee1, oEmployee2])

# Call methods of the Employee objects
print('Employee name:', oEmployee1.getName())
print('Employee salary:', '{:,.2f}'.format(oEmployee1.payPerYear()))
print('Employee name:', oEmployee2.getName())
print('Employee salary:', '{:,.2f}'.format(oEmployee2.payPerYear()))
print()

# Call methods of the Manager object
managerName = oManager.getName()
```

```
print('Manager name:', managerName)

# Give the manager a bonus
print('Manager salary:', '{:,.2f}'.format(oManager.payPerYear(True)))
print(managerName, '(' + oManager.getTitle() + ')', 'direct reports:')
reportsList = oManager.getReports()
for oEmployee in reportsList:
    print('   ', oEmployee.getName(),
          '(' + oEmployee.getTitle() + ')')
```

When we run this code, we see the following output, as we would expect:

```
Employee name: Joe Schmoe
Employee salary: 33,280.00
Employee name: Chris Smith
Employee salary: 29,120.00

Manager name: Sue Jones
Sue Jones gets a bonus for good work
Manager salary: 60,500.00
Sue Jones (Pizza Restaurant Manager) direct reports:
    Joe Schmoe (Pizza Maker)
    Chris Smith (Cashier)
```

## The Client's View of a Subclass

The discussion so far has been focused on the details of implementation. But classes can look different depending on whether you are the developer of a class or are writing code to use a class. Let's change focus and take a look at inheritance from the client's point of view. As far as client code is concerned, a subclass has all the functionality of the base class, plus anything defined in the subclass itself. It may help to think about the resulting collection of methods as layers of paint on a wall. When a client looks at the Employee class, the client sees all the methods defined in that class (Figure 10-3).

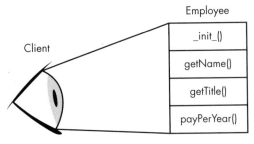

Figure 10-3: What a client would see looking at the interface of the Employee class

When we introduce the `Manager` class that inherits from the `Employee` class, it's like adding paint to touch up the places where we want to add or change methods. For methods that we don't want to change, we just leave the old layer of paint (Figure 10-4).

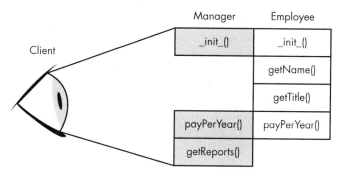

Figure 10-4: What a client would see looking at the interface of the Manager class

As the developer, we know that the `Manager` class inherits from the `Employee` class and overrides some methods. As the client, we just see five methods. The client doesn't need to know that some methods are implemented in the `Manager` class and others come from the inherited `Employee` class.

## Real-World Examples of Inheritance

Let's take a look at two real-world examples of inheritance. First, I'll show you how to build an input field that only allows you to enter numbers. I'll then build an output field that formats monetary values.

### InputNumber

In this first example, we'll create an input field that allows the user to input only numerical data. As a general user interface design principle, it's much better to restrict the input to allow only for correctly formatted data while the user is entering the data, rather than allowing any input and checking its correctness later. Entering letters or other symbols in this input field, or attempting to enter multiple decimal points or multiple minus signs, should not be allowed.

The `pygwidgets` package contains an `InputText` class that allows the user to input any characters. We'll write an `InputNumber` class to allow only valid numbers as input. The new `InputNumber` class will inherit much of its code from `InputText`. We'll only need to override three methods of `InputText`: `_init_()`, `handleEvent()`, and `getValue()`. Listing 10-3 shows the `InputNumber` class that overrides these methods.

## File: MoneyExamples/InputNumber.py

```python
# InputNumber class - allows the user to enter only numbers
#
# Demo of inheritance

import pygame
from pygame.locals import *
import pygwidgets

BLACK = (0, 0, 0)
WHITE = (255, 255, 255)
# Tuple of legal editing keys
LEGAL_KEYS_TUPLE = (pygame.K_RIGHT, pygame.K_LEFT, pygame.K_HOME,
                    pygame.K_END, pygame.K_DELETE, pygame.K_BACKSPACE,
                    pygame.K_RETURN, pygame.K_KP_ENTER)
# Legal keys to be typed
LEGAL_UNICODE_CHARS = ('0123456789.-')


#
#   InputNumber inherits from InputText
#
class InputNumber(pygwidgets.InputText):

    def __init__(self, window, loc, value='', fontName=None, ❶
                 fontSize=24, width=200, textColor=BLACK,
                 backgroundColor=WHITE, focusColor=BLACK,
                 initialFocus=False, nickName=None, callback=None,
                 mask=None, keepFocusOnSubmit=False,
                 allowFloatingNumber=True, allowNegativeNumber=True):
        self.allowFloatingNumber = allowFloatingNumber
        self.allowNegativeNumber = allowNegativeNumber

        # Call the __init__ method of our base class
        super().__init__(window, loc, value, fontName, fontSize, ❷
                         width, textColor, backgroundColor,
                         focusColor, initialFocus, nickName, callback,
                         mask, keepFocusOnSubmit)

    # Override handleEvent so we can filter for proper keys
    def handleEvent(self, event): ❸
        if (event.type == pygame.KEYDOWN):
            # If it's not an editing or numeric key, ignore it
            # Unicode value is only present on key down
            allowableKey = (event.key in LEGAL_KEYS_TUPLE) or
                            (event.unicode in LEGAL_UNICODE_CHARS))
            if not allowableKey:
                return False

            if event.unicode == '-':  # user typed a minus sign
                if not self.allowNegativeNumber:
                    # If no negatives, don't pass it through
                    return False
                if self.cursorPosition > 0:
```

```
                    return False # can't put minus sign after 1st char
            if '-' in self.text:
                return False  # can't enter a second minus sign

        if event.unicode == '.':
            if not self.allowFloatingNumber:
                # If no floats, don't pass the period through
                return False
            if '.' in self.text:
                return False  # can't enter a second period

    # Allow the key to go through to the base class
    result = super().handleEvent(event)
    return result

def getValue(self): ❹
    userString = super().getValue()
    try:
        if self.allowFloatingNumber:
            returnValue = float(userString)
        else:
            returnValue = int(userString)
    except ValueError:
        raise ValueError('Entry is not a number, needs to have at least one digit.')

    return returnValue
```

*Listing 10-3: InputNumber only allows the user to enter numeric data.*

The __init__() method allows for the same parameters as the InputText base class, plus a few more ❶. It adds two Booleans: allowFloatingNumber to determine if the user should be allowed to enter floating-point numbers and allowNegativeNumber to determine if the user can enter a number starting with a minus sign. Both default to True, so the default case allows the user to enter a floating-point number and both positive and negative numbers. You could use these to restrict the user to, for example, only entering a positive integer value by setting both to False. The __init__() method saves the values of these two additional parameters in instance variables, then calls the __init__() method of the base class using the call to super() ❷.

The significant code is in the handleEvent() method ❸, which restricts the allowed keys to a small subset: the numbers zero through nine, the minus sign, a period (decimal point), ENTER, and a few editing keys. When the user presses a key, this method is called and a KEYDOWN or KEYUP event is passed in. The code first ensures that the key pressed is in the restricted set. If the user enters a key not in that set (for example, any letter), we return False to indicate that nothing important has happened in this widget, and that key is ignored.

The handleEvent() method then does a few more checks to ensure that the number being entered is legal (for example, doesn't have two periods, only has one minus sign and, so on). Whenever a valid key press is detected, the code calls the handleEvent() method of the InputText base class to do whatever it needs to do with that key (display or edit the field).

When the user presses RETURN or ENTER, client code calls the get-Value() method ❹ to get the user's entry. The getValue() method in this class calls getValue() in the InputText class to get the string from the field, then attempts to convert that string to a number. If that conversion fails, it raises an exception.

By overriding methods, we have built a very powerful new reusable class that extends the functionality of the InputText class, without changing a single line in the base class. InputText will continue to function as a class by itself, without any changes to its functionality whatsoever.

## DisplayMoney

As a second real-world example, we'll create a field to display an amount of money. To make this general, we'll display the amount with a chosen currency symbol, place that currency symbol to the left or the right of the text (as appropriate), and format the number by adding commas between every three digits, followed by a period and then two decimal digits. For example, we would like to be able to display 1234.56 US dollars as $1,234.56.

The pygwidgets package already has a DisplayText class. We can instantiate an object from that class using the following interface:

```
def __init__(self, window, loc=(0, 0), value='',
            fontName=None, fontSize=18, width=None, height=None,
            textColor=PYGWIDGETS_BLACK, backgroundColor=None,
            justified='left', nickname=None):
```

Let's assume that we have some code that creates a DisplayText object named oSomeDisplayText using the appropriate arguments. Any time that we want to update the text in a DisplayText object, we must call its setValue() method, like this:

```
oSomeDisplayText.setValue('1234.56')
```

The functionality of displaying a number (as a string) with a DisplayText object already exists. We want to create a new class named DisplayMoney that is similar to DisplayText but adds functionality, so we'll inherit from DisplayText.

Our DisplayMoney class will have an enhanced version of the setValue() method that overrides the base class's setValue() method. The DisplayMoney version will add the desired formatting, by adding a currency symbol, adding commas, optionally truncating to two decimal digits, and so on. At the end, the method will call the inherited setValue() method of the DisplayText base class and pass in a string version of the formatted text to display in the window.

We'll also add some additional setup parameters in the __init__() method to allow client code to:

- Choose the currency symbol (defaults to $)
- Place the currency symbol on the left or right (defaults to left)
- Show or hide two decimal places (defaults to show)

Listing 10-4 shows the code of our new `DisplayMoney` class.

**File: MoneyExamples/DisplayMoney.py**

```python
# DisplayMoney class - displays a number as an amount of money
#
#   Demo of inheritance

import pygwidgets

BLACK = (0, 0, 0)

#
#   DisplayMoney class inherits from DisplayText class
#
❶ class DisplayMoney(pygwidgets.DisplayText):

❷     def __init__(self, window, loc, value=None,
                   fontName=None, fontSize=24, width=150, height=None,
                   textColor=BLACK, backgroundColor=None,
                   justified='left', nickname=None, currencySymbol='$',
                   currencySymbolOnLeft=True, showCents=True):

❸         self.currencySymbol = currencySymbol
           self.currencySymbolOnLeft = currencySymbolOnLeft
           self.showCents = showCents
           if value is None:
               value = 0.00

           # Call the __init__ method of our base class
❹         super().__init__(window, loc, value,
                       fontName, fontSize, width, height,
                       textColor, backgroundColor, justified)

❺     def setValue(self, money):
           if money == '':
               money = 0.00

           money = float(money)

           if self.showCents:
               money = '{:,.2f}'.format(money)
           else:
               money = '{:,.0f}'.format(money)

           if self.currencySymbolOnLeft:
               theText = self.currencySymbol + money
           else:
               theText = money + self.currencySymbol

           # Call the setValue method of our base class
❻         super().setValue(theText)
```

*Listing 10-4: DisplayMoney displays a number formatted as a monetary value.*

In the class definition, we explicitly inherit from pygwidgets.DisplayText ❶. The DisplayMoney class only contains two methods: __init__() and setValue(). These two methods override the methods with the same names in the base class.

A client instantiates a DisplayMoney object like this:

```
oDisplayMoney = DisplayMoney(widow, (100, 100), 1234.56)
```

With this line, the __init__() method in DisplayMoney ❷ will run and override the __init__() method in the base class. This method does some initialization, including saving any client preferences for the currency symbol, the side on which to show the symbol, and whether or not we should show cents, all in instance variables ❸. The method ends with a call to the __init__() method of the base class, DisplayText ❹ (which it finds by calling super()), and passes on the data required by that method.

Later, the client makes a call like this to show a value:

```
oDisplayMoney.setValue(12233.44)
```

The setValue() method ❺ in the DisplayMoney class runs to create a version of the amount of money formatted as a currency value. The method ends by calling the inherited setValue() method in the DisplayText class ❻ to set the new text to display.

When a call is made to any other method with an instance of DisplayMoney, the version residing in DisplayText will run. Most importantly, every time through the loop, the client code should call oDisplayMoney.draw(), which draws the field in the window. Since DisplayMoney does *not* have a draw() method, that call will go to the DisplayText base class, which does have a draw() method.

## Example Usage

Figure 10-5 shows the output of an example program that takes advantage of both the InputNumber and DisplayMoney classes. The user enters a number into an InputNumber field. When the user presses OK or ENTER, that value will be displayed in the two DisplayMoney fields. The first field shows the number with decimal places, and the second rounds to the closest dollar using different initial settings.

Listing 10-5 contains the full code of the main program. Notice that the code creates a single InputNumber object and two DisplayMoney objects.

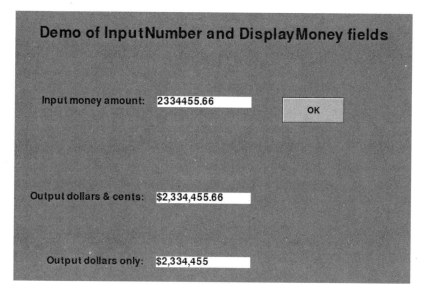

Figure 10-5: A client program where the user enters an amount into an InputNumber field and the amount is displayed in two DisplayMoney fields

## File: MoneyExamples/Main_MoneyExample.py

```
#   Money example
#
#   Demonstrates overriding inherited DisplayText and InputText methods

# 1 - Import packages
import pygame
from pygame.locals import *
import sys
import pygwidgets
from DisplayMoney import *
from InputNumber import *

# 2 - Define constants
BLACK = (0, 0, 0)
BLACKISH = (10, 10, 10)
GRAY = (128, 128, 128)
WHITE = (255, 255, 255)
BACKGROUND_COLOR = (0, 180, 180)
WINDOW_WIDTH = 640
WINDOW_HEIGHT = 480
FRAMES_PER_SECOND = 30

# 3 - Initialize the world
pygame.init()
window = pygame.display.set_mode([WINDOW_WIDTH, WINDOW_HEIGHT])
clock = pygame.time.Clock()

# 4 - Load assets: image(s), sound(s), etc.
```

```python
# 5 - Initialize variables
title = pygwidgets.DisplayText(window, (0, 40),
                              'Demo of InputNumber and DisplayMoney fields',
                              fontSize=36, width=WINDOW_WIDTH, justified='center')

inputCaption = pygwidgets.DisplayText(window, (20, 150),
                                      'Input money amount:', fontSize=24,
                                      width=190, justified='right')
inputField = InputNumber(window, (230, 150), '', width=150, inputFocus=True)
okButton = pygwidgets.TextButton(window, (430, 150), 'OK')

outputCaption1 = pygwidgets.DisplayText(window, (20, 300),
                                        'Output dollars & cents: ', fontSize=24,
                                        width=190, justified='right')
moneyField1 = DisplayMoney(window, (230, 300), '', textColor=BLACK,
                           backgroundColor=WHITE, width=150)

outputCaption2 = pygwidgets.DisplayText(window, (20, 400),
                                        'Output dollars only: ', fontSize=24,
                                        width=190, justified='right')
moneyField2 = DisplayMoney(window, (230, 400), '', textColor=BLACK,
                           backgroundColor=WHITE, width=150,
                           showCents=False)

# 6 - Loop forever
while True:

    # 7 - Check for and handle events
    for event in pygame.event.get():
        # If the event was a click on the close box, quit pygame and the program
        if event.type == pygame.QUIT:
            pygame.quit()
            sys.exit()

        # Pressing Return/Enter or clicking OK triggers action
        if inputField.handleEvent(event) or okButton.handleEvent(event): ❶
            try:
                theValue = inputField.getValue()
            except ValueError:  # any remaining error
                inputField.setValue('(not a number)')
            else:  # input was OK
                theText = str(theValue)
                moneyField1.setValue(theText)
                moneyField2.setValue(theText)

    # 8  Do any "per frame" actions

    # 9 - Clear the window
    window.fill(BACKGROUND_COLOR)

    # 10 - Draw all window elements
    title.draw()
    inputCaption.draw()
    inputField.draw()
    okButton.draw()
```

```
outputCaption1.draw()
moneyField1.draw()
outputCaption2.draw()
moneyField2.draw()

# 11 - Update the window
pygame.display.update()

# 12 - Slow things down a bit
clock.tick(FRAMES_PER_SECOND)  # make pygame wait
```

*Listing 10-5: The main program to demonstrate the `InputNumber` and `DisplayMoney` classes*

The user enters the number into an `InputNumber` field. As the user types, any inappropriate characters are filtered out and ignored by the `handleEvent()` method. When the user clicks OK ❶, the code reads the input and passes it to the two `DisplayMoney` fields. The first shows the dollar and cents amount (with two decimal digits), while the second shows the value in dollars only. Both add a $ as the currency symbol and add commas every three digits.

## Multiple Classes Inheriting from the Same Base Class

Multiple different classes can inherit from the same base class. You can build a very general base class, then construct any number of subclasses that inherit from it. Figure 10-6 is a representation of this relationship.

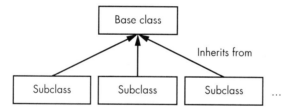

*Figure 10-6: Three or more different subclasses inheriting from a common base class*

Each of the different subclasses can then be a variant (a more specific version) of the generic base class. Each subclass can override any methods of the base class that it wants to or needs to, independent of any other subclass.

Let's walk through an example using the Shapes program from Chapter 9 that created and drew circles, squares, and triangles. The code also allowed the user to click on any shape in the window to see the area of that shape.

The program was implemented with three different shape classes: `Circle`, `Square`, and `Triangle`. If we look back at those three classes, we find that each one has this exact same method:

```
def getType(self):
    return self.shapeType
```

Further, looking at the __init__() methods of the three classes, we find that there is some common code that remembers the window, chooses a random color, and chooses a random location:

```
self.window = window
self.color = random.choice((RED, GREEN, BLUE))
self.x = random.randrange(1, maxWidth - 100)
self.y = random.randrange(1, maxHeight - 100)
```

Finally, each class sets the instance variable self.shapeType to an appropriate string.

Whenever we find a set of classes that implement the exact same method and/or share some code in a commonly named method, we should recognize that this is a good candidate for inheritance.

Let's extract the common code from the three classes and build a common base class named Shape, shown in Listing 10-6.

### File: InheritedShapes/ShapeBasic.py

```
# Shape class - basic

import random

# Set up the colors
RED = (255, 0, 0)
GREEN = (0, 255, 0)
BLUE = (0, 0, 255)

class Shape():

❶   def __init__(self, window, shapeType, maxWidth, maxHeight):
        self.window = window
        self.shapeType = shapeType
        self.color = random.choice((RED, GREEN, BLUE))
        self.x = random.randrange(1, maxWidth - 100)
        self.y = random.randrange(25, maxHeight - 100)

❷   def getType(self):
        return self.shapeType
```

Listing 10-6: The Shape class, to be used as a base class

The class consists of only two methods: __init__() and getType(). The __init__() method ❶ remembers the data passed in in instance variables, then randomly chooses a color and a starting location (self.x and self.y). The getType() method ❷ just returns the type of the shape given at initialization.

We can now write any number of subclasses that inherit from Shape. We'll create three subclasses that will call the __init__() method of the Shape class, passing in a string that identifies its type and the size of the window. The getType() method will only appear in the Shape class, so any client calls to getType() will be handled by that method in the inherited Shape class. We'll start with the code for the Square class, shown in Listing 10-7.

## File: InheritedShapes/Square.py

```
# Square class

import pygame
from Shape import *

class Square(Shape):  ❶

    def __init__(self, window, maxWidth, maxHeight):
        super().__init__(window, 'Square', maxWidth, maxHeight)  ❷
        self.widthAndHeight = random.randrange(10, 100)
        self.rect = pygame.Rect(self.x, self.y,
                                self.widthAndHeight, self.widthAndHeight)

    def clickedInside(self, mousePoint):  ❸
        clicked - self.rect.collidcpoint(mousePoint)
        return clicked

    def getArea(self):  ❹
        theArea = self.widthAndHeight * self.widthAndHeight
        return theArea

    def draw(self):  ❺
        pygame.draw.rect(self.window, self.color,
                         (self.x, self.y, self.widthAndHeight, self.widthAndHeight))
```

Listing 10-7: The Square class that inherits from the Shape class

The Square class starts by inheriting from the Shape class ❶. The __init__() method calls the __init__() method of its base class (or superclass) ❷, identifying this shape as a square and randomly choosing its size.

Next we have three methods whose implementation is specific to a square. The clickedInside() method only needs to make a call to rect.collidepoint() to determine if a click happened inside its rectangle ❸. The getArea() method simply multiplies the widthAndHeight by the widthAndHeight ❹. Finally, the draw() method draws a rectangle using the value of widthAndHeight ❺.

Listing 10-8 shows the Circle class, which has also been modified to inherit from the Shape class.

## File: InheritedShapes/Circle.py

```
# Circle class

import pygame
from Shape import *
import math
```

```
class Circle(Shape):

    def __init__(self, window, maxWidth, maxHeight):
        super().__init__(window, 'Circle', maxWidth, maxHeight)
        self.radius = random.randrange(10, 50)
        self.centerX = self.x + self.radius
        self.centerY = self.y + self.radius
        self.rect = pygame.Rect(self.x, self.y, self.radius * 2, self.radius * 2)

    def clickedInside(self, mousePoint):
        theDistance = math.sqrt(((mousePoint[0] - self.centerX) ** 2) +
                                ((mousePoint[1] - self.centerY) ** 2))
        if theDistance <= self.radius:
            return True
        else:
            return False

    def getArea(self):
        theArea = math.pi * (self.radius ** 2)
        return theArea

    def draw(self):
        pygame.draw.circle(self.window, self.color, (self.centerX, self.centerY),
                           self.radius, 0)
```

Listing 10-8: The Circle class that inherits from the Shape class

The Circle class also contains the clickedInside(), getArea(), and draw() methods, whose implementation is specific to a circle.

Finally, Listing 10-9 shows the code of the Triangle class.

**File: InheritedShapes/Triangle.py**

```
# Triangle class

import pygame
from Shape import *

class Triangle(Shape):

    def __init__(self, window, maxWidth, maxHeight):
        super().__init__(window, 'Triangle', maxWidth, maxHeight)
        self.width = random.randrange(10, 100)
        self.height = random.randrange(10, 100)
        self.triangleSlope = -1 * (self.height / self.width)
        self.rect = pygame.Rect(self.x, self.y, self.width, self.height)

    def clickedInside(self, mousePoint):
        inRect = self.rect.collidepoint(mousePoint)
        if not inRect:
            return False

        # Do some math to see if the point is inside the triangle
        xOffset = mousePoint[0] - self.x
```

```
        yOffset = mousePoint[1] - self.y
        if xOffset == 0:
            return True

        pointSlopeFromYIntercept = (yOffset - self.height) / xOffset  # rise over run
        if pointSlopeFromYIntercept < 1:
            return True
        else:
            return False

    def getArea(self):
        theArea = .5 * self.width * self.height
        return theArea

    def draw(self):
        pygame.draw.polygon(self.window, self.color, (
                            (self.x, self.y + self.height),
                            (self.x, self.y),
                            (self.x + self.width, self.y)))
```

Listing 10-9: The `Triangle` class that inherits from the `Shape` class

The main code we used for testing in Chapter 9 doesn't have to change at all. As a client of these new classes, it instantiates Square, Circle, and Triangle objects without having to worry about the implementation of those classes. It doesn't need to know that each is subclassed from a common Shape class.

## Abstract Classes and Methods

Unfortunately, our Shape base class has a potential bug. At the moment, a client could instantiate a generic Shape object, which is too generic to have its own getArea() method. Further, all classes that inherit from the Shape class (like Square, Circle, and Triangle) *must* implement clickedInside(), getArea(), and draw(). To solve both of these problems, I'll introduce the concepts of an *abstract class* and an *abstract method*.

---

**abstract class**    A class that is *not* intended to be instantiated directly, but only to be used as a base class by one or more subclasses. (In some other languages, an abstract class is referred to as a *virtual class*.)

---

**abstract method**    A method that *must* be overridden in every subclass.

---

Often, a base class cannot correctly implement an abstract method because it cannot know the detailed data it should operate on, or it may not be possible to implement a general algorithm. Instead, all subclasses need to implement their own version of the abstract method.

In our shapes example, we want the Shape class to be an abstract class so no client code can instantiate a Shape object. Further, our Shape class should indicate that all its subclasses need to implement the clickedInside(), getArea(), and draw() methods.

Python does not have a keyword to designate a class or method as abstract. However, the Python Standard Library contains the abc module, short for *abstract base class*, which is designed to help developers build abstract base classes and methods.

Let's take a look at what we need to do to build an abstract class with abstract methods. To begin, we need to import two things from the abc module:

```
from abc import ABC, abstractmethod
```

Next, we need to indicate that the class we want to act as an abstract base class should inherit from the ABC class, which we do by putting ABC inside parentheses after the class name:

```
class <classWeWantToDesignateAsAbstract>(ABC):
```

We then must use the special decorator @abstractmethod before any methods that must be overwritten by all subclasses:

```
@abstractmethod
def <someMethodThatMustBeOverwritten>(self, ...):
```

Listing 10-10 shows how we can mark our Shape class as an abstract base class and indicate its abstract methods.

**File: InheritedShapes/Shape.py**

```
# Shape class
#
# To be used as a base class for other classes

import random
from abc import ABC, abstractmethod

# Set up the colors
RED = (255, 0, 0)
GREEN = (0, 255, 0)
BLUE = (0, 0, 255)

❶ class Shape(ABC):   # identifies this as an abstract base class

❷     def __init__(self, window, shapeType, maxWidth, maxHeight):
           self.window = window
           self.shapeType = shapeType
           self.color = random.choice((RED, GREEN, BLUE))
           self.x = random.randrange(1, maxWidth - 100)
           self.y = random.randrange(25, maxHeight - 100)

❸     def getType(self):
           return self.shapeType
```

```
❹ @abstractmethod
   def clickedInside(self, mousePoint):
       raise NotImplementedError

❺ @abstractmethod
   def getArea(self):
       raise NotImplementedError

❻ @abstractmethod
   def draw(self):
       raise NotImplementedError
```

*Listing 10-10: The Shape base class that inherits from ABC with abstract methods*

The Shape class inherits from the ABC class ❶, telling Python to prevent client code from instantiating a Shape object directly. Any attempt to do so results in the following error message:

```
TypeError: Can't instantiate abstract class Shape with abstract methods
clickedInside, draw, getArea
```

The __init__() ❷ and getType() ❸ methods contain code that will be shared by all subclasses of Shape.

The clickedInside() ❹, getArea() ❺, and draw() ❻ methods are all preceded by the @abstractmethod decorator. This decorator indicates that these methods *must* be overwritten by all subclasses of Shape. Since these methods in this abstract class will never run, the implementation here consists only of raise NotImplementedError to further emphasize that the method doesn't do anything.

Let's extend the shape demonstration program to add a new Rectangle class, as shown in Listing 10-11. The Rectangle class inherits from the abstract Shape class and therefore must implement the clickedInside(), getArea(), and draw() methods. I'll make an intentional error in this subclass to show what happens.

**File: InheritedShapes/Rectangle.py**

```
# Rectangle class

import pygame
from Shape import *

class Rectangle(Shape):

    def __init__(self, window, maxWidth, maxHeight):
        super().__init__(window, 'Rectangle', maxWidth, maxHeight)
        self.width = random.randrange(10, 100)
        self.height = random.randrange(10, 100)
        self.rect = pygame.Rect(self.x, self.y, self.width, self.height)

    def clickedInside(self, mousePoint):
```

```
        clicked = self.rect.collidepoint(mousePoint)
        return clicked

    def getArea(self):
        theArea = self.width * self.height
        return theArea
```

*Listing 10-11: The* Rectangle *class that implements* clickedInside() *and* getArea()*, but not* draw()

As a demonstration, this class mistakenly does not contain a draw() method. Listing 10-12 shows a modified version of the main code that includes the creation of Rectangle objects.

### File: InheritedShapes/Main_ShapesWithRectangle.py

```
shapesList = []
shapeClassesTuple = ('Square', 'Circle', 'Triangle', 'Rectangle')
for i in range(0, N_SHAPES):
    randomlyChosenClass = random.choice(shapeClassesTuple)
    oShape = randomlyChosenClass(window, WINDOW_WIDTH, WINDOW_HEIGHT)
    shapesList.append(oShape)
```

*Listing 10-12: The main code that randomly creates* Squares, Circles, Triangles, *and* Rectangles

When this code attempts to create a Rectangle object, Python generates this error message:

```
TypeError: Can't instantiate abstract class Rectangle with abstract method
draw
```

This tells us that we cannot instantiate a Rectangle object because we did not write a draw() method in our Rectangle class. Adding a draw() method to the Rectangle class (with appropriate code to draw the rectangle) fixes the error.

## How pygwidgets Uses Inheritance

The pygwidgets module uses inheritance to share common code. For example, consider the two button classes we discussed in Chapter 7: TextButton and CustomButton. The TextButton class requires a string to be used as a label on the button, while the CustomButton class requires you to supply your own art. The way that you create an instance of each of these classes is different—you need to specify a different set of arguments. However, once created, all the remaining methods of both objects are exactly the same. That's because the two classes inherit from a common base class, named PygWidgetsButton (Figure 10-7).

PygWidgetsButton is an abstract class. Client code is not supposed to create an instance of it, and attempting to do so will generate an error message.

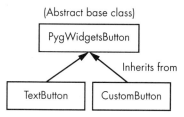

Figure 10-7: The pygwidgets TextButton and CustomButton classes both inherit from PygWidgetsButton.

Instead, PygWidgetsButton is subclassed by the TextButton and CustomButton classes. Those classes each provide the single method, __init__(), which will do whatever is needed to initialize their type of button. Each will then pass on identical arguments to the __init__() method of the base class, PygWidgetsButton.

The TextButton class is used to build a text-based button with minimal art. This is helpful when trying to get programs up and running quickly. Here is the interface for creating a TextButton object:

```
def __init__(self, window, loc, text, width=None, height=40,
            textColor=PYGWIDGETS_BLACK,
            upColor= PYGWIDGETS_NORMAL_GRAY,
            overColor= PYGWIDGETS_OVER_GRAY,
            downColor=PYGWIDGETS_DOWN_GRAY,
            fontName=None, fontSize=20, soundOnClick=None,
            enterToActivate=False, callBack=None, nickname=None)
```

While many of the parameters default to reasonable values, the caller must provide a value for text, which will appear on the button. The __init__() method itself creates "surfaces" (images) for the button that are used in displaying a standard button. The code to create a typical TextButton object looks like this:

```
oButton = pygwidgets.TextButton(window, (50, 50), 'Text Button')
```

When drawn, the user sees a button that looks like Figure 10-8.

**Text Button**

Figure 10-8: An example of a typical TextButton

The CustomButton class is used to build a button using artwork the client supplies. Here is the interface for creating a CustomButton:

```
def __init__(self, window, loc, up, down=None, over=None,
            disabled=None, soundOnClick=None,
            nickname=None, enterToActivate=False):
```

The key difference is that this version of the __init__() method requires the caller to supply a value for the up parameter (remember, a button has four images: up, down, disabled, and over). You can optionally also supply down, over, and disabled images. For any image that is not supplied, CustomButton makes a copy of the up image of the button and uses that.

The last line of the __init__() methods for *both* the TextButton and CustomButton classes is a call to the __init__() method of the common base class, PygWidgetsButton. Both calls pass in four images for the button, along with other arguments:

```
super().__init__(window, loc, surfaceUp, surfaceOver,
                 surfaceDown, surfaceDisabled, buttonRect,
                 soundOnClick, nickname, enterToActivate, callBack)
```

From the client's point of view, you see two completely different classes with many methods (most of which are identical). But from the implementer's point of view, you can now see how inheritance allowed us to override the single __init__() method in the base class to provide client programmers with two similar, but very useful, ways of creating buttons. The two classes share everything other than the __init__() method. Therefore, the way that the buttons function, and the method calls that are available (handleEvent(), draw(), disable(), enable(), and so on), must be identical.

There are a number of benefits to this kind of inheritance. First, it provides consistency for both the client code and the end user: TextButton and CustomButton objects work the same way. It also makes bugs easier to fix—fixing a bug in a base class means you have then fixed the bug in all subclasses that inherit from it. Finally, if you add functionality in the base class, it is available immediately in all classes that inherit from the base class.

## Class Hierarchy

Any class can be used as a base class, even a subclass that already inherits from another base class. This kind of relationship, known as a *class hierarchy*, is depicted in Figure 10-9.

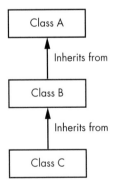

*Figure 10-9: A class hierarchy*

In this figure, class C inherits from class B, which inherits from class A. Therefore, class C is a subclass and class B is a base class, but class B is also a subclass of class A. So, class B serves in both roles. In cases like this, class C inherits not only all the methods and instance variables in class B, but also all the methods and instance variables in class A. This type of hierarchy can be very useful when building more and more specific classes. Class A can be very general, class B more detailed, and class C even more specific.

Figure 10-10 provides a different way to think about the relationships in a class hierarchy.

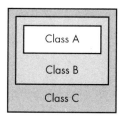

*Figure 10-10: A different way of portraying a class hierarchy*

Here, the client sees only class C, but this class is made up of all the methods and instance variables defined collectively in classes C, B, and A.

The pygwidgets package uses a class hierarchy for all widgets. The first class in pygwidgets is the abstract class PygWidget, which supplies basic functionality to all widgets in the package. Its code consists of methods that allow for showing and hiding, enabling and disabling, getting and setting the location, and getting the nickname (internal name) of any widget.

There are other classes in pygwidgets that are used as abstract classes, including the aforementioned PygWidgetsButton, which is the base class of both TextButton and CustomButton. Figure 10-11 should help make this relationship clear.

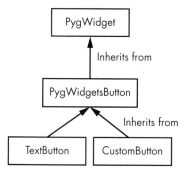

*Figure 10-11: Class hierarchy in* pygwidgets

As you can see, the `PygWidgetsButton` class is both a subclass of `PygWidget` and a base class for `TextButton` and `CustomButton`.

## The Difficulty of Programming with Inheritance

When developing using inheritance, it can be difficult to understand what to put where. You're constantly asking yourself questions like: Should this instance variable be in the base class? Is there enough common code in subclasses to create a method in the base class? What are appropriate parameters for a method in a subclass? What are appropriate parameters and defaults to be used in a base class that expects to be overridden or called from a subclass?

Attempting to understand the interactions among all the variables and methods in a hierarchy of classes can be an extremely difficult, tricky, and frustrating task. This is especially true when reading the code of a class hierarchy developed by another programmer. To fully understand what's going on, you often have to become familiar with the code in the base classes all the way up the hierarchy.

For example, imagine a hierarchy in which class D is a subclass of C, which is a subclass of B, which is a subclass of the base class A. In class D, you may encounter code that branches based on the value of an instance variable, but that variable might never be set in the code of class D. In cases like this, you must look for the instance variable in the code of class C. If it is not found there, then you must look in the code of class B, and so on.

When designing a class hierarchy, perhaps the best way to avoid this problem is to only call methods and use instance variables inherited from one layer up in the hierarchy. In our example, code in class D should only make calls to methods in class C, while class C should only make calls to methods in class B, and so on. This is a simplistic version of the *Law of Demeter*. Stated simply, you (meaning objects) should only talk to your immediate friends (nearby objects) and never talk to strangers (distant objects). A detailed discussion is beyond the scope of this book, but there are many references available on the internet.

Another approach, which we first talked about in Chapter 4, is to take advantage of *composition*, where an object instantiates one or more other objects. The key difference is that inheritance is used to model an "is a" relationship, whereas composition uses a "has a" relationship. For example, if we wanted to have a spinbox widget (an editable text number field with an up and a down arrow), we could build a `SpinBox` class that instantiates a `DisplayNumber` object and two `CustomButton` objects for the arrows. Each of these objects already knows how to handle its user interactions.

## MULTIPLE INHERITANCE

You've seen how a class can inherit from another class. In fact, Python (like some other programming languages) allows a class to inherit from more than just one class. This is known as *multiple inheritance*. The Python syntax is for inheriting from more than one class is quite straightforward:

```
class SomeClass(<BaseClass1>, <BaseClass2>, ...):
```

However, it's important to be aware that multiple inheritance can potentially introduce conflicts when the base classes you inherit from contain identically named methods and/or instance variables. Python does have rules (known as the *method resolution order*, or *MRO*) to resolve these potential problems. I consider this an advanced topic and will not cover it here, but if you want to look into it, a detailed discussion can be found at *https://www .python.org/download/releases/2.3/mro*.

## Summary

This was a very ambitious chapter on the topic of inheritance: the art of "programming by difference." The basic idea of inheritance is to build a class (a subclass) that incorporates all the methods and instance variables of another class (a base class), thereby allowing you to reuse existing code. Your new subclass can choose to use or override the methods of the base class, as well as define its own methods. A method in a subclass can find the base class by using a call to super().

We built two classes, InputNumber and DisplayMoney that provide highly reusable functionality. These classes are implemented as subclasses that use classes in the pygwidgets package as base classes.

Any client code that uses your subclass will see an interface that incorporates methods defined in both the subclass and the base class. Any number of subclasses can be built using the same base class. An abstract class is one that is not intended to be instantiated by client code, but rather is intended only to be inherited from by subclasses. An abstract method in a base class is one that *must* be overridden in each subclass.

We worked through a number of examples to demonstrate inheritance in the pygwidgets package, including how the TextButton and CustomButton classes both inherit from a common base class, PygWidgetsButton.

I showed how you can build a class hierarchy, where a class inherits from another class, which in turn inherits from a third class, and so on.

Inheritance can be complex—reading someone else's code can be confusing—but as we've seen, inheritance can be extremely powerful.

# 11

## MANAGING MEMORY USED BY OBJECTS

This chapter will explain a few important concepts of Python and OOP, such as the lifetime of an object (including deleting an object) and class variables, that didn't fit well in the earlier chapters in this section. To tie all of this together, we'll build a small game. I'll also introduce slots, a memory management technique for objects. This chapter should give you a better understanding of how your code can affect the way that memory is used by objects.

# Object Lifetime

In Chapter 2, I defined an object as "Data, plus code that acts on that data, over time." I've talked quite a bit about data (instance variables) and the code that acts on that data (methods), but I haven't explained much about the time aspect. That will be my focus here.

You already know that a program can create an object at any time. Often, a program will create one or more objects at startup and use those objects throughout its operation. However, in many cases a program will want to create an object when it needs it, but release or remove the object when it's done using it to free up the resources that the object uses (memory, files, network connections, and so on). Here are a few examples:

- A "transaction" object that's used while a customer is making an electronic purchase. When the purchase is completed, the object is destroyed.
- An object to handle communication over the internet that's released when the communication is completed.
- Transient objects in a game. The program could instantiate many copies of bad guys, aliens, spaceships, and so on; as the player destroys each one, the program can eliminate the underlying object.

The period of time from the instantiation of an object until it is destroyed is known as the object's *lifetime*. To understand the lifetime of an object, you first need to know about a related underlying concept having to do with the implementation of objects in Python (and some other OOP languages): the reference count.

## Reference Count

There are a number of different implementations of Python. The following discussion of reference counts applies to the official version released by the Python Software Foundation—the version downloaded from *python.org*—that's commonly known as *CPython*. Other implementations of Python may use a different approach.

Part of the philosophy of Python is that programmers should never have to worry about the details of managing memory. Python takes care of that for you. However, having a basic idea of how Python manages memory will be helpful in understanding how and when objects are released back to the system.

Whenever a program instantiates an object from a class, Python allocates memory for the storage of the instance variables defined in the class. Each object also contains an extra internal field called a *reference count*, which keeps track of how many different variables refer to that object. I show how this works in Listing 11-1.

**File: ReferenceCount.py**

```
# Reference count example

class Square():
    def __init__(self, width, color):
        self.width = width
        self.color = color

    # Instantiate an object
oSquare1 = Square(5, 'red')
print(oSquare1)
# Reference count of the Square object is 1

# Now set another variable to the same object
oSquare2 = oSquare1
print(oSquare2)
# Reference count of the Square object is 2
```

❶ at `class Square():`, ❷ at `oSquare1 = Square(5, 'red')`, ❸ at `oSquare2 = oSquare1`

*Listing 11-1: A simple Square class for demonstrating reference counting*

We can use Python Tutor (*http://pythontutor.com/*) to step through our code. We start with a simple Square class ❶ containing a few instance variables. We then instantiate an object and assign it to the variable oSquare1 ❷. Figure 11-1 shows what we see after instantiating the first object: as you can see, the variable oSquare1 refers to an instance of the Square class.

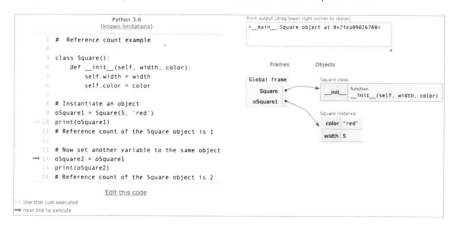

*Figure 11-1: A single variable (oSquare1) referring to an object*

Next, we set a second variable to refer to the same Square object ❸ and print the value of the new variable. Note that the statement oSquare2 = oSquare1 does not make a new copy of the Square object! Figure 11-2 shows what we see after executing these two lines.

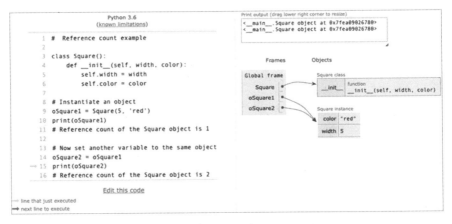

Figure 11-2: Two variables referring to the same object

The variables oSquare1 and oSquare2 both refer to the same Square object. You can also see in the top box that the two calls to print() show the same memory address. Therefore, the reference count of the object is now 2. If we were to assign another variable:

```
oSquare3 = oSquare2  # or oSquare1
```

the reference count would be incremented to 3 (because all three variables would refer to the same object), and so on.

The reference count of an object is important because when it reaches zero, Python marks the relevant memory as no longer in use by the program. This is known as being *marked as garbage*. Python has a garbage collector that runs to reclaim any blocks of memory that have been marked as garbage; I'll discuss that later in this chapter.

The Python Standard Library contains the getrefcount() function, which returns the number of variables that refer to an object. Here, we use it to see the reference count after the first instantiation of a Square object from the Square class:

```
oSquare1 = Square(5, 'red')
print('Reference count is', sys.getrefcount(oSquare1))
```

This prints a count of 2. This may be surprising—you likely expected that the count would be 1. However, as the documentation of this function explains, "The count returned is generally one higher than you might expect, because it includes the (temporary) reference as an argument to getrefcount()."

## Incrementing the Reference Count

There are a few ways that an object's reference count is incremented:

1. When an additional variable is assigned to refer to the same object:

```
oSquare2 = oSquare1
```

2. When an object is passed into a function and therefore a local parameter variable is set to refer to the object:

```
def myFunctionOrMethod(oLocalSquareParam):
    # oLocalSquareParam now refers to wherever the argument refers to
    <body of myFunctionOrMethod>

myFunctionOrMethod(oSquare1)   # call the function and pass in the object
```

3. When an object is put into a container such as a list or a dictionary:

```
myList = [oSquare1, someValue, someOtherValue]
```

If oSquare1 already refers to an object, after executing this line, the list contains an additional reference to the same Square object.

## Decrementing the Reference Count

Decrementing the reference count also happens in a few ways. To demonstrate this, let's create an object and increment its reference count:

```
oSquare1 = Square(20, BLACK)
oSquare2 = oSquare1
myList = [oSquare1]
myFunctionOrMethod(oSquare1)   # call the function and pass in the object
```

When myFunctionOrMethod() starts, the reference to the object is copied into a local parameter variable for use inside the function. The reference count of this Square object is currently 4: two object variables, one copy inside a list, plus a local parameter variable inside the function. This reference count can be decremented:

1. When any variable that refers to an object is reassigned. For example:

```
oSquare2 = 5
```

2. Whenever a local variable that refers to an object goes out of scope. When a variable is created inside of a function or method, the scope of that variable is limited to that function or method. When the execution

of the current function or method ends, that variable literally goes away. In this example, when `myFunctionOrMethod()` ends, the local variable that refers to the object is eliminated.

3. When an object is removed from a container like a list, tuple, or dictionary, for example with:

```
myList.pop()
```

Calling the `remove()` method of a list would also decrement the reference count.

4. When you use the `del` statement to explicitly delete a variable that refers to an object. This eliminates the variable and reduces the reference count of the object:

```
del oSquare3  # delete the variable
```

5. If the reference count of the object's container (in this case, `myList`) goes to zero:

```
del myList  # where myList has an element that refers to an object
```

If you have a variable that refers to an object, and you want to keep the variable but lose the reference to the object, you can execute a statement like the following:

```
oSquare1 = None
```

That keeps the variable name, but lowers the reference count of the object.

### Death Notice

When the reference count of an object goes to zero, Python knows that the object can be safely deleted. Right before destroying an object, Python calls a magic method of that object named __del__() to inform the object of its impending demise.

In any class, you can write your own version of the __del__() method. In your version, you can include any code you want your object to execute (ha! interesting word choice here) before the object disappears forever. For example, your object may want to close a file, close a network connection, and so on.

When an object is deleted, Python checks to see if any of its instance variables refer to other objects. If so, the reference counts of those objects are also decremented. If this results in another object's reference count going to zero, then that object is deleted as well. This type of chained or *cascading* deletion can go on as many layers deep as is necessary. Listing 11-2 provides an example.

**File: DeleteExample_Teacher_Student.py**

```
# Student class

class Student():
    def __init__(self, name):
        self.name = name
        print('Creating Student object', self.name)

❶ def __del__(self):
        print('In the __del__ method for student:', self.name)

# Teacher class
class Teacher():
    def __init__(self):
        print('Creating the Teacher object')
❷       self.oStudent1 = Student('Joe')
        self.oStudent2 = Student('Sue')
        self.oStudent3 = Student('Chris')

❸ def __del__(self):
        print('In the __del__ method for Teacher')

# Instantiate the Teacher object (that creates Student objects)
❹ oTeacher = Teacher()

# Delete the Teacher object
❺ del oTeacher
```

*Listing 11-2: Classes demonstrating __del__() methods*

Here we have two classes, Student and Teacher. The main code instantiates one Teacher object ❹, and its __init__() method creates three instances of the Student class ❷, one each for Joe, Sue, and Chris. Therefore, after starting up, the Teacher object has three instance variables that are Student objects. The output from the first part is:

```
Creating the Teacher object
Creating Student object Joe
Creating Student object Sue
Creating Student object Chris
```

Next, the main code uses the del statement to delete the Teacher object ❺. Since we wrote a __del__() method in the Teacher class ❸, that method of the Teacher *object* is called—which, for demonstration purposes, only prints a message.

When the Teacher object is deleted, Python sees that it contains three other objects (the three Student objects). So, Python lowers the reference count of each of those objects from 1 to 0.

Once this happens, the __del__() method of the Student objects is called ❶, and each outputs a message. The memory used by all three of the Student objects is then marked as garbage. The output from the end of the program is:

```
In the __del__ method for Teacher
In the __del__ method for student: Joe
In the __del__ method for student: Sue
In the __del__ method for student: Chris
```

Because Python keeps track of reference counts for all objects, you rarely, if ever, have to worry about memory management in Python and rarely need to include a __del__() method. However, you might consider using a del statement to explicitly tell Python to delete objects that use a very large amount of memory when you are no longer using them. For example, you might want to delete an object that loads a large number of records from a database, or loads many images, when you are done using it. Also, it is not guaranteed that Python will call the __del__() method when a program exits, so you should avoid putting any program-ending critical code in this method.

### Garbage Collection

When an object is deleted, either through the reference count going to zero or though the explicit use of a del statement, as the programmer you should consider the object inaccessible.

However, the specific implementation of the garbage collector is completely up to Python. The details of the algorithm that decides when the actual garbage collection code runs are not important to you as the programmer. It may run when your program instantiates an object and Python needs to allocate memory, or at random times, or at certain scheduled times. The algorithm may change from one release of Python to another. Whichever it is, Python will take care of garbage collection, and you needn't worry about the specifics.

## Class Variables

I have talked extensively about how instance variables are defined in a class and how each object instantiated from a class gets its own set of all the instance variables. The prefix self. is used to identify each instance variable. However, you can also create *class variables* at the class level.

**class variable**   A variable that is defined in and owned by a class. Only one of each class variable exists, independent of how many instances of that class are created.

You create a class variable with an assignment statement, which by convention is placed between the class statement and the first def statement, like so:

```
class MyDemoClass():
    myClassVariable = 0  # create a class variable and assign 0 to it
```

```
def __init__(self, <otherParameters>):
    # More code here
```

Because this class variable is owned by the class, in methods of the class you would refer to it as MyDemoClass.myClassVariable. Every object instantiated from a class has access to all class variables defined in the class.

There are two typical uses for class variables: defining a constant and creating a counter.

## Class Variable Constants

You can create a class variable to be used as a constant, like so:

```
class MyClass():
    DEGREES_IN_CIRCLE = 360  # creating a class variable constant
```

To access this constant in methods of the class, you would write MyClass.DEGREES_IN_CIRCLE.

As a reminder, Python does not actually have constants. Instead, there is a convention among Python programmers that any variable whose name consists of all uppercase letters, with words separated by underscores, is meant to be treated as a constant. That is, this type of variable should never be reassigned.

We can also use class variable constants to save on resources (memory and time). Imagine we're writing a game where we create many instances of a SpaceShip class. We create a picture of a spaceship and place the file in a folder named *images*. Before considering class variables, the __init__() method of our SpaceShip class would start by instantiating an Image object like this:

```
class SpaceShip():
    def __init__(self, window, ...):
        self.image = pygwidgets.Image(window, (0, 0),
                                      'images/ship.png')
```

This technique works fine. However, coding it this way means that not only does every object instantiated from the SpaceShip class have to take the time to load the image, but each object takes up all the memory needed to represent a copy of the same image. Instead, we can have the class load the image once, and each SpaceShip object then uses the single image kept in the class, like this:

```
class SpaceShip():
    SPACE_SHIP_IMAGE = pygame.image.load('images/ship.png')
    def __init__(self, window, ...):
        self.image = pygwidgets.Image(window, (0, 0),
                                      SpaceShip.SPACE_SHIP_IMAGE)
```

An Image object (in pygwidgets, as used here) can use either a path to an image or an already loaded image. Allowing the class to load the image only *once* makes startup faster and results in lower memory usage.

## Class Variables for Counting

A second way to use a class variable is to keep track of how many objects have been instantiated from a class. Listing 11-3 shows an example.

**File: ClassVariable.py**

```
# Sample class

class Sample():
❶ nObjects = 0  # this is a class variable of the Sample class
    def __init__(self, name):
        self.name = name
❷     Sample.nObjects = Sample.nObjects + 1

    def __del__(self):
❸     Sample.nObjects = Sample.nObjects - 1

# Instantiate 4 objects
oSample1 = Sample('A')
oSample2 = Sample('B')
oSample3 = Sample('C')
oSample4 = Sample('D')

# Delete 1 object
del oSample3

# See how many we have
print('There are', Sample.nObjects, 'Sample objects')
```

*Listing 11-3: Using a class variable for counting objects instantiated from a class*

In the `Sample` class, `nObjects` is a class variable because it is defined in the class scope, typically between the `class` statement and the first `def` statement ❶. It is used to count the number of `Sample` objects that exist and is initialized to zero. All methods refer to this variable using the name `Sample.nObjects`. Whenever a `Sample` object is instantiated, the count is incremented ❷. When one is deleted, the count is decremented ❸. The last line accesses the class variable and reports the current count.

The main code creates four objects, then deletes one. When run, this program outputs:

```
There are 3 Sample objects
```

# Putting It All Together: Balloon Sample Program

In this section, we'll take a number of different concepts we've covered and put them all together in a relatively simple game—at least, simple from the user's point of view. The game will present some number of balloons in three sizes that move upward in the window. The goal for the user is to pop as many balloons as possible before they float off the top of the window. Small balloons are worth 30 points, medium balloons are worth 20 points, and large balloons are worth 10 points.

The game could be extended to include many levels with faster-moving balloons, but for now, there is only a single level. The size and location of each balloon is chosen at random. Before each round, a Start button becomes available that allows the user to play again. Figure 11-3 is a screenshot of the game in action.

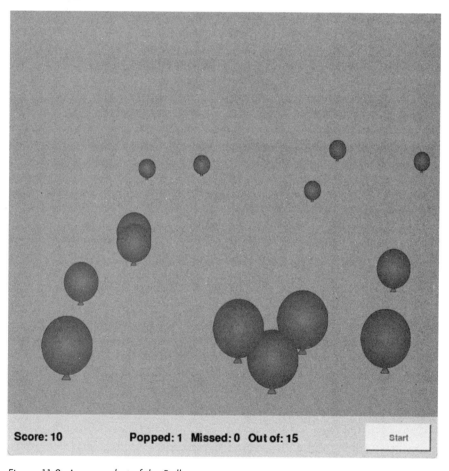

Figure 11-3: A screenshot of the Balloon game

Figure 11-4 shows the project folder for the game.

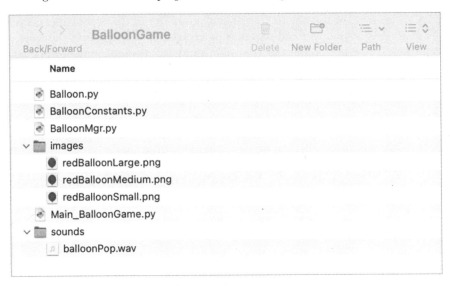

Figure 11-4: The Balloon game project folder

The game is implemented with four Python source files:

***Main_BalloonGame.py***    Main code, runs the main loop

***BalloonMgr.py***    Contains the `BalloonMgr` class that handles all `Balloon` objects

***Balloon.py***    Contains the `Balloon` class and `BalloonSmall`, `BalloonMedium`, and `BalloonLarge` subclasses

***BalloonConstants.py***    Contains constants used by more than one file

Figure 11-5 shows an object diagram of the implementation.

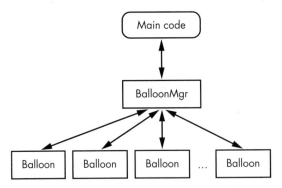

Figure 11-5: An object diagram of the Balloon game

The main code (found in *Main_BalloonGame.py*) instantiates a single balloon manager (oBalloonMgr) object from the `BalloonMgr` class. The balloon manager then instantiates a number of balloons, each chosen randomly from the `BalloonSmall`, `BalloonMedium`, and `BalloonLarge` classes, and keeps this list of objects in an instance variable. Each `Balloon` object sets its own speed, point value, and random starting position off the bottom of the window.

Given this structure, the main code is responsible for presenting the overall user interface. It only communicates with the `oBalloonMgr`. The `oBalloonMgr` talks to all the `Balloon` objects. Therefore, the main code doesn't even know that the `Balloon` objects exist. It relies on the balloon manager to take care of them. Let's walk through the different parts of the program and see how each piece works.

## Module of Constants

This organization introduces a new technique for working with multiple Python files, each of which is commonly referred to as a *module*. If you find yourself in a situation where multiple Python modules require access to the same constants, a good solution is to create a module of constants and import that module into all modules that use the constants. Listing 11-4 shows some constants defined in *BalloonConstants.py*.

### File: BalloonGame/BalloonConstants.py

```
# Constants used by more than one Python module

N_BALLOONS = 15    # number of balloons in a round of the game
BALLOON_MISSED = 'Missed'    # balloon went off the top
BALLOON_MOVING = 'Balloon Moving'    # balloon is moving
```

*Listing 11-4: A module of constants that's imported by other modules*

This is just a simple Python file that contains constants shared by more than one module. The main code needs to know how many balloons there are in order to display that number. The balloon manager needs to know the number so it can instantiate the correct number of `Balloon` objects. This approach makes it extremely simple to modify the number of `Balloon` objects. If we added levels with different numbers of balloons, we could build a list or a dictionary in this file alone, and all other files would have access to that information.

The other two constants are used in each `Balloon` object as status indicators as the balloon moves up the window. When I get to the discussion of the game play, you'll see that the balloon manager (`oBalloonMgr`) asks each `Balloon` object for its status, and each responds with one of these two constants. Placing shared constants in a module and importing that module in modules that use the constants is a simple and effective technique for ensuring that different parts of a program use consistent values. This is a good example of applying the Don't Repeat Yourself (DRY) principle by only defining values in a single place.

## Main Program Code

The main code of our sample program, shown in Listing 11-5, follows the 12-step template I've used throughout this book. It shows the user's score, the game status, and a Start button at the bottom of the window, and it reacts to the user clicking the Start button.

**File: BalloonGame/Main_BalloonGame.py**

```
#  Balloon game main code

# 1 - Import packages
from pygame.locals import *
import pygwidgets
import sys
import pygame
from BalloonMgr import *

# 2 - Define constants
BLACK = (0, 0, 0)
GRAY = (200, 200, 200)
BACKGROUND_COLOR = (0, 180, 180)
WINDOW_WIDTH = 640
WINDOW_HEIGHT = 640
PANEL_HEIGHT = 60
USABLE_WINDOW_HEIGHT = WINDOW_HEIGHT - PANEL_HEIGHT
FRAMES_PER_SECOND = 30

# 3 - Initialize the world
pygame.init()
window = pygame.display.set_mode((WINDOW_WIDTH, WINDOW_HEIGHT))
clock = pygame.time.Clock()

# 4 - Load assets: image(s), sound(s), etc.
oScoreDisplay = pygwidgets.DisplayText(window, (10, USABLE_WINDOW_HEIGHT + 25),
                            'Score: 0', textColor=BLACK,
                            backgroundColor=None, width=140, fontSize=24)
oStatusDisplay = pygwidgets.DisplayText(window, (180, USABLE_WINDOW_HEIGHT + 25),
                            '', textColor=BLACK, backgroundColor=None,
                            width=300, fontSize=24)
oStartButton = pygwidgets.TextButton(window,
                            (WINDOW_WIDTH - 110, USABLE_WINDOW_HEIGHT + 10),
                            'Start')

# 5 - Initialize variables
oBalloonMgr = BalloonMgr(window, WINDOW_WIDTH, USABLE_WINDOW_HEIGHT)
playing = False ❶  # wait until user clicks Start

# 6 - Loop forever
while True:
    # 7 - Check for and handle events
    nPointsEarned = 0
    for event in pygame.event.get():
```

```
        if event.type == pygame.QUIT:
            pygame.quit()
            sys.exit()

        if playing:  ❷
            oBalloonMgr.handleEvent(event)
            theScore = oBalloonMgr.getScore()
            oScoreDisplay.setValue('Score: ' + str(theScore))
        elif oStartButton.handleEvent(event):  ❸
            oBalloonMgr.start()
            oScoreDisplay.setValue('Score: 0')
            playing = True
            oStartButton.disable()

    # 8 - Do any "per frame" actions
    if playing:  ❹
        oBalloonMgr.update()
        nPopped = oBalloonMgr.getCountPopped()
        nMissed = oBalloonMgr.getCountMissed()
        oStatusDisplay.setValue('Popped: ' + str(nPopped) +
                        '  Missed: ' + str(nMissed) +
                        '  Out of: ' + str(N_BALLOONS))

        if (nPopped + nMissed) == N_BALLOONS:  ❺
            playing = False
            oStartButton.enable()

    # 9 - Clear the window
    window.fill(BACKGROUND_COLOR)

    # 10 - Draw all window elements
    if playing:  ❻
        oBalloonMgr.draw()

    pygame.draw.rect(window, GRAY, pygame.Rect(0,
                    USABLE_WINDOW_HEIGHT, WINDOW_WIDTH, PANEL_HEIGHT))
    oScoreDisplay.draw()
    oStatusDisplay.draw()
    oStartButton.draw()

    # 11 - Update the window
    pygame.display.update()

    # 12 - Slow things down a bit
    clock.tick(FRAMES_PER_SECOND)  # make pygame wait
```

Listing 11-5: The Balloon game's main code

The code is based on a single Boolean variable, playing, set to False by default to let the user begin the game by pressing Start ❶.

When playing is True, the main code calls the handleEvent() method ❷ of the balloon manager, oBalloonMgr, to handle all events. We call the balloon manager's getScore() method to get the score, and we update the score field's text.

When the game is over, the program waits for the user to press the Start button ❸. When the button is clicked, the balloon manager is told to start the game, and the user interface is updated.

In every frame, if the game is running, we send the update() message to the balloon manager ❹, triggering it to pass on the update() message to all balloons. Then we ask the balloon manager for the numbers of balloons remaining and balloons popped. We use that information to update the user interface.

When the user pops all balloons or the last balloon floats off the top of the window, we set the playing variable to False and enable the Start button ❺.

The drawing code is very straightforward ❻. We tell the balloon manager to draw, which triggers all the balloons to draw themselves. Then we draw the bottom bar with its status data and the Start button.

## Balloon Manager

The balloon manager is responsible for keeping track of all balloons, including creating the Balloon objects, telling each one to draw itself, telling each to move, and keeping track of how many were popped and missed. Listing 11-6 contains the code of the BalloonMgr class.

### File: BalloonGame/BalloonMgr.py

```
# BalloonMgr class

import pygame
import random
from pygame.locals import *
import pygwidgets
from BalloonConstants import *
from Balloon import *

# BalloonMgr manages a list of Balloon objects
class BalloonMgr():
  ❶ def __init__(self, window, maxWidth, maxHeight):
        self.window = window
        self.maxWidth = maxWidth
        self.maxHeight = maxHeight

  ❷ def start(self):
        self.balloonList = []
        self.nPopped = 0
        self.nMissed = 0
        self.score = 0

      ❸ for balloonNum in range(0, N_BALLOONS):
            randomBalloonClass = random.choice((BalloonSmall,
                                                BalloonMedium,
                                                BalloonLarge))
            oBalloon = randomBalloonClass(self.window, self.maxWidth,
                                          self.maxHeight, balloonNum)
```

```
                self.balloonList.append(oBalloon)

        def handleEvent(self, event):
      ❹ if event.type == MOUSEBUTTONDOWN:
                # Go 'reversed' so topmost balloon gets popped
                for oBalloon in reversed(self.balloonList):
                    wasHit, nPoints = oBalloon.clickedInside(event.pos)
                    if wasHit:
                        if nPoints > 0:  # remove this balloon
                            self.balloonList.remove(oBalloon)
                            self.nPopped = self.nPopped + 1
                            self.score = self.score + nPoints
                        return  # no need to check others

    ❺ def update(self):
          for oBalloon in self.balloonList:
              status = oBalloon.update()
              if status == BALLOON_MISSED:
                  # Balloon went off the top, remove it
                  self.balloonList.remove(oBalloon)
                  self.nMissed = self.nMissed + 1

    ❻ def getScore(self):
          return self.score

    ❼ def getCountPopped(self):
          return self.nPopped

    ❽ def getCountMissed(self):
          return self.nMissed

    ❾ def draw(self):
          for oBalloon in self.balloonList:
              oBalloon.draw()
```

Listing 11-6: The BalloonMgr class

When instantiated, the balloon manager is told the width and height of
the window ❶, and it saves this information in instance variables.

The concept behind the start() method ❷ is important. Its purpose
is to initialize any instance variables needed for one round of the game,
so it's called whenever the user starts a round of the game. In this game,
start() resets the count of popped balloons and the count of missed balloons. It then goes through a loop that creates all the Balloon objects (randomly chosen among three different sizes using three different classes)
and stores them in a list ❸. Whenever the method creates a Balloon object,
it passes the window and the width and height of the window. (For future
expansion, each Balloon object is given a unique number.)

Each time through the main loop, the main code calls the handleEvent()
method of the balloon manager ❹. Here, we check if the user has clicked
on any Balloon. If the event detected was a MOUSEDOWNEVENT, the code loops
through all the Balloon objects, asking each one if the click occurred inside
that balloon. Each Balloon returns a Boolean indicating if it was hit and, if

so, the number of points the user should get for popping it. (The code is set up this way for future expansion, as discussed in the note at the end of this section.) The balloon manager then uses the remove() method to eliminate that Balloon from its list, increments the number of popped balloons, and updates the score.

In each iteration of the main loop, the main code also calls the update() method of the balloon manager ❺, which passes this call on to all of the balloons, telling them to update themselves. Each balloon moves up the screen based on its own speed setting and returns its status: either that it is still moving (BALLOON_MOVING) or that it has moved beyond the top of the window (BALLOON_MISSED). If a balloon was missed, the balloon manager removes that balloon from its list and increments its count of missed balloons.

The balloon manager provides three getter methods that allow the main code to get the score ❻, the number of popped balloons ❼, and the number of missed balloons ❽.

Each time through the main loop, the main code calls the balloon manager's draw() method ❾. The balloon manager doesn't have anything to draw by itself, but loops though all the Balloon objects and calls the draw() method of each. (Notice the polymorphism here. The balloon manager has a draw() method, and each Balloon object has a draw() method.)

**NOTE** *As a challenge, try to expand this game to include a new type (subclass) of Balloon, a MegaBalloon. The difference is that a MegaBalloon will take three clicks to pop. Artwork is included in the download for this game.*

## Balloon Class and Objects

Finally, we have the balloon classes. To reinforce the concept of inheritance from Chapter 10, the *Balloon.py* module includes an abstract base class named Balloon and three subclasses: BalloonSmall, BalloonMedium, and BalloonLarge. The balloon manager instantiates Balloon objects from these subclasses. The subclasses each only include an __init__() method, which overrides and then calls the abstract method __init__() in the Balloon class. Each balloon image will start at some randomized location (below the bottom of the window) and will move up a few pixels in every frame. Listing 11-7 shows the code of the Balloon class and its subclasses.

### File: BalloonGame/Balloon.py

```
# Balloon base class and 3 subclasses

import pygame
import random
from pygame.locals import *
import pygwidgets
from BalloonConstants import *
from abc import ABC, abstractmethod
```

```
❶ class Balloon(ABC):

    popSoundLoaded = False
    popSound = None  # load when first balloon is created

    @abstractmethod
❷ def __init__(self, window, maxWidth, maxHeight, ID,
                oImage, size, nPoints, speedY):
        self.window = window
        self.ID = ID
        self.balloonImage = oImage
        self.size = size
        self.nPoints = nPoints
        self.speedY = speedY
        if not Balloon.popSoundLoaded:  # load first time only
            Balloon.popSoundLoaded = True
            Balloon.popSound = pygame.mixer.Sound('sounds/balloonPop.wav')

        balloonRect = self.balloonImage.getRect()
        self.width = balloonRect.width
        self.height = balloonRect.height
        # Position so balloon is within the width of the window,
        # but below the bottom
        self.x = random.randrange(maxWidth - self.width)
        self.y = maxHeight + random.randrange(75)
        self.balloonImage.setLoc((self.x, self.y))

❸ def clickedInside(self, mousePoint):
        myRect = pygame.Rect(self.x, self.y, self.width, self.height)
        if myRect.collidepoint(mousePoint):
            Balloon.popSound.play()
            return True, self.nPoints  # True here means it was hit
        else:
            return False, 0  # not hit, no points

❹ def update(self):
        self.y = self.y - self.speedY  # update y position by speed
        self.balloonImage.setLoc((self.x, self.y))
        if self.y < -self.height:  # off the top of the window
            return BALLOON_MISSED
        else:
            return BALLOON_MOVING

❺ def draw(self):
        self.balloonImage.draw()

❻ def __del__(self):
        print(self.size, 'Balloon', self.ID, 'is going away')

❼ class BalloonSmall(Balloon):
    balloonImage = pygame.image.load('images/redBalloonSmall.png')
    def __init__(self, window, maxWidth, maxHeight, ID):
        oImage = pygwidgets.Image(window, (0, 0),
                                  BalloonSmall.balloonImage)
```

```
        super().__init__(window, maxWidth, maxHeight, ID,
                        oImage, 'Small', 30, 3.1)

❽ class BalloonMedium(Balloon):
    balloonImage = pygame.image.load('images/redBalloonMedium.png')
    def __init__(self, window, maxWidth, maxHeight, ID):
        oImage = pygwidgets.Image(window, (0, 0),
                        BalloonMedium.balloonImage)
        super().__init__(window, maxWidth, maxHeight, ID,
                        oImage, 'Medium', 20, 2.2)

❾ class BalloonLarge(Balloon):
    balloonImage = pygame.image.load('images/redBalloonLarge.png')
    def __init__(self, window, maxWidth, maxHeight, ID):
        oImage = pygwidgets.Image(window, (0, 0),
                        BalloonLarge.balloonImage)
        super().__init__(window, maxWidth, maxHeight, ID,
                        oImage, 'Large', 10, 1.5)
```

*Listing 11-7: The Balloon classes*

The Balloon class is an abstract class ❶, so the BalloonMgr instantiates objects (randomly) from the BalloonSmall ❼, BalloonMedium ❽, and BalloonLarge ❾ classes. Each of those classes creates a pygwidgets Image object, then calls the __init__() method in the Balloon base class. We differentiate the balloons with the arguments representing the image, size, number of points, and speed.

The __init__() method in the Balloon class ❷ stores the information about each balloon in instance variables. We get the rectangle of the balloon image and remember its width and height. We set a randomized horizontal position that will ensure that the balloon image will fully show within the window.

Every time a MOUSEDOWNEVENT happens, the balloon manager loops through the Balloon objects and calls the clickedInside() method of each ❸. The code here checks to see if the MOUSEDOWNEVENT that was detected happened inside the current balloon. If it did, the Balloon plays the pop sound and returns a Boolean to say that it was clicked on, as well as the number of points that balloon was worth. If it was not hit, it returns False and zero.

In each frame, the balloon manager calls the update() method of each Balloon ❹, which updates that Balloon's y position by subtracting its own speed in order to move higher in the window. After changing the position, the update() method returns either BALLOON_MISSED (if it has moved completely off the top of the window) or BALLOON_MOVING (to indicate that it is still in play).

The draw() method simply draws the image of the balloon at the appropriate (x, y) location ❺. Although the y position is kept as a floating-point value, pygame automatically converts it to an integer for pixel placement in the window.

The last method, __del__() ❻, has been added for debugging and for future development. Whenever the balloon manager deletes a balloon, the __del__() method of that Balloon object is called. For demonstration purposes, for now it simply prints a message that displays the balloon's size and ID number.

When the program is run and the user starts clicking on the balloons, we see output like this in the shell or console window:

```
Small Balloon 2 is going away
Small Balloon 8 is going away
Small Balloon 3 is going away
Small Balloon 7 is going away
Small Balloon 9 is going away
Small Balloon 12 is going away
Small Balloon 11 is going away
Small Balloon 6 is going away
Medium Balloon 14 is going away
Large Balloon 1 is going away
Medium Balloon 10 is going away
Medium Balloon 13 is going away
Medium Balloon 0 is going away
Medium Balloon 4 is going away
Large Balloon 5 is going away
```

When the game is over, the program waits for the user to click on the Start button. When that button is clicked, the balloon manager re-creates the list of Balloon objects and resets its instance variables, and the game begins again.

## Managing Memory: Slots

As we have discussed, when you instantiate an object, Python must allocate space for the instance variables defined in the class. By default, Python does this using a dictionary with a special name: \_\_dict\_\_. To see this in action, you can add this line to the end of the \_\_init\_\_() method of any class:

```
print(self.__dict__)
```

A dictionary is an excellent way to represent all the instance variables because it is dynamic—it can grow whenever Python encounters an instance variable that it has not seen before in a class. While I recommend that you initialize all your instance variables in your \_\_init\_\_() method, you can in fact define instance variables in any method, and those instance variables will be added when the method is executed for the first time. While I personally think the following is a bad idea, it demonstrates the ability to add an instance variable to an object dynamically:

```
myObject = MyClass()
myObject.someInstanceVariable = 5
```

In order to allow for this dynamic capability, dictionaries are typically implemented starting with enough empty space to represent some number of instance variables (the exact number is an internal detail of Python).

Whenever a new instance variable is encountered, it's added to the dictionary. If the dictionary runs out of space, Python adds more. This generally works well, and programmers do not experience any problems with this implementation.

However, imagine you have a class like the following with two instance variables created in the __init__() method, and you know that you will not need to add any more instance variables:

```python
class Point():
    def __init__(self, x, y):
        self.x = x
        self.y = y
        # More methods
```

Now, let's assume that you need to instantiate a very large number (hundreds of thousands, or even millions) of objects from this class. A case like this could cumulatively account for a large amount of wasted memory space (RAM).

To combat this potential waste, Python gives us a different approach, known as *slots*, to represent the instance variables. The idea is that you can tell Python the names of all the instance variables up front, and Python will use a data structure that allocates exactly enough space for just those instance variables. To use slots, you need to include the special class variable __slots__ to define a list of variables:

```python
__slots__ = [<instanceVar1>, <instanceVar2>, ... <instanceVarN>]
```

Here is what a modified version of our example class would look like:

```python
class PointWithSlots():
    # Define slots for only two instance variables
    __slots__ = ['x', 'y']

    def __init__(self, x, y):
        self.x = x
        self.y = y
        print(x, y)
```

These two classes will work identically, but objects instantiated from PointWithSlots will take up considerably less memory. To demonstrate the difference, we'll add this line to the end of the __init__() method of both classes:

```python
        # Try to create an additional instance variable
        self.color = 'black'
```

Now when we try to instantiate an object from both classes, the Point class has no problem adding another instance variable, but the PointWithSlots class fails with the following error:

```
AttributeError: 'PointWithSlots' object has no attribute 'color'
```

Using slots is highly memory-efficient at the expense of a loss of dynamic instance variables. If you're dealing with a very large number of objects from a class, this trade-off may very well be worthwhile.

## Summary

This chapter focused on a few concepts that didn't readily fit in the previous chapters. First, I discussed the circumstances under which you might want to delete an object. We looked at reference counts and how they track how many variables refer to the same object, which led to a discussion of object lifetimes and garbage collection. When the reference count goes to zero, the object is available for garbage collection. If a class has a __del__() method, then any objects created from the class can use the __del__() method for any cleanup that they might want to do.

Next, I discussed how class variables are different from instance variables. Every object instantiated from a class gets its own set of all the instance variables in the class. However, there is only one of each class variable, and that is accessible by all objects created from the class. Class variables are often used as constants or counters, or for loading something large and making it available to all objects instantiated from the class.

To put a number of techniques and concepts together, we built a balloon-popping game and organized it very efficiently. We had one file that contained only constants used by other files. The main code consisted of the main loop and a status display, and the balloon manager did the work of managing the objects. Such a division of labor allows for splitting up the game into smaller, logical pieces. The role of each part is well defined, making the overall program more manageable.

Finally, I explained how a technique called slots allows for a memory-efficient representation of instance variables.

# PART IV

## USING OOP IN GAME DEVELOPMENT

In this part of the book, we'll build some sample games using `pygwidgets`. I'll also introduce the `pyghelpers` module, which includes a number of classes and functions that can be useful in building game programs.

Chapter 12 revisits the Higher or Lower game from Chapter 1. We'll build a version of the game with a graphical user interface, and I'll introduce `Deck` and `Card` classes that can be reused in any card game program.

Chapter 13 focuses on timers. We'll build a number of different timer classes that allow your program to keep running while concurrently checking for a certain time limit.

Chapter 14 discusses different animation classes you can use to show sequences of images. This will allow you to easily build more artistic games and programs.

Chapter 15 introduces an approach to building a program that can contain many scenes, like a start scene, a play scene, and a game over scene. I'll show a `SceneMgr` class that is designed to manage any number of programmer-built scenes, and we'll use it to build a Rock, Paper, Scissors game.

Chapter 16 demonstrates how to show and react to different types of dialog boxes. You'll then use everything you've learned to build a fully functioning animated game.

Chapter 17 introduces the concept of design patterns, using the model, view, controller pattern as an example. It then provides a short wrap-up for the book.

# 12

## CARD GAMES

In the remaining chapters of this book, we'll build a few demo programs using pygame and pygwidgets. Each program will present one or more reusable classes and show how they can be used in a sample project.

In Chapter 1, I presented a text-based Higher or Lower card game. In this chapter we'll create a GUI version of the game, as shown in Figure 12-1.

To quickly recap the game rules: we start with seven cards face down and one card face up. The player guesses whether the next card to be turned over will be higher or lower than the last visible card by pressing Lower or Higher. When the game is over, the user can click New Game to start a new round of the game. The player starts with 100 points, gains 15 points for a correct answer, and loses 10 points for an incorrect answer.

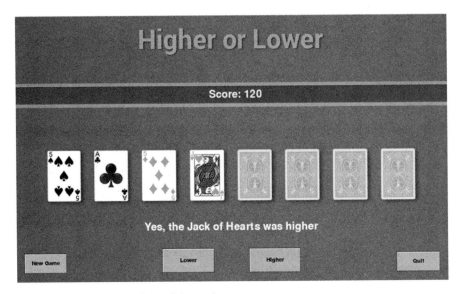

Figure 12-1: The user interface of the Higher or Lower game

## The Card Class

In the original text-based version of the game, the code dealing with the deck of cards was not easily reusable in other projects. To solve this problem, here we'll create a highly reusable Deck class that manages cards from a Card class.

To represent a card in pygame, we need to store the following data in instance variables for each Card object:

- Rank (ace, 2, 3, ... 10, jack, queen, king)
- Suit (clubs, hearts, diamonds, spades)
- Value (1, 2, 3, ... 12, 13)
- Name (built using the rank and suit: for example, 7 of clubs)
- Image of the back of the card (a single image shared by all Card objects)
- Image of the front of the card (a unique image for each Card object)

Each card must be able to perform the following behaviors, for which we will create methods:

- Mark itself as concealed (face down)
- Mark itself as revealed (face up)
- Return its name
- Return its value
- Set and get its location in the window
- Draw itself (either the revealed image or the concealed image)

While the following card behaviors are not used in the Higher or Lower game, we'll add these too in case they are needed in some other game:

- Return its rank
- Return its suit

Listing 12-1 shows the code of the Card class.

**File: HigherOrLower/Card.py**

```
# Card class

import pygame
import pygwidgets

class Card():

❶   BACK_OF_CARD_IMAGE = pygame.image.load('images/BackOfCard.png')

❷   def __init__(self, window, rank, suit, value):
        self.window = window
        self.rank = rank
        self.suit = suit
        self.cardName = rank + ' of ' + suit
        self.value = value
❸       fileName = 'images/' + self.cardName + '.png'
        # Set some starting location; use setLoc below to change
❹       self.images = pygwidgets.ImageCollection(window, (0, 0),
                        {'front': fileName,
                         'back': Card.BACK_OF_CARD_IMAGE}, 'back')

❺   def conceal(self):
        self.images.replace('back')

❻   def reveal(self):
        self.images.replace('front')

❼   def getName(self):
        return self.cardName

    def getValue(self):
        return self.value

    def getSuit(self):
        return self.suit

    def getRank(self):
        return self.rank

❽   def setLoc(self, loc):   # call the setLoc method of the ImageCollection
        self.images.setLoc(loc)
```

```
❾ def getLoc(self):   # get the location from the ImageCollection
        loc = self.images.getLoc()
        return loc

❿ def draw(self):
        self.images.draw()
```

*Listing 12-1: The Card class*

The Card class assumes that image files for all 52 cards, plus an image for the back of all the cards, are available in a folder named *images* inside the project folder. If you download the files associated with this chapter, you will see that the *images* folder contains the full set of *.png* files. The files are available via my GitHub repository at *https://github.com/IrvKalb/Object-Oriented-Python-Code/*.

The class loads the image of the back of the cards once and saves it in a class variable ❶. That image is available to all Card objects.

When called for each card, the __init__() method ❷ starts by storing the window; building and storing the name of the card; and storing its rank, value, and suit in instance variables. It then builds the path to the file in the *images* folder that contains the image for that specific card ❸. For example, if the rank is ace and the suit is spades, we build a path of *images/Ace of Spades.png*. We use an ImageCollection object to remember the paths to both the front and back images ❹; we'll use 'back' to say that we want to show the back of the card as the starting image.

The conceal() method ❺ tells ImageCollection to set the back of the card as the current image. The reveal() method ❻ tells ImageCollection to set the front of the card as the current image.

The getName(), getValue(), getSuit(), and getRank() methods ❼ are getter methods that allow the caller to retrieve the name, value, suit, and rank of the given card.

The setLoc() method sets a new location for the card ❽, and getLoc() retrieves the current location ❾. The location is kept in the ImageCollection.

Finally, draw() ❿ draws the image of the card in the window. More specifically, it tells the ImageCollection to draw the currently indicated image at the remembered location.

# The Deck Class

A Deck object is a classic example of an object manager object. Its job is to create and manage 52 Card objects. Listing 12-2 contains the code of our Deck class.

### File: HigerOrLower/Deck.py

```
# Deck class

import random
from Card import *
```

```
class Deck():
❶ SUIT_TUPLE = ('Diamonds', 'Clubs', 'Hearts', 'Spades')
    # This dict maps each card rank to a value for a standard deck
    STANDARD_DICT = {'Ace':1, '2':2, '3':3, '4':4, '5':5,
                     '6':6, '7':7, '8': 8, '9':9, '10':10,
                     'Jack':11, 'Queen':12, 'King':13}

❷ def __init__(self, window, rankValueDict=STANDARD_DICT):
       # rankValueDict defaults to STANDARD_DICT, but you can call it
       # with a different dict, e.g., a special dict for Blackjack
       self.startingDeckList = []
       self.playingDeckList = []
       for suit in Deck.SUIT_TUPLE:
           ❸ for rank, value in rankValueDict.items():
               oCard = Card(window, rank, suit, value)
               self.startingDeckList.append(oCard)

       self.shuffle()

❹ def shuffle(self):
       # Copy the starting deck and save it in the playing deck list
       self.playingDeckList = self.startingDeckList.copy()
       for oCard in self.playingDeckList:
           oCard.conceal()
       random.shuffle(self.playingDeckList)

❺ def getCard(self):
       if len(self.playingDeckList) == 0:
           raise IndexError('No more cards')
       # Pop one card off the deck and return it
       oCard = self.playingDeckList.pop()
       return oCard

❻ def returnCardToDeck(self, oCard):
       # Put a card back into the deck
       self.playingDeckList.insert(0, oCard)
```

*Listing 12-2: A Deck class that manages 52 Card objects*

We begin the Deck class by creating a few class variables ❶ that we'll use to create 52 cards with the proper suits and values. There are only four methods.

To the __init__() method ❷, we pass a reference to the window and an optional dictionary that maps card ranks to their values. If none is passed in, we use the dictionary for a standard deck of values. We build a deck of 52 cards, saved in self.startingDeckList, by iterating through all suits, then iterating through all card ranks and values. In the inner for loop ❸, we use a call to the items() method of a dictionary that allows us to easily get the key and value (here, the rank and value) in a single statement. Each time through the inner loop we instantiate a Card object, passing the rank, suit, and value of the new card. We append each Card object to the list self.startingDeckList to create a full deck of cards.

The final step is to call the shuffle() method ❹ to randomize the deck. The purpose of this method may seem obvious: to shuffle the deck. However, it does an extra little trick. The __init__() method built the self.startingDeckList, and that work should only be done once. So, whenever we shuffle the deck, rather than re-creating all the Card objects, we make a copy of the starting deck list, save it in self.playingDeckList, and shuffle that. The copy is what will be used and manipulated as the game runs. With this approach, we can remove cards from self.playingDeckList and not have to worry about adding them back into the deck later or reloading cards. The two lists, self.startingDeckList and self.playingDeckList, share references to the same 52 Card objects.

Note that when we call shuffle() for subsequent runs of the game, some of the Card objects may be in the "revealed" state. So, before proceeding, we iterate through the entire deck and call the conceal() method on each card, so that all cards will initially appear face down. The shuffle() method finishes by randomizing the cards in the playing deck using random.shuffle().

The getCard() method ❺ retrieves a card from the deck. It first checks to see if the deck is empty and, if so, raises an exception. Otherwise, since the deck is already shuffled, it pops a card off the deck and returns that card to the caller.

Together, Deck and Card provide a highly reusable combination of classes that can be used in most card games. The Higher or Lower game only uses eight cards for each round and shuffles the entire deck at the start of each game. Therefore, in this game it is not possible for the Deck object to run out of cards. For a card game where you need to know if the deck runs out of cards, you can build a try block around the call to getCard() and use an except clause to catch an exception. The choice of what to do there is up to you.

While not used in this game, the returnCardToDeck() method ❻ allows you to put a card back into the deck.

## The Higher or Lower Game

The code of the actual game is fairly simple: the main code implements the main loop, and a Game object contains the logic for the game itself.

### Main Program

Listing 12-3 is the main program that sets up the world and contains the main loop. It also creates the Game object that runs the game.

#### File: HigherOrLower/Main_HigherOrLower.py

```
# Higher or Lower - pygame version
# Main program

--- snip ---
# 4 - Load assets: image(s), sound(s), etc.
❶ background = pygwidgets.Image(window, (0, 0),
```

```
                                        'images/background.png')
newGameButton = pygwidgets.TextButton(window, (20, 530),
                                        'New Game', width=100, height=45)
higherButton = pygwidgets.TextButton(window, (540, 520),
                                        'Higher', width=120, height=55)
lowerButton = pygwidgets.TextButton(window, (340, 520),
                                        'Lower', width=120, height=55)
quitButton = pygwidgets.TextButton(window, (880, 530),
                                        'Quit', width=100, height=45)

    # 5 - Initialize variables
❷ oGame = Game(window)

    # 6 - Loop forever
    while True:

        # 7 - Check for and handle events
        for event in pygame.event.get():
            if ((event.type == QUIT) or
                ((event.type == KEYDOWN) and (event.key == K_ESCAPE)) or
                (quitButton.handleEvent(event))):
                pygame.quit()
                sys.exit()

        ❸ if newGameButton.handleEvent(event):
                oGame.reset()
                lowerButton.enable()
                higherButton.enable()

            if higherButton.handleEvent(event):
                gameOver = oGame.hitHigherOrLower(HIGHER)
                if gameOver:
                    higherButton.disable()
                    lowerButton.disable()

            if lowerButton.handleEvent(event):
                gameOver = oGame.hitHigherOrLower(LOWER)
                if gameOver:
                    higherButton.disable()
                    lowerButton.disable()

        # 8 - Do any "per frame" actions

        # 9 - Clear the window before drawing it again
    ❹ background.draw()

        # 10 - Draw the window elements
        # Tell the game to draw itself
    ❺ oGame.draw()
        # Draw remaining user interface components
        newGameButton.draw()
        higherButton.draw()
        lowerButton.draw()
        quitButton.draw()
```

```
    # 11 - Update the window
    pygame.display.update()

    # 12 - Slow things down a bit
    clock.tick(FRAMES_PER_SECOND)
```

*Listing 12-3: The main code of the Higher or Lower game*

The main program loads the background image and builds four buttons ❶, then instantiates the Game object ❷.

In the main loop, we listen for any of the buttons being pressed ❸, and when one is, we call the appropriate method in the Game object.

At the bottom of the loop, we draw the window elements ❹, starting with the background. Most significantly, we call the draw() method of the Game object ❺. As you will see, the Game object passes this message on to each of the Card objects. Finally, we draw all four buttons.

### Game Object

The Game object handles the actual game logic. Listing 12-4 contains the code of the Game class.

**File: HigherOrLower/Game.py**

```
# Game class

import pygwidgets
from Constants import *
from Deck import *
from Card import *

class Game():
    CARD_OFFSET = 110
    CARDS_TOP = 300
    CARDS_LEFT = 75
    NCARDS = 8
    POINTS_CORRECT = 15
    POINTS_INCORRECT = 10

    def __init__(self, window):  ❶
        self.window = window
        self.oDeck = Deck(self.window)
        self.score = 100
        self.scoreText = pygwidgets.DisplayText(window, (450, 164),
                                        'Score: ' + str(self.score),
                                        fontSize=36, textColor=WHITE,
                                        justified='right')

        self.messageText = pygwidgets.DisplayText(window, (50, 460),
                                        '', width=900, justified='center',
                                        fontSize=36, textColor=WHITE)

        self.loserSound = pygame.mixer.Sound("sounds/loser.wav")
```

```
        self.winnerSound = pygame.mixer.Sound("sounds/ding.wav")
        self.cardShuffleSound = pygame.mixer.Sound("sounds/cardShuffle.wav")

        self.cardXPositionsList = []
        thisLeft = Game.CARDS_LEFT
        # Calculate the x positions of all cards, once
        for cardNum in range(Game.NCARDS):
            self.cardXPositionsList.append(thisLeft)
            thisLeft = thisLeft + Game.CARD_OFFSET

        self.reset()  # start a round of the game

    def reset(self): ❷  # this method is called when a new round starts
        self.cardShuffleSound.play()
        self.cardList = []
        self.oDeck.shuffle()
        for cardIndex in range(0, Game.NCARDS):  # deal out cards
            oCard = self.oDeck.getCard()
            self.cardList.append(oCard)
            thisXPosition = self.cardXPositionsList[cardIndex]
            oCard.setLoc((thisXPosition, Game.CARDS_TOP))

        self.showCard(0)
        self.cardNumber = 0
        self.currentCardName, self.currentCardValue = \
                        self.getCardNameAndValue(self.cardNumber)

        self.messageText.setValue('Starting card is ' + self.currentCardName +
                            '. Will the next card be higher or lower?')

    def getCardNameAndValue(self, index):
        oCard = self.cardList[index]
        theName = oCard.getName()
        theValue = oCard.getValue()
        return theName, theValue

    def showCard(self, index):
        oCard = self.cardList[index]
        oCard.reveal()

    def hitHigherOrLower(self, higherOrLower): ❸
        self.cardNumber = self.cardNumber + 1
        self.showCard(self.cardNumber)
        nextCardName, nextCardValue = self.getCardNameAndValue(self.cardNumber)

        if higherOrLower == HIGHER:
            if nextCardValue > self.currentCardValue:
                self.score = self.score + Game.POINTS_CORRECT
                self.messageText.setValue('Yes, the ' + nextCardName + ' was higher')
                self.winnerSound.play()
            else:
                self.score = self.score - Game.POINTS_INCORRECT
                self.messageText.setValue('No, the ' + nextCardName + ' was not higher')
                self.loserSound.play()
```

```
    else:  # user hit the Lower button
        if nextCardValue < self.currentCardValue:
            self.score = self.score + Game.POINTS_CORRECT
            self.messageText.setValue('Yes, the ' + nextCardName + ' was lower')
            self.winnerSound.play()
        else:
            self.score = self.score - Game.POINTS_INCORRECT
            self.messageText.setValue('No, the ' + nextCardName + ' was not lower')
            self.loserSound.play()

    self.scoreText.setValue('Score: ' + str(self.score))

    self.currentCardValue = nextCardValue  # set up for the next card

    done = (self.cardNumber == (Game.NCARDS - 1))  # did we reach the last card?
    return done

def draw(self): ❹
    # Tell each card to draw itself
    for oCard in self.cardList:
        oCard.draw()

    self.scoreText.draw()
    self.messageText.draw()
```

*Listing 12-4: The Game object that runs the game*

In the __init__() method ❶, we initialize a number of instance variables that only need to be set up once. We create the Deck object, set the starting score, and create a DisplayText object for displaying the score and the result of each move. We also load a number of sound files for use during play. Lastly, we call the reset() method ❷, which contains any code needed for one play of the game: that is, to shuffle the deck, play the shuffling sound, deal out eight cards, display them in previously computed positions, and show the face of the first card.

When the user presses the Higher or Lower button, the main code calls hitHigherOrLower() ❸, which turns over the next card, compares the value with the previous face-up card, and awards or subtracts points.

The draw() method ❹ iterates through all the cards in the current game, telling each to draw itself (by calling each Card object's draw() method). It then draws the text of the score and the feedback for the current move.

## Testing with __name__

When you write a class, it's always a good idea to write some test code to ensure that an object created from that class will work correctly. As a reminder, any file containing Python code is called a *module*. A standard practice is to write one or more classes in a module, then use an import statement to bring that module into some other module. When you write a module that contains a class (or classes), you can add some test code that's intended to run *only* when the module is run as the main program, and doesn't run in the typical case when the module is imported by another Python file.

In a project with multiple Python modules, you typically have one main module and several other modules. When your program runs, Python creates the special variable _name_ in every module. In whichever module is given control first, Python sets the value of _name_ to the string '_main_'. Therefore, you can write code to check the value of _name_ and execute some test code only if a module is running as the main program.

I'll use the Deck class as an example. At the end of *Deck.py*, after the code of the class, I've added this code to create an instance of the Deck class and print out the cards that it creates:

```
--- snip code of the Deck class ---
if __name__ == '__main__':
    # Main code to test the Deck class

    import pygame

    # Constants
    WINDOW_WIDTH = 100
    WINDOW_HEIGHT = 100

    pygame.init()
    window = pygame.display.set_mode((WINDOW_WIDTH, WINDOW_HEIGHT))

    oDeck = Deck(window)
    for i in range(1, 53):
        oCard = oDeck.getCard()
        print('Name: ', oCard.getName(), ' Value:', oCard.getValue())
```

This checks if the *Deck.py* file is running as the main program. In the typical case where the Deck class is imported by some other module, the value of _name_ will be 'Deck', so this code does nothing. But if we run *Deck.py* as the main program, for testing purposes only, Python sets the value of _name_ to '_main_' and this test code runs.

In the test code, we build a minimal pygame program that creates an instance of the Deck class, then prints out the name and value of all 52 cards. The output of running *Deck.py* as the main program looks like this in the shell or console window:

```
Name:  4 of Spades    Value: 4
Name:  4 of Diamonds    Value: 4
Name:  Jack of Hearts    Value: 11
Name:  8 of Spades    Value: 8
Name:  10 of Diamonds    Value: 10
Name:  3 of Clubs    Value: 3
Name:  Jack of Diamonds    Value: 11
Name:  9 of Spades    Value: 9
Name:  Ace of Diamonds    Value: 1
Name:  2 of Clubs    Value: 2
Name:  7 of Clubs    Value: 7
```

```
Name:   4 of Clubs      Value: 4
Name:   8 of Hearts     Value: 8
Name:   3 of Diamonds      Value: 3
Name:   7 of Spades     Value: 7
Name:   7 of Diamonds      Value: 7
Name:   King of Diamonds      Value: 13
Name:   10 of Spades     Value: 10
Name:   Ace of Hearts     Value: 1
Name:   8 of Diamonds      Value: 8
Name:   Queen of Diamonds      Value: 12
...
```

Code like this is useful for testing that the class is generally working as we expect, without having to deal with a larger main program to instantiate it. It gives us a quick way to make sure the class isn't broken. Depending on our needs, we could go further and add some example code to illustrate typical calls to the methods of the class.

# Other Card Games

There are many card games that use a standard 52-card deck. We could use the Deck and Card classes as is to build games like Bridge, Hearts, Gin Rummy, and most Solitaire games. However, there are some card games that use different card values or different numbers of cards. Let's look at a few examples and see how our classes could be adapted for these cases.

## Blackjack Deck

While a deck for Blackjack, also known as 21, uses the same cards as a standard deck, the *values* of the cards are different: the card values for 10, jack, queen, and king are all 10. The __init__() method of the Deck class starts like this:

```
def __init__(self, window, rankValueDict=STANDARD_DICT):
```

To create a Blackjack deck, you would only need to supply a different dictionary for rankValueDict, like this:

```
blackJackDict = {'Ace':1, '2':2, '3':3, '4':4, '5':5,
                 '6':6, '7':7, '8': 8, '9':9, '10':10,
                 'Jack':10, 'Queen':10, 'King':10}
oBlackjackDeck = Deck(window, rankValueDict=blackJackDict)
```

Once you create the oBlackjackDeck this way, you can then call the existing shuffle() and getCard() methods with no change. In the implementation of Blackjack, you would also have to deal with the fact that an ace can have a value of 1 or 11. But that, as we say, is an exercise left to the reader!

### Games with Unusual Card Decks

There are a number of card games that do not use a standard deck of 52 cards. The game of canasta requires at least two decks with jokers, for a total of 108 cards. A pinochle deck consists of two copies of 9, 10, jack, queen, king, and ace for each suit, for a total of 48 cards.

For games like these, you could still use the Deck class, but you would need to create a subclass with Deck as the base class. The new CanastaDeck or PinochleDeck class would need to have its own __init__() method that builds a deck as a list consisting of the appropriate Card objects. However, the shuffle() and getCard() methods could be inherited from the Deck class. Therefore, a CanastaDeck or PinochleDeck class would subclass the Deck class and consist of only an __init__() method.

## Summary

In this chapter, we built a GUI version of the Higher or Lower card game from Chapter 1 using highly reusable Deck and Card classes. The main code instantiates a Game object, which creates a Deck object that instantiates 52 Card objects, one for each card in the resulting deck. Each Card object is responsible for drawing its appropriate image in the window and can respond to queries about its name, rank, suit, and value. The Game class, which contains the logic of the game, is separate from the main code, which runs the main loop.

I demonstrated how Python creates a special variable called __name__ and gives it different values depending on whether a file is being run as the main program or not. You can use this feature to add some test code that runs when you run the file as a main program (to test the code in the module), but will not run in the typical case when the file is imported by another module.

Finally, I showed how you can build different types of card decks, depending on how different they are from the Deck class.

# 13

## TIMERS

This chapter is about timers. A *timer* allows your program to count or wait for a given amount of time before moving on to perform some other action. In the world of text-based Python programs, this is easily achieved with `time.sleep()` by specifying a number of seconds to sleep. To pause for two and a half seconds, you could write:

```
import time
time.sleep(2.5)
```

However, in the world of pygame, and event-driven programming in general, the user should always be able to interact with the program, so pausing in this way is inappropriate. A call to `time.sleep()` would make the program nonreactive during the sleeping period.

Instead, the main loop needs to continue to run at whatever frame rate you have chosen. You need a way for the program to continue to loop, but also count time from a given starting point to some time in the future. There are three different ways this can be accomplished:

- Measure time by counting frames.
- Use pygame to create an event that is issued in the future.
- Remember a start time and continuously check for the elapsed time.

I will quickly discuss the first two, but I'll focus on the third, as it provides the cleanest and most accurate approach.

## Timer Demonstration Program

To illustrate the different approaches, I'll use different implementations of the test program shown in Figure 13-1.

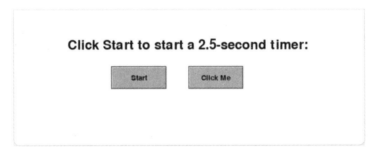

Figure 13-1: The timer demonstration program

When the user clicks Start, a 2.5-second timer starts and the window changes to look like Figure 13-2.

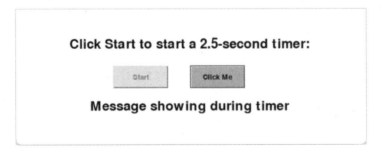

Figure 13-2: The message displayed while the timer is running

For two and a half seconds, the Start button becomes disabled and a message is displayed below the buttons. When the time expires, the message goes away and the Start button is re-enabled. Independent of the timer running, anything else that the user wants to do in the program still needs to be responsive. In this example, clicking Click Me prints a message to the shell window, whether the timer is running or not.

# Three Approaches for Implementing Timers

In this section, I'll discuss three different approaches to implementing timers: counting frames, generating a pygame event, and checking for elapsed time. To make these concepts clear, the following code examples are built directly in the main loop.

## Counting Frames

A straightforward approach to creating a timer is to count the number of frames that go by. One frame is the same as one loop iteration. If you know the frame rate of a program, you can calculate how long to wait by multiplying the time to wait by the frame rate. The following code shows the key parts of the implementation:

### File: InLineTimerExamples/CountingFrames.py

```
FRAMES_PER_SECOND = 30  # takes 1/30th of a second for each frame
TIMER_LENGTH = 2.5
--- snip ---
timerRunning = False
```

This code shows what happens when the user clicks the Start button:

```
if startButton.handleEvent(event):
    timerRunning = True
    nFramesElapsed = 0  # initialize a counter
    nFramesToWait = int(FRAMES_PER_SECOND * TIMER_LENGTH)
    startButton.disable()
    timerMessage.show()
```

The program calculates that it should wait for 75 frames (2.5 seconds × 30 frames per second), and we set timerRunning to True to indicate that the timer has started. Inside the main loop, we use this code to check for when the timer ends:

```
if timerRunning:
    nFramesElapsed = nFramesElapsed + 1  # increment the counter
    if nFramesElapsed >= nFramesToWait:
        startButton.enable()
        timerMessage.hide()
        print('Timer ended by counting frames')
        timerRunning = False
```

When the timer ends, we re-enable the Start button, hide the message, and reset the timerRunning variable. (If you prefer, you could set the count to the number of frames to wait and count down to zero instead.) This approach works fine, but it is tied to the program's frame rate.

## Timer Event

As a second approach, we'll take advantage of pygame's built-in timer. Pygame allows you to add a new event to the event queue—this is known as *posting* an event. Specifically, we'll ask pygame to create and post a timer event. We only need to specify how far into the future we want the event to happen. After the given amount of time, pygame will issue a timer event in the main loop, in the same way that it issues other standard events such as KEYUP, KEYDOWN, MOUSEBUTTONUP, MOUSEBUTTONDOWN, and so on. Your code will need to look for and react to this type of event.

The following documentation is from *https://www.pygame.org/docs/ref/ time.html*:

pygame.time.set_timer()

> *Repeatedly create an event on the event queue*
>
> set_timer(eventid, milliseconds) -> None
>
> set_timer(eventid, milliseconds, once) -> None

Set an event type to appear on the event queue every given number of milliseconds. The first event will not appear until the amount of time has passed.

Every event type can have a separate timer attached to it. It is best to use the value between pygame.USEREVENT and pygame.NUMEVENTS.

To disable the timer for an event, set the milliseconds argument to 0.

If the once argument is True, then only send the timer once.

Every event type in pygame is represented by unique identifier. As of pygame 2.0, you can now make a call to pygame.event.custom_type() to get an identifier for a custom event.

### File: InLineTimerExamples /TimerEvent.py

```
TIMER_EVENT_ID = pygame.event.custom_type()   # new in pygame 2.0
TIMER_LENGTH = 2.5   # seconds
```

When the user clicks Start, the code creates and posts the timer event:

```
if startButton.handleEvent(event):
    pygame.time.set_timer(TIMER_EVENT_ID,
                          int(TIMER_LENGTH * 1000), True)
    --- snip disable button, show message ---
```

The value calculated is 2,500 milliseconds. True means that the timer should only run once (generate only one event). We now need code in the event loop that checks for the event happening:

```
if event.type == TIMER_EVENT_ID:
    --- snip enable button, hide message ---
```

Since we specified True in the call to set the timer, this event is issued only once. If we want to repeat events every 2,500 milliseconds, we could set the last argument in the original call to False (or just let it default to False). To end repeated timer events, we would make a call to set_timer() and pass 0 (zero) as the second argument.

## Building a Timer by Calculating Elapsed Time

The third approach for implementing a timer uses the current time as a starting point. We can then continuously query the current time and perform a simple subtraction to calculate the elapsed time. The code shown for this example runs in the main loop; later, we'll extract the timer-related code and build a reusable Timer class.

The time module of the Python Standard Library has this function:

```
time.time()
```

Calling this function returns the current time in seconds as a floating-point number. The value returned is the number of seconds that have passed since "epoch time," which is defined as 00:00:00 UTC on January 1, 1970.

The code in Listing 13-1 creates a timer by remembering the time when the user clicks Start. While the timer is running, we check in every frame to see if the desired amount of time has elapsed. You've already seen the user interface, so I'll omit those details and some of the setup code for brevity.

### File: InLineTimerExamples/ElapsedTime.py

```
# Timer in the main loop

--- snip ---

TIMER_LENGTH = 2.5  # seconds
--- snip ---
timerRunning = False

# 6 - Loop forever
while True:

    # 7 - Check for and handle events
    for event in pygame.event.get():
        if event.type == pygame.QUIT:
            pygame.quit()
            sys.exit()

    ❶ if startButton.handleEvent(event):
            timeStarted = time.time()  # remember the start time
            startButton.disable()
            timerMessage.show()
            print('Starting timer')
            timerRunning = True
```

```
        if clickMeButton.handleEvent(event):
            print('Other button was clicked')

    # 8 - Do any "per frame" actions
❷ if timerRunning:  # if the timer is running
        elapsed = time.time() - timeStarted
      ❸ if elapsed >= TIMER_LENGTH:  # True here means timer has ended
            startButton.enable()
            timerMessage.hide()
            print('Timer ended')
            timerRunning = False

    # 9 - Clear the window
    window.fill(WHITE)

    # 10 - Draw all window elements
    headerMessage.draw()
    startButton.draw()
    clickMeButton.draw()
    timerMessage.draw()

    # 11 - Update the window
    pygame.display.update()

    # 12 - Slow things down a bit
    clock.tick(FRAMES_PER_SECOND)  # make pygame wait
```

*Listing 13-1: A timer built into the main loop*

The important variables to notice in this program are:

**TIMER_LENGTH**   A constant that says how long we want our timer to run

**timerRunning**   A Boolean that tells us whether the timer is running

**timeStarted**   The time at which the user pressed the Start button

When the user clicks Start, timerRunning is set to True ❶. We initialize the variable startTime to the current time. We then disable the Start button and show the message below the buttons.

Each time through the loop, if the timer is running ❷, we subtract the starting time from the current time to see how much time has elapsed since the timer started. When the amount of time elapsed becomes greater than or equal to TIMER_LENGTH, whatever action we want to happen when the time is up can happen. In this sample program, we enable the Start button, remove the bottom message, print a short text output, and reset the timerRunning variable to False ❸.

The code in Listing 13-1 works fine . . . for a single timer. However, this is a book on object-oriented programming, so we want this to be scalable. To generalize the functionality, we'll turn the timing code into a class. We'll take the important variables, turn them into instance variables, and split the code into methods. That way, we can define and use any number of timers in a program. The `Timer` class, along with other classes used to display timing in pygame programs, are available in a module named pyghelpers.

# Installing pyghelpers

To install `pyghelpers`, open the command line and enter the following two commands:

```
python3 -m pip install -U pip --user
```

```
python3 -m pip install -U pyghelpers --user
```

These commands download and install `pyghelpers` from PyPI into a folder that is available to all your Python programs. Once installed, you can use `pyghelpers` by including the following statement at the beginning of your programs:

```
import pyghelpers
```

You can then instantiate objects from the classes in the module and call the methods of those objects. The most current documentation of `pyghelpers` is at *https://pyghelpers.readthedocs.io/en/latest/*, and the source code is available via my GitHub repository at *https://github.com/IrvKalb/pyghelpers/*.

# The Timer Class

Listing 13-2 contains the code of a very simple timer as a class. This code is built into the `pyghelpers` package as the `Timer` class (I've omitted some of the documentation here for brevity).

### File: (Available as part of the pyghelpers module)

```
# Timer class

class Timer():
--- snip ---
❶ def __init__(self, timeInSeconds, nickname=None, callBack=None):
        self.timeInSeconds = timeInSeconds
        self.nickname = nickname
        self.callBack = callBack
        self.savedSecondsElapsed = 0.0
        self.running = False

❷ def start(self, newTimeInSeconds=None):
```

```
        --- snip ---
        if newTimeInSeconds != None:
            self.timeInSeconds = newTimeInSeconds
        self.running = True
        self.startTime = time.time()

❸ def update(self):
        --- snip ---
        if not self.running:
            return False
        self.savedSecondsElapsed = time.time() - self.startTime
        if self.savedSecondsElapsed < self.timeInSeconds:
            return False   # running but hasn't reached limit

        else:   # timer has finished
            self.running = False
            if self.callBack is not None:
                self.callBack(self.nickname)

            return True   # True here means that the timer has ended

❹ def getTime(self):
        --- snip ---
        if self.running:
            self.savedSecondsElapsed = time.time() - self.startTime

        return self.savedSecondsElapsed

❺ def stop(self):
        """Stops the timer"""
        self.getTime()   # remembers final self.savedSecondsElapsed
        self.running = False
```

*Listing 13-2: A simple `Timer` class*

When you create a `Timer` object, the only required argument is the number of seconds you want the timer to run ❶. You can optionally supply a nickname for the timer and a function or method to be called back when the time has elapsed. If you specify a callback, the nickname will be passed in when the callback happens.

You call the `start()` method ❷ to start the timer running. The `Timer` object remembers the start time in the instance variable `self.startTime`.

The `update()` method ❸ must be called every time through the main loop. If the timer is running and the appropriate amount of time has elapsed, this method returns `True`. In any other call, this method returns `False`.

If a `Timer` is running, calling `getTime()` ❹ returns how much time has elapsed for that `Timer`. You can call the `stop()` method ❺ to immediately stop the `Timer`.

We can now rewrite the timer demonstration program shown in Figure 13-1 to use this `Timer` class from the `pyghelpers` package. Listing 13-3 shows how we use a `Timer` object in the code.

## File: TimerObjectExamples/SimpleTimerExample.py

```
# Simple timer example

--- snip ---

❶ oTimer = pyghelpers.Timer(TIMER_LENGTH)  # create a Timer object

# 6 - Loop forever
while True:

    # 7 - Check for and handle events
    for event in pygame.event.get():
        if event.type == pygame.QUIT:
            pygame.quit()
            sys.exit()

        if startButton.handleEvent(event):
          ❷ oTimer.start()  # start the timer
            startButton.disable()
            timerMessage.show()
            print('Starting timer')

        if clickMeButton.handleEvent(event):
            print('Other button was clicked')

    # 8 - Do any "per frame" actions
  ❸ if oTimer.update():  # True here means timer has ended
        startButton.enable()
        timerMessage.hide()
        print('Timer ended')

    # 9 - Clear the screen
    window.fill(WHITE)

    # 10 - Draw all screen elements
    headerMessage.draw()
    startButton.draw()
    clickMeButton.draw()
    timerMessage.draw()

    # 11 - Update the screen
    pygame.display.update()

    # 12 - Slow things down a bit
    clock.tick(FRAMES_PER_SECOND)  # make pygame wait
```

*Listing 13-3: A main program that uses an instance of the* Timer *class*

Again, I've cut the setup code. Before the main loop starts, we create a
Timer object ❶. When the user clicks Start, we call oTimer.start() ❷ to start
the timer running.

Each time through the loop, we call the update() method of the Timer object ❸. There are two ways to know when the timer ends. The simple way is to check for this call returning True. The sample code in Listing 13-3 uses this approach. Alternatively, if we specified a value for callBack in the __init__() call, when the timer finished, whatever was specified as the callBack value would be called back. In most cases, I would suggest using the first approach.

There are two advantages to using a Timer class. First, it hides the details of the timing code; you only create a Timer object when you want to, and you call the methods of that object. Second, you can create as many Timer objects as you wish, and each will run independently.

## Displaying Time

Many programs will need to count and display time to the user. For example, in a game, the elapsed time might be constantly displayed and updated, or the user might have a set amount of time to complete a task, requiring a countdown timer. I'll demonstrate how to do both of these using the Slider Puzzle game pictured in Figure 13-3.

Figure 13-3: The Slider Puzzle user interface

When you start this game, the tiles are randomly rearranged, and there is one empty black space. The goal of the game is to move tiles one at a time to put them in order from 1 to 15. You are only allowed to click a tile that is horizontally or vertically adjacent to the empty square. Clicking a valid tile swaps it with the space. I won't get into the details of the full implementation of the game (although the source code is available online, with the rest of the book's resources). Instead, I will focus on how to integrate a timer.

The pyghelpers package contains two classes that allow programmers to track time. The first is CountUpTimer, which starts at zero and counts up indefinitely, or until you tell it to stop. The second is CountDownTimer, which starts at a given amount of time and counts down to zero. I've built a version of the game for each. The first version lets the user see how long it takes them to solve the puzzle. In the second one, the user is given a certain amount of time when they start the game, and if they have not completed it when the timer reaches zero, they lose the game.

## CountUpTimer

With the CountUpTimer class, you create a timer object and tell it when to start. Then, in every frame, you can call one of three different methods to get the time elapsed in different formats.

Listing 13-4 contains the implementation of the CountUpTimer class from pyghelpers. The code is a good example of how the different methods of a class share instance variables.

**File: (Available as part of the pyghelpers module)**

```
# CountUpTimer class

class CountUpTimer():
    --- snip ---

    def __init__(self): ❶
        self.running = False
        self.savedSecondsElapsed = 0.0
        self.secondsStart = 0  # safeguard

    def start(self): ❷
    --- snip ---
        self.secondsStart = time.time()  # get the current seconds and save the value
        self.running = True
        self.savedSecondsElapsed = 0.0

    def getTime(self): ❸
        """Returns the time elapsed as a float"""
        if not self.running:
            return self.savedSecondsElapsed  # do nothing

        self.savedSecondsElapsed = time.time() - self.secondsStart
        return self.savedSecondsElapsed  # returns a float

    def getTimeInSeconds(self): ❹
        """Returns the time elapsed as an integer number of seconds"""
        nSeconds = int(self.getTime())
        return nSeconds

    # Updated version using fStrings
    def getTimeInHHMMSS(self, nMillisecondsDigits=0): ❺
    --- snip ---
        nSeconds = self.getTime()
        mins, secs = divmod(nSeconds, 60)
        hours, mins = divmod(int(mins), 60)

        if nMillisecondsDigits > 0:
```

```
            secondsWidth = nMillisecondsDigits + 3
        else:
            secondsWidth = 2

        if hours > 0:
            output = 
                f'{hours:d}:{mins:02d}:{secs:0{secondsWidth}.{nMillisecondsDigits}f}'
        elif mins > 0:
            output = f'{mins:d}:{secs:0{secondsWidth}.{nMillisecondsDigits}f}'
        else:
            output = f'{secs:.{nMillisecondsDigits}f}'

        return output

    def stop(self): ❻
        """Stops the timer"""
        self.getTime()  # remembers final self.savedSecondsElapsed
        self.running = False
```

Listing 13-4: The CountUpTimer class

The implementation depends on three key instance variables ❶:

- self.running is a Boolean that indicates whether the timer is running or not.
- self.savedSecondsElapsed is a float that represents the elapsed time of a timer.
- self.secondsStart is the time that the timer started running.

The client calls the start() method ❷ to start a timer. In response, the method calls time.time(), stores the start time in self.secondsStart, and sets self.running to True to indicate that the timer is running.

The client can call any of these three methods to get the elapsed time associated with the timer, in different formats:

- getTime() ❸ returns the elapsed time as a floating-point number.
- getTimeInSeconds() ❹ returns the elapsed time as an integer number of seconds.
- getTimeInHHMMSS() ❺ returns the elapsed time as a formatted string.

The getTime() method calls time.time() to get the current time and subtracts the starting time to get the elapsed time. The other two methods each make a call to the getTime() method of this class to calculate the elapsed time, then do different processing on the output: getTimeInSeconds() converts the time into an integer number of seconds, and getTimeInHHMMSS() formats the time into a string in *hours:minutes:seconds* format. The output of each of these methods is intended to be sent to a DisplayText object (defined in the pygwidgets package) to be shown in the window.

The stop() method ❻ can be called to stop the timer (for example, when the user completes the puzzle).

The main file for this version of the Slider Puzzle game is available with the rest of the book's resources, at *SliderPuzzles/Main_SliderPuzzleCountUp.py*. It instantiates a CountUpTimer object before the main loop begins and saves it in the variable oCountUpTimer. It then calls the start() method right away. It also creates a DisplayText field to display the time. Each time through the main loop, the main code calls the getTimeInHHMMSS() method and shows the result in the field:

```
timeToShow = oCountUpTimer.getTimeInHHMMSS()   # ask the Timer object for the elapsed time
oTimerDisplay.setValue('Time: ' + timeToShow)  # put that into a text field
```

The variable oTimerDisplay is an instance of the pygwidgets.DisplayText class. The setValue() method of the DisplayText class is optimized to check whether the new text to be displayed is the same as the previous text. Therefore, even though we are telling the field to display the amount of time 30 times every second, there is not much work done until the time changes, once per second.

The game code checks for a solved puzzle and, when the puzzle is solved, calls the stop() method to freeze the time. If the user clicks the Restart button to start a new game, the game calls start() to restart the timer object.

### CountDownTimer

The CountDownTimer class has some subtle differences. Instead of counting up from zero, you initialize a CountDownTimer by providing a starting number of seconds, and it counts down from that value. The interface for creating a CountDownTimer looks like this:

```
CountDownTimer(nStartingSeconds, stopAtZero=True, nickname=None,
               callBack=None):
```

There is a second optional parameter, stopAtZero, that defaults to True— which assumes that you want the timer to stop when it reaches zero. You can also optionally specify a function or method as a callback when the timer reaches zero. Lastly, you can supply a nickname to be used if and when a callback is made.

The client calls the start() method to begin counting down.

From the client's point of view, the getTime(), getTimeInSeconds(), getTimeInHHMMSS(), and stop() methods appear identical to their counterparts in the CountUpTimer class.

CountDownTimer has an additional method named ended(). The application needs to call the ended() method every time through its main loop. It returns False while the timer is active, but returns True when the timer ends (that is, reaches zero).

The countdown version of the Slider Puzzle game's main file is available with the book's resources, at *SliderPuzzles/Main_SliderPuzzleCountDown.py*.

The code is very similar to the previous version that counts up, but this version creates an instance of CountDownTimer instead and supplies a set number of seconds it allows to solve the puzzle. It also calls getTimeInHHMMSS(2) every frame and updates the time with two decimal digits. Finally, it includes a call to the ended() method in every frame to see if the time has run out. If the timer ends before the user has solved the puzzle, it plays a sound and displays a message telling the user that they ran out of time.

## Summary

This chapter gave you a number of ways to handle timing in programs. I discussed three different approaches: first by counting frames, second by creating a custom event, and finally by remembering a start time and subtracting it from the current time to get the time elapsed.

Using the third approach, we built a generic reusable Timer class (which you can find in the pyghelpers package). I also showed two additional classes from this package, CountUpTimer and CountDownTimer, that can be used to handle timing in programs where you want to show a timer to the user.

# 14

## ANIMATION

This chapter is about animation—
specifically, traditional image animation.
On a very simple level, you can think of
this like a flip-book: a series of images, each
slightly different from the previous one, that are
shown in succession. The user sees each image for a
short amount of time and experiences the illusion of
movement. Animation provides a good opportunity
for building a class because the mechanics of displaying the images over time are well understood and
easily coded.

To show the general principles, we'll begin by implementing two animation classes: a SimpleAnimation class based on a series of individual image files,
and a SimpleSpriteSheetAnimation class built using a single file that contains

a sequence of many images. Then I'll show you two more-robust animation classes from the pygwidgets package, Animation and SpriteSheetAnimation, and explain how they are built using a common base class.

# Building Animation Classes

The basic idea behind an animation class is relatively straightforward. The client will provide an ordered set of images and an amount of time. The client code will tell the animation when to start playing and will periodically tell the animation to update itself. The images in the animation will be displayed in order, each for the given amount of time.

## SimpleAnimation Class

The general technique is to begin by loading the complete set of images, storing them in a list, and displaying the first image. When the client tells the animation to start, the animation begins tracking time. Each time the object is told to update itself, our code checks to see if the specified amount of time has passed and, if so, displays the next image in the sequence. When the animation is finished, we display the first image again.

### Creating the Class

Listing 14-1 contains the code of a SimpleAnimation class, which handles an animation made up of separate image files. To keep things clearly organized, I strongly recommend that you place all the image files associated with an animation in a subfolder inside an *images* folder inside your project folder. The examples given here will use this structure, and the associated art and main code are available with the rest of the book's resources.

**File: SimpleAnimation/SimpleAnimation.py**

```
# SimpleAnimation class

import pygame
import time

class SimpleAnimation():
    def __init__(self, window, loc, picPaths, durationPerImage): ❶
        self.window = window
        self.loc = loc
        self.imagesList = []
        for picPath in picPaths:
            image = pygame.image.load(picPath)  # load an image
            image = pygame.Surface.convert_alpha(image) ❷ # optimize blitting
            self.imagesList.append(image)

        self.playing = False
        self.durationPerImage = durationPerImage
        self.nImages = len(self.imagesList)
```

```
        self.index = 0

    def play(self): ❸
        if self.playing:
            return
        self.playing = True
        self.imageStartTime = time.time()
        self.index = 0

    def update(self): ❹
        if not self.playing:
            return

        # How much time has elapsed since we started showing this image
        self.elapsed = time.time() - self.imageStartTime

        # If enough time has elapsed, move on to the next image
        if self.elapsed > self.durationPerImage:
            self.index = self.index + 1

            if self.index < self.nImages: # move on to next image
                self.imageStartTime = time.time()
            else:  # animation is finished
                self.playing = False
                self.index = 0  # reset to the beginning

    def draw(self): ❺
        # Assumes that self.index has been set earlier - in the update() method.
        # It is used as the index into the imagesList to find the current image.
        theImage = self.imagesList[self.index]  # choose the image to show

        self.window.blit(theImage, self.loc)  # show it
```

Listing 14-1: The SimpleAnimation class

When a client instantiates a SimpleAnimation object, it must pass in the following:

**window**    The window to draw into.

**loc**    The location in the window to draw the images.

**picPaths**    A list or tuple of paths to images. The images will be displayed in the order given here.

**durationPerImage**    How long (in seconds) to show each image.

In the __init__() method ❶, we save these parameter variables into similarly named instance variables. The method loops through the list of paths, loads each image, and saves the resulting images into a list. A list is a perfect way to represent an ordered set of images. The class will use the self.index variable to keep track of the current image in the list.

The format of an image in a file is different from the format of an image when displayed on the screen. The call to convert_alpha() ❷ converts from the file format to the screen format to optimize performance when showing an image in the window. The actual drawing is done later, in the draw() method.

The play() method ❸ starts an animation running. It first checks to see if the animation is already running, and if it is, the method just returns. Otherwise, it sets self.playing to True to indicate that the animation is now running.

When a SimpleAnimation is created, the caller specifies the amount of time that each image should be shown, and this is saved in self.durationPerImage. Therefore, we must keep track of time as a SimpleAnimation runs to know when to switch to the next image. We call time.time() to get the current time (in milliseconds) and save that in an instance variable. Making the class time based means that any SimpleAnimation object built from this class will work correctly, independent of the frame rate used for the main loop. Finally, we set the variable self.index to 0 to indicate that we should be showing the first image.

The update() method ❹ needs to be called in every frame of the main loop. If the animation is not playing, update() does nothing and just returns. Otherwise, update() calculates how much time has elapsed since the current image started showing by getting the current time using the system time.time() function and subtracting that from the time at which the current image started showing.

If the elapsed time is greater than the amount of time that each image should be showing, it's time move to the next image. In this case, we increment self.index so that the upcoming call to the draw() method will draw the appropriate image. We then check whether the animation has finished. If not, we save the start time for the new image. If the animation is done, we set self.playing back to False (to indicate that we are no longer playing the animation), and we reset self.index to 0 so that the draw() method will show the first image again.

Finally, we call draw() in every frame ❺ to draw the current image of the animation. The draw() method assumes that self.index has been set correctly by a previous method, and uses it to index into the list of images. It then draws that image in the window at the specified location.

### Example Main Program

Listing 14-2 shows a main program that creates and uses a SimpleAnimation object. This will animate a dinosaur riding a bicycle.

### File: SimpleAnimation/Main_SimpleAnimation.py

```
# Animation example
# Shows example of SimpleAnimation object

# 1 - Import library
import pygame
from pygame.locals import *
import sys
import pygwidgets
from SimpleAnimation import *

# 2 Define constants
SCREEN_WIDTH = 640
```

```
SCREEN_HEIGHT = 480
FRAMES_PER_SECOND = 30
BGCOLOR = (0, 128, 128)

# 3 - Initialize the world
pygame.init()
window = pygame.display.set_mode([SCREEN_WIDTH, SCREEN_HEIGHT])
clock = pygame.time.Clock()

# 4 - Load assets: images(s), sound(s), etc.
❶ dinosaurAnimTuple = ('images/Dinobike/f1.gif',
                        'images/Dinobike/f2.gif',
                        'images/Dinobike/f3.gif',
                        'images/Dinobike/f4.gif',
                        'images/Dinobike/f5.gif',
                        'images/Dinobike/f6.gif',
                        'images/Dinobike/f7.gif',
                        'images/Dinobike/f8.gif',
                        'images/Dinobike/f9.gif',
                        'images/Dinobike/f10.gif')

# 5 - Initialize variables
oDinosaurAnimation = SimpleAnimation(window, (22, 140),
                                     dinosaurAnimTuple, .1)
oPlayButton = pygwidgets.TextButton(window, (20, 240), "Play")

# 6 - Loop forever
while True:

    # 7 - Check for and handle events
    for event in pygame.event.get():
        if event.type == QUIT:
            pygame.quit()
            sys.exit()

    ❷ if oPlayButton.handleEvent(event):
            oDinosaurAnimation.play()

    # 8 - Do any "per frame" actions
❸ oDinosaurAnimation.update()

    # 9 - Clear the window
    window.fill(BGCOLOR)

    # 10 - Draw all window elements
❹ oDinosaurAnimation.draw()
    oPlayButton.draw()

    # 11 - Update the window
    pygame.display.update()

    # 12 - Slow things down a bit
    clock.tick(FRAMES_PER_SECOND)   # make pygame wait
```

*Listing 14-2: The main program that instantiates and plays a `SimpleAnimation`*

All the images for the animated dinosaur are in the folder *images/ DinoBike/*. We first build a tuple of the images ❶. Then, using that tuple, we create a SimpleAnimation object and specify that each image should be shown for a tenth of a second. We also instantiate a Play button.

In the main loop, we call the update() and draw() methods of the oDinosaurAnimation object. The program loops while continuously drawing the current image of the animation and the Play button. When the animation is not running, the user just sees the first image.

When the user clicks the Play button ❷, the program calls the play() method of oDinosaurAnimation to start the animation running.

In the main loop, we call the update() method of oDinosaurAnimation ❸, which determines whether enough time has elapsed for the animation to move on to the next image.

Finally, we call draw() ❹, and the object draws the appropriate image.

## SimpleSpriteSheetAnimation Class

The second type of animation is implemented in the SimpleSpriteSheetAnimation class. A *sprite sheet* is a single image made up of a number of equally sized smaller images, intended to appear in order to create an animation. From a developer's point of view, there are three advantages to a sprite sheet. First, all the images are in a single file, so there is no need to worry about building a name for each separate file. Second, it's possible to see the progression of an animation in a single file, rather than having to flip through a sequence of images. Finally, loading a single file is faster than loading a list of files that make up an animation.

Figure 14-1 shows an example of a sprite sheet.

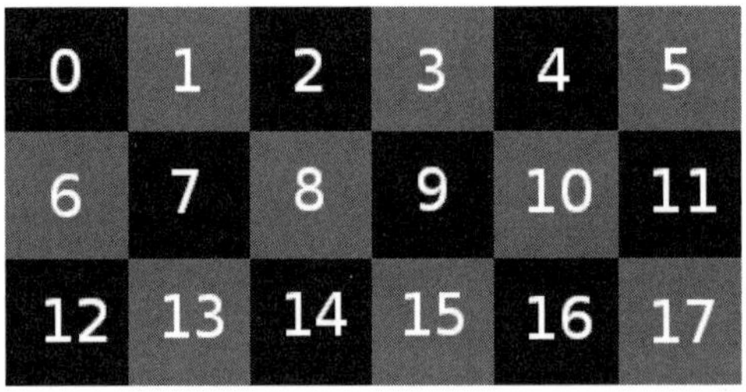

Figure 14-1: A sprite sheet image made up of 18 smaller images

This example is designed to show the numbers from 0 to 17. The original file contains an image that is 384×192 pixels. A quick division shows that each individual number image is 64×64 pixels. The key idea here is that we use pygame to create *subimages* of a larger image to give us a set of 18 new 64×64 pixel images. The smaller images can then be displayed using the same technique as we used in the SimpleAnimation class.

### Creating the Class

Listing 14-3 contains the SimpleSpriteSheetAnimation class to handle sprite sheet–based animations. During initialization, the contents of the single sprite sheet image are split up into a list of smaller images, which are then displayed by the other methods.

**File: SimpleSpriteSheetAnimation/SimpleSpriteSheetAnimation.py**

```
# SimpleSpriteSheetAnimation class

import pygame
import time

class SimpleSpriteSheetAnimation():
    def __init__(self, window, loc, imagePath, nImages, width, height, durationPerImage): ❶
        self.window = window
        self.loc = loc
        self.nImages = nImages
        self.imagesList = []

        # Load the sprite sheet
        spriteSheetImage = pygame.image.load(imagePath)
        # Optimize blitting
        spriteSheetImage = pygame.Surface.convert_alpha(spriteSheetImage)

        # Calculate the number of columns in the starting image
        nCols = spriteSheetImage.get_width() // width

        # Break up the starting image into subimages
        row = 0
        col = 0
        for imageNumber in range(nImages):
            x = col * height
            y = row * width

            # Create a subsurface from the bigger spriteSheet
            subsurfaceRect = pygame.Rect(x, y, width, height)
            image = spriteSheetImage.subsurface(subsurfaceRect)
            self.imagesList.append(image)

            col = col + 1
            if col == nCols:
                col = 0
                row = row + 1

        self.durationPerImage = durationPerImage
        self.playing = False
        self.index = 0

    def play(self):
        if self.playing:
            return
        self.playing = True
```

```
        self.imageStartTime = time.time()
        self.index = 0

    def update(self):
        if not self.playing:
            return

        # How much time has elapsed since we started showing this image
        self.elapsed = time.time() - self.imageStartTime

        # If enough time has elapsed, move on to the next image
        if self.elapsed > self.durationPerImage:
            self.index = self.index + 1

            if self.index < self.nImages:  # move on to next image
                self.imageStartTime = time.time()

            else:  # animation is finished
                self.playing = False
                self.index = 0  # reset to the beginning

    def draw(self):
        # Assumes that self.index has been set earlier - in the update() method.
        # It is used as the index into the imagesList to find the current image.
        theImage = self.imagesList[self.index]  # choose the image to show

        self.window.blit(theImage, self.loc)  # show it
```

*Listing 14-3: The SimpleSpriteSheetAnimation class*

This class is very similar to SimpleAnimation, but because this animation is based on a sprite sheet, the __init__() method must be passed different information ❶. The method requires the standard window and loc parameters, as well as:

**imagePath**   A path to a sprite sheet image (single file)

**nImages**   The number of images in the sprite sheet

**width**   The width of each subimage

**height**   The height of each subimage

**durationPerImage**   How long (in seconds) to show each image

Given these values, the __init__() method loads the sprite sheet file, and it uses a loop to split up the larger image into a list of smaller subimages through a call to the pygame subsurface() method. The smaller images are then appended into the self.imagesList list for use by the other methods. The __init__() method uses a counter to count the number of subimages, up to the number specified by the caller; therefore, the last row of images does not need to be a full row. For example, we could have used a sprite sheet image that only had the numbers 0 through 14, rather than needing to fill the row to 17. The nImages parameter is the key to making this work.

This rest of this class has the exact same methods as the previous SimpleAnimation class: play(), update(), and draw().

## Example Main Program

Listing 14-4 provides a sample main program that creates and shows a `SimpleSpriteSheetAnimation` object that shows an animated drop of water landing and spreading out. If you download everything in the *SpriteSheetAnimation* folder of this book's resources, you will get the code and the appropriate artwork.

### File: SimpleSpriteSheetAnimation/Main_SimpleSpriteSheetAnimation.py

```
# Shows example of SimpleSpriteSheetAnimation object

# 1 - Import library
import pygame
from pygame.locals import *
import sys
import pygwidgets
from SimpleSpriteSheetAnimation import *

# 2 Define constants
SCREEN_WIDTH = 640
SCREEN_HEIGHT = 480
FRAMES_PER_SECOND = 30
BGCOLOR = (0, 128, 128)

# 3 - Initialize the world
pygame.init()
window = pygame.display.set_mode([SCREEN_WIDTH, SCREEN_HEIGHT])
clock = pygame.time.Clock()

# 4 - Load assets: images(s), sound(s), etc.

# 5 - Initialize variables
❶ oWaterAnimation = SimpleSpriteSheetAnimation(window, (22, 140),
                                    'images/water_003.png',
                                    50, 192, 192, .05)
oPlayButton = pygwidgets.TextButton(window, (60, 320), "Play")

# 6 - Loop forever
while True:

    # 7 - Check for and handle events
    for event in pygame.event.get():
        if event.type == QUIT:
            pygame.quit()
            sys.exit()

        if oPlayButton.handleEvent(event):
            oWaterAnimation.play()

    # 8 - Do any "per frame" actions
    oWaterAnimation.update()
```

```
# 9 - Clear the window
window.fill(BGCOLOR)

# 10 - Draw all window elements
oWaterAnimation.draw()
oPlayButton.draw()

# 11 - Update the window
pygame.display.update()

# 12 - Slow things down a bit
clock.tick(FRAMES_PER_SECOND)   # make pygame wait
```

*Listing 14-4: A sample main program that creates and uses a SimpleSpriteSheetAnimation object*

The only significant difference with this example is that it instantiates a SimpleSpriteSheetAnimation object ❶ instead of a SimpleAnimation object.

### Merging Two Classes

The __init__() methods in SimpleAnimation and SimpleSpriteSheetAnimation have different parameters, but the other three methods (start(), update(), and draw()) are identical. Once you instantiate either of these classes, the way that you access the resulting objects is exactly the same. The "Don't Repeat Yourself" (DRY) principle says that having these duplicated methods is a bad idea, because any bug fixes and/or enhancements would have to be applied in both copies of the methods.

Instead, this is a good opportunity to merge classes. We can create a common abstract base class for these classes to inherit from. The base class will have its own __init__() method that includes any common code from the __init__() methods of both original classes, and it will contain the play(), update(), and draw() methods.

Each original class will inherit from the new base class and implement its own __init__() method using the appropriate parameters. Each will do its own work to create self.imagesList, which is then used in the other three methods in the new base class.

Rather than showing the result of merging these two "simple" classes, I'll show the result of this merge in the "professional strength" Animation and SpriteSheetAnimation classes that are part of the pygwidgets package.

## Animation Classes in pygwidgets

The pygwidgets module contains the following three animation classes:

**PygAnimation**  An abstract base class for the Animation and SpriteSheetAnimation classes

**Animation**  A class for image-based animations (separate image files)

**SpriteSheetAnimation**  A class for sprite sheet–based animations (a single large image)

We'll look at each class in turn. The `Animation` and `SpriteSheetAnimation` classes use the same basic concepts discussed, but also have more options available via initialization parameters.

## Animation Class

You use pygwidget's `Animation` class to create an animation from many different image files. Here is the interface:

```
Animation(window, loc, animTuplesList, autoStart=False,
        loop=False, showFirstImageAtEnd=True, nickname=None, callBack=None, nIterations=1):
```

The required parameters are:

**window**

The window to draw in.

**loc**

The upper-left corner where images should be drawn.

**animTuplesList**

A list (or tuple) of tuples describing the sequence of the animation. Each inner tuple contains:

**pathToImage**   The relative path to an image file.

**Duration**   The duration this image should be shown (in seconds, floating point).

**offset (optional)**   If present, an (x, y) tuple used as an offset from the main loc to show this image.

These parameters are all optional:

**autoStart**

True if you want the animation to start right away; defaults to False.

**loop**

True if you want the animation to loop continuously; defaults to False.

**showFirstImageAtEnd**

When an animation ends, show the first image again; defaults to True.

**nickname**

An internal name to assign to this animation, used as an argument when a callBack is specified.

**callBack**

The function or object method to call when the animation is done.

**nIterations**

The number of times to loop through the animation; defaults to 1.

Unlike `SimpleAnimation`, which uses a single duration for all images, the `Animation` class lets you specify a duration for *each* image, allowing for greater flexibility in the timing of how the images are displayed. You can also specify an x, y offset when drawing each image, but in general this isn't needed. Here is some sample code that creates an Animation object that shows a running T-rex dinosaur:

```
TRexAnimationList = [('images/TRex/f1.gif', .1),
                     ('images/TRex/f2.gif', .1),
                     ('images/TRex/f3.gif', .1),
                     ('images/TRex/f4.gif', .1),
                     ('images/TRex/f5.gif', .1),
                     ('images/TRex/f6.gif', .1),
                     ('images/TRex/f7.gif', .1),
                     ('images/TRex/f8.gif', .1),
                     ('images/TRex/f9.gif', .1),
                     ('images/TRex/f10.gif', .4)]

# 5 - Initialize variables
oDinosaurAnimation = pygwidgets.Animation(window, (22, 145),
        TRexAnimationList, callBack=myFunction, nickname='Dinosaur')
```

This creates an Animation object that will show 10 different images. The first nine images each show for one-tenth of a second, but the last image shows for four-tenths of a second. The animation will only play once and will not automatically start playing. When the animation is finished, myFunction() will be called with the argument 'Dinosaur'.

### SpriteSheetAnimation Class

For SpriteSheetAnimation, you pass in a path to the single sprite sheet file. In order for SpriteSheetAnimation to break up the large animation into many smaller images, you must specify the width and height of all subimages. For durations, you have two choices: you can specify a single value to say that all images should be shown for the same amount of time, or you can specify a list or tuple of durations, one for each image. Here's the interface:

```
SpriteSheetAnimation(window, loc, imagePath, nImages,
            width, height, durationOrDurationsList,
            autoStart=False, loop=False, showFirstImageAtEnd=True, nickname=None,
            callBack=None, nIterations=1):
```

The required parameters are:

window   The window to draw in

loc   The upper-left corner where images should be drawn

imagePath   The relative path to the sprite sheet image file

nImages   The total number of subimages in the sprite sheet subimage

width   The width of each single resulting subimage

height   The height of each single resulting subimage

durationOrDurationsList   The amount of time for which each subimage should be shown during animation or a list of durations, one per subimage (the length must be nImages)

These are the optional parameters:

**autoStart**

True if you want the animation to start right away; defaults to False.

**loop**

True if you want to animation to loop continuously; defaults to False.

**showFirstImageAtEnd**

When an animation ends, show the first image again; defaults to True.

**nickname**

An internal name to assign to this animation, used as an argument when a callBack is specified.

**callBack**

The function or object method to call when the animation is done.

**nIterations**

The number of times to loop through the animation; defaults to 1.

Here is a typical statement to create a SpriteSheetAnimation object:

```
oEffectAnimation = pygwidgets.SpriteSheetAnimation(window, (400, 150),
                        'images/effect.png', 35, 192, 192, .1,
                        autoStart=True, loop=True)
```

This creates a SpriteSheetAnimation object using a single image file found at the given path. The original image contains 35 subimages. Each smaller image is 192×192 pixels, and each subimage will be shown for one-tenth of a second. The animation will start automatically and loop continuously.

## Common Base Class: PygAnimation

The Animation and SpriteSheetAnimation classes each consist only of an __init__() method and inherit from a common abstract base class, PygAnimation. The __init__() methods of both classes call the inherited __init__() method of the PygAnimation base class. Therefore, the __init__() methods of the Animation and SpriteSheetAnimation classes only initialize the unique data in their classes.

After creating an Animation or SpriteSheetAnimation object, client code needs to include calls to update() and draw() in every frame. The following is a list of the methods available to both classes through the base class:

**handleEvent(*event*)**

Must be called in every frame if you want to check if the user has clicked on the animation. If so, you pass in the event supplied by pygame. This method returns False most of the time, but returns True when the user clicks down on the image, in which case you would typically call play().

**play()**

Starts the animation playing.

**stop()**

>Stops the animation wherever it is, and resets to showing only the first image.

**pause()**

>Causes the animation to temporarily stop on the current image. You can continue playing with a call to play().

**update()**

>Should be called in every frame. When the animation is running, this method takes care of calculating the proper time to advance to the next image. It typically returns False, but returns True when the animation ends (and it is not set to loop).

**draw()**

>Should be called in every frame. This method draws the current image of the animation.

**setLoop(*trueOrFalse*)**

>Pass in True or False to indicate whether the animation should loop or not.

**getLoop()**

>Returns True if the animation is set to loop or False if it is not.

**NOTE** *The location of an animation in the window is determined by the original value of loc that's passed to __init__(). Both Animation and SpriteSheetAnimation inherit from the common PygAnimation class, and that class inherits from PygWidget. Since all the methods available in PygWidget are therefore available in both animation classes, you could easily construct an animation that also changes its location while it is playing. You can make any animation move by calling setLoc(), inherited from PygWidget, and supplying any x and y location you like for each image.*

## Example Animation Program

Figure 14-2 shows a screenshot of a sample program that demonstrates multiple animations built from the Animation and SpriteSheetAnimation classes.

The little dinosaur on the left is an Animation object. It's set to autoStart so the animation plays when the program begins, but only once. Clicking the buttons below the small dinosaur makes appropriate calls to the Animation object. If you click Play, the animation plays again. While the animation is playing, clicking Pause will freeze the animation until you click Play again. If you play the animation and then click Stop, the animation will stop and show the first image. Below those buttons are two checkboxes. By default, this animation will not loop. If you check Loop, then press Play, the animation repeats until you uncheck Loop. The Show checkbox makes the animation visible or invisible.

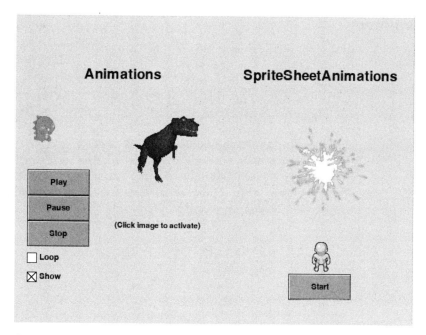

Figure 14-2: An example animation program using the Animation and
SpriteSheetAnimation classes

The second (T-rex) Animation object is not set to autoStart, so you only
see the first image of the animation. If you click this image, the animation is set to iterate through all its images three times (three loops) before
stopping.

At the top right is a firework SpriteSheetAnimation object, which comes
from a single image containing 35 subimages. This animation is set to loop,
so you see it run continuously.

At the bottom right is a walking SpriteSheetAnimation from a single image
with 36 subimages. When you click Start, the animation plays through all
the images once.

The full source code of this program is available in the *AnimationExample/
Main_AnimationExample.py* file along with the rest of the book's resources.

The program instantiates two Animation objects (the small dinosaur and
the T-rex) and two SpriteSheetAnimation objects (the firework and the walking person). When a button below the little dinosaur is clicked, we call the
appropriate method of the dinosaur animation object. A click on the little
dinosaur or T-rex results in a call to the start() method of that animation.

The program shows that multiple animations can run at the same
time. This works because the main loop calls the update() and draw() methods of *each* animation in every frame in the main loop, and each animation
makes its own decision about keeping the current image or showing the
next image.

## Summary

In this chapter, we explored the mechanisms required in an animation class by building our own SimpleAnimation and SimpleSpriteSheetAnimation classes. The former is made up of multiple images, whereas the latter uses a single larger image that contains multiple subimages.

These two classes have different initializations, but the remaining methods of the classes are identical. I explained the process of merging the two classes by building a common abstract base class.

I then introduced the Animation class and the SpriteSheetAnimation class in pygwidgets. I explained that these two classes only implement their own versions of the __init__() method, inheriting their other methods from the common base class, PygAnimation. I concluded by showing a demonstration program that provides examples of animations and sprite sheet animations.

# 15

## SCENES

Games and programs will often need to present different scenes to the user. For the purpose of this discussion, I'll define a *scene* as any window layout and related user interactions that are significantly different from any other. For example, a game like *Space Invaders* may have a starting or *splash* scene, a main game play scene, a high scores scene, and perhaps an ending or goodbye scene.

In this chapter I will discuss two different approaches to writing a program that has multiple scenes. First, I'll introduce the state machine technique, which works well for relatively small programs. Then I'll show a fully object-oriented approach where each scene is implemented as an object, under the control of a scene manager. The latter is much more scalable for larger programs.

# The State Machine Approach

At the beginning of this book, we developed a software simulation of a light switch. In Chapter 1, we first implemented a light switch using procedural code, and then we rewrote it using a class. In both cases, the position (or state) of the switch was represented by a single Boolean variable; True represented on and False represented off.

There are many situations where a program or an object can be in one of a number of different states, and different code needs to run based on the current state. For example, consider the series of steps involved in using an ATM. There is a starting (greeting) state, then you need to put in your ATM card; after this you're prompted to enter your PIN, choose which action you want to do, and so on. At any point, you may need to go back a step or even start over. The general implementation approach is to use a *state machine*.

---

**state machine**  A model that represents and controls the flow of execution through a series of states.

---

The implementation of a state machine consists of:

- A collection of predefined states, typically expressed as constants whose values are strings comprised of a word or short phrase that describes what happens in the state
- A single variable to track the current state
- A starting state (from the set of predefined states)
- A set of clearly defined transitions between states

A state machine can only be in one state at any given time, but can move to a new state, typically based on specific input from the user.

In Chapter 7 we discussed the GUI button classes in the pygwidgets package. When rolling over and clicking a button, a user sees three different images—up, over, and down—which correspond to different states of the button. The image switching is done in the handleEvent() method (which is called whenever an event occurs). Let's take a closer look at how this is implemented.

The handleEvent() method is built as a state machine. The state is kept in an instance variable, self.state. Each button starts in the up state, showing the "up" image. When the user moves the cursor over a button, we show the "over" image and the code transitions to the over state. When the user clicks down on the button, we show the "down" image and the code moves into the down state (internally called the *armed* state). When the user releases the mouse button (clicks up), we again show the "over" image, and the code transitions back to the over state (and handleEvent() returns True to indicate that a click has happened). If the user then moves the cursor off the button, we show the "up" image again and transition back to the up state.

Next, I'll show you how we can use a state machine to represent different scenes that a user can encounter in a larger program. As a generic example, we'll have the following scenes: *Splash* (starting), *Play*, and *End*. We'll create a set of constants that represent the different states, create a variable called state, and assign it the value of the starting state:

```
STATE_SPLASH = 'splash'
STATE_PLAY = 'play'
STATE_END = 'end'
state = STATE_SPLASH  # initialize to starting state
```

In order to perform different actions in the different states, in the program's main loop we use an if/elif/elif/.../else construct that branches based on the current value of the state variable:

```
while True:
    if state == STATE_SPLASH:
        # Do whatever you want to do in the Splash state here
    elif state == STATE_PLAY:
        # Do whatever you want to do in the Play state here
    elif state == STATE_END:
        # Do whatever you want to do in the End state here
    else:
        raise ValueError('Unknown value for state: ' + state)
```

Since state is initially set to STATE_SPLASH, only the first branch of the if statement will run.

The idea of a state machine is that under certain circumstances, typically triggered by some event, the program changes its state by assigning a different value to the state variable. For example, the starting Splash scene could just show a game introduction with a Start button. When the user clicks the Start button, the game will execute an assignment statement that changes the value of the state variable to transition into the Play state:

```
state = STATE_PLAY
```

Once that line runs, only the code in the first elif runs and completely different code will execute—the code to show and react to the Play state.

Similarly, whenever and however the program reaches the ending condition for the game, it will execute the following line to transition to the End state:

```
state = STATE_END
```

From then on, every time the program goes around the while loop, the code of the second elif branch will run.

In summary, a state machine has a set of states, one variable to keep track of which state the program is in, and a set of events that cause the program to transition from one state to another. Since there is a single variable that keeps track of the state, the program can be in only one of the states at any time. Different actions that the user takes (clicking a button, pressing a key, dragging an item, and so on) or other events (such as a timer running out) can cause the program to transition from one state to another. Depending on which state it is in, the program may listen for different events and will typically execute different code.

## A pygame Example with a State Machine

Next, we'll build a Rock, Paper, Scissors game that uses a state machine. The user chooses rock, paper, or scissors; then the computer randomly chooses among the three. If the person and computer choose the same item, it's a tie. Otherwise, one point is awarded to the player or the computer, according to the following rules:

- Rock crushes scissors.
- Scissors cuts paper.
- Paper covers rock.

The user will see the game as three scenes: an opening or Splash scene (Figure 15-1), a Play scene (Figure 15-2), and a Results scene (Figure 15-3).

*Figure 15-1: The Rock, Paper, Scissors Splash scene*

The Splash scene waits for the user to click the Start button.

Figure 15-2: The Rock, Paper, Scissors Play scene

The Play scene is where the user makes a choice. After the user clicks an icon to indicate their choice, the computer makes a randomized choice.

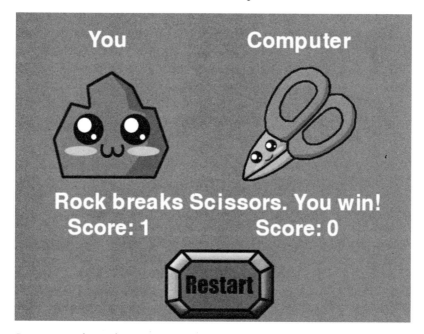

Figure 15-3: The Rock, Paper, Scissors Results scene

The Results scene shows the outcome of the round and the score. It waits for the user to click Restart to play another round.

In this game, each value of state corresponds to a different scene. Figure 15-4 is a *state diagram* that shows the states and transitions (the actions or events that cause the program to move from one state to another).

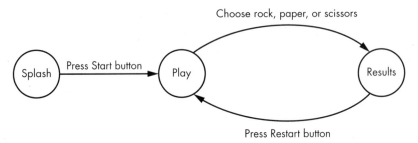

*Figure 15-4: Rock, Paper, Scissors state diagram*

When sitting idle (waiting for the user), the current scene will typically remain unchanged. That is, inside the main event loop, the program will usually not change the value of the state variable. (The state might change when a timer ends, but this will be rare.) This game starts in the Splash scene, and when the user presses the Start button, the game moves to the Play scene. The play of the game then alternates between the Play and Results scenes. Though this is a simple example, a state diagram can be very useful in understanding the flow of more complicated programs.

Listing 15-1 provides the code of the Rock, Paper, Scissors program, with the boilerplate code omitted to save space.

### File: RockPaperScissorsStateMachine/RockPaperScissors.py

```
# Rock, Paper, Scissors in pygame
# Demonstration of a state machine

--- snip ---

ROCK = 'Rock'
PAPER = 'Paper'
SCISSORS = 'Scissors'

# Set constants for each of the three states
STATE_SPLASH = 'Splash' ❶
STATE_PLAYER_CHOICE = 'PlayerChoice'
STATE_SHOW_RESULTS = 'ShowResults'

# 3 - Initialize the world
--- snip ---

# 4 - Load assets: image(s), sound(s), etc.
--- snip ---
```

```
# 5 - Initialize variables
playerScore = 0
computerScore = 0
state = STATE_SPLASH ❷   # the starting state

# 6 - Loop forever
while True:

    # 7 - Check for and handle events
    for event in pygame.event.get():
        if event.type == pygame.QUIT:
            pygame.quit()
            sys.exit()

        if state == STATE_SPLASH: ❸
            if startButton.handleEvent(event):
                state = STATE_PLAYER_CHOICE

        elif state == STATE_PLAYER_CHOICE: ❹   # let the user choose
            playerChoice = ''   # indicates no choice yet
            if rockButton.handleEvent(event):
                playerChoice = ROCK
                rpsCollectionPlayer.replace(ROCK)

            elif paperButton.handleEvent(event):
                playerChoice = PAPER
                rpsCollectionPlayer.replace(PAPER)

            elif scissorButton.handleEvent(event):
                playerChoice = SCISSORS
                rpsCollectionPlayer.replace(SCISSORS)

            if playerChoice != '':   # player has made a choice, make computer choice
                # Computer chooses from tuple of moves
                rps = (ROCK, PAPER, SCISSORS)
                computerChoice = random.choice(rps) # computer chooses
                rpsCollectionComputer.replace(computerChoice)

                # Evaluate the game
                if playerChoice == computerChoice: # tie
                    resultsField.setValue('It is a tie!')
                    tieSound.play()

                elif playerChoice == ROCK and computerChoice == SCISSORS:
                    resultsField.setValue('Rock breaks Scissors. You win!')
                    playerScore = playerScore + 1
                    winnerSound.play()

                elif playerChoice == ROCK and computerChoice == PAPER:
                    resultsField.setValue('Rock is covered by Paper. You lose.')
                    computerScore = computerScore + 1
                    loserSound.play()
```

```
            elif playerChoice == SCISSORS and computerChoice == PAPER:
                resultsField.setValue('Scissors cuts Paper. You win!')
                playerScore = playerScore + 1
                winnerSound.play()

            elif playerChoice == SCISSORS and computerChoice == ROCK:
                resultsField.setValue('Scissors crushed by Rock. You lose.')
                computerScore = computerScore + 1
                loserSound.play()

            elif playerChoice == PAPER and computerChoice == ROCK:
                resultsField.setValue('Paper covers Rock. You win!')
                playerScore = playerScore + 1
                winnerSound.play()

            elif playerChoice == PAPER and computerChoice == SCISSORS:
                resultsField.setValue('Paper is cut by Scissors. You lose.')
                computerScore = computerScore + 1
                loserSound.play()

            # Show the player's score
            playerScoreCounter.setValue('Your Score: '+ str(playerScore))
            # Show the computer's score
            computerScoreCounter.setValue('Computer Score: '+ str(computerScore))

            state = STATE_SHOW_RESULTS  # change state

    elif state == STATE_SHOW_RESULTS: ❺
        if restartButton.handleEvent(event):
            state = STATE_PLAYER_CHOICE  # change state

    else:
        raise ValueError('Unknown value for state:', state)

# 8 - Do any "per frame" actions
if state == STATE_PLAYER_CHOICE:
    messageField.setValue('        Rock          Paper          Scissors')
elif state == STATE_SHOW_RESULTS:
    messageField.setValue('You                      Computer')

# 9 - Clear the window
window.fill(GRAY)

# 10 - Draw all window elements
messageField.draw()

if state == STATE_SPLASH: ❻
    rockImage.draw()
    paperImage.draw()
    scissorsImage.draw()
    startButton.draw()

# Draw player choices
elif state == STATE_PLAYER_CHOICE: ❼
    rockButton.draw()
```

```
    paperButton.draw()
    scissorButton.draw()
    chooseText.draw()

# Draw the results
elif state == STATE_SHOW_RESULTS: ❽
    resultsField.draw()
    rpsCollectionPlayer.draw()
    rpsCollectionComputer.draw()
    playerScoreCounter.draw()
    computerScoreCounter.draw()
    restartButton.draw()

# 11 - Update the window
pygame.display.update()

# 12 - Slow things down a bit
clock.tick(FRAMES_PER_SECOND)   # make pygame wait
```

*Listing 15-1: The Rock, Paper, Scissors game*

In this listing, I have snipped the code that creates images, buttons, and text fields for the Splash, Play, and Results scenes. The downloadable files for the book contain the full source code and all the associated art.

Before the program goes into the main loop, we define all three states ❶, instantiate and load all the screen elements, and set the starting state ❷.

We do different event checks depending on which state the program is in. In the Splash state, we only check for clicking the Start button ❸. In the Play state, we check for a click on the Rock, Paper, or Scissors icon buttons ❹. In the Results state, we only check for a click on the Restart button ❺.

Pressing a button or making a selection in one scene changes the value of the state variable and therefore moves the game into a different scene. At the bottom of the main loop ❻ ❼ ❽, we draw different screen elements depending on which state the program is currently in.

This technique works well for a small number of states/scenes. However, in a program with more complicated rules or one that has many scenes and/or states, keeping track of what should be done where can become very difficult. Instead, we can take advantage of many of the object-oriented programming techniques introduced earlier in this book and build a different architecture based on independent scenes, all controlled by an object manager object.

# A Scene Manager for Managing Many Scenes

The second approach to building a program with multiple scenes is to use a *scene manager*: an object that centralizes the handling of different scenes. We'll create a SceneMgr class and instantiate a single oSceneMgr object from it. In the following discussion, I'll refer to the oSceneMgr object as the scene manager, since we only instantiate one. As you'll see, the scene manager and the related scenes take advantage of encapsulation, inheritance, and polymorphism.

Using the scene manager can be a little tricky, but the resulting program architecture results in a highly modular, easy-to-modify program. A program that uses the scene manager will be made up of the following files:

**Main program**    The small main program (that you write) must first create an instance of every scene identified in your program, then create an instance of the scene manager, passing a list of the scenes and a frame rate. To start your program, you call the run() method of the scene manager. For each new project you build, you must write a new main program.

**Scene manager**    The scene manager is written for you and is available as the SceneMgr class in the *pyghelpers.py* file. It keeps track of all the different scenes, remembers which one is current, calls methods in the current scene, allows for switching between scenes, and handles communication between scenes.

**Scenes**    Your program can have as many scenes as you want or need. Each scene is typically developed as a separate Python file. Each scene class must inherit from the prewritten Scene base class and have a set of methods whose names are predefined. The scene manager uses polymorphism to call these methods in the current scene. I have provided a template *SceneExample.py* file to show you how to build a scene.

The code for the SceneMgr class and the code for the Scene base class live in the pyghelpers package. The scene manager is an object manager object that manages any number of Scene objects.

## A Demo Program Using a Scene Manager

As a demonstration, we'll build a Scene Demo program that contains three simple scenes: Scene A, Scene B, and Scene C. The idea is that from any scene, you can click a button to get to any other scene. Figures 15-5 through 15-7 show screenshots of the three scenes.

*Figure 15-5: What the user sees in Scene A*

From Scene A, you can get to Scene B or Scene C.

Figure 15-6: What the user sees in Scene B

From Scene B, you can get to Scene A or Scene C.

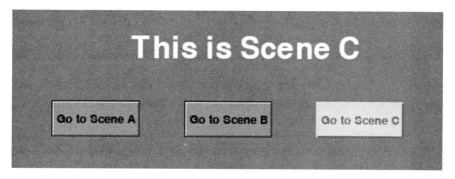

Figure 15-7: What the user sees in Scene C

From Scene C, you can get to Scene A or Scene B.

The structure of the project folder is shown in Figure 15-8. Note that this assumes that you have already installed the pygwidgets and pyghelpers modules in the proper *site-packages* folder.

Name

- Constants.py
- Main_SceneDemo.py
- SceneA.py
- SceneB.py
- SceneC.py
- SceneExample.py

Figure 15-8: The project folder showing the main program and the different scene files

*Main_SceneDemo.py* is the main program. *Constants.py* contains a few constants shared by the main program and all the scenes. *SceneA.py*, *SceneB.py*, and *SceneC.py* are the actual scenes, each containing a related scene class. *SceneExample.py* is a sample file that shows what a typical scene file might look like. It's not used in this program, but you can refer to it to get an understanding of the basics of writing a typical scene.

Figure 15-9 shows how the objects in the program relate to each other.

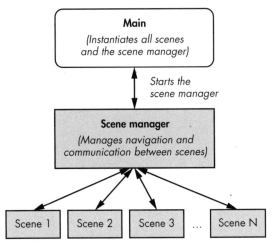

All scenes inherit from the Scene base class

Figure 15-9: The hierarchy of objects in a project

Let's see how the different parts of a program using the scene manager work together, starting with the main program.

## The Main Program

The main program will be unique for every project. Its purpose is to initialize the pygame environment, instantiate all the scenes, create an instance of the SceneMgr, then transfer control to the scene manager, oSceneMgr. Listing 15-2 presents the code of the demo main program.

### File: SceneDemo/Main_SceneDemo.py

```
# Scene Demo main program with three scenes

--- snip ---
# 1 - Import packages
import pygame
❶ import pyghelpers

from SceneA import *
from SceneB import *
from SceneC import *

# 2 - Define constants
❷ WINDOW_WIDTH = 640
WINDOW_HEIGHT = 180
FRAMES_PER_SECOND = 30
```

```
# 3 - Initialize the world
pygame.init()
window = pygame.display.set_mode((WINDOW_WIDTH, WINDOW_HEIGHT))

# 4 - Load assets: image(s), sound(s), etc.

# 5 - Initialize variables
# Instantiate all scenes and store them into a list
❸ scenesList = [SceneA(window),
                SceneB(window),
                SceneC(window)]

# Create the scene manager, passing in the scenes list and the FPS
❹ oSceneMgr = pyghelpers.SceneMgr(scenesList, FRAMES_PER_SECOND)

# Tell the scene manager to start running
❺ oSceneMgr.run()
```

*Listing 15-2: A sample main program using the scene manager*

The code of the main program is relatively short. We start by importing pyghelpers, then all the scenes (in this case, Scene A, Scene B, and Scene C) ❶. We then define a few more constants, initialize pygame, and create the window ❷. Next, we create an instance of each scene and store all the scenes in a list ❸. After this line executes, we have an initialized object for each scene.

We then instantiate the scene manager object (oSceneMgr) ❹ from the SceneMgr class. When we create this object, we need to pass in two values:

- The list of scenes, so the scene manager can be aware of all the scenes. The first scene in the list of scenes is used as the starting scene for the program.
- The frames per second (frame rate) that the program should maintain.

Finally, we tell the scene manager to start running by calling its run() method ❺. The scene manager always maintains a single scene as the current scene—the one that the user sees and interacts with.

Notice that with this approach, the main program implements the initialization of a typical pygame program but does *not* build the main loop. Instead, the main loop is built into the scene manager itself.

## Building the Scenes

To understand the interaction between the scene manager and any individual scene, I'll explain how a typical scene is built.

Each time through its loop, the scene manager calls a predefined set of methods in the current scene that are intended to handle events, do any per-frame actions, and draw anything that needs to be drawn in that scene. Therefore, the code of each scene must be split up into these methods. The approach makes use of polymorphism: each scene needs to implement a common set of methods.

## Methods to Implement in Each Scene

Each scene is implemented as a class that inherits from the Scene base class defined in the *pyghelpers.py* file. Therefore, each scene must import pyghelpers. At a minimum, a scene needs to contain an __init__() method and must override the getSceneKey(), handleInputs(), and draw() methods from the base class.

Every scene must have a unique *scene key*—a string used by the scene manager to identify each scene. I recommend that you build a file with a name like *Constants.py* that contains the keys for all the scenes and import this file into each scene file. For example, the *Constants.py* file for the sample program contains:

```
# Scene keys (any unique values):
SCENE_A = 'scene A'
SCENE_B = 'scene B'
SCENE_C = 'scene C'
```

During its initialization, the scene manager calls the getSceneKey() method of each scene, which simply returns its unique scene key. The scene manager then builds an internal dictionary of scene keys and scene objects. When any scene in the program wants to switch to a different scene, it will call self.goToScene() (described in the following section) and pass in the scene key of the target scene. The scene manager uses this key in the dictionary to find the associated scene object; it then sets the new scene object as the current scene and calls its methods.

Each scene must contain its own version of handleInputs() to handle any events that would typically be handled in the main loop and its own version of draw() to draw anything the scene wants to draw in the window. If your scene does not override these two methods, it will not be able to respond to any events and will not draw anything in the window.

Let's take a closer look at the four methods you need to implement for each scene:

### def __init__(self, window):

Each scene should begin with its own __init__() method. The window parameter is the window into which your program draws. You should start your method with this statement to save the window parameter for use in the draw() method:

```
self.window = window
```

After that, you can include any other initialization code you want or need, such as code for instantiating buttons and text fields, loading images and sounds, and so on.

### def getSceneKey(self):

This method must be implemented in every scene that you write. Your method must return the unique scene key associated with this scene.

```
def handleInputs(self, events, keyPressedList):
```

This method must be implemented in every scene that you write. It should do everything needed to deal with events or keys. The `events` parameter is a list of events that happened since the last frame, and `keyPressedList` is a list of Booleans representing the state of all keyboard keys (`True` means down). To find whether a particular key is up or down, you should use a constant rather than an integer index. The constants representing all keys of the keyboard are available in the pygame documentation (*https://www.pygame.org/docs/ref/key.html*).

Your implementation of this method should contain a `for` loop that loops through all events in the list that is passed in. If you want, it can also contain code to implement the continuous mode of handling the keyboard, as described in Chapter 5.

```
def draw(self):
```

This method must be implemented in every scene that you write. It should draw everything that needs to be drawn in the current scene.

The scene manager also calls the following methods in each scene. In the `Scene` base class, these methods each contain a simple `pass` statement, so they don't do anything. You can override any or all of them to execute any code you want for a particular scene:

```
def enter(self, data):
```

This method is called after the scene manager has made the transition into this scene. There is a single `data` parameter, with `None` as a default. If `data` is not `None`, then the information it contains was sent from the previous scene when it called `goToScene()` (described in the next section). The value of `data` can take any form—from a single string or numeric value to a list or dictionary to an object—as long as the leaving scene and the entering scene agree on the type of data being passed. The `enter()` method should do whatever it needs to do when this scene is about to be given control.

```
def update(self):
```

This method is called in every frame. Here, you can perform any actions you would have done in step 8 of the original 12-step template introduced in Chapter 5. For example, you might want this method to move images on the screen, check for collisions, and so on.

```
def leave(self):
```

This method is called by the scene manager whenever the program is about to transition to a different scene. It should do any cleanup that needs to be done before leaving, such as writing information to a file.

### Navigating Between Scenes

The scene manager and the Scene base class provide a simple way to navigate between scenes. When the program wants to transition to another scene, the current scene should call its own goToScene() method, which is in the inherited Scene base class, like this:

```
self.goToScene(nextSceneKey, data)
```

The goToScene() method communicates to the scene manager that you want to transition to a different scene, whose scene key is nextSceneKey. You should make all scene keys available via a file such as *Constants.py*. The data parameter is any optional information that you want to pass on to the next scene. If no data needs to be transferred, you can eliminate this argument. Typical calls would look like this:

```
self.goToScene(SOME_SCENE_KEY)   # no data to be passed
# Or
self.goToScene(ANOTHER_SCENE_KEY, data=someValueOrValues)   # go to a scene and pass data
```

The value of data can take any form, as long as the scenes being left and entered both understand the format. In response to this call, before leaving the current scene, the scene manager calls that scene's leave() method. When the next scene is about to be activated, the scene manager calls that scene's enter() method and passes the value of data to the new scene.

### Quitting the Program

The scene manager takes care of three different ways that the user can quit the currently running program:

- By clicking the close button at the top of the window.
- By pressing the ESCAPE key.
- Through any additional mechanism such as a Quit button. In this case, make the following call (which is also built into the Scene base class):

```
self.quit()   # quits the program
```

## A Typical Scene

Listing 15-3 shows an example of a typical scene—this is the *SceneA.py* file that implements Scene A in the demo program, shown in Figure 15-5. Remember that the main loop is implemented by the scene manager. Inside its main loop, the scene manager calls the handleInputs(), update(), and draw() methods for the current scene.

## File: SceneDemo/SceneA.py

```
# Scene A

import pygwidgets
import pyghelpers
import pygame
from pygame.locals import *
from Constants import *

class SceneA(pyghelpers.Scene):
  ❶ def __init__(self, window):

        self.window = window

        self.messageField = pygwidgets.DisplayText(self.window,
                (15, 25), 'This is Scene A', fontSize=50,
                textColor=WHITE, width=610, justified='center')

        self.gotoAButton = pygwidgets.TextButton(self.window,
                (250, 100), 'Go to Scene A')
        self.gotoBButton = pygwidgets.TextButton(self.window,
                (250, 100), 'Go to Scene B')
        self.gotoCButton = pygwidgets.TextButton(self.window,
                (400, 100), 'Go to Scene C')

        self.gotoAButton.disable()

  ❷ def getSceneKey(self):
        return SCENE_A

  ❸ def handleInputs(self, eventsList, keyPressedList):
        for event in eventsList:
            if self.gotoBButton.handleEvent(event):
              ❹ self.goToScene(SCENE_B)
            if self.gotoCButton.handleEvent(event):
              ❺ self.goToScene(SCENE_C)

    --- snip (testing code to send messages) ---
  ❻ def draw(self):
        self.window.fill(GRAYA)
        self.messageField.draw()
        self.gotoAButton.draw()
        self.gotoBButton.draw()
        self.gotoCButton.draw()

    --- snip (testing code to respond to messages) ---
```

*Listing 15-3: A typical scene (Scene A in the Scene Demo program)*

In the __init__() method ❶, we save away the window parameter in an instance variable. We then create an instance of a DisplayText field to show a title and create some TextButtons to allow for navigation to the other scenes.

The getSceneKey() method ❷ just returns the unique scene key (found in *Constants.py*) for this scene. In the handleInputs() method ❸, if the user has clicked the button for a different scene, we call the self.goToScene() navigation method ❹ ❺ to transfer control to the new scene. In the draw() method ❻, we fill the background, draw the message field, and draw the buttons. This example scene does very little, so we don't need to write our own enter(), update(), and leave() methods. Calls to these methods will be handled by methods of the same names in the Scene base class, and those methods don't do anything—they simply execute a pass statement.

The two other scene files are *SceneB.py* and *SceneC.py*. The only differences are the titles shown, the buttons drawn, and the effects of clicking the buttons to transfer to the appropriate new scene.

## Rock, Paper, Scissors Using Scenes

Let's build an alternate implementation of the Rock, Paper, Scissors game using the scene manager. To the user, the game will work exactly the same way as the earlier state machine version. We'll build a Splash scene, a Play scene, and a Results scene.

All of the source code is available, so I won't go through every Python file. The Splash scene is just a background picture with a Start button. When the user presses the Start button, the code executes goToScene(SCENE_PLAY) to transfer to the Play scene. In the Play scene, the user is presented with a set of images (rock, paper, and scissors) and asked to choose one. Clicking an image transfers control to the Results scene. Listing 15-4 contains the code of the Play scene.

**File: RockPaperScissorsWithScenes/ScenePlay.py**

```
# The Play scene
# The player chooses among rock, paper, or scissors

import pygwidgets
import pyghelpers
import pygame
from Constants import *
import random

class ScenePlay(pyghelpers.Scene):
    def __init__(self, window):

        self.window = window

        self.RPSTuple = (ROCK, PAPER, SCISSORS)
```

```
--- snip ---
def getSceneKey(self): ❶
    return SCENE_PLAY

def handleInputs(self, eventsList, keyPressedList): ❷
    playerChoice = None

    for event in eventsList:
        if self.rockButton.handleEvent(event):
            playerChoice = ROCK

        if self.paperButton.handleEvent(event):
            playerChoice = PAPER

        if self.scissorButton.handleEvent(event):
            playerChoice = SCISSORS

        if playerChoice is not None: ❸   # user has made a choice
            computerChoice = random.choice(self.RPSTuple)   # computer chooses
            dataDict = {'player': playerChoice, 'computer': computerChoice} ❹
            self.goToScene(SCENE_RESULTS, dataDict) ❺   # go to Results scene

# No need to include update method, defaults to inherited one which does nothing

def draw(self):
    self.window.fill(GRAY)
    self.titleField.draw()
    self.rockButton.draw()
    self.paperButton.draw()
    self.scissorButton.draw()
    self.messageField.draw()
```

*Listing 15-4: The Play scene in Rock, Paper, Scissors*

I've snipped the code to create text fields and the rock, paper, and scissors buttons. The getSceneKey() method ❶ simply returns the scene key for this scene.

The most important method is handleInputs() ❷, which is called in every frame. If any button is clicked, we set a variable named playerChoice to an appropriate constant ❸, and we make a random choice for the computer. We then take the player's choice and the computer's choice and build a simple dictionary ❹ incorporating both, so we can pass this information as data to the Results scene. Finally, to transfer to the Results scene, we call goToScene() and pass the dictionary ❺.

The scene manager receives this call, calls leave() for the current scene (Play), changes the current scene to the new scene (Results), and calls enter() for the new scene (Results). It passes the data from the leaving scene into the enter() method of the new scene.

Listing 15-5 contains the code of the Results scene. There's a lot of code here, but most of it deals with showing the appropriate icons and the evaluation of the results of the round.

```
# The Results scene
# The player is shown the results of the current round

import pygwidgets
import pyghelpers
import pygame
from Constants import *

class SceneResults(pyghelpers.Scene):
    def __init__(self, window, sceneKey):
        self.window = window

        self.playerScore = 0
        self.computerScore = 0

    ❶ self.rpsCollectionPlayer = pygwidgets.ImageCollection(
                        window, (50, 62),
                        {ROCK: 'images/Rock.png',
                        PAPER: 'images/Paper.png',
                        SCISSORS: 'images/Scissors.png'}, '')

        self.rpsCollectionComputer = pygwidgets.ImageCollection(
                        window, (350, 62),
                        {ROCK: 'images/Rock.png',
                        PAPER: 'images/Paper.png',
                        SCISSORS: 'images/Scissors.png'}, '')

        self.youComputerField = pygwidgets.DisplayText(
                        window, (22, 25),
                        'You                    Computer',
                        fontSize=50, textColor=WHITE,
                        width=610, justified='center')

        self.resultsField = pygwidgets.DisplayText(
                        self.window, (20, 275), '',
                        fontSize=50, textColor=WHITE,
                        width=610, justified='center')

        self.restartButton = pygwidgets.CustomButton(
                        self.window, (220, 310),
                        up='images/restartButtonUp.png',
                        down='images/restartButtonDown.png'
                        over='images/restartButtonHighlight.png')

        self.playerScoreCounter = pygwidgets.DisplayText(
                        self.window, (86, 315), 'Score:',
                        fontSize=50, textColor=WHITE)

        self.computerScoreCounter = pygwidgets.DisplayText(
                        self.window, (384, 315), 'Score:',
                        fontSize=50, textColor=WHITE)
```

```
                # Sounds
                self.winnerSound = pygame.mixer.Sound("sounds/ding.wav")
                self.tieSound = pygame.mixer.Sound("sounds/push.wav")
                self.loserSound = pygame.mixer.Sound("sounds/buzz.wav")

❷   def enter(self, data):
                # data is a dictionary (comes from the Play scene) that looks like:
                #      {'player': playerChoice, 'computer': computerChoice}
                playerChoice = data['player']
                computerChoice = data['computer']

                # Set the player and computer images
❸       self.rpsCollectionPlayer.replace(playerChoice)
                self.rpsCollectionComputer.replace(computerChoice)

                # Evaluate the game's win/lose/tie conditions
❹   if playerChoice == computerChoice:
                    self.resultsField.setValue("It's a tie!")
                    self.tieSound.play()

                elif playerChoice == ROCK and computerChoice == SCISSORS:
                    self.resultsField.setValue("Rock breaks Scissors. You win!")
                    self.playerScore = self.playerScore + 1
                    self.winnerSound.play()

                --- snip ---

                # Show the player's and computer's scores
                self.playerScoreCounter.setValue(
                                        'Score: ' + str(self.playerScore))
                self.computerScoreCounter.setValue(
                                        'Score: ' + str(self.computerScore))

❺   def handleInputs(self, eventsList, keyPressedList):
                for event in eventsList:
                    if self.restartButton.handleEvent(event):
                        self.goToScene(SCENE_PLAY)

        # No need to include update method,
        # defaults to inherited one which does nothing

❻   def draw(self):
                self.window.fill(OTHER_GRAY)
                self.youComputerField.draw()
                self.resultsField.draw()
                self.rpsCollectionPlayer.draw()
                self.rpsCollectionComputer.draw()
                self.playerScoreCounter.draw()
                self.computerScoreCounter.draw()
                self.restartButton.draw()
```

Listing 15-5: The Results scene in Rock, Paper, Scissors

Here, I've snipped some of the game evaluation logic. The enter() method ❷ is the most important method in this class. When the player makes a choice in the previous Play scene, the program transitions to this Results scene. First, we extract the player's and computer's choices that were passed in from the Play scene as a dictionary, which looks like this:

```
{'player': playerChoice, 'computer': computerChoice}
```

In the __init__() method ❶, we create ImageCollection objects for the player and computer, each containing the rock, paper, and scissors images. In the enter() method ❷, we use the replace() method of ImageCollection ❸ to show the images that represent the player's and the computer's choices.

Then, the evaluation is quite simple ❹. If the computer and the player made the same choice, we have a tie, and we play an appropriate tie sound. If the player wins, we increment the player's score and play a happy sound. If the computer wins, we increment the computer's score and play a sad sound. We update the player's or the computer's score and show the scores in the matching text display fields.

After the enter() method runs (one time for each round), the handleInputs() method ❺ is called in every frame by the scene manager. When the user clicks Restart, we call the inherited goToScene() method to transfer back to the Play scene.

The draw() method ❻ draws everything in the window for this scene.

In this scene, we don't do any additional work in each frame, so we don't need to write an update() method. When the scene manager calls update(), the inherited method in the Scene base class runs and just executes a pass statement.

## Communication Between Scenes

The scene manager provides a set of methods that allow scenes to communicate with each other by sending or requesting information. This communication won't be needed by all programs but can be highly useful. The scene manager allows any scene to:

- Request information from another scene
- Send information to another scene
- Send information to all other scenes

In the following sections, I'll call the scene the user is seeing the *current* scene. The scene that the current scene is sending information to or requesting information from is the *target* scene. The methods used to transfer information are all implemented in the Scene base class. Therefore, all scenes (which must inherit from the Scene base class) have access to these methods using self.<method>().

## Requesting Information from a Target Scene

To request information from any other scene, a scene makes a call to the inherited request() method, like this:

```
self.request(targetSceneKey, requestID)
```

This call allows the current scene to ask for information from a target scene, identified by its scene key (targetSceneKey). The requestID uniquely identifies the information you are asking for. The value used for a requestID would normally be a constant defined in a file like *Constants.py*. The call returns the requested information. A typical call would look like this:

```
someData = self.request(SOME_SCENE_KEY, SOME_INFO_CONSTANT)
```

This effectively says, "Issue a request to the *SOME_SCENE_KEY* scene asking for information identified by *SOME_INFO_CONSTANT*." The data is returned and assigned to the someData variable.

The scene manager acts as an intermediary: it receives the call to request() and turns it into a call to respond() in the target scene. To make a target scene able to give information, you must implement a respond() method in that scene's class. The method should start like this:

```
def respond(self, requestID):
```

The typical code of a respond() method checks the value of the requestID parameter and returns the appropriate data. The data returned can be formatted in any way that the current scene and the target scene agree on.

## Sending Information to a Target Scene

To send information to a target scene, the current scene makes a call to the inherited send() method, like this:

```
self.send(targetSceneKey, sendID, info)
```

This call allows the current scene to send information to a target scene, identified by its scene key (targetSceneKey). The sendID uniquely identifies the information you are sending. The info parameter is the information you want to send to the target scene.

A typical call would look like this:

```
self.send(SOME_SCENE_KEY, SOME_INFO_CONSTANT, data)
```

This effectively says, "Send information to the *SOME_SCENE_KEY* scene. The information is identified by *SOME_INFO_CONSTANT*, and the information is in the value of the variable data."

The scene manager receives the call to send() and turns it into a call to receive() in the target scene. To allow a scene to send information to another scene, you must implement a receive() method in your target scene class, like this:

```
def receive(self, receiveID, info):
```

The receive() method can contain an if/elif/else construct if it needs to handle different values for receiveID. The transmitted information can be formatted in any way that the current scene and the target scene agree on.

### Sending Information to All Scenes

As an additional convenience, a scene can send information to all other scenes using the single method sendAll():

```
self.sendAll(sendID, info)
```

This call allows the current scene to send information to all the other scenes. The sendID uniquely identifies the information you are sending. The info parameter is the information you want to send to all scenes.

A typical call would look like this:

```
self.sendAll(SOME_INFO_CONSTANT, data)
```

This effectively says, "Send information to all scenes. The information is identified by *SOME_INFO_CONSTANT*, and the information is in the value of the variable data."

For this to work, all scenes other than the current scene must implement the receive() method, as described in the previous section. The scene manager sends the message to all scenes (other than the current scene). The current scene may contain a receive() method for information sent by other scenes.

### Testing Communications Among Scenes

The Scene Demo program (with Scene A, Scene B, and Scene C), discussed earlier with Listings 15-2 and 15-3, contains code in each scene that demonstrates calls to send(), request(), and sendAll(). In addition, the scenes each implement simple versions of the receive() and respond() methods. In the demo program, you can send a message to another scene by pressing A, B, or C. Pressing X sends a message to all scenes. Pressing 1, 2, or 3 sends a request to get data from a target scene. The target scene responds with a string.

## Implementation of the Scene Manager

Here we'll look at how the scene manager is implemented. However, one important lesson of OOP is that the developer of client code doesn't need to understand the implementation of a class, only the interface. With respect to the scene manager, you don't need to know how it works, only what methods you must implement in your scenes, when they are called, and what methods you can call. Therefore, if you're not interested in the internals, you can go right to the Summary. If you are interested, this section goes through the implementation details, and along the way you'll learn an interesting technique to allow for two-way communication between objects.

The scene manager is implemented in a class named SceneMgr in the pyghelpers module. As explained previously, in your main program, you create a single instance of the scene manager like this:

```
oSceneMgr = SceneMgr(scenesList, FRAMES_PER_SECOND)
```

The last line of your main program needs to be:

```
oSceneMgr.run()
```

Listing 15-6 contains the code of the __init__() method of the SceneMgr class.

```
--- snip ---
def __init__(self, scenesList, fps):

# Build a dictionary, each entry of which is a sceneKey : scene object
❶    self.scenesDict = {}
❷    for oScene in scenesList:
        key = oScene.getSceneKey()
        self.scenesDict[key] = oScene

    # The first element in the list is used as the starting scene
❸    self.oCurrentScene = scenesList[0]
    self.framesPerSecond = fps

    # Give each scene a reference back to the SceneMgr.
    # This allows any scene to do a goToScene, request, send,
    # or sendAll, which gets forwarded to the scene manager.
❹    for key, oScene in self.scenesDict.items():
        oScene._setRefToSceneMgr(self)
```

Listing 15-6: The __init__() method of the SceneMgr class

The __init__() method keeps track of all scenes in a dictionary ❶. It iterates through the list of scenes, asking each scene for its scene key, and builds a dictionary ❷. The first scene object in the list of scenes is used as the starting scene ❸.

The last part of the __init__() method does some interesting work. The scene manager holds a reference to every scene, so it can send messages to any and every scene. But every scene also needs to be able to send messages to the scene manager. To allow each scene to do that, the last for loop in the __init__() method calls the special method _setRefToSceneMgr() ❹ that lives in the base class of every scene, and it passes self, which is a reference to the scene manager. The entire code of this method consists of a single line:

```
def _setRefToSceneMgr(self, oSceneMgr):
--- snip ---
    self.oSceneMgr = oSceneMgr
```

This method just stores this reference back to the scene manager in an instance variable, self.oSceneMgr. Each scene can use this variable to make calls to the scene manager. I'll show how scenes use this a little later in this section.

## run() Method

For every project you build, you have to write a small main program that instantiates the scene manager. The last step in your main program is a call to the run() method of the scene manager. This is where the main loop of the whole program lives. Listing 15-7 contains the code of that method.

```
def run(self):

--- snip ---
    clock = pygame.time.Clock()

    # 6 - Loop forever
    while True:

      ❶ keysDownList = pygame.key.get_pressed()

        # 7 - Check for and handle events
      ❷ eventsList = []
        for event in pygame.event.get():
            if (event.type == pygame.QUIT) or \
                    ((event.type == pygame.KEYDOWN) and
                    (event.key == pygame.K_ESCAPE)):
                # Tell the current scene we're leaving
                self.oCurrentScene.leave()
                pygame.quit()
                sys.exit()

            eventsList.append(event)

        # Here, we let the current scene process all events,
        # do any "per frame" actions in its update method,
        # and draw everything that needs to be drawn.
      ❸ self.oCurrentScene.handleInputs(eventsList, keysDownList)
      ❹ self.oCurrentScene.update()
      ❺ self.oCurrentScene.draw()

        # 11 - Update the window
      ❻ pygame.display.update()

        # 12 - Slow things down a bit
        clock.tick(self.framesPerSecond)
```

Listing 15-7: The run() method of the SceneMgr class

The run() method is the key to how the scene manager works. Remember that all scenes must be polymorphic—at a minimum, each must implement a handleInputs() and a draw() method. Each time through the loop, the run() method does the following:

- Gets a list of all keyboard keys ❶ (False means up, True means down).
- Builds a list of events ❷ that have happened since the last time through the loop.
- Makes calls to the polymorphic methods ❸ of the current scene. The current scene is always kept in an instance variable named self.oCurrentScene. In the call to the scene's handleInputs() method, the scene manager passes in the list of events that have happened and the list of keys. Each scene is responsible for handling the events and for dealing with the state of the keyboard.
- Calls the update() method ❹ to allow the scene to do any per-frame actions. The Scene base class implements an update() method that just contains a pass statement, but a scene can override this method with any code it wants to execute.
- Calls the draw() method ❺ to allow the scene to draw anything it needs to draw in the window.

At the bottom of the loop (identical to the standard main loop without a scene manager), the method updates the window ❻ and waits for an appropriate amount of time.

## Main Methods

The remaining methods of the SceneMgr class implement the navigation and communication between scenes:

**_goToScene()**   Called to transfer to a different scene

**_request_respond()**   Called to query data in another scene

**_send_receive()**   Called to send information from one scene to another

**_sendAll_receive()**   Called to send information from one scene to all other scenes

The code of any scenes that you write should not call these methods directly, and they should not be overwritten. The underscore in front of their names implies that these are private (internal) methods. While they are not called directly within the scene manager itself, they are called by the Scene base class.

To explain how these methods work, I'll start by giving an overview of the steps involved when a scene wants to navigate to another scene. To make a transition to a target scene, the current scene calls:

```
self.goToScene(SOME_SCENE_KEY)
```

When a scene makes this call, the call goes to the goToScene() method in the inherited Scene base class. The code of the inherited method consists of a single line:

```
def goToScene(self, nextSceneKey, data=None):
--- snip ---
    self.oSceneMgr._goToScene(nextSceneKey, data)
```

This makes a call to the private _goToScene() method in the scene manager. Within the scene manager's method, we need to give the current scene an opportunity to do any cleanup that might be needed, then transfer control to the new scene. Here is the code of the _goToScene() method of the scene manager:

```
def _goToScene(self, nextSceneKey, dataForNextScene):
--- snip ---
    if nextSceneKey is None:  # meaning, exit
        pygame.quit()
        sys.exit()

    # Call the leave method of the old scene to allow it to clean up.
    # Set the new scene (based on the key) and
    # call the enter method of the new scene.
 ❶ self.oCurrentScene.leave()
    pygame.key.set_repeat(0) # turn off repeating characters
    try:
     ❷ self.oCurrentScene = self.scenesDict[nextSceneKey]
    except KeyError:
        raise KeyError("Trying to go to scene '" + nextSceneKey +
                "' but that key is not in the dictionary of scenes.")
 ❸ self.oCurrentScene.enter(dataForNextScene)
```

The _goToScene() method performs a number of steps to transition from the current scene to the target scene. First, it calls leave() in the current scene ❶ so the current scene can do any necessary cleanup. Then, using the target scene key that was passed in, it finds the object for the target scene ❷ and sets that as the current scene. Finally, it calls enter() for the new current scene ❸ to allow the new current scene to do any required setup.

From this point on, the run() method of the scene manager loops and calls the handleInputs(), update(), and draw() methods of the current scene. These methods will be called in the current scene until the program executes another call to self.goToScene() to transition to yet another scene or the user quits the program.

## Communication Between Scenes

Finally, let's discuss how one scene communicates with another scene. To request information from another scene, a scene only needs to make a call to self.request(), which lives in the Scene base class, like this:

```
dataRequested = self.request(SOME_SCENE_KEY, SOME_DATA_IDENTIFIER)
```

The target scene must have a respond() method. That method needs to be defined like this:

```
def respond(self, requestID):
```

It uses the value of requestID to uniquely identify what data to retrieve and returns that data. Again, the requesting scene and the target scene must agree on the value of any identifier(s). The full process is shown in Figure 15-10.

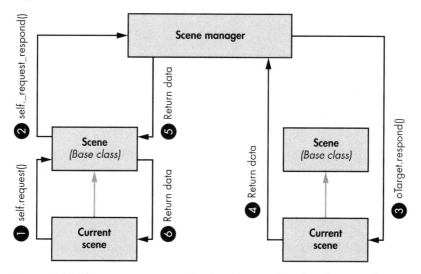

Figure 15-10: The communication path of one scene asking for information from another scene

The current scene cannot get information from another scene directly, since the current scene does not have a reference to any other scene. Instead, it uses the scene manager as an intermediary. Here is how it all works:

1. The current scene makes a call to self.request(), which lives in the inherited Scene base class.

2. The Scene base class has a reference to the scene manager in its instance variable self.oSceneMgr, to allow its methods to call methods of the scene manager. The self.request() method calls the scene manager's _request_respond() method to request information from a target scene.

3. The scene manager has a dictionary of all scene keys and related objects, and it uses the parameter that's passed in to find the object associated with the target scene. It then calls the respond() method in the target scene.

4. The respond() method in the target scene (which you must write) does whatever it needs to do to generate the data that was asked for, then returns the data to the scene manager.

5. The scene manager returns the data to the request() method in the Scene base class inherited by the current scene.

6. Finally, the request() method in the Scene base class returns the data to the original caller.

The same mechanism is used to implement send() and sendAll(). The only difference is that when sending a message to a scene or to all scenes, there is no data to be returned to the original caller.

## Summary

In this chapter, I introduced two different ways to implement a program that incorporates multiple scenes. A state machine is a technique for representing and controlling the flow of execution through a series of states; you can use it to implement a program with a small number of scenes. The scene manager is designed to help you build larger multi-scene applications by providing navigation and a general way for scenes to communicate with each other. I also explained how the scene manager implements all this functionality.

The scene manager and the Scene base class provide clear examples of the three main tenets of object-oriented programming: encapsulation, polymorphism, and inheritance. Each scene is a good example of encapsulation because all the code and data of a scene is written as a class. Each scene class must be polymorphic, in that it must implement a common set of methods in order for it to work with calls from the scene manager. Finally, each scene inherits from a common Scene base class. Two-way communication between the scene manager and the Scene base class is implemented by every scene using the inherited methods and instance variables in the base class.

# 16

## FULL GAME: DODGER

In this chapter we'll build a full game called Dodger that uses many of the techniques and concepts that have been explained in this book. This is a fully object-oriented extended version of a game originally developed by Al Sweigart in his book *Invent Your Own Computer Games with Python* (No Starch, 2016; the basic game concept, graphics, and sounds are used by permission).

Before I get into the game itself, I'll introduce a set of functions that present modal dialogs that we'll use in the game. A *modal dialog* is one that forces the user to interact with it—choosing an option, for example—before they can continue using the underlying program. These dialogs stop the program from running until an option is clicked.

# Modal Dialogs

The pyghelpers module has two types of modal dialogs:

- *Yes/No dialogs* present a question and wait for the user to click one of two buttons. The text of these buttons defaults to Yes and No, though you can use any text you like (for example, OK and Cancel). If no text is specified for the No button, this dialog can be used as an alert, with only a Yes (or typically, OK) button.

- *Answer dialogs* present a question, a text field for the user to type in, and a set of buttons with text defaulting to OK and Cancel. The user can answer the question and click OK or cancel (close) the dialog by clicking Cancel.

You present each type of dialog to the user by calling a particular function in the pyghelpers module. Each dialog comes in two flavors: a simple TextButton-based version and a more complicated custom version. The simple text version uses a default layout with two TextButton objects that's great for quick prototyping. In the custom version, you can provide a background for the dialog, customize the question text, customize the answer text (with an Answer dialog), and provide customized artwork for the buttons.

## Yes/No and Alert Dialogs

We'll first look at the Yes/No dialog, starting with the text version.

### Text Version

Here is the interface of the textYesNoDialog() function:

```
textYesNoDialog(theWindow, theRect, prompt, yesButtonText='Yes',
        noButtonText='No',
        backgroundColor=DIALOG_BACKGROUND_COLOR,
        textColor=DIALOG_BLACK)
```

When you call this function, you need to pass in the window to draw into, a rectangle object or tuple representing the location and size of the dialog to create, and a text prompt to be shown. You can also optionally specify the text of the two buttons, a background color, and the color of the prompt text. If not specified, the button text defaults to Yes and No.

Here is a typical call to this function:

```
returnedValue = pyghelpers.textYesNoDialog(window,
            (75, 100, 500, 150),
            'Do you want fries with that?')
```

This call shows the dialog in Figure 16-1.

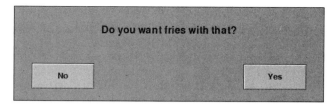

*Figure 16-1: A typical* textYesNoDialog *dialog*

The Yes and No buttons are instances of the TextButton class in pygwidgets. The main program stops while the dialog shows. When the user clicks a button, the function returns True for Yes or False for No. Your code does whatever needs to be done based on the returned Boolean value; then the main program continues running where it left off.

You can also use this function to create a simple Alert dialog with only one button. If the value passed in for noButtonText is None, that button will not be shown. For example, you can make a call like this to show only one button:

```
ignore = pyghelpers.textYesNoDialog(window, (75, 80, 500, 150),
                                    'This is an alert!', 'OK', None)
```

Figure 16-2 shows the resulting Alert dialog.

*Figure 16-2: A* textYesNoDialog *used as an Alert dialog*

### Custom Version

Setting up a custom Yes/No dialog is more complicated but allows for much more control. Here is the interface of the customYesNoDialog() function:

```
customYesNoDialog(theWindow, oDialogImage, oPromptText, oYesButton,
                  oNoButton)
```

Before you can call this function, you need to create objects for the background of the dialog, the prompt text, and the Yes and No buttons. You would typically use Image, DisplayText, and CustomButton (or TextButton) objects created from pygwidgets classes for this purpose. The customYesNoDialog() code demonstrates polymorphism by calling the handleEvent() method of the buttons, so it doesn't matter whether you use CustomButtons or TextButtons, and by calling the draw() method of all objects that make up the dialog. Because you create all these objects, you can customize the look of any or all of them. You will need to supply your own artwork for any Image and CustomButton objects and customarily place them in the *images* folder of the project.

When implementing a custom Yes/No dialog, typically you would write an intermediate function like showCustomYesNoDialog(), shown in Listing 16-1. Then, at the place in your code where you want to show the dialog, rather than calling customYesNoDialog() directly, you instead call the intermediate function, which both instantiates the widgets and makes the actual call.

```
def showCustomYesNoDialog(theWindow, theText):
  ❶ oDialogBackground = pygwidgets.Image(theWindow, (60, 120),
                                'images/dialog.png')
  ❷ oPromptDisplayText = pygwidgets.DisplayText(theWindow, (0, 170),
                                theText, width=WINDOW_WIDTH,
                                justified='center', fontSize=36)
  ❸ oNoButton = pygwidgets.CustomButton(theWindow, (95, 265),
                                'images/noNormal.png',
                                over='images/noOver.png',
                                down='images/noDown.png',
                                disabled='images/noDisabled.png')
    oYesButton = pygwidgets.CustomButton(theWindow, (355, 265),
                                'images/yesNormal.png',
                                over='images/yesOver.png',
                                down='images/yesDown.png',
                                disabled='images/yesDisabled.png')
  ❹ userAnswer = pyghelpers.customYesNoDialog(theWindow,
                                oDialogBackground,
                                oPromptDisplayText,
                                oYesButton, oNoButton)
  ❺ return userAnswer
```

*Listing 16-1: An intermediate function to create a custom Yes/No dialog*

Inside the function you write code to create an Image object for the background using an image you specify ❶. You also create a DisplayText object for the prompt ❷, in which you specify the placement, text size, font, and so on. Then you create buttons as either TextButton objects or, more likely, CustomButton objects so you can show custom images ❸. Finally, this function calls customYesNoDialog(), passing in all the objects you just created ❹. The call to customYesNoDialog() returns the user's choice to this intermediate function, and the intermediate function returns the user's choice to the original caller ❺. This approach works well because the widget objects (oDialogBackground, oPromptDisplayText, oYesButton, and oNoButton) created inside this function are all local variables and therefore will all go away when the intermediate function ends.

When you call this function, you only need to pass in the window and the text prompt to be displayed. For example:

```
returnedValue = showCustomYesNoDialog(window,
                                'Do you want fries with that?')
```

Figure 16-3 shows the resulting dialog. This is just one example; you can design any layout you like.

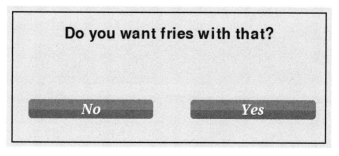

*Figure 16-3: A typical* customYesNoDialog *dialog*

As with the simple text version, if the value passed in for oNoButton is None, that button will not be shown, which is useful for building and displaying an Alert dialog.

Internally, the textYesNoDialog() and customYesNoDialog() functions each run their own while loop that handles events and updates and draws the dialog. That way, the calling program is suspended (its main loop does not run) until the user clicks a button and the modal dialog returns the selected answer. (The source code of both functions is available in the pyghelpers module.)

## Answer Dialogs

An Answer dialog adds an input text field where the user can type a response. The pyghelpers module also contains functions textAnswerDialog() and customAnswerDialog() to handle these dialogs, which work similarly to their Yes/No counterparts.

### Text Version

Here is the interface of the textAnswerDialog() function:

```
textAnswerDialog(theWindow, theRect, prompt, okButtonText='OK'
                cancelButtonText='Cancel',
                backgroundColor=DIALOG_BACKGROUND_COLOR,
                promptTextColor=DIALOG_BLACK,
                inputTextColor=DIALOG_BLACK)
```

If the user clicks the OK button, the function returns whatever text the user entered. If the user clicks the Cancel button, the function returns None. Here is a typical call:

```
userAnswer = pyghelpers.textAnswerDialog(window, (75, 100, 500, 200),
                    'What is your favorite flavor of ice cream?')
if userAnswer is not None:
    # User pressed OK, do whatever you want with the variable userAnswer
else:
    # Here do whatever you want knowing that the user pressed Cancel
```

This will display the dialog in Figure 16-4.

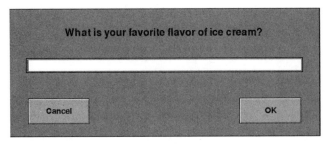

Figure 16-4: A typical textAnswerDialog dialog

## Custom Version

To implement a custom Answer dialog, you should write an intermediate function, similar to the approach shown with customYesNoDialog(). Your main code calls the intermediate function, which in turn calls customAnswerDialog(). Listing 16-2 shows the code of a typical intermediate function.

```
def showCustomAnswerDialog(theWindow, theText):
    oDialogBackground = pygwidgets.Image(theWindow, (60, 80),
                            'images/dialog.png')
    oPromptDisplayText = pygwidgets.DisplayText(theWindow, (0, 120),
                            theText, width=WINDOW_WIDTH,
                            justified='center', fontSize=36)
    oUserInputText = pygwidgets.InputText(theWindow, (225, 165), '',
                            fontSize=36, initialFocus=True)
    oNoButton = pygwidgets.CustomButton(theWindow, (105, 235),
                            'images/cancelNormal.png',
                            over='images/cancelOver.png',
                            down='images/cancelDown.png',
                            isabled='images/cancelDisabled.png')
    oYesButton = pygwidgets.CustomButton(theWindow, (375, 235),
                            'images/okNormal.png',
                            over='images/okOver.png',
                            down='images/okDown.png',
                            disabled='images/okDisabled.png')
    response = pyghelpers.customAnswerDialog(theWindow,
                            oDialogBackground, oPromptDisplayText,
                            oUserInputText,
                            oYesButton, oNoButton)
    return response
```

Listing 16-2: An intermediate function to create a custom Answer dialog

You can customize the entire appearance of the dialog: background image, fonts, and sizes and placement of the display and input text fields and the two buttons. To show a custom dialog, your main code would call the intermediate function and pass in the prompt text, like this:

```
userAnswer = showCustomAnswerDialog(window,
                    'What is your favorite flavor of ice cream?')
```

That call displays a custom Answer dialog like the one shown in Figure 16-5.

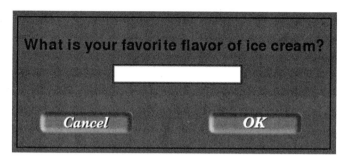

Figure 16-5: A typical customAnswerDialog dialog

If user clicks OK, the function returns the text the user entered. If the user clicks the Cancel button, the function returns None.

A demo program that demonstrates all the types of dialogs, *DialogTester/ Main_DialogTester.py*, is available with the downloadable resources for the book.

## Building a Full Game: Dodger

In this section, we'll put all the material from this part of the book together in the context of a game called Dodger. From the user's point of view, the game is extremely simple: get as many points as you can by dodging the red Baddies and making contact with the green Goodies.

### Game Overview

Red Baddies will drop from the top of the window, and the user must avoid them. Any Baddie that makes it all the way down to the bottom of the game area is removed, and the user gains one point. The user moves the mouse to control a Player icon. If the Player touches any Baddie, the game is over. A small number of green Goodies show up randomly and move horizontally, and the user gets 25 points for any Goodie they touch.

The game has three scenes: a starting or Splash scene with instructions, a Play scene where you play the game, and a High Scores scene where you can view the top 10 high scores. If you score within the top 10, you're given the option of entering your name and score into the high scores table. Figure 16-6 shows the three scenes.

 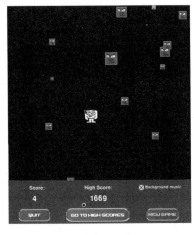 

Figure 16-6: The Splash, Play, and High Score scenes (left to right)

## Implementation

The contents of the *Dodger* project folder are as follows (filenames are in italic):

**__init__.py**   Empty file that indicates that this is a Python package

**Baddies.py**   Contains the `Baddie` and `BaddieMgr` classes

**Constants.py**   Contains constants used by multiple scenes

**Goodies.py**   Contains the `Goodie` and `GoodieMgr` classes

**HighScoresData.py**   Contains the `HighScoresData` class

**images**   Folder that contains all the artwork for the game

**Main_Dodger.py**   The main program

**Player.py**   Contains the `Player` class

**SceneHighScores.py**   The scene that shows and records high scores

**ScenePlay.py**   The main Play scene

**Scene.Splash.py**   The Splash scene

**sounds**   Folder that contains all the sound files for the game

The project folder is included with the book's resources. I won't talk through the entirety of the code, but I'll go through the source files and explain how the key parts work.

### File: Dodger/Constants.py

This file contains constants that can be used by more than one source file. The most important constants are the scene keys:

```
# Scene keys
SCENE_SPLASH = 'scene splash'
SCENE_PLAY = 'scene play'
SCENE_HIGH_SCORES = 'scene high scores'
```

The values of these constants are unique strings that identify the different scenes.

## File: Main_Dodger.py

The main file performs the necessary initialization, then passes control to the scene manager. The most important code in the file is this:

```
# Instantiate all scenes and store them in a list
scenesList = [SceneSplash(window)
            SceneHighScores(window)
            ScenePlay(window)]

# Create the scene manager, passing in the scenes list and the FPS
oSceneMgr = pyghelpers.SceneMgr(scenesList, FRAMES_PER_SECOND)

# Tell the scene manager to start running
oSceneMgr.run()
```

Here we create an instance of each scene, instantiate the scene manager, then turn over control to the scene manager. The scene manager's run() method gives control to the first scene in the list. In this game, it gives control to the Splash scene.

As discussed in the previous chapter, each scene class inherits from the Scene base class. In addition to providing its own __init__() method, each of these classes is required to override the getSceneKey(), handleInputs(), and draw() methods from the base class.

## File: Dodger/SceneSplash.py

The Splash scene shows the user a graphic with the rules of the game and three buttons: Start, Quit, and Go to High Scores. The code for this scene's class only contains the required methods; all other methods default to the ones in the Scene base class.

The __init__() method creates an Image object for the background image and three CustomButton objects for the user's options.

The getSceneKey() method must be implemented in all scenes; it just returns a unique key for the scene.

The handleInputs() method checks for the user clicking any of the buttons. If the user clicks Start, we call the inherited self.goToScene() method to ask the scene manager to transfer control to the Play scene. Similarly, clicking the Go to High Scores button takes the user to the High Scores scene. If the user clicks Quit, we call the scene's inherited self.quit() method, which quits the program.

In the draw() method, the program draws the background and all three buttons.

## File: Dodger/ScenePlay.py

The Play scene manages the actual playing of the game: the user moving the Player icon, generation and movement of the Baddies and Goodies, and collision detection. It also manages the display elements at the bottom of the window, including the current game score and high score, and responds to clicks on the Quit, Go to High Scores, and Start buttons and the Background Music checkbox.

There is quite a bit of code for the Play scene, so I'll break it up into smaller chunks (Listings 16-3 through 16-7) to explain the methods. The scene adheres to the design rules established in Chapter 15 by implementing the __init__(), handleInputs(), update(), and draw() methods. It also implements an enter() method to handle what the scene should do when it becomes the active scene and a leave() method for what the scene should do when the user navigates away. Finally, it has a reset() method for resetting the state before starting a new round. Listing 16-3 shows the initialization code.

```python
#  Play scene - the main game play scene
--- snip imports and showCustomYesNoDialog ---


BOTTOM_RECT = (0, GAME_HEIGHT + 1, WINDOW_WIDTH,
               WINDOW_HEIGHT - GAME_HEIGHT)
STATE_WAITING = 'waiting'
STATE_PLAYING = 'playing'
STATE_GAME_OVER = 'game over'


class ScenePlay(pyghelpers.Scene):

    def __init__(self, window):
    ❶ self.window = window

        self.controlsBackground = pygwidgets.Image(self.window,
                            (0, GAME_HEIGHT),
                            'images/controlsBackground.jpg')

        self.quitButton = pygwidgets.CustomButton(self.window,
                            (30, GAME_HEIGHT + 90),
                            up='images/quitNormal.png',
                            down='images/quitDown.png',
                            over='images/quitOver.png',
                            disabled='images/quitDisabled.png')

        self.highScoresButton = pygwidgets.CustomButton(self.window,
                            (190, GAME_HEIGHT + 90),
                            up='images/gotoHighScoresNormal.png',
                            down='images/gotoHighScoresDown.png',
                            over='images/gotoHighScoresOver.png',
                            disabled='images/gotoHighScoresDisabled.png')

        self.startButton = pygwidgets.CustomButton(self.window,
                            (450, GAME_HEIGHT + 90),
                            up='images/startNewNormal.png',
                            down='images/startNewDown.png',
                            over='images/startNewOver.png',
                        disabled='images/startNewDisabled.png',
                            enterToActivate=True)
```

```
        self.soundCheckBox = pygwidgets.TextCheckBox(self.window,
                             (430, GAME_HEIGHT + 17),
                             'Background music',
                             True, textColor=WHITE)

        self.gameOverImage = pygwidgets.Image(self.window, (140, 180),
                             'images/gameOver.png')

        self.titleText = pygwidgets.DisplayText(self.window,
                             (70, GAME_HEIGHT + 17),
                             'Score:                          High Score:',
                             fontSize=24, textColor=WHITE)

        self.scoreText = pygwidgets.DisplayText(self.window,
                             (80, GAME_HEIGHT + 47), '0',
                             fontSize=36, textColor=WHITE,
                             justified='right')

        self.highScoreText = pygwidgets.DisplayText(self.window,
                             (270, GAME_HEIGHT + 47), '',
                             fontSize=36, textColor=WHITE,
                             justified='right')

        pygame.mixer.music.load('sounds/background.mid')
        self.dingSound = pygame.mixer.Sound('sounds/ding.wav')
        self.gameOverSound = pygame.mixer.Sound('sounds/gameover.wav')

        # Instantiate objects
❷    self.oPlayer = Player(self.window)
        self.oBaddieMgr = BaddieMgr(self.window)
        self.oGoodieMgr = GoodieMgr(self.window)

        self.highestHighScore = 0
        self.lowestHighScore = 0
        self.backgroundMusic = True
        self.score = 0
❸    self.playingState = STATE_WAITING

❹ def getSceneKey(self):
        return SCENE_PLAY
```

*Listing 16-3: The __init__() and getSceneKey() methods of the ScenePlay class*

When run, the main code of the game instantiates all the scenes. In the
Play scene, the __init__() method creates all the buttons and text display
fields for the bottom of the window ❶, then loads the sounds. Very importantly, we use composition, discussed in Chapters 4 and 10, to create a
Player object (oPlayer), a Baddie manager object (oBaddieMgr), and a Goodie
manager object (oGoodieMgr) ❷. The Play scene object creates these managers and expects them to create and manage all the Baddies and Goodies.
The __init__() method runs when the program starts, but doesn't actually
start the game. Instead, it implements a state machine (as discussed in
Chapter 15) that starts in the waiting state ❸. A round of the game starts
when the user presses New Game.

All scenes must have a getSceneKey() method ❹ that returns a string representing the current scene. Listing 16-4 shows the code that retrieves the scores and resets the game upon request.

```
❶ def enter(self, data):
      self.getHiAndLowScores()

❷ def getHiAndLowScores(self):
      # Ask the High Scores scene for a dict of scores
      # that looks like this:
      #  {'highest': highestScore, 'lowest': lowestScore}
❸     infoDict = self.request(SCENE_HIGH_SCORES, HIGH_SCORES_DATA)
      self.highestHighScore = infoDict['highest']
      self.highScoreText.setValue(self.highestHighScore)
      self.lowestHighScore = infoDict['lowest']

❹ def reset(self):   # start a new game
      self.score = 0
      self.scoreText.setValue(self.score)
      self.getHiAndLowScores()

      # Tell the managers to reset themselves
❺     self.oBaddieMgr.reset()
      self.oGoodieMgr.reset()

      if self.backgroundMusic:
          pygame.mixer.music.play(-1, 0.0)
❻     self.startButton.disable()
      self.highScoresButton.disable()
      self.soundCheckBox.disable()
      self.quitButton.disable()
      pygame.mouse.set_visible(False)
```

Listing 16-4: The enter(), getHiAndLowScores(), and reset() methods of the ScenePlay class

When navigating to the Play scene, the scene manager calls enter() ❶, which in turn calls the getHiAndLowScores() method ❷. That method issues a request to the High Scores scene ❸ to retrieve the highest and lowest scores from the high scores table, so we can draw the highest score from that table in the bar at the bottom of the window. At the end of each game, it compares the game's score to the lowest top 10 score to see if this game ranks in the top 10.

When the user clicks the New Game button, the reset() method ❹ is called to reinitialize everything that needs to be reset before starting a new round of the game. The reset() method tells the Baddie manager and the Goodie manager to reinitialize themselves by calling their own reset() methods ❺, disables the buttons at the bottom of the screen so they cannot be pressed during game play ❻, and hides the pointer cursor. During play, the user moves the mouse to control the Player icon in the window.

The code in Listing 16-5 deals with user input.

```
❶ def handleInputs(self, eventsList, keyPressedList):
❷     if self.playingState == STATE_PLAYING:
          return  # ignore button events while playing

      for event in eventsList:
❸         if self.startButton.handleEvent(event):
              self.reset()
              self.playingState = STATE_PLAYING

❹         if self.highScoresButton.handleEvent(event):
              self.goToScene(SCENE_HIGH_SCORES)

❺         if self.soundCheckBox.handleEvent(event):
              self.backgroundMusic = self.soundCheckBox.getValue()

❻         if self.quitButton.handleEvent(event):
              self.quit()
```

*Listing 16-5: The* handleInputs() *method of the* ScenePlay *class*

The handleInputs() method ❶ is responsible for click events. If the state machine is in the playing state, the user cannot click the buttons, so we don't bother checking for events ❷. If the user presses New Game ❸, we call reset() to reinitialize variables and change the state machine to the playing state. If the user presses Go to High Scores ❹, we navigate to the High Scores scene using the inherited self.goToScene() method. If the user toggles the Background Music checkbox ❺, we call its getValue() method to retrieve its new setting; the reset() method uses this setting to decide if background music should be played. If the user presses Quit ❻, we call the inherited self.quit() method from the base class. Listing 16-6 shows the code for the actual game play.

```
❶ def update(self):
      if self.playingState != STATE_PLAYING:
          return  # only update when playing

      # Move the Player to the mouse position, get back its rect
❷     mouseX, mouseY = pygame.mouse.get_pos()
      playerRect = self.oPlayer.update(mouseX, mouseY)

      # Tell the GoodieMgr to move all Goodies
      # Returns the number of Goodies that the Player contacted
❸     nGoodiesHit = self.oGoodieMgr.update(playerRect)
      if nGoodiesHit > 0:
          self.dingSound.play()
          self.score = self.score + (nGoodiesHit * POINTS_FOR_GOODIE)

      # Tell the BaddieMgr to move all the Baddies
      # Returns the number of Baddies that fell off the bottom
❹     nBaddiesEvaded = self.oBaddieMgr.update()
      self.score = self.score + (nBaddiesEvaded * POINTS_FOR_BADDIE_EVADED)
      self.scoreText.setValue(self.score)
```

```
                  # Check if the Player has hit any Baddie
❺ if self.oBaddieMgr.hasPlayerHitBaddie(playerRect):
       pygame.mouse.set_visible(True)
       pygame.mixer.music.stop()

       self.gameOverSound.play()
       self.playingState = STATE_GAME_OVER
❻ self.draw()   # force drawing of game over message

❼ if self.score > self.lowestHighScore:
       scoreAsString = 'Your score: ' + str(self.score) + '\n'
       if self.score > self.highestHighScore:
           dialogText = (scoreString +
                           'is a new high score, CONGRATULATIONS!')
       else:
           dialogText = (scoreString +
                           'gets you on the high scores list.')

       result = showCustomYesNoDialog(self.window, dialogText)
       if result:   # navigate
           self.goToScene(SCENE_HIGH_SCORES, self.score)

   self.startButton.enable()
   self.highScoresButton.enable()
   self.soundCheckBox.enable()
   self.quitButton.enable()
```

Listing 16-6: The update() method of the ScenePlay class

The scene manager calls the update() method of the ScenePlay class ❶ in every frame. This method handles everything that happens while the game is being played. First, it tells the Player object to move the Player's icon to the position of the mouse. Then it calls the Player's update() method ❷, which returns the current rectangle of the icon in the window. We use this to see if the Player's icon has contacted any Goodies or Baddies.

Next, it calls the Goodie manager's update() method ❸ to move all the Goodies. This method returns the number of Goodies that the Player has contacted, which we use to increase the score.

This is followed by a call to the Baddie manager's update() method ❹ to move all the Baddies. That method returns the number of Baddies that have fallen off the bottom of the game area.

We then check to see if the Player has contacted any Baddies ❺. If so, the game is over and we display a Game Over graphic. We also make a special call to our draw() method ❻ because we may put up a dialog for the user, and the game's main loop will not draw the Game Over graphic until the user clicks one of the buttons in the dialog.

Finally, when the game ends, if the current game score is higher than the tenth-best score ❼, we put up a dialog giving the user the option of recording their score into the high scores list. If the score of the current game is a new all-time high score, we give a special message in the dialog.

The code in Listing 16-7 draws the game characters.

```
❶ def draw(self):
       self.window.fill(BLACK)

       # Tell the managers to draw all the Baddies and Goodies
       self.oBaddieMgr.draw()
       self.oGoodieMgr.draw()

       # Tell the Player to draw itself
       self.oPlayer.draw()

       # Draw all the info at the bottom of the window
❷      self.controlsBackground.draw()
       self.titleText.draw()
       self.scoreText.draw()
       self.highScoreText.draw()
       self.soundCheckBox.draw()
       self.quitButton.draw()
       self.highScoresButton.draw()
       self.startButton.draw()

❸      if self.playingState == STATE_GAME_OVER:
           self.gameOverImage.draw()

❹ def leave(self):
       pygame.mixer.music.stop()
```

*Listing 16-7: The draw() and leave() methods of the ScenePlay class*

The draw() method tells the Player to draw itself and the Goodie and Baddie managers to draw all the Goodies and Baddies ❶. We then draw the bottom portion of the window ❷ with all the buttons and text display fields. If we are in the game over state ❸, we draw the Game Over image.

When the user navigates away from this scene, the scene manager calls the leave() method ❹ and we stop any music.

### File: Dodger/Baddies.py

The *Baddies.py* file contains two classes: Baddie and BaddieMgr. The Play scene creates the single Baddie manager object, which creates and maintains a list of all Baddies. The Baddie manager instantiates objects from the Baddie class every few frames, based on a timer. Listing 16-8 contains the code for the Baddie class.

```
# Baddie class
--- snip imports ---

class Baddie():
    MIN_SIZE = 10
    MAX_SIZE = 40
    MIN_SPEED = 1
    MAX_SPEED = 8
    # Load the image only once
```

```
❶ BADDIE_IMAGE = pygame.image.load('images/baddie.png')

   def __init__(self, window):
       self.window = window
       # Create the image object
       size = random.randrange(Baddie.MIN_SIZE, Baddie.MAX_SIZE + 1)
       self.x = random.randrange(0, WINDOW_WIDTH - size)
       self.y = 0 - size  # start above the window
    ❷ self.image = pygwidgets.Image(self.window, (self.x, self.y),
                                     Baddie.BADDIE_IMAGE)

       # Scale it
       percent = (size * 100) / Baddie.MAX_SIZE
       self.image.scale(percent, False)
       self.speed = random.randrange(Baddie.MIN_SPEED,
                                     Baddie.MAX_SPEED + 1)

❸ def update(self):  # move the Baddie down
       self.y = self.y + self.speed
       self.image.setLoc((self.x, self.y))
       if self.y > GAME_HEIGHT:
           return True  # needs to be deleted
       else:
           return False  # stays in the window

❹ def draw(self):
       self.image.draw()

❺ def collide(self, playerRect):
       collidedWithPlayer = self.image.overlaps(playerRect)
       return collidedWithPlayer
```

*Listing 16-8: The Baddie class*

We load the image of the Baddie as a class variable ❶ so the single image is shared by *all* Baddies.

The __init__() method ❷ chooses a random size for each new Baddie, so the user sees differently sized Baddies. It chooses a random x-coordinate and a y-coordinate that will place the image just above the window. It then creates an Image object and scales the image down to the selected size ❷. Lastly, it chooses a random speed.

The Baddie manager, the code for which I'll show in a moment, calls the update() method ❸ in every frame: the code here moves the location of the Baddie down by the number of pixels that represents its speed. If the Baddie has moved off the bottom of the game area, we return True to say this Baddie is ready to be removed. Otherwise, we return False to tell the Baddie manager to leave this Baddie in the window.

The draw() method ❹ draws the Baddie at its new location.

The collide() method ❺ checks to see if the Player and the Baddie intersect.

The `BaddieMgr` class, shown in Listing 16-9, creates and manages a list of Baddie objects; this is a classic example of an object manager object.

```
# BaddieMgr class
class BaddieMgr():
    ADD_NEW_BADDIE_RATE = 8  # how often to add a new Baddie

❶ def __init__(self, window):
        self.window = window
        self.reset()

❷ def reset(self):  # called when starting a new game
        self.baddiesList = []
        self.nFramesTilNextBaddie = BaddieMgr.ADD_NEW_BADDIE_RATE

❸ def update(self):
        # Tell each Baddie to update itself
        # Count how many Baddies have fallen off the bottom
        nBaddiesRemoved = 0
    ❹ baddiesListCopy = self.baddiesList.copy()
        for oBaddie in baddiesListCopy:
        ❺ deleteMe = oBaddie.update()
            if deleteMe:
                self.baddiesList.remove(oBaddie)
                nBaddiesRemoved = nBaddiesRemoved + 1

        # Check if it's time to add a new Baddie
    ❻ self.nFramesTilNextBaddie = self.nFramesTilNextBaddie - 1
        if self.nFramesTilNextBaddie == 0:
            oBaddie = Baddie(self.window)
            self.baddiesList.append(oBaddie)
            self.nFramesTilNextBaddie = BaddieMgr.ADD_NEW_BADDIE_RATE

        # Return the count of Baddies that were removed
        return nBaddiesRemoved

❼ def draw(self):
        for oBaddie in self.baddiesList:
            oBaddie.draw()

❽ def hasPlayerHitBaddie(self, playerRect):
        for oBaddie in self.baddiesList:
            if oBaddie.collide(playerRect):
                return True
        return False
```

Listing 16-9: The BaddieMgr class

The `__init__()` method calls ❶ the `BaddieMgr`'s own reset() method to set the list of Baddie objects to the empty list. We use the frame-counting approach to create a new Baddie relatively often, to keep things interesting. We use the instance variable `self.nFramesTilNextBaddie` for counting frames.

The reset() method ❷ is called when starting a new round of the game. It clears the list of Baddies and resets the frame counter.

The update() method ❸ is where the real management of Baddies happens. Our intent here is to loop through all the Baddies, telling each one to update its own position and removing any that have fallen off the bottom of the window. However, there is a potential bug. If you simply iterate through a list and remove an element that matches your criteria for deletion, the list is immediately compacted. When this happens, the element directly following the one that was deleted will be skipped; in this loop, that element will not be told to update itself. Though I didn't go into detail at the time, we encountered the same problem in Chapter 11 in the Balloon game, where we needed to eliminate balloons that floated off the top of the window. There I employed a solution using the reversed() function applied to the list, to iterate in the reverse order (see Listing 11-6).

Here I've implemented a more generalized solution ❹. The approach used in the BaddieMgr class is to make a copy of the list and iterate over the *copied* list; then, if we find an element that meets the criteria for deletion (in this case a Baddie that has fallen off the bottom of the window), we remove that element (that specific Baddie) from the *original* list. With this approach, we are iterating over a different list than the one from which we are removing elements.

As we iterate through the Baddies, the call to the update() method of each Baddie ❺ returns a Boolean: False to indicate it's still moving down the window or True to indicate that it has fallen off the bottom. We count the number of Baddies that fall off the bottom and remove each one from the list. At the end of the method, we return the count to the main code so it can update the score.

In every frame, we also check to see if it's time to create a new Baddie ❻. When we've gone through the constant ADD_NEW_BADDIE_RATE number of frames, we create a new Baddie object and add it to the list of Baddies.

The draw() method ❼ iterates through the list of Baddies and calls the draw() method of each Baddie to draw itself at its appropriate location.

Finally, the hasPlayerHitBaddie() method ❽ checks to see if the Player's rectangle intersects any Baddie. The code iterates through the list of Baddies and calls the collide() method of each. If there was an intersection (overlap) with any Baddie, then we report that back to the main code, which ends the game.

### File: Dodger/Goodies.py

The GoodieMgr and Goodie classes are very similar to the BaddieMgr and Baddie classes. The Goodie manager is an object manager object that maintains a list of Goodies. The difference from the Baddie manager is that it will randomly place a Goodie at either the left edge of the window (in which case it moves right) or the right edge (so it moves left). It also creates new Goodies after a randomized number of frames. When the Player intersects with a Goodie, the user is rewarded with 25 points. The update() method of the Goodie manager uses the technique described in the previous section: it makes a copy of the Goodies list and iterates through the copy.

**File: Dodger/Player.py**

The Player class, shown in Listing 16-10, manages the Player icon and keeps track of where it should appear in the game window.

```
# Player class
--- snip imports ---

class Player():
❶ def __init__(self, window):
        self.window = window
        self.image = pygwidgets.Image(window,
                                (-100, -100), 'images/player.png')
        playerRect = self.image.getRect()
        self.maxX = WINDOW_WIDTH - playerRect.width
        self.maxY = GAME_HEIGHT - playerRect.height

    # Every frame, move the Player icon to the mouse position
    # Limits the x- and y-coordinates to the game area of the window
❷ def update(self, x, y):
        if x < 0:
            x = 0
        elif x > self.maxX:
            x = self.maxX
        if y < 0:
            y = 0
        elif y > self.maxY:
            y = self.maxY

        self.image.setLoc((x, y))
        return self.image.getRect()

❸ def draw(self):
        self.image.draw()
```

*Listing 16-10: The Player class*

The __init__() method ❶ loads the Player icon image and sets up a number of instance variables for use later.

The update() method ❷ is called in every frame by the Play scene. The basic idea is to show the Player icon at the mouse location, which is passed in. We do a few checks to ensure that the icon remains within the rectangle of the playable area. In every frame, the update() method returns the updated rectangle of the Player icon so the main Play code in Listing 16-6 can check if the Player's rectangle intersects with any Baddie or Goodie.

Finally, the draw() method ❸ draws the Player icon at the new location.

The use of the Goodie manager, the Baddie manager, and the Player object clearly demonstrates the power of OOP. We can just send messages to these objects, asking them to update or reset themselves, and they do whatever they need to do in response. The Goodie and Baddie managers pass these messages on to all the Goodies and Baddies that they manage.

**File: Dodger/SceneHighScores.py**

The High Scores scene displays the top 10 high scores (and the names of the players) in a table. It also allows a user who has scored in the top 10 to optionally enter their name and score into the table. The scene instantiates a HighScoresData object to manage the actual data, which includes reading and writing the data file. This allows the High Scores scene to update the table and to respond to requests from the Play scene for the current high and low scores in the table.

Listings 16-11 through 16-13 contain the code of the SceneHighScores class. We'll start with the __init__() and getSceneKey() methods in Listing 16-11.

```
# High Scores scene
--- snip imports, showCustomAnswersDialog, and showCustomResetDialog ---

class SceneHighScores(pyghelpers.Scene):
    def __init__(self, window):
        self.window = window
 ❶  self.oHighScoresData = HighScoresData()

        self.backgroundImage = pygwidgets.Image(self.window,
                                (0, 0),
                                'images/highScoresBackground.jpg')

        self.namesField = pygwidgets.DisplayText(self.window,
                                (260, 84), '', fontSize=48,
                                textColor=BLACK,
                                width=300, justified='left')

        self.scoresField = pygwidgets.DisplayText(self.window,
                                (25, 84), '', fontSize=48,
                                textColor=BLACK,
                                width=175, justified='right')

        self.quitButton = pygwidgets.CustomButton(self.window,
                                (30, 650),
                                up='images/quitNormal.png',
                                down='images/quitDown.png',
                                over='images/quitOver.png',
                                disabled='images/quitDisabled.png')

        self.backButton = pygwidgets.CustomButton(self.window,
                                (240, 650),
                                up='images/backNormal.png',
                                down='images/backDown.png',
                                over='images/backOver.png',
                                disabled='images/backDisabled.png')

        self.resetScoresButton = pygwidgets.CustomButton(self.window,
                                (450, 650),
                                up='images/resetNormal.png',
                                down='images/resetDown.png',
                                over='images/resetOver.png',
```

```
                                     disabled='images/resetDisabled.png')

 ❷ self.showHighScores()

 ❸ def getSceneKey(self):
       return SCENE_HIGH_SCORES
```

*Listing 16-11: The __init__() and getSceneKey() methods of the SceneHighScores class*

The __init__() method ❶ creates an instance of the HighScoresData class, which maintains all the data for the High Scores scene. We then create all the images, fields, and buttons for this scene. At the end of the initialization, we call self.showHighScores() ❷ to populate the name and score fields.

The getSceneKey() method ❸ returns a unique key for the scene and must be implemented in all scenes.

Listing 16-12 shows the code for the enter() method of the SceneHighScores class.

```
 ❶ def enter(self, newHighScoreValue=None):
       # This can be called two different ways:
       # 1. If no new high score, newHighScoreValue will be None
       # 2. newHighScoreValue is score of the current game - in top 10
 ❷     if newHighScoreValue is None:
           return  # nothing to do

 ❸     self.draw()  # draw before showing dialog
       # We have a new high score sent in from the Play scene
       dialogQuestion = ('To record your score of ' +
                          str(newHighScoreValue) + ',\n' +
                          'please enter your name:')
 ❹     playerName = showCustomAnswerDialog(self.window,
                                            dialogQuestion)
 ❺     if playerName is None:
           return  # user pressed Cancel

       # Add user and score to high scores
       if playerName == '':
           playerName = 'Anonymous'
 ❻     self.oHighScoresData.addHighScore(playerName,
                                          newHighScoreValue)

       # Show the updated high scores table
       self.showHighScores()
```

*Listing 16-12: The enter() method of the SceneHighScores class*

The scene manager calls the enter() method of the High Scores scene ❶ when navigating to that scene from the Play scene. If the game the user just finished did not have a score in the top 10, this method just returns ❷. But if the user did earn a top 10 score, the enter() method is called with an extra value—the score of the game that the user just completed.

In that case, we call draw() ❸ to draw the contents of the High Scores scene before showing the dialog offering the user the choice to add their score to the list. We then call an intermediate function, showCustom AnswerDialog(), that builds and displays the custom dialog ❹, as shown in Figure 16-7.

*Figure 16-7: A* customAnswerDialog *to let the user add their name to the high scores list*

If the user selects No Thanks, we get a returned value of None and we skip the rest of this method ❺. Otherwise, we take the name that is returned and add the name and score to the table ❻ by calling a method in the HighScoresData object. Finally, we update the fields by calling the showHighScores() method. If there is no score in the call to this method ❷, there is nothing to do, since the current list is already displayed.

Listing 16-13 contains the code for the remaining methods of this class.

```
def showHighScores(self): ❶
    # Get the scores and names, show them in two fields
    scoresList, namesList = self.oHighScoresData.getScoresAndNames()
    self.namesField.setValue(namesList)
    self.scoresField.setValue(scoresList)

def handleInputs(self, eventsList, keyPressedList): ❷
    for event in eventsList:
        if self.quitButton.handleEvent(event):
            self.quit()

        elif self.backButton.handleEvent(event):
            self.goToScene(SCENE_PLAY)

        elif self.resetScoresButton.handleEvent(event):
            confirmed = showCustomResetDialog(self.window, ❸
                        'Are you sure you want to \nRESET the high scores?')
            if confirmed:
                self.oHighScoresData.resetScores()
                self.showHighScores()

def draw(self): ❹
    self.backgroundImage.draw()
    self.scoresField.draw()
    self.namesField.draw()
    self.quitButton.draw()
    self.resetScoresButton.draw()
    self.backButton.draw()
```

```
    def respond(self, requestID): ❺
        if requestID == HIGH_SCORES_DATA:
            # Request from Play scene for the highest and lowest scores
            # Build a dictionary and return it to the Play scene
            highestScore, lowestScore = self.oHighScoresData.getHighestAndLowest()
            return {'highest':highestScore, 'lowest':lowestScore}
```

*Listing 16-13: The showHighScores(), handleInputs(), draw(), and respond() methods of the SceneHighScores class*

The showHighScores() method ❶ starts by asking the HighScoresData object for two lists: the top 10 names and scores. It takes the lists that are returned and sends them to two display fields to be shown. If you pass a list to the setValue() method of a DisplayText object, it will display each element on a separate line. We use two DisplayText objects because self.namesField is left justified, while self.scoresField is right justified.

The handleInputs() method ❷ only needs to check for and respond to the user clicking the Quit, Back, and Reset Scores buttons. Because the Reset Scores button wipes data, we should ask for confirmation before performing this action. Therefore, when the user clicks this button, we call an intermediate function, showCustomResetDialog() ❸, to put up a dialog asking the user to confirm that they really want to clear out all the current scores.

The draw() method ❹ draws all the elements in the window.

Finally, the respond() method ❺ allows another scene to ask this scene for information. This is what allows the Play scene to request the highest current score and the tenth-highest score—the minimum score to qualify a player for the high scores list. The caller sends a value that indicates what information it's looking for. In this case, the requested info is HIGH_SCORES_DATA, a constant that is shared from the *Constants.py* file. This method builds up a dictionary of the two requested values and returns it to the calling scene.

### File: Dodger/HighScoresData.py

The final class is HighScoresData, responsible for managing the high score information. It reads and writes the data as a file in JSON format. The data is always kept in order, from the highest to the lowest score. For example, the file representing the 10 highest scores might look like this:

```
[['Moe', 987], ['Larry', 812], ... ['Curly', 597]]
```

Listing 16-14 shows the code of the HighScoresData class.

```
# HighScoresData class
from Constants import *
from pathlib import Path
import json

class HighScoresData():
    """The data file is stored as a list of lists in JSON format.
    Each list is made up of a name and a score:
        [[name, score], [name, score], [name, score] ...]
    In this class, all scores are kept in self.scoresList.
```

```
          The list is kept in order of scores, highest to lowest.
          """
❶ def __init__(self):
        self.BLANK_SCORES_LIST = N_HIGH_SCORES * [['-----', 0]]
    ❷ self.oFilePath = Path('HighScores.json')

        # Try to open and load the data from the data file
        try:
          ❸ data = self.oFilePath.read_text()
        except FileNotFoundError:  # no file, set to blank scores and save
          ❹ self.scoresList = self.BLANK_SCORES_LIST.copy()
            self.saveScores()
            return

            # File exists, load the scores from the JSON file
          ❺ self.scoresList = json.loads(data)

❻ def addHighScore(self, name, newHighScore):
        # Find the appropriate place to add the new high score
        placeFound = False
        for index, nameScoreList in enumerate(self.scoresList):
            thisScore = nameScoreList[1]
            if newHighScore > thisScore:
                # Insert into proper place, remove last entry
                self.scoresList.insert(index, [name, newHighScore])
                self.scoresList.pop(N_HIGH_SCORES)
                placeFound = True
                break
        if not placeFound:
            return  # score does not belong in the list

        # Save the updated scores
        self.saveScores()

❼ def saveScores(self):
        scoresAsJson = json.dumps(self.scoresList)
        self.oFilePath.write_text(scoresAsJson)

❽ def resetScores(self):
        self.scoresList = self.BLANK_SCORES_LIST.copy()
        self.saveScores()

❾ def getScoresAndNames(self):
        namesList = []
        scoresList = []
        for nameAndScore in self.scoresList:
            thisName = nameAndScore[0]
            thisScore = nameAndScore[1]
            namesList.append(thisName)
            scoresList.append(thisScore)

        return scoresList, namesList

❿ def getHighestAndLowest(self):
        # Element 0 is the highest entry, element -1 is the lowest
```

```
highestEntry = self.scoresList[0]
lowestEntry = self.scoresList[-1]
# Get the score (element 1) of each sublist
highestScore = highestEntry[1]
lowestScore = lowestEntry[1]
return highestScore, lowestScore
```

*Listing 16-14: The HighScoresData class*

In the __init__() method ❶, we first create a list of all blank entries. We use the Path module to create a path object with the location of the data file ❷.

**NOTE**   *The path shown in this listing is in the same folder as the code. This is fine for learning the concept of file input and output. However, if you intend to share your program with other people to play on their computers, it would be better to use a different path in the user's home folder. This path can be constructed like this:*

```
import os.path
DATA_FILE_PATH = os.path.expanduser('~/DodgerHighScores.json')
```

*or:*

```
from pathlib import Path
DATA_FILE_PATH = Path('~/DodgerHighScores.json').expanduser()
```

Next, we check if we already have some high scores saved by checking for the existence of the data file ❸. If the file is not found ❹, we set the scores to the list of blank entries, call saveScores() to save the scores, and return. Otherwise, we read the contents of the file ❺ and convert from JSON format to a list of lists.

The addHighScores() method ❻ is responsible for adding a new high score to the list. Since the data is always kept in order, we iterate through the list of scores until we find the appropriate index and insert the new name and score. Because that operation will extend the list, we remove the last element to only keep the top 10. We also check that the new score should actually be inserted into the list. Finally, we call saveScores() to save the scores to the data file.

The saveScores() method ❼ saves the score data to a JSON-formatted file. It's called from various places.

The resetScores() method ❽ is called when the user says that they wish to reset all the names and scores to the starting point (all blank names and all scores set to zero). We call saveScores() to rewrite the data file.

The getScoresAndNames() method ❾ is called by the High Scores scene to get the top 10 scores and names. We iterate through the list of lists of high scores data to create one list of scores and another of names; both lists are returned.

Finally, the getHighestAndLowest() method ❿ is called by the High Scores scene to get the highest and lowest scores in the table. It uses these results to determine if a user's score qualifies the user to enter their name and score into the high scores table.

### Extensions to the Game

The overall architecture is modular, allowing for ease of modification. Each scene encapsulates its own data and methods, while communication and navigation are handled by the scene manager. Extensions can be handled in one scene without affecting anything in other scenes.

For example, rather than the game ending as soon as the Player icon hits a Baddie, you might want the user to start with some number of lives; when the Player icon hits a Baddie, the number of lives is decremented by one, and the game is over when the player runs out of lives. This kind of change would be relatively easy to implement and would affect only the Play scene.

As another idea, the user might start with a small number of bombs that they can detonate when they're in a bind, eliminating all Baddies within a given radius around the Player icon. The count of bombs would be decremented each time one is used, until it reaches zero. This change would affect only the code of the Play scene and the Baddie manager.

Or maybe you want to keep track of more high scores—say, 20 instead of 10. A change like that can be made in the High Scores scene without affecting the Play or Splash scenes.

## Summary

This chapter demonstrated how to create and use Yes/No and Answer dialogs—both text and customizable versions. We then focused on building a full object-oriented game program, Dodger.

We used the `pygwidgets` module for all the buttons, text displays, and input text fields. We used the `pyghelpers` module for all the dialogs. The `SceneMgr` allowed us to split up the game into smaller, more manageable pieces (Scene objects) and to navigate between scenes.

The game used or demonstrated the following object-oriented concepts:

**Encapsulation**    Each scene handles only the things specific to the scene.

**Polymorphism**    Each scene implements the same methods.

**Inheritance**    Each scene inherits from the Scene base class.

**Object manager object**    The Play scene uses composition to create a Baddie manager object, `self.oBaddieMgr`, and a Goodie manager object, `self.oGoodieMgr`, each of which manages a list of its objects.

**Shared constants**    We use separate modules for Goodies and Baddies, and a *Constants.py* file allows us to easily share constants across modules.

# 17

## DESIGN PATTERNS
## AND WRAP-UP

In this final chapter, I'll introduce the object-oriented programming concept of *design patterns,* which are reusable OOP solutions to commonly occurring software problems. We've already seen one design pattern in this book: using an object manager object to manage a list or dictionary of objects. Many full books have been written on the topic of design patterns, so we obviously cannot discuss all of them. In this chapter we'll focus on the Model View Controller pattern that's used to break a system into smaller, more manageable and more modifiable parts. Lastly, I'll give a wrap-up on OOP.

## Model View Controller

The *Model View Controller (MVC)* design pattern enforces a clear split between a collection of data and the way that data is represented to the user. The pattern separates the functionality into three parts: the model, the view, and the controller. Each part has a clearly defined responsibility, and each is implemented by one or more objects.

The model stores data. The view is responsible for drawing the information from the model in one of perhaps multiple ways. The controller typically creates the model and view objects, handles all user interactions, communicates changes to the model, and tells the view to display the data. This separation makes the overall system highly maintainable and modifiable.

## File Display Example

As a good example of the MVC pattern, consider the way files are displayed in the macOS Finder or the Windows File Explorer. Say we have a folder that contains four files and a subfolder. The end user can choose to display these items as a list, as in Figure 17-1.

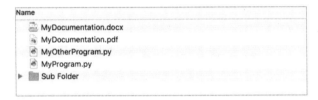

*Figure 17-1: Files in a folder shown as a list*

Alternatively, the user can choose to display the same items as icons, as in Figure 17-2.

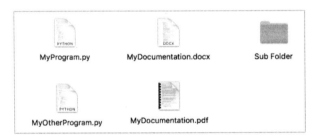

*Figure 17-2: Files in a folder shown as icons*

The underlying data for both displays is identical, but the representation of the information to the user is different. In this example, the data is the list of files and subfolders; it's kept in a model object. The view object displays the data in whatever way the user chooses: as a list, as icons, as a detailed list, and so on. The controller tells the view to display the information in the layout chosen by the user.

## Statistical Display Example

As a more extensive example of the MVC pattern, let's consider a program that simulates rolling a pair of dice many times and shows the results. In each roll we'll add the values of the two dice, so the sum—which we'll call an *outcome*—must be between 2 and 12. The data consists of the count of the number of times each outcome is rolled and the percentage of the total number of rolls each outcome makes up. The program can display this data in three different representations: a bar chart, a pie chart, and a text table. It defaults to a bar chart and displays the result after simulating rolling a pair of dice 2,500 times. Since this program is just intended as a working demonstration of the MVC pattern, we'll generate the output using pygame and `pygwidgets`. For more professional-looking charts and displays, I suggest that you look into Python data visualization libraries such as Matplotlib, Seaborn, Plotly, Bokeh, and others that are designed for this purpose.

Figure 17-3 shows the data displayed as a bar chart.

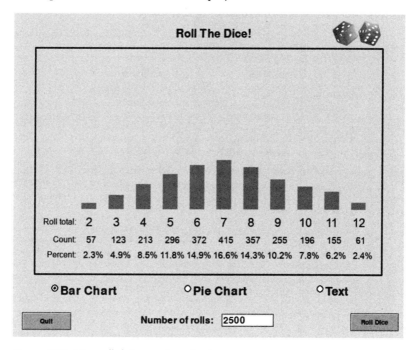

Figure 17-3: Dice roll data as a bar chart

Beneath each bar is the outcome, the count of the number of times that outcome was rolled, and the percentage of the total number of rolls that count represents. The height of each bar corresponds to the count (or percentage). Clicking Roll Dice runs the simulation again, using the number of rolls specified in the input field. The user can click the different radio buttons to show different views of the same data. If the user selects the Pie Chart radio button, the data is displayed as in Figure 17-4.

Roll The Dice!
2: 2.3%
3: 4.9%
4: 8.5%
5: 11.8%
6: 14.9%
7: 16.6%
8: 14.3%
9: 10.2%
12: 2.4%
Bar Chart
Pie Chart
Text
Quit
Number of rolls: 2500
Roll Dice

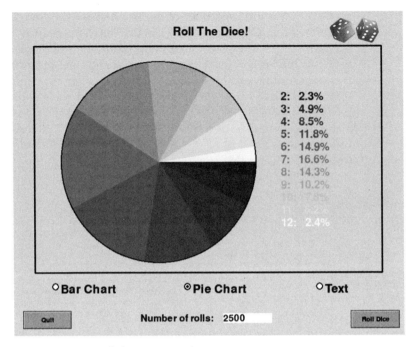

*Figure 17-4: Dice roll data as a pie chart*

If the user selects the Text radio button, the data is displayed as in Figure 17-5.

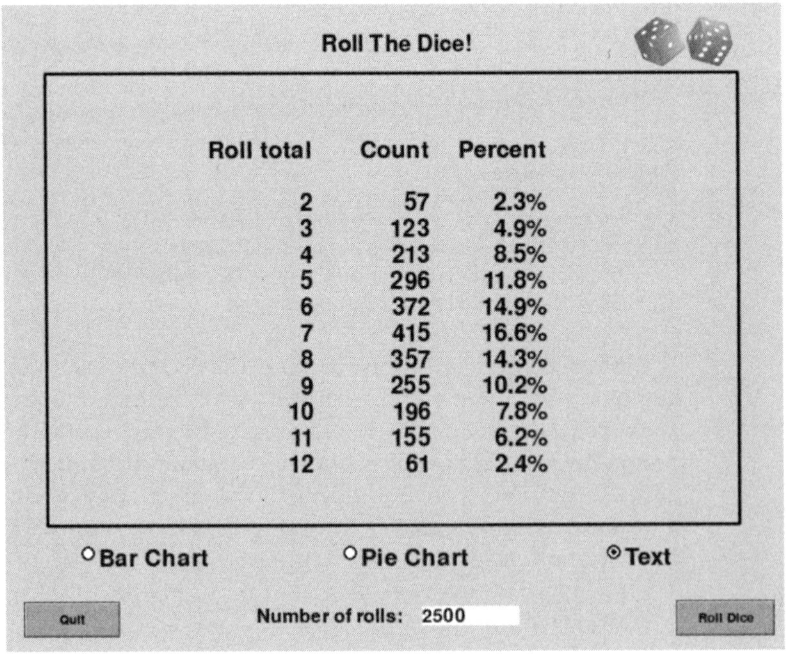

Roll The Dice!
Roll total Count Percent
2 57 2.3%
3 123 4.9%
4 213 8.5%
5 296 11.8%
6 372 14.9%
7 415 16.6%
8 357 14.3%
9 255 10.2%
10 196 7.8%
11 155 6.2%
12 61 2.4%
Bar Chart
Pie Chart
Text
Quit
Number of rolls: 2500
Roll Dice

*Figure 17-5: Dice roll data as text*

The user can change the value in the "Number of rolls" field to roll the dice as many times as they wish. This data in this program is based on statistics and randomness. With different sample sizes the exact counts will obviously vary, but the percentages should always be approximately the same.

I won't show the full listing of the program here, but will focus on a few key lines that demonstrate the setup and the flow of control in the MVC pattern. The full program is available for download with the rest of the book's resources, in the *MVC_RollTheDice* folder. The folder contains the following files:

*Main_MVC.py*   The main Python file

*Controller.py*   Contains the Controller class

*Model.py*   Contains the Model class

*BarView.py*   Contains the BarView class that displays the bar chart

*Bin.py*   Contains the Bin class that draws a single bar in the bar chart

*PieView.py*   Contains the PieView class that displays the pie chart

*TextView.py*   Contains the TextView class that displays the text view

*Constants.py*   Contains constants that are shared by multiple modules

The main program instantiates a Controller object and runs the main loop. Code in the main loop forwards all events (other than the pygame.QUIT event) to the controller to handle.

## The Controller

The controller is the supervisor of the whole program. It starts by instantiating the Model object. It then instantiates one of each of the different view objects: BarView, PieView, and TextView. Here is the startup code in the __init__() method of the Controller class:

```
# Instantiate the model
self.oModel = Model()
# Instantiate different view objects
self.oBarView = BarView(self.window, self.oModel)
self.oPieView = PieView(self.window, self.oModel)
self.oTextView = TextView(self.window, self.oModel)
```

When the Controller object instantiates these View objects, it passes in the Model object so each View object can request information directly from the model. Different implementations of the MVC pattern might handle communication between these three elements differently; for example, a controller could act as an intermediary, requesting data from the model and forwarding it on to the current view, rather than allowing the model and view to communicate directly.

The controller draws and reacts to everything outside the black rectangle in the window, including the title, the image of the dice, and the radio buttons. It draws the Quit and Roll Dice buttons and reacts when they're clicked, and it handles any changes the user makes to the number of rolls.

The `Controller` object keeps a current `View` object, which determines which view is currently displayed. We set it by default to the `BarView` object (the bar chart):

```
self.oView = self.oBarView
```

When the user clicks a radio button, the `Controller` sets its current `View` object to the newly selected view and tells the new `View` object to update itself by calling its `update()` method:

```
if self.oBarButton.handleEvent(event):
    self.oView = self.oBarView
    self.oView.update()
elif self.oPieButton.handleEvent(event):
    self.oView = self.oPieView
    self.oView.update()
elif self.oTextButton.handleEvent(event):
    self.oView = self.oTextView
    self.oView.update()
```

At startup, and whenever the user clicks Roll Dice, the controller validates the number of rolls specified in the "Number of rolls" field and tells the model to generate new data:

```
self.oModel.generateRolls(nRounds)
```

All the views are polymorphic, so in each frame the `Controller` object calls the `draw()` method of the current `View` object:

```
self.oView.draw()   # tell the current view to draw itself
```

## The Model

The model is responsible for obtaining (and potentially updating) information. In this program, the `Model` object is simple: it simulates rolling a pair of dice many times, stores the results in instance variables, and reports the data when a `View` object requests it.

When asked to generate data, the model runs a loop simulating rolling the dice and stores its data in two dictionaries: `self.rollsDict`, which uses each outcome as a key and the count as a value, and `self.percentsDict`, which uses each outcome as a key and the percentage of rolls as a value.

In more complex programs, the model could get its data from a database, the internet, or other sources. For example, a `Model` object could maintain stock information, population data, city housing data, temperature readings, and so on.

In this model, the `getRoundsRollsPercents()` method is called by the `View` objects to retrieve all the data at once. However, a model may contain more information than any one view might need. Therefore, different `View` objects can call different methods in the `Model` object to request different information from the same model. To support this, in the sample program

I've included a number of additional getter methods (getNumberOfRounds(), getRolls(), and getPercents()) that a programmer could use when building a new View object, to get only the data that the new view might want to display.

### The View

A View object is responsible for displaying data to the user. In our sample program, we have three different View objects that display the same underlying information in three different forms; each displays the information within the black rectangle in the window. At startup, and when the user clicks Roll Dice, the controller calls the update() method of the current View object. All View objects then make the same call to the Model object to get the current data:

```
nRounds, resultsDict, percentsDict = self.oModel.getRoundsRollsPercents()
```

The View object then formats the data in its own way and presents it to the user.

## *Advantages of the MVC Pattern*

The MVC design pattern breaks up responsibility into separate classes that act independently but work collectively. Building the components as distinct classes and minimizing the interactions between the resulting objects allows each individual component to be less complex and less error prone. Once the interface of each component is defined, the code of the classes can even be written by different programmers.

With the MVC approach, each component demonstrates the core OOP concepts of encapsulation and abstraction. Using an MVC object structure, the model can change the way it represents the data internally without affecting the controller or the view. As mentioned previously, the model might contain more data than any single view needs. And as long as the controller doesn't change the way it communicates with the model, and the model continues to return the requested information to the view in an agreed-upon way, the model can add new data without breaking the system.

The MVC model also makes it easy to add enhancements. For example, in our dice-rolling program, the model could keep track of the count of the different combinations of rolls of the two dice that make up each outcome, such as getting a 5 by rolling a 1 and a 4 or a 2 and a 3. We could then modify the BarChart view to obtain this additional information from the model and show each bar split into smaller bars to display the percentages of each combination.

Each of the View objects is entirely customizable. The TextView could use different fonts and font sizes, or a different layout. The PieView could show the wedges in different colors. The bars in the BarView could be thicker or taller, or be shown in different colors, or even be displayed horizontally. Any such changes would be made only in the appropriate View object, completely independent of the model or the controller.

The MVC pattern also makes it easy to add a new way to view the data, by writing a new View class. The only additional changes required would be to have the controller draw another radio button, instantiate the new View object, and call the new View object's update() method when the user selects the new view.

*MVC and other design patterns are independent of any specific computer language and can be used in any language that supports OOP. If you're interested in learning more, I suggest that you search the web for OOP design patterns such as the Factory, Flyweight, Observer, and Visitor patterns; there are numerous video and text tutorials (as well as books) available on all of these. For a general introduction,* Design Patterns: Elements of Reusable Object-Oriented Software *(Addison-Wesley) by Erich Gamma, Richard Helm, Ralph Johnson, and John Vlissides (the Gang of Four) is considered the bible of design patterns.*

# Wrap-Up

When thinking about object-oriented programming, remember my initial definition of an object: data plus code that acts on that data over time.

OOP gives you a new way to think about programming, offering an easy and convenient way to group together data and code that acts on that data. You write classes and instantiate objects from those classes. Each object gets a set of all instance variables defined in the class, but the instance variables in different objects can contain different data and remain independent of each other. The methods of the objects can work differently because they're working on different data. Objects can be instantiated at any time and can be destroyed at any time.

When instantiating multiple objects from one class, you typically build a list or dictionary of objects, then later iterate over that list or dictionary, calling methods of each object.

As a final reminder, the three main tenets of OOP are:

**Encapsulation**   Everything in one place, objects own their data.

**Polymorphism**   Different objects can implement the same methods.

**Inheritance**   A class can extend or modify the behavior of another class.

Objects often work in hierarchies; they can use composition to instantiate other objects and can call methods of lower-level objects to ask them to do work or provide information.

To give you a clear visual representation of OOP in action, most of the examples in this book focused on widgets and other objects that can be useful in a gaming environment. I developed the pygwidgets and pyghelpers packages to demonstrate many different OOP techniques and to allow you to easily use GUI widgets in pygame programs. I hope you find these packages useful and go on to use them to develop fun or useful programs of your own.

More importantly, I hope that you recognize that object-oriented programming is a general-purpose approach that can be applied in a wide variety of circumstances. Any time you see two or more functions that need to operate on a shared set of data, you should consider building a class and instantiating an object. You may also want to consider building an object manager object to manage a group of objects.

With all that said, I'd like to offer my congratulations: you've made it to the end of the book! Although actually, this should be considered the beginning of your journey into object-oriented programming. Hopefully, the concepts described in this book have given you a framework that you can build on—but the only way to truly get a handle on how OOP works is to write lots and lots of code. Over time, you will start to notice patterns that you will use again and again in your code. Understanding how to structure your classes is a difficult process. Only through experience will it begin to become easier to ensure that you have the proper methods and instance variables in the correct classes.

Practice, practice, practice!

# INDEX

graphic file formats, using with pygame, 100–101
greater than (>), magic method name, 196
greater than or equal to (>=), magic method name, 196
__gt__() magic method name, 196, 198
GUI programs, event-driven model, 95–96

# H

handleEvent() method used with pygwidgets, 150, 192, 221, 307, 312
handleInputs() method used with scenes, 363
help() function, 152
Higher or Lower card game, 268. *See also* card games
    Game object, 274–276
    implementation, 4–7
    main program, 272–274
    representing data, 4
    reusable code, 7
HighScoresData class, 363

# I

IDLE development environment, 90, 100–101
Image class, pygwidgets package, 149. *See also* subimages
ImageCollection class, pygwidgets package, 149, 157
implementation vs. interface, 84–85, 137
importing class code, 60–61
import statements, 98
inheritance. *See also* multiple inheritance
    abstract classes and methods, 231–234
    base class, 212
    class hierarchy, 236–238
    client's view of subclass, 218–219
    and composition, 238
    difficulty of programming with, 238–239
    DisplayMoney class, 222–227

employee and manager example, 214–218
    example usage, 224–227
    implementing, 213–214
    InputNumber class, 219–222, 224–227
    "is a" relationship, 213
    Law of Demeter, 238
    in object-oriented programming, 212–213
    and pygwidgets, 234–236
    real-world examples, 219–227
    from same base class, 227–231
    subclass, 212
    test code, 217–218
    use by pygwidgets, 234–236
initialization parameters, 43–44
__init__() method, 28, 37, 43, 216
    Account class, 59, 79
    Ball class, 123
    Bank class, 73
    inheritance examples, 228–229, 232–233
    InputNumber, 221
    pronouncing, 194
    property decorators, 175–176
    SceneMgr class, 335
    subclass in inheritance, 216
    using, 27
input() function, 133, 155
InputNumber class, 219–222, 224–227
InputText class, 149, 219, 222
installing
    pygame, 90–91
    pyghelpers, 287
    pygwidgets package, 149–150
instance and scope variables, 27–28
instances, 26, 31–32, 41–43. *See also* multiple instances
instance scope, 27
instance variables. *See also* slots
    changing into calculations, 167–168
    changing names of, 166–167
    using, 27, 165
instantiate, explained, 26
instantiation process, 25–33
interactive menu, building, 68–70

interface vs. implementation, 84–85, 137
*Invent Your Own Computer Games with Python*, 341
"is a" relationship, inheritance, 213
isInstance() function, 196
items() method, 271

**J**

JSON format, 363–365

**K**

keyword parameters, pygame, 145–146

**L**

Law of Demeter, inheritance, 238
__le__() magic method name, 196
leave() method used with scenes, 325
len() function, 15, 164
less than (<), magic method name, 196
less than or equal to (<=), magic
method name, 196
LIFO (last in, first out) order, 179
LightSwitch class and test code, 30
light switch example, 22–23, 25–31
LightSwitch object, instantiating, 29
line, drawing, 119
Lingo language, 178
local scope, 27
__lt__() magic method name, 196,
198, 200

**M**

Macromedia project, 178
magic methods, 194–201. *See also*
methods
Manager class, inheritance, 219
memory management, slots, 261–263
memory used by objects. *See also* objects
Balloon sample program, 251–261
class variables, 248–250
managing with slots, 261–263
mental models, 49–52
menu, making interactive, 68–70
methods. *See also* abstract classes and
methods; magic methods
calling, 30, 41
calling for objects, 30–31
calling on lists of objects, 83–84

and classes, 51
vs. functions, 28
passing arguments to, 40–41
modal dialogs, Dodger game, 342–347
Model object, 371–372
module of constants, Balloon game, 253
mouse click, detecting in pygame,
102–104
MOUSEDOWN event, 257
multiple inheritance, 239. *See also*
inheritance
multiple instances, 41–43. *See also*
instances
music, playing in pygame, 115–116
MVC (Model View Controller) design
pattern
advantages of, 373–374
Controller object, 371–372
dice roll data, 369–370
file display example, 368
Model object, 372–373
overview, 367–368
statistical display example, 368–371
View object, 373

**N**

__name__, testing card games with,
276–278
naming convention, 26
__ne__() magic method name, 196
not equal to (!=), magic method
name, 196

**O**

object composition, 71
object lifetime
cascading deletion, 246–248
death notice, 246–248
garbage collection, 246–248
reference count, 242–246
transaction objects, 242
transient objects, 242
object manager object, creating, 70–76
object-oriented programming (OOP)
explained, 3
as solution, 45
tenets, 374
wrap-up, 374–375

object-oriented pygame.
*See also* pygame
Ball class, 122–125
Ball objects, 125–127
callbacks, 137–141
demo ball with SimpleText and
SimpleButton, 135–137
interface vs. implementation, 137
program with buttons, 131–132
reusable object-oriented button,
127–132
reusable object-oriented text
display, 133–135
SimpleButton, 130–131
SimpleText class, 133–135
steps to display text, 133
object-oriented solutions
classes, 19–20
objects. *See also* memory used by
objects; physical objects
calling methods of, 30–31
calling methods on lists of,
83–84
and classes, 23–25
counting, 250
creating from classes, 28–30
definition of, 33
encapsulation with, 164
garbage collection, 248
inside vs. outside, 164–165
owning data, 165
reference count, 242–248
sending messages to, 184
string representations of values in,
203–205
transient type, 242
with unique identifiers, 66
variables referring to, 244
object scope, 27
OOP (object-oriented programming)
explained, 3
as solution, 45
tenets, 374
wrap-up, 374–375
operators
magic methods, 194–201
polymorphism for, 193–203
o prefix, 26

## P

parent class, inheritance, 212
path, using with pygame, 100
pathname, using with pygame, 100
patterns, extending with
polymorphism, 192
physical objects. *See also* objects
building software models of,
22–23
classes and objects, 23–25, 45
classes, objects, and instantiation,
25–33
complicated classes, 33–44
OOP as solution, 45
representing as classes, 35–44
PIE (polymorphism, inheritance,
encapsulation), 161
PinochleDeck class, 279
pixels
colors, 94–95
in window coordinate
system, 91
playing sounds, 114–116
Play scene, Rock, Paper, Scissors
game, 315
polygon, drawing, 119
polymorphism
classic example of, 184–185
extending patterns, 192
Fraction class with magic methods,
205–208
magic methods, 194–201
main program creating shapes,
190–192
for operators, 193–203
pygame shapes, 185–192
and pygwidgets, 192–193
sending messages to real-world
objects, 184
string representations of values in
objects, 203–205
vector example, 201–203
pop operation, using with
stacks, 179
positional parameters, pygame, 145
primitive shapes, drawing in pygame,
116–120
print() function, 133, 205

## R

raise statement and custom exceptions, 77–78

RAM memory space, 262

random package, 104

real-world objects, sending messages to, 184

receive() method used with scenes, 334

rectangle, drawing, 120

Rectangle class

inheritance example, 233–234

with magic methods, 196–198

reference count, 242–246

decrementing, 245–246

incrementing, 245

relative path, using with pygame, 100–101

respond() method used with scenes, 333

Results scene, Rock, Paper, Scissors game, 315–316

reusable object-oriented button, building, 127–132

reusable object-oriented text display, building, 133–135

RGB (red, green, blue), 94

Rock, Paper, Scissors game

Play scene, 315

Results scene, 315–316

Splash scene, 314

using scenes, 328–332

run() method of the scene manager, 336, 349

## S

Sample class, 250

Scene base class, 322

scene manager

building scenes, 323–326

communication between scenes, 338–340

demo program, 320–328

example scene, 326–328

features, 319–320

implementation of, 334–340

main methods, 337–338

main program, 322–323

methods for implementing scenes, 324–325

navigating between scenes, 326

project folder, 321

quitting program, 326

Rock, Paper, Scissors, 328–332

run() method, 336–337

using, 319–320

SceneMgr class, 337

ScenePlay class, Dodger game, 351–355

scenes

communication between, 332–334

current and target, 332

state machine approach, 312–319

testing communications among, 334

scope and instance variables, 27–28

screensaver ball, building with object-oriented pygame, 121–127

"self," meaning of, 52–55

self parameter, 41–42

self. prefix, 27

send() method used with scenes, 333

sendAll() method used with scenes, 334

setters and getters, 170–171, 175–176

Shape class

inheritance example, 232–233

using as base class, 228

shapes, drawing in pygame, 116–120

SimpleAnimation class, 296–300

SimpleButton class, 129, 131–132, 139–141

SimpleButton objects, 130–131, 137–138, 141

SimpleText class, 133–137

SimpleText object, 135

Slider class, 193

Slider Puzzle user interface, 290, 293

slots, using for memory management, 261–263. *See also* instance variables

software models, building for physical objects, 22–23

sound effects, playing in pygame, 114–116

SpaceShip class, 249

special methods, 194

Splash scene, 313–314, 347

SpriteSheetAnimation class, 149, 304,
    306–307
sprite sheet image, 300
Square class, 195, 227
    inheritance example, 229
    pygame shapes, 186–187
    for reference counting, 243
Square object, 243
Stack class, 181
stack operations, 179–180
state diagram, 316
state machine, pygame example,
    312–319
statistical display example, 368–373
__str__() method, 203–204
subclasses
    client's view of, 218–219
    inheritance, 212–213, 215–217
    inheriting from base class, 227
subimages, creating, 300.
        *See also* Image class
superclass, inheritance, 212
super() function, 216
Sweigart, Al, 341

## T

temporary variable, using, 66
test code
    accounts, 62–64
    creating, 61–62
    inheritance, 217–218
test programming, 177
textAnswerDialog dialog, Dodger
    game, 346
TextButton class, 148, 235
TextCheckBox class, pygwidgets
    package, 149
text display, building, 133–135
TextRadioButton class, pygwidgets
    package, 149
textYesNoDialog dialog, Dodger
    game, 343
throwing exceptions, 76
time, displaying, 290–294
Timer class, 287–290
timer demonstration program, 282
timer event, 284–285
Timer object, 288

timers
        building into main loop, 286
        calculating elapsed time,
            285–287
        counting frames, 283
        demonstration program, 282
        implementing, 283–287
        installing pyghelpers, 287
        overview, 281–282
toggle, using, 38
transaction objects, 242
transient objects, 242
Triangle class, 187, 227, 230–231
try/except techniques, 76–81
tuple, setting x- and y-coordinates
        as, 151
TV class, creating, 35–40
TV objects, creating, 42
type() function, 32

## U

update() method used with scenes, 325

## V

variables. *See also* class variables
        referring to same object, 244
        using temporarily, 66
vars() function, 52
vector example, polymorphism,
        201–203
View object, 371, 373

## W

WidgetWithFrills class, 214
window coordinate system, pygame,
        91–95
working directory, using with
        pygame, 100

## X

x- and y-coordinates, setting as
        tuple, 151
XTRAs and objects, accessing
        databases with, 178–179

## Y

Yes/No and Alert dialogs, Dodger
        game, 342–345

Never before has the world relied so heavily on the Internet to stay connected and informed. That makes the Electronic Frontier Foundation's mission—to ensure that technology supports freedom, justice, and innovation for all people—more urgent than ever.

For over 30 years, EFF has fought for tech users through activism, in the courts, and by developing software to overcome obstacles to your privacy, security, and free expression. This dedication empowers all of us through darkness. With your help we can navigate toward a brighter digital future.

# RESOURCES

Visit *https://nostarch.com/object-oriented-python/* for errata and more information.

*More no-nonsense books from*  **NO STARCH PRESS**

**BEYOND THE BASIC STUFF WITH PYTHON**
**Best Practices for Writing Clean Code**
*BY* AL SWEIGART
384 PP., $34.95
ISBN: 978-1-59327-966-0

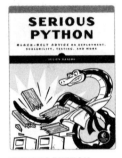

**SERIOUS PYTHON**
**Black-Belt Advice on Deployment, Scalability, Testing, and More**
*BY* JULIEN DANJOU
240 PP., $34.95
ISBN: 978-1-59327-878-6

**THE MISSING README**
**A Guide for the New Software Engineer**
*BY* CHRIS RICCOMINI AND DMITRIY RYABOY
288 PP., $24.99
ISBN: 978-1-7185-0183-6

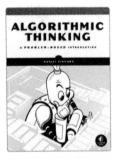

**ALGORITHMIC THINKING**
**A Problem-Based Introduction**
*BY* DANIEL ZINGARO
408 PP., $49.95
ISBN: 978-1-7185-0080-8

**THE SECRET LIFE OF PROGRAMS**
**Understand Computers—Craft Better Code**
*BY* JONATHAN E. STEINHART
504 PP., $44.95
ISBN: 978-1-59327-970-7

**WRITE GREAT CODE, VOLUME 3**
**Engineering Software**
*BY* RANDALL HYDE
376 PP., $49.95
ISBN: 978-1-59327-979-0

**PHONE:**
800.420.7240 OR
415.863.9900

**EMAIL:**
SALES@NOSTARCH.COM
**WEB:**
WWW.NOSTARCH.COM